MW00584256

When Life Strikes the President

When Life Strikes the President

Scandal, Death, and Illness in the White House

EDITED BY JEFFREY A. ENGEL

AND

THOMAS J. KNOCK

OXFORD
UNIVERSITY PRESS

Oxford University Press is a department of the University of Oxford. It furthers the University's objective of excellence in research, scholarship, and education by publishing worldwide. Oxford is a registered trade mark of Oxford University Press in the UK and certain other countries.

Published in the United States of America by Oxford University Press
198 Madison Avenue, New York, NY 10016, United States of America.

Library of Congress Cataloging-in-Publication Data
Names: Engel, Jeffrey A., editor. | Knock, Thomas J., editor.
Title: When life strikes the president : scandal, death, and illness in the White House / edited by Jeffrey A. Engel and Thomas J. Knock.
Description: New York, NY : Oxford University Press, 2017. | Includes index.
Identifiers: LCCN 2016042216 (print) | LCCN 2017000855 (ebook) | ISBN 9780190650759 (hardcover : alk. paper) | ISBN 9780190650766 (Updf) | ISBN 9780190650773 (Epub)
Subjects: LCSH: Presidents—United States—Health—Case studies. | Presidents--United States—Psychology—Case studies. | Presidents—United States—Decision making—Case studies. | Political corruption—United States—Case studies.
Classification: LCC E176.1 .W565 2017 (print) | LCC E176.1 (ebook) | DDC 973.09/9—dc23
LC record available at https://lccn.loc.gov/2016042216

1 3 5 7 9 8 6 4 2

Printed by Sheridan Books, Inc., United States of America

CONTENTS

Acknowledgments vii
Contributors ix

Introduction 1
Jeffrey A. Engel and Thomas J. Knock

1. A Crisis of His Own Contrivance: Andrew Jackson's Break with John C. Calhoun 13
Daniel Feller

2. "I am President": John Tyler, Presidential Succession, the Crisis of Legitimacy, and the Defense of Presidential Power 39
Aaron Scott Crawford

3. Personal Loss and Franklin Pierce's Presidency 65
Michael F. Holt

4. Abraham Lincoln and the Death of His Son Willie 83
Michael Burlingame

5. "One Long Wilderness of Despair": Woodrow Wilson's Stroke and the League of Nations 105
Thomas J. Knock

6. Calvin Coolidge: "When he went the power and the glory of the Presidency went with him" 131
Amity Shlaes

7. The Splendid Deception of "Doctor" Roosevelt 161
Frank Costigliola

8. The Kennedy Family through Sickness and Death 189
David Nasaw

9. Lyndon Johnson at Home and Abroad 211
Randall B. Woods

10. A Depressed and Self-Destructive President: Richard Nixon in the White House 233
Jeremi Suri

11. Governing During a Time of Crisis: The Reagan Presidency 257
Kiron K. Skinner

12. The Clintons: The Politics of the Personal 293
William Chafe

Index 325

ACKNOWLEDGMENTS

It takes a village to raise a child, but it takes a university and, in this case, an entire city's historical community to conceive, coordinate, and produce a book about crises. This effort in particular began as symposium at Southern Methodist University in February of 2014: "When Life Strikes the White House: Death, Scandal, and Illness and the Responsibility of a President." The timing mattered, offering a culmination, of sorts, for the year-long Dallas commemoration of the fiftieth anniversary of the assassination of President John F. Kennedy, a true presidential crisis if there ever was one. Coordinated by SMU's Center for Presidential History, the symposium was generously supported by campus partners, including the John G. Tower Center for Political Studies, the Cary M. Maguire Center for Ethics and Public Responsibility, the Office of the Provost, the Office of the Dean of Dedman College, and the William P. Clements Department of History. Local partners included the George W. Bush Presidential Library and the Sixth Floor Museum of Dallas, Texas.

Thereon, the editors wish to thank, in particular, those who led the aforementioned organizations or contributed their expertise to the symposium, including Provost Paul Ludden, Dean Bill Tsutsui, Bush Library Directory Alan Lowe, Sixth Floor Museum Director Nicola Longford, Tower Center Director James Hollifield, and Maguire Center Director Rita Kirk. For their staffs and successors who made the symposium possible and this volume a reality, we sincerely thank Candy

Crespo, Nancy Kress, Andy Graybill, Talmage Boston, Denis Simon, Provost Steve Currall, and Dean Tom DiPiero. The editors also would like to express their appreciation to the contributing authors for their expertise and responsiveness; to Susan Ferber, Alexandra Dauler, and Julie Mullins of Oxford University Press for their friendly, insightful counsel along the way; to Margaret Spellings and the George W. Bush Institute, which hosted an keynote event with Karen Hughes for an insider's perspective on White House crises; and to our respective spouses, Katherine Carté Engel and George D. Sellers, for keeping all other crises isolated during this book's long gestation. Finally and most importantly, our most profound thanks must go to Brian Franklin, Ronna Spitz, Aaron Crawford, Clara Johnson, and Andrew Oh, not only for helping to make this book a reality but for making our center the ideal place for "doing" presidential history.

CONTRIBUTORS

Michael Burlingame holds the Chancellor Naomi B. Lynn Distinguished Chair in Lincoln Studies at the University of Illinois at Springfield. Author of *Abraham Lincoln: A Life* (two volumes) and *The Inner World of Abraham Lincoln*, he has also edited for publication numerous diaries, essays, and letters concerning Abraham Lincoln and the Civil War.

William Chafe is the Alice Mary Baldwin Professor of History at Duke University. Author or editor of thirteen books, his work has focused on civil rights history, women's history, and modern political history. Chafe served as president of the Organization of American Historians in 1999–2000 and on the executive board of the organization for more than ten years. In 2011 he was awarded the Roy Rozenzweig Prize for Distinguished Service by the Organization of American Historians.

Frank Costigliola teaches at the University of Connecticut and is the recipient of fellowships from the Guggenheim Foundation, the Institute for Advanced Study at Princeton, and the National Endowment for the Humanities. His most recent publications include the prize-winning *Roosevelt's Lost Alliances: How Personal Politics Helped Start the Cold War* and *The Kennan Diaries*.

Aaron Scott Crawford is a fellow at the Center for Presidential History at Southern Methodist University. He previously served as associate editor of the first scholarly edition of the *Memoirs of Ulysses S. Grant*, and as editor of the Correspondence of James K. Polk. He is currently writing a history of presidential memoirs.

Jeffrey A. Engel is the founding director of the Center for Presidential History at Southern Methodist University.

Daniel Feller is Distinguished Professor of History and editor/director of *The Papers of Andrew Jackson* at the University of Tennessee in Knoxville. Author of *The Public Lands in Jacksonian Politics, The Jacksonian Promise: America 1815–1840*, and a new edition of Harriet Martineau's 1838 American tour narrative, *Retrospect of Western Travel*, he and his team have published volumes of *The Papers of Andrew Jackson*, covering Jackson's presidency from 1829 through 1832.

Michael F. Holt is the Langbourne M. Williams Professor of American History Emeritus at the University of Virginia. A specialist in nineteenth-century American political history, among his eight books are *The Political Crisis of the 1850s, The Rise and Fall of the American Whig Party*, and *Franklin Pierce*. He has held research fellowships from Stanford's Center for Advanced Study in the Behavioral Sciences and the National Humanities Center, and in the academic year 1993–1994 he was Pitt Professor of American History and Institutions at the University of Cambridge.

Thomas J. Knock is Professor of History and Altshuler Distinguished Teaching Professor in the Clements Department of History at Southern Methodist University. In addition to book chapters and articles in leading scholarly journals, he is the author of *To End All Wars: Woodrow Wilson and the Quest for a New World Order* and *Rise of a Prairie Statesman: The Life and Times of George McGovern*, and co-author of *Wilsonianism in the 21st Century*.

David Nasaw is the Arthur M. Schlesinger Jr. Professor of History at the Graduate Center of the City University of New York. His publications include *The Patriarch: The Remarkable Life and Turbulent Times of Joseph P. Kennedy, Andrew Carnegie, The Chief: The Life of William Randolph Hearst, Going Out: The Rise and Fall of Public Amusements*, and *Schooled to Order: A Social History of Public Schooling*.

Amity Shlaes chairs the board of the Calvin Coolidge Presidential Foundation. A frequent essayist and news commentator, she is also author of four *New York Times* best-sellers: *Coolidge, The Forgotten Man Graphic, The Forgotten Man*, and *The Greedy Hand.*

Kiron K. Skinner is the founding director of Carnegie Mellon University's Institute for Politics and Strategy. A member of the Council on Foreign Relations and a research fellow at Stanford University's Hoover Institution, she is the editor of *Stories in His Own Hand: The Everyday Wisdom of Ronald Reagan* and *Reagan: A Life in Letters.*

Jeremi Suri holds the Mack Brown Distinguished Chair for Leadership in Global Affairs at the University of Texas at Austin, where he is a professor in the university's Department of History and the Lyndon B. Johnson School of Public Affairs. Author of six books on contemporary politics and foreign policy, he has recently published an edited volume, *Foreign Policy Breakthroughs: Cases in Successful Diplomacy*, and he is completing a new book, *The Promethean President: Why Strong Leaders Fail.*

Randall B. Woods was John A. Cooper Professor of American History and a Distinguished Professor at the University of Arkansas, where he also served as Associate Dean, Interim Dean, and Dean of Fulbright College of Arts and Sciences. He has published seven books, most notably, *Fulbright: A Biography, LBJ: Architect of American Ambition*, and *Prisoners of Hope: Lyndon B. Johnson, the Great Society, and the Limits of Liberalism.*

When Life Strikes the President

Introduction

JEFFREY A. ENGEL AND THOMAS J. KNOCK ■

Americans demand much from their presidents. They practically require them to be superhuman in all circumstances—cool in moments of stress, compassionate amidst tragedy, resolute in time of war. Yet they are also human. Presidents bleed, grieve, and err like any other citizen, though they enjoy none of the privacy most take for granted when dealing with life's personal trials. Once inaugurated, they will rarely again be alone. Contemporary presidents never drive themselves on public streets, walk unannounced into a restaurant, or even quietly browse the shelves of a local store without their every move observed and every utterance recorded.

Other famous people can at least take days off from the scrutiny, but a president's responsibilities never fully abate. "Six mornings a week . . . the CIA briefed me on what they called the Threat Matrix, a summary of potential attacks on the homeland," President George W. Bush once explained of his time in office. "On Sundays I received a written intelligence briefing."[1] Such briefings occur irrespective of fatigue, travel schedules, a night at the theater, or sickness or health. The problems of the world never fully sleep so far as a president is concerned.

Sometimes their personal problems become the world's as well. This collection of essays explores just that dynamic: what happens when life strikes the president of the United States and, specifically, how personal crises—in the form of illness, the loss of a loved one, and scandal—have throughout American history shaped presidential decision making in critical moments, at times altering the course of events and the fate of the nation. The stories that follow reveal the flaws and frailties, the humanity, the sins, and the strength of character of some twelve presidents from the early national period to the early twenty-first century. Together they show that not all of American history can be found within the broad strokes of politics, war, or economic policy. Personal crises, too, influence the nation's course and, by the same token, personality frequently matters most of all to a president's choices, successes, and failures.

The essays in this volume generally focus on one of the aforementioned broad categories of personal crisis—illness, loss of a loved one, and scandal—but occasionally intertwine two and even all three. Presented chronologically, these twelve stories present recurrent themes with regard to both physical and mental illness in the White House; the burden of coping with a death in the family, especially of children; the strain on presidential marriages; and the changing role that women, and First Ladies in particular, have played in Oval Office politics.

For example, the volume's opening piece offers a prime example of the way scandal and a spouse's death intersect with politics high and low. Daniel Feller shows how Andrew Jackson's temperament and the death of his wife, Rachel, shortly after his election in 1828, affected his entire presidency, sparking in particular an unseemly quarrel with Vice President John C. Calhoun over Peggy Eaton, the secretary of war's "saucy wife." When the wives of other cabinet members ostracized Mrs. Eaton, the mourning president stirred to her defense. The Eaton affair in turn reignited Jackson's fury over Calhoun's attempt, ten years earlier, to have him censured for his invasion of Spanish Florida. "Jackson as president was his own best friend and potential worst enemy," Feller writes. He became "at times nearly unhinged." His temperament "created perils which his strengths armed him to survive ... [and] propelled him into nearly unending crisis and made every crisis personal." The story of Peggy Eaton is well known to historians of the Jacksonian age, yet Feller demonstrates with fresh clarity how a president's personal affairs directly altered the entire country's politics.

William Chafe applies a comparable analytical lens to Bill Clinton and Hillary Rodham Clinton in the collection's concluding essay. This president's brilliant political talents seemed forever at odds with lapses in personal discipline. Chafe does not, however, explore the notorious sex scandal that nearly exploded Clinton's second term. He concentrates instead on the president's "disastrous first term" (in particular, the collapse of health-care legislation under Hillary's supervision and the Republican victories in the 1994 midterm elections) and squarely locates blame for those disasters in "the chemistry of the Clintons' personal relationship."

Rumors of infidelity had long dogged Bill Clinton's personal rise, and Chafe suggests such personal tribulations formed the recurring or, more aptly, the ongoing crisis of the Clinton presidency. She offered salvation. It was Hillary who "saved Clinton's presidency," Chafe writes, when accusations of an affair led to impeachment. Wounded and betrayed, she nonetheless defended him. "Public opinion," impressed by her loyalty, consequently "moved to his side." As Americans "learned to live with the idea that their President was a flawed human being," Chafe concludes, "Bill Clinton had only his wife to thank for rescuing him from a fate he had done all too much to deserve."

John Tyler's crisis was neither one of passion or peccadillos but was rather embedded both in his personality and his unprecedented path to power. The first vice president to assume the presidency upon his predecessor's death, his elevation occurred only four weeks after William Henry Harrison's inauguration. "I am President," Tyler declared, emphasizing the middle word of that short declaration, while deciding to act not as a caretaker for Harrison's agenda but instead as a fully functional chief executive in his own right even if voters had just recently cast ballots for someone else. Myriad critics, however, including Harrison supporters, simply did not take to the Virginian's bluster. Many referred to him as "His Accidency." Others insisted upon calling him "acting" rather than "mister" president.

Even so, Aaron Crawford explains, Tyler left a lasting legacy from his single tumultuous term in the way he asserted the validity of his ascension (thereby determining how subsequent generations would view those others who came into office unexpectedly)—and in his expansion of presidential prerogative by using the veto as a powerful executive tool. By taking his opponents' rejection of his legitimacy personally, in effect creating a personal crisis out of a political one, he enlarged the power of the presidency, strengthening in particular the executive powers used to great effect by Abraham Lincoln to subdue Southern secessionists during the Civil War that soon after rent the country apart. It was an ironic legacy indeed, as Crawford makes clear. A president who fought so passionately in his own day for states rights, by defending his own right to be president in every fashion, laid the groundwork for a successor to defeat his cause and people. Tyler's personal crisis, in other words, ultimately gave Lincon the means to save the Union.

Deaths in the family, indeed the worst of all when children are lost, forms this book's second category of personal crises. Few could imagine a more horrific experience than that of Franklin Pierce, who witnessed his sole remaining son's violent death mere weeks before assuming office. Michael F. Holt reveals how this tragic loss (unfamiliar to most Americans) and Pierce's reaction to it helped set the conditions for the great national dramas of the 1850s and the crisis of civil war in the ensuing decade. Pierce, a Democrat from New Hampshire, became president in 1853. His four years in the White House witnessed the sectional unraveling of the Democratic Party, the birth of the Republican Party, the misbegotten Kansas-Nebraska Act, and the presentation of the Dred Scott case before the Supreme Court.

Nearly undone by their son's gruesome death, Pierce and his wife soon found comfort in the company of Jefferson Davis, senator from Mississippi, in large measure because Davis's own little boy became a surrogate for the one the Pierces had recently lost. The heartbroken couple in the White House doted on Davis's son, Sam, drawing their families closer together. Holt reflects on how this intimacy and his grief helped put Pierce under Davis's sway, contributing to the ruin of his presidency, while "pushing the U.S. down the road to Civil War."

Abraham Lincoln knew Pierce's pain all too well. He too suffered the loss of a cherished eleven-year-old child, in Lincoln's case amidst the broader tragedy of the Civil War. By practically all accounts, Willie was his father's favorite of three sons. As Michael Burlingame tells the story, "Lincoln and Willie were so close that the father could almost read the son's mind." ("They were intimates—often seen hand in hand," a family friend observed.) Yet Burlingame makes the boy's passing all the more poignant, and Lincoln's burden and humanity the more impressive, as he considers the ways that Willie's death profoundly affected the president who had to cope with depression, the problems of a mentally unbalanced wife, and the greatest crisis in American history. Willie's death tore Lincoln apart. But in Burlingame's accounting, the personal did not affect the national in this instance—an important observation on presidential crises: sometimes the pain experienced in private stays there. Some losses, scandals, or illnesses directly affect a presidency, though not all. Although Lincoln grieved deeply, Burlingame finds no specific case where Willie's death altered the nation's fate or his father's decision making. He did not suffer alone, but neither did he force the nation to suffer in consequence of his personal loss.

Amity Shlaes presents a similar portrait of another desperate president who, some sixty years later, also held a dying son in his arms. Calvin Coolidge forever asked himself "why such a price was exacted for occupying the White House." As for the impact, Shlaes holds that his sixteen-year-old son's untimely death actually made Coolidge "a more efficient president." He was able in the aftermath to pull himself together, to compartmentalize, and thus to emerge from the tragedy "more determined to act on principle." His sorrow, Shlaes maintains, as well as the solace he consciously took from Lincoln's example, reinforced his ideological conservatism and his fundamental aversion to spending and taxation. "We can see that what Coolidge said of Lincoln holds also for Coolidge himself," she writes, "he did not stop part way."

John F. Kennedy experienced a different sort of loss as president. He lost an infant son while in office, but the focus within this chapter is the loss of his father, not to death, but rather to a debilitating stroke suffered in December of 1961, at the end of his son's first year in office. Joseph

P. Kennedy, the former chair of the Security and Exchange Commission and ambassador to the Court of St. James, had never hesitated to offer his son guidance on the road to the White House. He was indubitably Jack's most trusted adviser. His money and ambition paved his son's way as well. David Nasaw's contribution ponders the famous family's emphasis on good health and good looks and the impact of the various health crises that the children endured, including JFK's illnesses in youth and maturity and his sister Rosemary's mental retardation and lobotomy.

Kennedys celebrated health and vitality, Nasaw writes, which further unscored the impact of the patriarch's illness, which denied the youthful president his father's counsel and encouragement during the grave crises of the Cold War that marked JFK's time in office. Joseph was not there to comfort and guide his son during the Cuban Missile Crisis, for example, as he had been during the Bay of Pigs fiasco. His enfeeblement affected Kennedy's presidency in other ways as well, Nasaw posits, making JFK more resolute about getting his Medicare bill enacted (though it failed to pass under his watch). John Kennedy's personal loss, in other words, changed his perspective on a highly important matter of social policy. It thus directly changed his presidency.

Presidential illness is our third typology. Thomas J. Knock begins with probably the most serious of all such cases: Woodrow Wilson's stroke of October 1919. Knock points out that Wilson remains one of the greatest legislators among presidents and that his authorship of the Covenant of the League of Nations at the end of World War I set in motion the most original idea for reducing the risk of war that ever emanated from the White House. The stroke occurred not long after Wilson returned from the Paris peace conference, however, just as the political fight over American membership in The League heated up. His wife, the second Mrs. Wilson, prevented a full disclosure about the extent of the president's incapacity. "Wilson should have resigned from office," Knock writes. "Had the 25th Amendment been in effect, he would have had no choice."

Historians often cite the affliction as the cause of the political gridlock that prevented the United States from entering the League; yet Knock concludes that other factors were just as decisive in bringing about the great debacle. "Even if Wilson had never suffered a severe stroke, it is probable that the changed political conditions of 1918–1919—the Republicans' parliamentary restoration on one hand and the unraveling of Wilson's once-ascendant progressive-left coalition on the other—had already made ratification of a *Wilsonian* league nearly impossible," Knock argues. "If this was so, then the crisis of the stroke did not matter quite as much as one might have reasonably assumed." Wilson's health dramatically affected his presidency and legacy, to say nothing of his personal life. But in this instance a medical crisis within the Oval Office did not necessarily change the nation's course.

Franklin Delano Roosevelt's illness was longer term. So, too, was the impact of his illness on American history. Polio acquired at the age of thirty-nine paralyzed his legs, and he later developed heart disease. Neither kept him from becoming president, of course. And as Frank Costigliola stresses, Roosevelt knew that he must travel the nation and the world extensively in order to lead the United States through the rending trials of the Great Depression and World War II. Costigliola explains that, during the pre–White House years, Roosevelt had learned ways of meeting the physically grueling challenges of his disabled condition and that this experience furnished the tools he needed to convince the American people that he was otherwise in fine physical condition and that he could actually "walk."

This "splendid deception," Costigliola writes, enhanced the president's capacity for flexibility and innovation in shaping the New Deal and forging the Grand Alliance. Thus, instead of imposing limitations on his leadership (as in the case of Woodrow Wilson), "his paralysis rendered him a more empathetic, effective leader and contributed to his historic greatness." Costigliola also holds that the wartime exertions eventually exhausted Roosevelt and led to his early death at the age of sixty-three—which, in turn, further strained relations between the world's great powers, and ultimately degraded into a Cold War that would last another two generations.

Randall Woods and Jeremy Suri each shed light upon another kind of presidential illness—psychological depression—by exploring its consequences in the cases of Lyndon Johnson and Richard Nixon. Living on the "emotional edge for most of his adult life," as Woods puts it, LBJ suffered since childhood from feelings of being unloved by his demanding mother. That relationship helped to create the insecure, intensely driven politician and president that he came to be. Notwithstanding all of the historic legislative achievements of his Great Society, Johnson endured fits of the "black dog" of depression. Woods limns manifestations of Johnson's personality traits in two dramatic illustrative episodes. The first was his near emotional breakdown in August 1964, upon the eve of his triumphal nomination for a term as president in his own right, when the Mississippi Democratic Freedom Party persisted in its efforts to have its delegates seated at the Democratic National Convention in Atlantic City. The second telling episode centers on crisis overseas. In April 1965 the Dominican Republic's civil war appeared to be careening toward Castroite revolution in Johnson's "fevered imagination." Down with a bad cold and fed by misleading reports from FBI director J. Edgar Hoover, Wood explains, the overwrought and clearly unwell Johnson launched an avoidable and unnecessary military invasion of the island involving more than 22,000 Marines.

In like manner, Jeremy Suri takes sharp aim at the behavior of Richard Nixon. Frequently depressed as president, Suri suggests his critical relationship with Henry Kissinger, his national security adviser and later, concurrently, his secretary of state, "created a strange co-dependency and isolation." Both were drawn to each other. As "self-conscious outsiders," they believed from the start that their opponents despised them personally and that they were bent on bringing them down. The two acted in kind, Suri observes, and developed a paranoid style of policymaking (a penchant for secrecy and revenge against political enemies not unlike that exemplified by Andrew Jackson) that ultimately led to Watergate and Nixon's resignation. The relationship and Nixon's depression (which Kissinger skillfully if cruelly manipulated) shaped American foreign policy as well. Thereon, as Suri demonstrates, the president "mixed strategic and emotional considerations" at crucial moments in his decisions about the ongoing war in Vietnam as well as his "mad man" theory and policy toward the Soviets and the Chinese and the nuclear crises of 1969 and 1973.

Finally there is the unique crisis of Ronald Reagan who, early in his first term, survived an attempted assassination that seriously complicated his health and, in his second term, helped to impel the Iran-Contra scandal that nearly brought about his impeachment. Kiron Skinner suggests that Reagan's incomplete recovery from the wounds, both physical and emotional, along with his hands-off managerial style and declining abilities, offers partial explanation for the latter incident: "The White House environment in the first hours after the president nearly died set the conditions for the Iran-Contra scandal."

The chief impact of the bullets that nearly killed Reagan lay elsewhere, however. To begin, the assassination crisis revealed confusion among his top aides regarding nuclear command-and-control procedures and shocking ignorance of constitutional guidelines for presidential disability and succession. But of far greater significance, Skinner argues, his near-death experience made Reagan more determined to reject traditional Cold War thinking and ultimately to pursue a radically different nuclear policy toward the Soviet Union. "His Soviet strategy grew in part out of his pre-presidential thinking," she writes, but most people "were unaware of how he redoubled his efforts on the geopolitical front in light of the assassination attempt." Once he found a willing partner in Soviet leader Mikhail Gorbachev—a "kind of chemistry," as Reagan called it, took hold between them—the president was able to achieve a historic, sweeping nuclear disarmament treaty and redirect the two superpowers onto the path to a safer world. But for nearly dying, she concludes, he might never had found the will to end the Cold War.

* * *

Collectively these essays prove a truism worth emphasizing: the power of the American presidency is awesome but not without its limits. Presidents are constrained by many things—by politics, public opinion, Congress and the Supreme Court, and of course by the actions of other governments. Sometimes, no matter how great their dreams or magnanimous their aspirations, they are also reined in or thwarted by their own bodies, by family tragedy, or by their own worst tendencies. Yet in spite of these constraints they must strive to complete the goals they have set for themselves and the nation. Their structural restraints and impediments are difficult enough. When exacerbated by illness, loss, or weakness, the job frequently borders on the impossible, with the nation's course directly altered by what happens in their personal lives.

These twelve essays pull back the Oval Office's heavy curtain in order to show that personal side of presidential leadership. They also remind us that tomorrow is promised to no one, not even to the most successful, and that perhaps the most any person, even a president, can hope to control is their response to unexpected turns. The presidency was never a job for the faint of heart and never more so than today. The takeaway from these essays should therefore give pause to anyone who would consider running for this highest of offices and to any who would cast a vote for one candidate or another while prompting a singular question: Is this a person who can handle the problems we know and can foresee? Can they also take on these problems when fate also intervenes, and when difficulties or tragedies in their own lives arise? Our study suggests the strongest presidents make for the hardiest bearers of personal blows. It would behoove us all, historians and citizens alike, to ponder, then, when choosing leaders capable of handling the nation's woes, who might also prove most able to manage their own.

NOTE

1. George W. Bush, *Decision Points* (New York: Crown, 2010), p. 153.

Andrew Jackson was the frequent subject of sharp caricature. The impact of his controversial presidency on the republic was immense. "More than one such president a century," wrote the scholar Clinton Rossiter, "would be hard to take." [Library of Congress Prints and Photographs Division.]

1

A Crisis of His Own Contrivance

Andrew Jackson's Break with John C. Calhoun

DANIEL FELLER

Controversy and crisis permeated Andrew Jackson's presidency. Indeed, they nearly defined his life. Jackson functioned in such a perpetual atmosphere of crisis that it sometimes seemed he needed crisis in order to function at all. A telling instance came at the very outset of his presidency. Staggered by the death of his wife just after his election in 1828, Jackson on the eve of leaving Tennessee felt listless and depressed and nearly incapacitated. As he confessed to his old companion John Coffee, "My dear friend my heart is nearly broke. I try to summons up my usual fortitude but it is vain." But soon after arriving in Washington, Jackson learned that Tennessee congressmen were objecting to the choice of his old friend John Eaton for a seat in the cabinet. "He is animated by the shew of opposition which has appeared against Eaton," Jackson's friend James A. Hamilton reported to Martin Van Buren, "& he consequently is more like himself [.] He said to me this makes me well [.] I was born for a storm and a calm does not suit me."[1]

Born for a storm, Jackson lived in tumultuous times, but in the view of some observers the tumult around him never surpassed the tumult within. If Jackson lived always surrounded by crisis, was it because his character demanded and created crisis? Were the storms that he braved merely tempests of his own making? Was he, at bottom, mentally stable?

The question of what made Andrew Jackson tick has mesmerized and bedeviled generations of historians, as indeed it mesmerized and bedeviled his contemporaries. The crux of the issue concerns the interrelated workings of his intellect, his will, and his temper. Jackson's admirers, from his own closest associates on down to such modern historians and biographers as Arthur Schlesinger Jr., Robert Remini, Sean Wilentz, and Jon Meacham, have portrayed him as a man of strongly rooted democratic convictions as well as indomitable will. If he also had a famously volcanic temper—well, that could have its uses, too, as long as it was kept under control. And at least during his presidential years, his temper was supposedly always under control. Jackson's closest confidants averred that his legendary tantrums and tirades were simply staged for political effect. Martin Van Buren, who witnessed some of these performances, remarked on the "contradiction between [Jackson's] apparent undue excitement and his real coolness and self-possession." Another intimate, Amos Kendall, explained that Jackson was "ardent and impetuous" but never reckless. He simply thought faster than other men and, after making up his mind, he never hesitated: "Though he acted rapidly, he never acted rashly." Kendall testified flatly that "I never saw him in a passion." Senator Thomas Hart Benton and Jackson's onetime private secretary Nicholas Trist said the same. Jackson's emotions, in this view, were firmly grounded and never ungovernable. They were the instrument of his political will, never the determinant of it.[2]

So spoke Jackson's admirers. Henry Clay saw it differently. In 1837, near the close of Jackson's presidency, he complained in the Senate that Jackson "has swept over the Government, during the last eight years, like a tropical tornado," his ambition, wrath, and vanity destroying everything in their path. This is the Jackson of legend: indomitable indeed but driven not by studied conviction and principle but by primitive passions and raging hatreds. This is the Jackson who had fought duels and streetbrawls, who as a general had defied superiors and shot prisoners and subordinates, and who, when offered citations on international law to justify one of his military adventures, reportedly exploded, "Damn Grotius! Damn Pufendorf! Damn Vattel! This is a mere matter between Jim Monroe and myself." This is also the Jackson who is said on leaving the presidency to have voiced only two regrets: that he had not shot Henry Clay nor hanged John C. Calhoun.[3]

The list of contemporaries and historians who have seen Jackson as out of control—willful, self-obsessed, choleric, perhaps pathological—is every bit as long and distinguished as that on the other side. It includes most recently Daniel Walker Howe, author of the Pulitzer-winning *Oxford History of the United States* volume on what he pointedly refuses to call the Age of Jackson; and Andrew Burstein, author of a book tellingly titled *The Passions of Andrew Jackson*.[4]

It also included James Parton, Jackson's first and still best scholarly biographer, who in 1860 completed a three-volume *Life of Andrew Jackson*. Parton confessed that a year of intensive preparatory reading on Jackson had left him merely baffled, unable to arrive "at any conclusion whatever." It seemed that Jackson was simply a maze of contradictions: "A democratic autocrat. An urbane savage. An atrocious saint." But after traversing the country in search of evidence, gathering documents and remembrances from everyone he could find, and penning 1800 pages of text, Parton thought he had finally figured Jackson out. "He appears always to have meant well. But his ignorance of law, history, politics, science, of every thing which he who governs a country ought to know, was extreme.... His ignorance was as a wall round about him—high, impenetrable. He was imprisoned in his ignorance, and sometimes raged round his little, dim enclosure like a tiger in his den." Where real statesmen had policy, Jackson, it seemed, had only ferocity. "Andrew Jackson, in fact, was a fighting man, and little more than a fighting man. It was not till a political controversy became personalized, that his force and strength were elicited. He hated the whig party much, but Henry Clay more; nullification much, but Calhoun more; the bank much, but Biddle more. He was a thorough-going human fighting-cock."[5]

In this view, temperament, not conviction, governed Jackson's actions; and the salient features of that temperament were pent-up rage and a petulant, spoiled-child pique whenever he did not get his way. It is not hard to postulate plausible sources for Jackson's rage, beginning with his fatherless childhood and war-torn youth; nor to trace out its possible influence on policy, since there is no denying that (very much unlike Henry Clay or Jackson's own right-hand man, Martin Van Buren), Jackson did indeed, as Parton observed, personalize political disputes and demonize political enemies.

So which was the true Jackson, calculating or crazed? As usual with such starkly phrased dichotomies, the probable answer is somewhere in between, or a little bit of both. This should not be a surprise. We are all complicated and contradictory characters in our own ways. But that still leaves the puzzle of exactly how Jackson's complexities worked themselves out in practice, because one peculiarity of his presidency stands out, and that is its success.

This is not to open up the can-of-worms question of whether Jackson was a great president, the answer to which hinges largely on how one chooses to define greatness. Nor is to pronounce on whether Jackson's policies and legacy were good for the country or not. We can identify a successful president more narrowly and neutrally as one who defines substantive policy aims, musters popular support behind them, and sees them through to fruition, leaving aside for this purpose whatever unintended consequences they may one day produce.

By this instrumental measure, Jackson was perhaps the most successful president ever. In eight years he accomplished a full agenda: he overhauled the patronage, removed the Indians, destroyed the Bank of the United States, thwarted nullification, stymied Henry Clay's "American System" of conjoined protective tariff and internal improvements, brought several diplomatic contretemps to resolution, asserted and exercised novel presidential prerogatives, humbled and heeled the US Senate, forged a diffuse personal coalition into a disciplined and durable political party, articulated that party's ethos in enduring terms, won landslide reelection over the opposition's best man, and at the end maneuvered his hand-picked successor Martin Van Buren into the presidency despite the man's manifest unpopularity. Taken all in all, Jackson's presidency was not merely successful but transformational. This is largely why his name graces an era in American history.

And yet traits that many observers have found dominant in Jackson's character would seem to foreclose such a result. Men consumed by rage and resentment rarely make good politicians, and even if they do manage to get elected, they rarely make successful presidents. When put under stress, their weaknesses do them in. It is hard to imagine George Washington or Thomas Jefferson or Abraham Lincoln (or later, Franklin Roosevelt or John Kennedy or Ronald Reagan) ever once behaving as Jackson behaved almost daily in the White House: penning vitriolic and splenetic letters to be sent out across the country, or exploding in wrath at casual visitors. The question then, bluntly put, is how, given his apparent volatility, Jackson escaped disaster: why did he not (as many thought he would) simply self-destruct?

To canvass this subject thoroughly would take an entire book. This essay approaches the issue by looking at a single crisis, one of the greatest of Jackson's presidency: his severance in 1830–1831 from the man he purportedly later regretted not hanging: his first vice president, John C. Calhoun of South Carolina. This is a fitting case study because it perfectly counterposes the two views of Jackson's character and his mental processes. Calhoun was Jackson's principal adversary over nullification and a secondary adversary over the Bank of the United States—two of the signature issues of Jackson's presidency. Calhoun was also Jackson's antagonist in the Eaton affair and the Seminole War controversy, both personal quarrels having little or no intrinsic policy content at all. So with Jackson and Calhoun, which drove which: the personal or the political?

The story as usually told centers on the Eaton affair, a lurid tale that has enlivened histories of Jackson's presidency from Parton on down. In 1829 the newly elected Jackson appointed John Henry Eaton of Tennessee as his first secretary of war. Eaton was Jackson's Tennessee friend and neighbor, a former comrade-in-arms and campaign biographer. Though he had risen to be a US senator, Eaton lacked the stature and experience of some of his predecessors, and there were whispered doubts of his competence. But as Jackson later explained, he wanted "one confidential friend" in the cabinet, whose other members—even Secretary of State Martin Van Buren, who would soon become his closest counselor—were at first nearly strangers to him. Eaton also shared Jackson's enthusiasm for Indian removal, on which Jackson wanted to move quickly. Indian affairs fell within Eaton's War Department, and his avid cooperation enabled Jackson to announce and begin to implement his removal policy within three weeks of taking office, before Van Buren even reached town.[6]

But while Eaton's elevation raised eyebrows on his own account, what really shocked official Washington was the character of his wife, Margaret (or "Peggy"). Margaret had just recently married Eaton in what seemed undue haste after the death at sea, apparently by suicide, of her first husband, a navy purser. Margaret had a conspicuously forward personality and a reputation, whether deserved or not, as a loose woman. Tales of her alleged past dalliances with Eaton and other swains passed freely in the capital's circles. Leading ladies of Washington's close-knit society—among them three other cabinet wives and Jackson's own niece and White House hostess, Emily Donelson—visibly avoided her, refusing to return her calls or admit her to their entertainments.[7]

Jackson came charging to Margaret Eaton's defense. Interpreting the whispers against her as both slanders on female character and political thrusts aimed at Eaton and himself, he set out to vindicate her character and confound her detractors. Jackson sent operatives to collect sworn affidavits disproving the stories of Mrs. Eaton's extramarital trysts; he compiled these in a large book, had copies made, and circulated them to friends. When the minister of Jackson's own Washington church revealed himself as one of Mrs. Eaton's accusers, Jackson haled him before the cabinet, shouted him down, and then quit his church in disgust. Emily Donelson and her husband, Jackson's nephew and private secretary Andrew Jackson Donelson, were dispatched back to Tennessee.

While the ladies of Washington and their politician husbands avoided Mrs. Eaton, Secretary of State Van Buren, a widower with no wife to contend with, conspicuously paid court to her. For two years the administration staggered toward paralysis, its members barely speaking to each other. Finally, in 1831, Eaton and Van Buren cut the knot by offering to resign, giving Jackson an opening to demand resignations from the other secretaries so that he could start anew with a fresh slate. After the cabinet breakup, the circumstance that lay behind it, the ostracism of Margaret Eaton as unfit for decent society—long known in Washington but as yet unspoken in print—was finally published in the papers. Eaton, seeing his wife traduced before the nation, sought vengeance on her tormenters. He challenged two of his former cabinet colleagues to duels; and when one of them, former US Treasury secretary Samuel Ingham, derisively refused, Eaton stalked him in the Washington streets, intending to thrash him. Of this conduct Jackson heartily approved.

Many historians have seen the Eaton affair as the crucial pivot in Jackson's presidency. As Parton famously pronounced in 1860, "The political history of the United States, for the last thirty years, dates from the moment when the soft hand of Mr. Van Buren touched Mrs. Eaton's knocker." It was for this, as the story goes, that Van Buren was elevated in Jackson's affections; while Calhoun, the presumed mastermind of Margaret Eaton's humiliation, was cast out. Within months of the cabinet upheaval, Van Buren joined Jackson's 1832 reelection ticket as vice president, displacing Calhoun. Van Buren became president next and Calhoun never; and Andrew Jackson's emerging Democratic Party bore the organizational stamp and ideological bent of Van Buren's New York rather than Calhoun's South Carolina. Thus, in a common telling, everything that followed, including Jackson's course in the nullification crisis on which perhaps hung the fate of the republic, turned on little more than an irascible old man's pigheaded spite at those who had slighted poor Mrs. Eaton. Historian Edward Pessen, among many, marveled that the American political system "permitted its Chief Executive the latitude it did to determine the fate of grown men over such matters."[8]

Thus construed, the Eaton affair certainly challenges the picture of emotional poise and self-control painted by Jackson's contemporary and scholarly admirers. But while no one can deny Jackson's extraordinary investment in Mrs. Eaton's vindication, there is some difficulty in pinning his estrangement from Calhoun upon it. For Calhoun was never a principal player in the Eaton affair. In fact, to appearances he was hardly a player at all. Jackson had been prompt to brand the Eatons' isolation as a conspiracy against himself and his administration, but he initially traced that conspiracy not to Calhoun but to his old enemy Henry Clay and to those he called Clay's "satalites," "minions," "tools," and "hired slanderers." And while Calhoun's wife Floride did abhor Mrs. Eaton, she had little to do with her concerted snubbing, which played out in Washington over a long stretch of months when Floride was back home in South Carolina. In fact, the Eaton affair smoldered on for more than a year, until mid-summer 1830, before Jackson started directly blaming it on Calhoun. By that time a number of other things had happened.[9]

The first serious breaches between Jackson and Calhoun had surfaced back in Jackson's first congressional session, in the winter of 1829–30, and they were pretty clearly not over social relations but weighty matters of policy. On New Year's Eve, 1829, Jackson wrote his friend and counselor John Overton to praise Van Buren and chide Calhoun. He did voice displeasure over the conduct of some of Calhoun's friends toward Eaton; but that was not his main complaint. Jackson had challenged the legitimacy of the Bank of the United States in his first message to Congress in December. He had also taken a middle position on the protective tariff, hoping that a modest amelioration of duties would allay sectional jealousies and forestall a constitutional showdown. Since a moderately, rather than drastically, reduced tariff would still yield more revenue than the government in his view could prudently spend, Jackson had lastly proposed to distribute the surplus by formula among the states, thus further cementing the union and averting "*flagicious logg-rolling legislation*" in Congress. On all these matters, Jackson rightly predicted resistance from Calhoun. Calhoun and his South Carolina coadjutors considered the protective tariff not only sectionally oppressive but flatly unconstitutional. Far from sanctioning distribution of the surplus revenue, they insisted there should be no surplus to distribute, as the government had no right to levy taxes beyond its own wants. And they were already threatening state nullification of the tariff if they did not get their way in Washington.[10]

Provocations for Jackson's disaffection with Calhoun multiplied into 1830. There was some trouble over appointments, which suggested to

Jackson that Duff Green, editor of the administration's Washington paper, the *United States' Telegraph*, had a perhaps overweening sense of his own importance and was perhaps more devoted to promoting Calhoun's interest than sustaining Jackson's. In the House of Representatives, a committee chaired by Calhoun's South Carolina henchman George McDuffie manhandled Jackson's proposal to replace the electoral college with a popular vote for president. In early April 1830 Jackson received word of a plan, undertaken in Calhoun's interest, to derail the Pennsylvania legislature's pending endorsement of Jackson's bid for reelection. On April 13 McDuffie delivered a House report savaging Jackson's proposed alternative to the Bank of the United States. That very evening, Jackson delivered his famous toast at the Jefferson birthday dinner, "Our Federal Union: It Must Be Preserved." Everyone understood this to be a shot aimed directly at the South Carolina nullifiers and at Calhoun, who replied with a toast of his own.[11]

By this time Jackson was pretty sure who was behind what appeared to be concerted resistance to all his favorite measures—who was, as he put it, "the great actor in this secrete drama." And, as he wrote his friend John Coffee three days before the Jefferson birthday toast, he also had "evidence to unfold to you, the base hypocracy of the great secrete agent, as it respects myself, as early as 1818."[12]

Thus began, or rather resumed, the famous Seminole War controversy, to understand which requires circling all the way back to 1818. At that time Calhoun, who was then secretary of war under President James Monroe, had ordered Jackson, who was then major general in the US Army, to cross the border into the Spanish province of Florida to subdue and chastise the Seminole Indians. Jackson did just that. He also seized the occasion to do something he had long hankered to do: conquer Florida itself. In a lightning campaign, Jackson assailed and captured the main Spanish bastions at St. Marks and Pensacola, deposed the Spanish authorities, and installed his own administration. Jackson wrote Monroe that if given another regiment and a frigate, he would gladly "in a few days" take Cuba, too.[13]

Militarily the campaign was a splendid success. But it aroused great consternation in Washington, since Jackson had, on his own initiative, launched an invasion against an ostensibly friendly foreign power. He had no orders to attack the Spanish. In fact, his immediate predecessor in command, General Edmund Gaines, had direct orders *not* to attack them—orders that the administration knew Jackson had seen and presumed he would be governed by.

Calhoun, Jackson's direct superior in the administration, at first thought that Jackson should be repudiated and perhaps disciplined for this arrant violation of orders. But in confidential cabinet meetings he was talked out of it by Secretary of State John Quincy Adams, who saw that Jackson's escapade could be turned to advantage in his own diplomatic efforts to pry Florida permanently loose from Spain. Privately both Calhoun and President Monroe made plain to Jackson that they thought he had misinterpreted and exceeded his orders. But publicly the entire administration united behind Jackson and embraced his own defense: that the Spanish had provoked him by abetting and sheltering the Seminoles, and had thus willingly cast themselves as belligerents. The administration clung to this line and successfully rode out a hail of subsequent public outcry and diplomatic complaint. Within months, the Spanish relinquished Florida.

Jackson got wind at the time that there was some pointed criticism of him within Monroe's cabinet. He naturally assumed that it came from Monroe's Treasury secretary, William Crawford of Georgia. Jackson and Crawford hated each other roundly, and when the Monroe administration did close ranks with a public defense of Jackson, it was then Crawford's friends in Congress who answered with speeches and committee reports that pilloried Jackson's conduct.

All this was in 1818–1819. Over the ensuing years, Jackson received several hints—and finally in 1828 some pretty definite evidence—that it was really Calhoun and not Crawford who had spoken against him in Monroe's cabinet. There was at the time no reason to follow up on this information. Jackson and Calhoun had long been political allies and were now running mates, and the Seminole campaign was past history. But by April 1830, when he confided to Coffee that he had the goods on Calhoun, Jackson was readying for a break. An electoral asset in 1828, Calhoun had since become an encumbrance. His policy views, especially on the tariff and nullification, were by this time clearly divergent from Jackson's, and his apparent presidential itchings crossed Jackson's own growing inclination to stand for a second term. Having found a helpmeet and worthy successor in Van Buren, Jackson no longer needed Calhoun. He had come to distrust him, and it was in Jackson's nature always to prefer an open antagonist to a suspect ally.

And so it now suited Jackson to reopen the old Seminole wound. On May 12, 1830, he received the smoking gun he had been seeking: a direct statement from William Crawford, now in retirement, that Calhoun (and not he) had favored punishing Jackson in Monroe's cabinet twelve years before. The very next day, Jackson wrote Calhoun demanding an explanation. The timing and manner of this challenge, let it be noted, were entirely of Jackson's choosing. There was no need to bring this old story up at this moment; indeed, no compelling reason to bring it up at all, ever. We need not doubt Jackson's genuine anger at learning of Calhoun's seeming betrayal back in 1818. But he had shown himself quite capable of parking such emotions when it suited him, as indeed he had parked them over this very incident for some years previous. Jackson's challenge to Calhoun reveals a man capable of encasing his wrath within cool and merciless calculation. As he explained to James A. Hamilton, who had helped him bait the trap:

> I have had the fullest confidence in Mr Calhoun's frankness, honor, & integrity—but should he not be able to clear up satisfactorously the conduct charged against him you can easily judge without my expressing, the feelings & opinions, I am forced, from his conduct, to form of him. I have never abandoned a friend, without being forced to do so, from his own course to me—and I never break with one, without giving him a fair opportunity, first, to explain. In pursuing this course, the moment I had any thing tangible, with my usual frankness, I addressed him—you shall in due time see the correspondence—but it is due to him, & to justice, to give him time to explain—*he shall have it*—but I am afraid, he is in a dilemma, how he will get out, I wait for him to shew.[14]

He did not have to wait long. Calhoun, thrown off guard, gulped and stuttered and then coughed up a reply that went on for fifty-two pages and that explained entirely too much. Yes, he had initially favored disciplining Jackson in Monroe's cabinet, but he had fully and faithfully supported the decision not to do so, once that decision was reached. Deliberating alternative courses of action was precisely what confidential cabinet meetings were for—and what went on in them was nobody else's business. He and Monroe had never disguised from Jackson their belief that he had exceeded his orders: they had told him so directly at the time. They had also told him and believed, then and still, that while his judgment had been mistaken his motives were fully honorable. All of these defenses and explanations offered up by Calhoun were perfectly sound and reasonable, and none of them had any effect on Jackson whatever. It was like arguing with a wall. John C. Calhoun was not a man who generally invites sympathy, but in this case one almost has to feel sorry for him. There was no reason to revive this ancient episode except to damage him politically. He was being set up, and he knew it.[15]

Jackson answered Calhoun's apologia brusquely and coldly: "I had a right to believe that you were my sincere friend, and until now, never expected to have occasion to say of you, in the language of Cesar—*et tu Brute*. . . . Understanding you now, no further communication with you on this subject is necessary."[16]

Indeed, Jackson had gotten just what he sought—an admission, however rationalized, that Calhoun had criticized him in Monroe's Cabinet in 1818 and concealed the fact ever since. Jackson had succeeded in throwing Calhoun on the defensive and had extracted ammunition for a public break if ever he chose to make it. Calhoun, writing to John Forsyth, understood the damage: "That there are those, who intend, that this affair shall operate against me politically by causing a rupture between the President and myself, and thereby affect, if possible, my standing with the nation, I cannot doubt." The timing of the next move, in Jackson's mind, was still tied to policy. He instructed James A. Hamilton, who was preparing a newspaper riposte to George McDuffie's defense of the Bank of the United States, to leave Calhoun carefully out of it for now: "It might be thought to arise from personal feeling, and arouse the sympathy of the people in his favor—you know an experienced Genl always keeps a *strong reserve*; and hereafter it may become necessary to pass in review the rise & progress of this Hydra of corruption [the Bank], when it will be proper to expose its founders & supporters by name—then, & then only, can his name be brought with advantage & propriety before the nation."[17]

But Calhoun could not let go. Like a man falsely convicted of crime (which in a political sense he was), he could not stop proclaiming his innocence. Rather than let the matter lie, he continued to offer up defenses to Jackson. He called on surviving witnesses, including James Monroe and John Quincy Adams, to testify in his behalf; he exposed contradictions in Jackson's stated motives for reopening the affair; and he challenged the veracity of William Crawford, who replied by calling him "a degraded and disgraced man, for whom no man of honor and character could feel any other than the most sovereign contempt." For his part, Jackson repeatedly tried to cut Calhoun off, writing in July that he would "leave you Mr Crawford & all concerned to settle the affair in your own way, and now close this correspondence for ever."[18]

So far, down to around mid-1830, Jackson seems to have been fully in control of both the situation and himself. But in the ensuing months that began to change. Having conjured up Calhoun as the evil genius of his administration, he began to believe in his own bogeyman—and to be increasingly spooked by it. He wrote off Calhoun's anguished declarations of innocence as "full evidence of the duplicity & insincerity of the man." In July he began calling him "the great Magician" and blaming him for the Eaton affair and for political difficulties everywhere, in Pennsylvania and Tennessee and Alabama as well as South Carolina. By Christmas 1830 Jackson was ready to ascribe all his travails to "the secrete workings of the great political magician who works in darkness, is plausible, but cunning, and as deceitful as Satan." Even his own niece and nephew, in refusing to associate with Mrs. Eaton, Jackson now believed had been "overreached by the designing and artful cunning of the puppets of J. C. Calhoun, who in secrete, worked the wiers, and who dreaded the popularity of Eaton, & that he would not be his supporter, & it is only the second Edition of the secrete lunge in the dark against me in 1818, under the open & avowed declarations of friendship, & support."[19]

In less than one year, Calhoun, without actually doing much of anything, had progressed in Jackson's mind from suspect supporter to ingrate and hypocrite to something very close to the devil incarnate. Jackson's private ventings by the end of 1830 suggest a man enwebbed in conspiracies of his own imagining, consumed by nearly paranoiac rage. And yet, just two days after penning the lurid phrases above, he could coolly note to Eaton himself that Crawford's most recent broadside to Calhoun over the Seminole business "places Mr C. in a very unpleasant dilemma."[20]

What was going on in Jackson's mind? He was at least correct in believing that Calhounites (whether or not Calhoun himself) had hoped to control the policy course of his administration and/or to ease him out of the presidency in Calhoun's favor after one term. He had come to view the isolation and degradation of Secretary of War Eaton as a calculated means to that end. So far, whether entirely accurate or not, this made political sense. And heading it off by provoking Calhoun over the Seminole business, whether fairly or not, likewise made political sense; for in a direct contest for popular favor, a matchup of public personas, Calhoun, whether in the right or not and no matter what the issue, could not hope to stand against Jackson—and both men knew it. Calhoun had sized up the matter correctly to Forsyth: a rupture would damage *his* "standing with the nation," not Jackson's. Personalizing his policy divisions with Calhoun, and thus politically enlisting his own vast popularity, was an adept way to tilt the verdict Jackson's way in the court of public opinion.

Nevertheless it was Calhoun, not Jackson, who made their quarrel public. In February 1831, seeking to defeat what he on his side saw as a giant conspiracy against himself, Calhoun made a decisive move. He published a fifty-page pamphlet disclosing the entire Seminole correspondence, including the recent back-and-forths between himself, Jackson, Crawford, Monroe, Adams, and others. Though the timing was not of Jackson's choice, there was no great reason for him to regret this publication. Indeed, Eaton, who Calhoun had approached through an intermediary, helped gull Calhoun into making it by offering private assurances that it would not further estrange him from Jackson—as, of course, it did. The break between the two men was now open and irrevocable.[21]

Considered simply in its political aspect, Jackson's resuscitating of the Seminole controversy was a brilliant maneuver. Driving Calhoun into open opposition helped dramatize their policy cleavages and rally Jackson's own following. Secondarily, it also helped cement Jacksonians and Crawfordites. This, too, was politically opportune; for, beginning with the Maysville Road Veto in May 1830, the same month he confronted Calhoun, Jackson's position on political economy began turning back to the Jeffersonian strict constructionism that Crawford had once stood for and that Jackson himself, as a post–War of 1812 nationalist, had once largely opposed.[22]

Still, as a political stroke, the Seminole affair was finished with the publication of Calhoun's exposition in February 1831. It had done its work and could not be improved upon. Calhoun and Crawford could, if they chose, go on calling each other liars in public (as indeed they did); there was, as Jackson himself had already declared, no need for him to say more. Jackson's friend John Overton reminded him so directly, and Jackson agreed that in exposing their correspondence Calhoun "has been cutting his own throat as fast as he can politically."[23]

And yet it was at precisely this point that Jackson's personal investment in the affair seems to have lost all compass. No matter its political effect, Calhoun's pamphlet had publicly challenged Jackson's integrity, his character; and Jackson could not let go of that. Instead, over the next year and a half, even while the bank and tariff issues both built to a head, he proceeded, with huge investment of time and energy, to construct, with the full intention of publishing, a rebuttal to Calhoun in the form of a narrative of the events in the Seminole controversy. If Jackson's behavior had so far exemplified a politician in control of himself, this carefully composed history suggests the opposite: a man whose craving for exoneration was so obsessive that it could drive him into either monstrous falsehood or paranoid fantasy, if not both.

The centerpiece of Jackson's intended exposition was the notorious "Rhea letter." Just before being put in command of the Seminole expedition back in 1818, Jackson had written President Monroe offering to conquer Florida on his own responsibility, "without implicating the Government," if Monroe would give him a private go-ahead through then Tennessee congressman John Rhea. Monroe had received Jackson's letter but had not answered it; in fact, according to his later word, he put it aside and did not even read it until months later. Through all the rehashing of the Seminole campaign that followed, from 1818 all the way down to 1830, the Rhea letter was never mentioned. There was good reason for this on both sides: on Monroe's side, because the letter was private and had played no part in official proceedings; on Jackson's side, because it offered damaging evidence of the very warlike proclivities and disdain for constitutional restraint for which, as a general and later presidential aspirant, he had been much criticized.[24]

The public first learned of Jackson's Rhea letter through allusions in Calhoun's pamphlet. The correspondence Calhoun published included an 1830 claim by Crawford that the Rhea letter had been before Monroe's cabinet during its consideration of the Seminole campaign—a claim countered by vehement denials from Calhoun, Monroe, and Monroe's attorney general William Wirt. While the disputants differed over whether the letter had been invoked in cabinet counsels, none of them suggested that Monroe had actually answered it. Yet now that its existence had been revealed, Jackson set out to prove that Monroe had indeed answered it: that he had given Jackson, through Rhea, direct prior authority for the conquest of Florida—and had then asked him to destroy the evidence.

Jackson first sought confirmation of this from Rhea himself. Rhea in 1831 was 77 years old and befuddled. His reply to Jackson's demand showed, in historian John Spencer Bassett's apt phrasing, that he "had no recollection of the affair but was willing to have one if he was told what it was about." Jackson supplied the compliant Rhea with his story of Monroe's pre-approval of the Seminole campaign and pushed him into writing Monroe a bumptious letter demanding that he confirm it. Monroe was now dying in New York. The very last time he raised pen to paper was to sign a statement declaring the whole concoction "utterly unfounded & untrue."[25]

Nothing deterred, Jackson sought proof elsewhere. One of his leading congressional critics back in 1819 was Senator Abner Lacock of Pennsylvania, a known Crawford partisan who had produced a devastating committee report attacking the Seminole campaign. Jackson now claimed, in drafts of his contemplated publication, that Calhoun had set Lacock up. Having failed to get Jackson condemned in the cabinet, Jackson now said, Calhoun had taken his Rhea letter proposing a conquest of Florida and shown it to Lacock while deliberately concealing the administration's approving response—the very response that Monroe on his deathbed swore he had never made. Thus (charged Jackson) Calhoun had made it look to Lacock as if Jackson had really intended to conquer Florida all along, from the beginning, with or without orders (which, by the way, was essentially true). And then (wrote Jackson), having provoked Lacock to produce a report condemning Jackson, Calhoun had paid Lacock off at the end of his Senate term with a government job.[26]

This was a literally fantastic set of allegations. Jackson was now claiming that Calhoun and Monroe had given him positive orders—in Jackson's exact words, "as effectually orders *to take and occupy the Province of Florida as if that object had been declared on their face*"—and had then devised an elaborate conspiracy to frame him for doing it. It would have been a perversely self-defeating conspiracy, one must note, because Jackson had been the administration's general and the administration had staked its own political survival on his defense. The whole thing made no sense.[27]

One tidbt was true. Lacock had indeed found employment as a federal contractor after his Senate term expired in 1819. But it was Crawford, not Calhoun, who had procured it for him. Jackson had noted this at the time and branded it as a payoff for Lacock's report. In fact, he had accused Crawford not only of suborning Lacock's report but of actually writing it. But all this was now forgotten.[28]

Taken as a whole, Jackson's history of the Seminole affair (one version of which runs twenty-one printed pages in *The Papers of Andrew Jackson*), painstakingly compiled over a period of more than a year, was a maze of distortions and fabrications, implausibilities and impossibilities, self-contradictory and indeed largely self-incriminating. And yet Jackson intended to publish all of this. He was stopped by a somewhat comical turn of events. Abner Lacock was still alive. Early in 1832 Jackson approached him through a political lackey, Henry Baldwin of Pennsylvania, whom Jackson had appointed to the Supreme Court (and who had returned the favor by filing a vigorous dissent in *Worcester v. Georgia*, the famous Cherokee Indian case). Baldwin, who had his own reasons for wanting some payback against Calhoun, sounded Lacock out and assured Jackson that he would confirm the whole story of how Calhoun had prompted him to condemn the Seminole campaign. Jackson craved the confirmation as putting the final seal on Calhoun's perfidy. Anticipating it, his draft narrative of the episode concluded: "These facts are stated *upon the authority of Mr. Lacock himself*."[29]

Lacock was no political friend of Jackson or of Calhoun, and he proved reluctant to enter into a moribund controversy for the benefit of either. But he finally consented to answer written questions from Jackson, provided that full copies of the exchange were furnished to Calhoun as well. Accordingly, at the end of May 1832, Jackson submitted, through Baldwin, a series of queries to Lacock.[30]

The answers that came back must have staggered him. To the first query, whether Calhoun had shown him Jackson's Rhea letter, Lacock replied: "Mr Calhoun never did at any time or upon any occasion, communicate to me, either verbally or in writing, his knowledge of the existence of such a letter," although he had learned of its contents from other sources. To Jackson's query whether Calhoun had opined to him on the Seminole campaign, Lacock replied that he had:

> Mr Calhoun calld upon me in the Senate Chamber, & askd me into a committee room, and when there said he wishd to converse with me in regard to your operations in Florida, as that subject was before a committee, of which he understood I was chairman. He then stated the subject had embarrass'd the administration, and presented many dificulties at first, but a course had been finally agreed upon, that he had flattered himself would have been generally acquiescd in, or

approved, and he was sorry to find himself mistaken, or words to this effect.

Calhoun had further explained that "when the subject was first presented by the President, he had been for taking pretty strong, & instituting an inquiry into your conduct, but after Mature consideration the Cabinet had made a different decision, and he had acquies'd and he observed he had yielded his opinion with less reluctance, finding the President strongly inclined to adopt a different course. and he added that while he was a member of the cabinet, he should consider it his duty to sustain the measures of the President if it could be done with any propriety." Calhoun had also declared Jackson's motives "pure and patriotic" and observed that he had dealt with the Spanish no more harshly than they deserved.[31]

In short, said Lacock, Calhoun had not tried to talk him into condemning Jackson in his report. He had tried to talk him out of it.

Lacock could not resist a mocking signoff. As Jackson had avowed to him that he aimed only at "'*the establishment of truth, and to do justice to all men,*'" Lacock declared his "sincere pleasure" in furthering such a laudable end, and thus, he hoped, in "producing harmony" and restoring "amicable relations" between Jackson and Calhoun.

Jackson's only answer was embarrassed silence—and what passed thereafter between Jackson and Baldwin, who had egged him on to query Lacock, can only be imagined. Lacock's testimony exploded the leading count in the indictment of Calhoun. Further, the formal cast of the exchange, with copies furnished to Calhoun, left no ambiguity or leeway for maneuver. Calhoun now held firsthand evidence that Jackson's central charge against him in the Seminole controversy was the precise reverse of the truth. Jackson had no recourse but to simply drop the matter. Perhaps providentially, just days later Congress passed a bill to recharter the Bank of the United States. As Jackson turned his attention first to his Bank Veto and then to the looming nullification crisis and presidential campaign, the Seminole controversy was thrust aside. Jackson never published his history, and from this point on the subject vanishes from his correspondence.

What can one make of all this? Were Jackson's mental processes diabolical, or delusional? And how can one reconcile this bizarre excursion with his previous shrewd circumspection in handling Calhoun? For what it is worth, if one begins with the premise that Calhoun had been conspiring ever since 1818 to destroy Jackson, then every piece of evidence that Jackson summoned to prove that point could indeed be fitted, or contorted, to that end. Then every seemingly innocent move by Calhoun became part of the deception; every friendly word a decoy, every explanation a lie. But even before Lacock's torpedo, there was no way a sober and level-headed judge could have reasoned on this evidence toward a judgment of Calhoun's persistent animus unless he had presumed it to start out with.

At first sight, the picture of Jackson that this episode thus presents is, if anything, even more disturbing than that of a man who had trouble controlling his temper, who could be excited by passion into occasional explosions of spleen. Rather, it shows Jackson in his study, apparently calm and composed, wallowing dangerously and self-indulgently in lurid conspiratorial fantasies about his own vice president, and spending inordinate time and psychic energy on pursuing them. Jackson had the reputation of a firebrand, but his true character was more that of a brooder. His psychosis, if psychosis it was, was chronic, not acute.

But—to return to our opening question—was it really psychosis, and if so how did Jackson survive it?

The Seminole controversy and the Eaton affair were only two beads in a long string of controversies in Jackson's public career. Indeed, controversy nearly made up that career. In every quarrel, Jackson seemed to be compelled by what one historian has called "the search for vindication." Three elements marked that search. First, Jackson had to be right. He saw his integrity, his character, his reputation constantly at risk. Therefore he could not readily admit error, nor brook contradiction. Secondly, he attributed any determined opposition to personal motives; he personalized disputes and demonized foes. Thirdly, he had a more than common ability to rearrange facts and adjust his memory to suit his purposes, to convince himself that what he needed at the moment to assert was true really was. He believed in his own contrivances, and could therefore proclaim them, even when false, with full honest conviction: not an admirable trait perhaps, but sometimes politically a very useful one.[32]

Taken together, these traits all but guaranteed entrapping Jackson in one vicious quarrel after another. Many of these blowups, including ones that had produced duels and near-duels in Jackson's pre-presidential years, were needless and pointless. The clashes with Calhoun were not pointless. Indeed, the political stakes could hardly have been higher, with not just the succession rivalry between Calhoun and Van Buren but the entire success of Jackson's policy agenda hanging in the balance. And as long as these larger objects were to be served, Jackson kept himself carefully in check, venting his wrath in private but restraining it in public. Even in the Eaton affair, which in touching his own family sorely taxed his emotional equilibrium, Jackson struck no public pose until after the Cabinet had already broken up. Unlike Calhoun, he knew when the best course politically was simply to keep silent.

It was not until after the Seminole controversy and the Eaton affair, as public events, had concluded and wrought their consequences that Jackson's judgment on them came increasingly unhinged. With no longer any calculation of political effect to restrain them, his resentments and revenge cravings were left free to run riot. It was, in other words, precisely when Jackson's personal quarrels became untethered from policy pursuits that his private demons came unloosed.

Yet even then he had two further safety nets to fall back on. The first was his friends. As president, the notoriously hotheaded Jackson surrounded himself with famously cool counselors. This was perhaps deliberate. It was certainly fortunate. Jackson rarely made a move without clearing it beforehand with an inner circle of advisors, among them Martin Van Buren, John Overton, John Coffee, and James A. Hamilton. These were even-tempered and politically astute men, and they saved him from embarrassment and perhaps disaster on many occasions. The Seminole controversy was likely one of them. In the spring of 1832, before Abner Lacock blew a hole in Jackson's narrative, he circulated drafts of it around to his confidential circle, asking their opinion. One copy went to Hamilton, who (in his words) "urgently advised him not to publish."[33]

And the bottom line was that Jackson did not publish. Having purged his wrath against Calhoun in drafts of his outlandish history, he consigned them to his private papers and so survived to fight another day. As the break with Calhoun illustrated, Jackson as president was his own best friend and potential worst enemy. His failings created perils that his strengths allowed him to survive. Jackson lacked equanimity and the ability to see things from an opposing point of view. While the presence of those traits helped steer some presidents from needless controversy, their absence in Jackson propelled him into nearly unending crisis and made every crisis personal. Yet when acting in crisis he tempered his famous vehemence with a sometimes astonishing political shrewdness and his impetuosity with a saving self-restraint. Even as Jackson acted deftly to politically disarm John C. Calhoun, he indulged in lurid imaginings of Calhoun's perfidy. His obsession with Calhoun brought him to the edge of a self-inflicted public disaster—but, in the end, not quite over it. In this crisis as in others of his presidency, Jackson's final line of defense against himself was a hard-earned self-possession that stopped him just short of irretrievable misstep. He never quite forgot himself so far as to lose sight of consequences. Andrew Jackson applied in politics a lesson he had learned in war: a good general always keeps a strong reserve.

NOTES

1. Jackson to John Coffee, Jan. 17, 1829, in *The Papers of Andrew Jackson: Volume VII, 1829* (henceforth *PAJ VII*), ed. Daniel Feller, et al. (Knoxville: University of Tennessee Press, 2007); James A. Hamilton to Martin Van Buren, Feb. 23, 1829, Van Buren Papers, Library of Congress.
2. Martin Van Buren, *Inquiry into the Origins and Course of Political Parties in the United States* (New York: Hurd and Houghton, 1867), 324–25; William Stickney, ed., *Autobiography of Amos Kendall* (Boston: Lee and Shepard, 1872), 634–35. See also Arthur M. Schlesinger Jr., *The Age of Jackson* (Boston, Little, Brown and Company, 1946), 36–43; Sean Wilentz, *The Rise of American Democracy: Jefferson to Lincoln* (New York: W. W. Norton & Company, 2005), 309; Robert V. Remini, *Andrew Jackson*, 3 vols. (New York: Harper & Row, 1977–84); Sean Wilentz, *Andrew*

Jackson (New York: Henry Holt and Company, 2005); Jon Meacham, *American Lion: Andrew Jackson in the White House* (New York: Random House, 2008).

3. *Register of Debates in Congress*, 24th Cong., 2nd sess., 438 (Jan. 16, 1837); Helen Nicolay, *Our Nation in the Building* (New York: The Century Co., 1916), 149; Augustus C. Buell, *History of Andrew Jackson* (New York: Charles Scribner's Sons, 1904), 2:363.
4. Daniel Walker Howe, *What Hath God Wrought: The Transformation of America, 1815–1848* (New York: Oxford University Press, 2007); Andrew Burstein, *The Passions of Andrew Jackson* (New York: Alfred A. Knopf, 2003).
5. James Parton, *Life of Andrew Jackson* (New York: Mason Brothers, 1860), 1:vii; 3:699, 695.
6. Jackson memorandum, c. 1831, in *The Papers of Andrew Jackson: Volume IX, 1831* (henceforth *PAJ IX*), ed. Daniel Feller, et al. (Knoxville: University of Tennessee Press, 2013), 795. Jackson announced his removal policy in a March 23, 1829, message to the Creeks, in *PAJ VII*, 112–13.
7. The standard account of the Eaton affair is John F. Marszalek, *The Petticoat Affair: Manners, Mutiny and Sex in Andrew Jackson's White House* (New York: The Free Press, 1997). See also Kirsten E. Wood, "'One Woman So Dangerous to Public Morals': Gender and Power in the Eaton Affair," *Journal of the Early Republic* 17 (Summer 1997): 237–75.
8. Parton, *Life of Jackson*, 3:287; Edward Pessen, *Jacksonian America: Society, Personality, and Politics* (Homewood, IL: The Dorsey Press, 1969), 312.
9. Jackson to Ezra S. Ely, Mar. 23, 1829, Jackson to John C. McLemore, Apr. 26, 1829, Jackson to John Coffee, Mar. 22, 1829, and Jackson to Richard K. Call, July 5, 1829, in *PAJ VII*, 114–16, 184, 108–9, 326. Jackson first linked Calhoun directly to the Eaton affair in a July 28, 1830, letter to William B. Lewis, in *The Papers of Andrew Jackson: Volume VIII, 1830* (henceforth *PAJ VIII*), ed. Daniel Feller, et al. (Knoxville: University of Tennessee Press, 2010), 455.
10. Jackson to John Overton, Dec. 31, 1829, in *PAJ VII*, 655–56.
11. Duff Green to Jackson, Jan. 4, 1830, in *PAJ VIII*, 11–12; Jackson to John Coffee, Apr. 10, 1830, in *PAJ VIII*, 183–84; Henry Petrikin to Jackson, Apr. 2, 1830, in *PAJ VIII*, 171–73; "Bank of the United States," House Report 358, 21st Cong., 1st sess.; "Toast at Jefferson Birthday Dinner" in *PAJ VIII*, 190–91.
12. Jackson to Coffee, Apr. 10, 1830, in *PAJ VIII*, 183.
13. Jackson to Monroe, June 2, 1818, in *The Papers of Andrew Jackson: Volume IV, 1816–1820* [henceforth *PAJ IV*], ed. Harold D. Moser, et al. (Knoxville: University of Tennessee Press, 1994), 215. On the Seminole War and subsequent controversy, see David S. Heidler and Jeanne T. Heidler, *Old Hickory's War: Andrew Jackson and the Quest for Empire* (Mechanicsburg, PA: Stackpole Books, 1996), and Daniel Feller, "The Seminole Controversy Revisited: A New Look at Andrew Jackson's 1818 Florida Campaign," *Florida Historical Quarterly* 88 (Winter 2010): 309–25.
14. Jackson to Calhoun, May 13, 1830, and Jackson to James A. Hamilton, May 29, 1830, in *PAJ VIII*, 255–59, 304–5.
15. Calhoun to Jackson, May 13 and 29, 1830, in *PAJ VIII*, 260, 305–21.
16. Jackson to Calhoun, May 30, 1830, in *PAJ VIII*, 321–22.

17. Calhoun to John Forsyth, June 1, 1830, and Jackson to Hamilton, June 3, 1830, in *PAJ VIII*, 341–42, 342–44.
18. William Crawford to Calhoun, Oct. 2, 1830, in Clyde N. Wilson, ed., *The Papers of John C. Calhoun: Volume XI, 1829–1832* (Columbia: University of South Carolina Press, 1978), 245; Jackson to Calhoun, July 19, 1830, in *PAJ VIII*, 434.
19. Jackson note on Calhoun to Jackson, Aug. 25, 1830, Jackson to Lewis, July 28, 1830, and Jackson to John C. McLemore, Dec. 25, 1830, in *PAJ VIII*, 506, 455, 707–14.
20. Jackson to John H. Eaton, Dec. 27, 1830, in *PAJ VIII*, 717.
21. *Correspondence between Gen. Andrew Jackson and John C. Calhoun, President and Vice-President of the U. States, on the Subject of the Course of the Latter, in the Deliberations of the Cabinet of Mr. Monroe, on the Occurrences in the Seminole War* (Washington, DC: Duff Green, 1831). The entire text also appeared in the *United States' Telegraph*, Feb. 17, 1831. Eaton had promised Calhoun's friend Felix Grundy that he would show the proposed publication to Jackson and relay word back of any objection. He then did not inform Jackson, leaving Calhoun to believe that he had. A subsequent *Telegraph* story implying that Jackson had seen and approved Calhoun's text infuriated Jackson. Jackson to Andrew J. Donelson, Mar. 24, 1831, in *PAJ VIII*, 141–45.
22. Although Jackson's 1828 campaign muted his policy positions to sustain a trans-sectional coalition, as a senator and presidential aspirant in 1824 he had supported both federal internal improvements and a protective tariff. The Maysville Road Veto repudiated the former, and in December 1831 Jackson withdrew his support for protection, endorsing a reduction of duties to meet the minimal wants of the government and silently dropping the idea of distributing the surplus revenue. The latter move, as he explained to Van Buren, would "annihilate the nullifiers as they will be left without any pretext of complaint." But it also bespoke a broader turn back toward Jeffersonian precept. Jackson to Van Buren, Nov. 14, 1831, in *PAJ IX*, 694.
23. John Overton to Jackson, Feb. 3, 1831, and Jackson to Overton, Feb. 8, 1831, in *PAJ IX*, 52–53, 68–69.
24. Jackson to James Monroe, Jan. 6, 1818, in *PAJ IV*, 166–67.
25. Jackson to John Rhea, Jan. 4, Apr. 23, and June 2, 1831, and Rhea to Monroe, June 3, 1831, in *PAJ IX*, 8–11, 209–10, 282–83, 286–88; Rhea to Jackson, [Feb. 1831], in *PAJ IX*, 109–10; *Correspondence of Andrew Jackson: Volume IV, 1829–1832*, ed. John Spencer Bassett (Washington: Carnegie Institution, 1929), 221; Stanislaus Murray Hamilton, ed., *The Writings of James Monroe: Volume VII, 1824–1831* (New York: G. P. Putnam's Sons, 1903), 234–36. On the Rhea letter generally, see the Seminole War citations in Note 13 above and also Richard R. Sternberg, "Jackson's 'Rhea Letter' Hoax," *Journal of Southern History* 2 (November 1936): 480–96.
26. Lacock's report is Senate Document 100, 15th Cong., 2d sess., Feb. 24, 1819. Jackson's draft publication, titled "An exposition of Mr. Calhoun's course towards General Jackson," is in *PAJ IX*, 804–26. A shorter and apparently earlier version is in *PAJ IX*, 797–804.
27. "Exposition," in *PAJ IX*, 808. Further on, Jackson repeated that his measures were "positively authorized by the President himself" ("Exposition," *PAJ IX*, 819).

28. Abner Lacock to James Monroe, Jan. 30, 1820, Monroe Papers, Library of Congress; Jackson to John Clark, Apr. 20, 1819, in *Correspondence of Andrew Jackson: Volume II, 1814–1819*, ed. John Spencer Bassett (Washington, DC: Carnegie Institution, 1927), 416; Jackson memorandum, c. Feb. 1822, in *Correspondence of Andrew Jackson: Volume III, 1820–1828*, ed. John Spencer Bassett (Washington: Carnegie Institution, 1928), 150–51.
29. "Exposition," in *PAJ IX*, 822.
30. Jackson to Baldwin and to John C. Calhoun, May 28, 1832, in *The Papers of Andrew Jackson: Volume X, 1832* [henceforth *PAJ X*], ed. Daniel Feller et al. (Knoxville: University of Tennessee Press, 2016), 287–89. The letters between Jackson, Baldwin, Lacock, and Calhoun arranging the approach are in *PAJ X*, 53–54, 128–31, 232–36, 254–55, 272–74, 292–93.
31. Lacock to Jackson, June 25, 1832, in *PAJ X*, 324–29.
32. James C. Curtis, *Andrew Jackson and the Search for Vindication* (Boston: Little, Brown and Company, 1976).
33. Jackson to Hamilton, April 26, 1832, in *PAJ X*, 237–38.

TYLER RECEIVING THE NEWS OF HARRISON'S DEATH.

The serenity of this pastoral scene would prove to be misleading. As the first president to assume the office upon the death of his predecessor, John Tyler was at constant pains to establish his legitimacy throughout this tumultuous single term. [Library of Congress, General Collection.]

2

"I am President"

John Tyler, Presidential Succession, the Crisis of Legitimacy, and the Defense of Presidential Power

AARON SCOTT CRAWFORD

Just at daybreak on April 5, 1841, Fletcher Webster knocked on the door of the colonial brick townhouse on Francis Street in Williamsburg. Only the day before, his father, Secretary of State Daniel Webster, had dispatched him from Washington with an urgent message for the vice president of the United States. The young Webster, a State Department clerk, rode furiously throughout the night. One-hundred-fifty miles later, John Tyler, in his bedclothes, answered the door. The Cabinet, which had pointedly addressed the message to the "Vice-President of the United States," had grave news: the president was dead.[1]

William Henry Harrison's death was no surprise. Secretary Webster had written to Tyler about the president's illness two weeks earlier. Though the Cabinet largely failed to keep Tyler adequately informed as his health declined, and though some newspapers reported that Harrison was improving, on April 3, Richmond attorney and Tyler friend James Lyon wrote to inform him of the president's grave condition. After Harrison's election the *Hudson River Chronicle* had posed a common sentiment: "General Harrison will be our next President, if he lives until the fourth of March next." Months before the 1840 election, political opponents had raised the likelihood of the sixty-eight-year-old Harrison failing to live out his term. Moreover, Tyler's friends and advisors had also warned him about his potential succession. Now, standing in the doorway of his home, Tyler read the news. Soon he heard the report of Harrison's final words, likely meant for him: "Sir—I wish you to understand the true principles of government. I wish them carried out. I ask nothing more."[2]

John Tyler, stubborn and resilient, allowed his devotion to republicanism to put him at the center of controversy and made him an unlikely defender of presidential power. Through the death of his wife, several Cabinet officers, and an unprecedented level of vilification, he proved indefatigable in his protection of the office. Tyler was the first man ever to learn he had been elevated to the presidency by death rather than election. Everything he would do in the ensuing hours, weeks, and months, was wholly without precedent. Nothing he did would prove easy, and indeed most of his actions generated significant criticism not only from the popular press but also from the men his predecessor had chosen to serve in his Cabinet. Although elected as vice president on a ticket dedicated to reducing executive power and subjugating the office to Congress, he fought all efforts to carry out those plans. Instead, Tyler became the most ardent defender of a powerful presidency between the American Revolution and the Civil War. Beginning with establishing the vice president as the legitimate successor to the president, he repeatedly defended challenges to his legitimacy. In doing so he ran contrary to his own party and, to a real extent, the national will.

His enemies vilified him in response, threatening ruination, impeachment, and even death. Tyler's vacillations, stubbornness, and ambitions often complicated matters. Through his struggle, he endured the deaths of his wife and several Cabinet members. While much of his presidency was spent in crises, Tyler often brought them upon himself in his effort to preserve what he believed was the executive's constitutional prerogatives. In the, end an unelected man did as much to define the modern presidency as any other chief executive in the nation's history, demonstrating that fate can indeed play a hand, and an unexpected hand at that, in the national story.

Little in Tyler's background foretold his becoming a great defender of executive power. Born to a distinguished planter family in 1790, he was shaped by the politics and society of Virginia. His father, John Tyler Sr., was a staunch Jeffersonian who feared centralized government and dedicated himself to the principles of states' rights and limited government, even fighting the ratification of the Constitution. The republicanism that shaped young Tyler came from Thomas Jefferson's Kentucky Resolutions of 1798. In those resolutions, Jefferson, a family friend, laid down a theory of states' rights that included nullification of federal law and even hinted at the right of secession. The growth of the market economy and increasing partisanship inspired fear in the senior Tyler about the future of republicanism. He instilled those "first principles" in his children and to his friend, Thomas Jefferson, swore: "I will die in the good old cause."[3]

Tyler's republican principles emanated from Virginia's slave society as well and in particular from its carefully stratified culture. As a white, propertied slaveowner, he resided at the top of the deeply paternalistic and racial social structure. Slavemasters such as Tyler became devoted to the strong Southern code of honor in life and governance to assure stability. Gentlemen ruled the patriarchal slave society of Virginia and derived their sense of masculinity from their idea of honor and the responsibility it bestowed. A man of honor consequently exercised ultimate power over his household, family, land, and slaves. To maintain order and dominance, a gentleman needed consistency of principles. While Tyler's manners, grace, and charm marked him as a gentleman, they masked the stubbornness that inspired his utter devotion to republican principles and resistance to submitting to the will of others.[4]

In 1816, the young Tyler entered national politics as a staunch Jeffersonian republican. In the House of Representatives, and later the Senate, he fought any legislation that threatened state sovereignty, including the Second Bank of the United States and the Missouri Compromise. His belief in limited government led him to support Andrew Jackson and join the burgeoning Democratic Party, in spite of his distaste for democracy. Tyler's dogged independence put him at odds with Jackson. Often he refused to vote for Jackson's nominees or support legislation if it violated his republican principles. Nothing violated those principles like Jackson's threat to subdue South Carolina when the state nullified federal tariff law.[5]

Before his elevation to the presidency in 1841, therefore, Tyler had already witnessed and participated in the slow-burning conflict between president and Congress over executive power, and the related contest over the limits of national power over the states. In the early 1830s Jackson's imperious behavior against the Second Bank of the United States led to Tyler's estrangement from the Democratic Party. While he agreed with Jackson that the bank was unconstitutional, he opposed the president's removal of the government's deposits from the bank. Tyler condemned the removal as a dangerous abuse of executive power: "Concede to the President the power to dispose of the public money as he pleases, and it is vain to talk of checker and balances. The presidential office swallows up all power, and the president becomes every inch a king." In 1834 he joined the emerging Whig party in voting for Jackson's censure and resigned his Senate seat when the Virginia legislature ordered him to vote to expunge the censure. By 1836 Tyler had joined the Whigs, who awarded him forty-seven electoral votes in that year's vice presidential election.[6]

The Whig party struggled to curtail the expansion of executive power exercised by Jackson and his hand-picked successor, Martin Van Buren. That struggle gained urgency after the financial collapse and subsequent Panic of 1837. The public came to believe Jackson's economic policies were responsible for the crisis, but President Van Buren refused to consider a new national bank or any substantive relief. In 1840, the Whigs were dedicated to defeating Van Buren and passed over the party's leader, Henry Clay, for war hero William Henry Harrison. The Democrats inadvertently established the patrician Harrison as a populist hero. Democrats inadvertently handed their opponents a powerful image for Harrison. "Give him a barrel of hard cider and settle a pension of two thousand a year on him," wrote a Democratic newspaper, "and take my word for it, he will sit the remainder of his days in a log cabin." Seizing the opportunity,

Whigs celebrated Harrison as the "log Cabin and Hard Cider" candidate although he came from one of the most distinguished families of Virginia and resided in a mansion in Ohio. In turn, the Whigs branded the president as Martin Van "Ruin," an out-of-touch and elite leader, and convincing the electorate that "Mat has a golden plate."[7]

The Whigs selected Tyler as the vice-presidential candidate, and the nomination of the states' rights Virginian helped solidify a disparate coalition. Delegates believed that the nomination of Tyler, a well-known supporter of Henry Clay, would soothe disappointed followers of the Kentucky Senator. The convention acted strategically, yet irresponsibly, since Tyler disagreed with most Whigs on the key issues of economic nationalism and a national bank. Indeed, the Whig convention refused to produce a platform in order to avoid disagreements among its members. What united Tyler with Harrison and Clay, or at least what seemed to, was their mutual mistrust of executive power. The party's irresistible slogan, "Tippecanoe and Tyler, too," put the candidates in the public conscience. Another Whig slogan ridiculed the seemingly inconsequential vice-presidential nomination. "We will vote for Tyler therefore, without a why or wherefore." The candidate's consistent record of opposition to a national bank was overlooked, and so was the possibility that, as president of the Senate, he could end up breaking a tie vote on a bank bill.[8]

Songs, slogans, and gimmicks masked one of the most substantial presidential campaigns of the era. Voters searched for answers to their economic hardships caused by the Panic of 1837. "We have many recruits in our ranks from the pressure of the times," Harrison said. In response to the public discontent, Harrison broke precedent and directly addressed voters. In the past, candidates maintained the notion that they did not seek the office, allowing surrogates to campaign for them. But from June to September 1840, he gave twenty-three speeches in Ohio and Indiana. In September, he addressed a crowd of 100,000 at Dayton, Ohio, where he specifically blamed the crisis on Jackson's abuse of executive power. In contrast, Harrison promised to follow Congress's lead in restoring economic prosperity, which included a new national bank. When Tyler was forced to make his own campaign trip, Democrats attempted to embarrass him by pointing out the inconsistency of the two candidates on the banking issue.[9]

An astounding 80 percent of the electorate showed up at the polls on Election Day, with 37 percent new voters, a turnout unparalleled in American political history. Though the popular vote was close—with the Whigs capturing 53 percent to the Democrats' 47 percent—the Electoral College vote was a rout: 234 to 60. The Whigs also won a majority in Congress, making their victory complete. Senator Henry Clay refused a Cabinet position and planned to lead the Whigs in Congress in enacting his economic nationalist plan, the American System. He insisted that waiting until the next session of Congress would be too long and urged President-elect Harrison to call a special session for the spring. Harrison appreciated neither Clay's persistence nor the widespread assumption of his power. "You are too imperious," he wrote to Clay a week after his inauguration. Despite being frustrated with Clay, the president called a special session for May.[10]

On March 4, 1841, fifty-thousand supporters attended the inauguration, where the nation's oldest president yet delivered a ninety-minute address in the chilly Washington morning. Amidst the classical allusions, Harrison reaffirmed his purpose: "[T]he great danger to our institutions does not appear to me to be in a usurpation by the Government of power not granted by the people, but by the accumulation in one of the departments of that which was assigned to others." Moreover, to ease concerns about executive power, he promised to serve only a single term. Tyler drew far less attention. After taking the oath in the Senate chamber of the capitol, he gave a gracious three-minute speech to the dignitaries assembled. He then departed Washington for Williamsburg, where he expected to spend the better part of an uneventful tenure. John Adams, the first vice president, had declared the office irrelevant, and no one had had challenged that description by 1841. The vice president's sole constitutional duty was to preside over the Senate, casting a vote in case of a tie. Two previous vice presidents had died in office leaving the office vacant. Few seemed to notice—a sign of the public's ambivalence to the office.[11]

During his month-long presidency, William Henry Harrison grew frustrated with Senator Henry Clay's attempt to seize the effort to enact the Whig agenda, dictating matters to the president himself. Harrison signaled a break from Clay and seemed willing to protect the power of the presidential office. His illness and death left Whigs anxious about their political program. Immediately after Harrison's death, his Cabinet met to compose the notification for Tyler. They puzzled over how to address it before deciding on "Vice President acting President." With no precedent, Secretary of State Daniel Webster asked Chief Justice Roger B. Taney his opinion, which he refused to offer lest he become involved. The Cabinet's confusion surrounding the succession was understandable. In 1787 the framers of the Constitution placed the same requirements on vice presidents as the president but were less than clear on succession.[12]

Upon hearing the news of Harrison's passing, Tyler immediately consulted with Nathaniel Beverley Tucker, an ardent Southern nationalist and distinguished professor of law at the College of William and Mary, who advised him to assume the office immediately and fully and to leave no question that he was the president. In order to offset any charges of usurpation, he advised Tyler to announce, like Harrison, that he would only serve one term—advice he refused to heed. Tyler arrived in Washington before dawn on April 6. By noon, fifty-three hours after Harrison's death, he was sworn into office by William Cranch, chief judge of the US Circuit Court of the District of Columbia. The ceremony took just five minutes. Though Tyler believed that his vice-presidential oath conferred upon him his new responsibilities, Daniel Webster and others convinced him that it would assure the public of the transfer of power. The oath would prove one of Tyler's most important actions establishing a precedent that symbolized the continuity of the government.[13]

Calling his first Cabinet meeting, Tyler made his position clear: he was the president. Secretary Webster told him that during Harrison's brief tenure decisions were made by binding Cabinet votes, with each member exercising a vote equal to the president's. Tyler would have none of it. He patiently heard Webster out before responding. "I am president," he told the group coolly, "and I shall be held responsible for my administration. I shall be pleased to avail myself of your counsel and advice. But I can never consent to being dictated to as to what I shall or shall not do. When you think otherwise, your resignations will be accepted."[14]

It was a rocky beginning. Tyler's stance immediately alienated his Cabinet. His written address to the nation three days later made much the same case for his assuming the full responsibilities of president. Reworking language from the Constitution, he notified Congress and the American people that for the first time in their history an elected vice president "has had devolved upon him the Presidential Office." To help establish his position as the legitimate successor, he referred to himself as "President" and "Chief Magistrate" In these early days of his administration, Tyler made decisions that underscored a desire to protect both his position and the office itself.[15]

Many Whigs refused to accept Tyler's actions and continued to call him "acting President." On April 16, Congressman and former president John Quincy Adams recorded his anger after meeting with Tyler, a man he deemed a "mediocrity." "I paid a visit this morning to Mr. Tyler, who styles himself President of the United States, and not Vice-President acting as President, which would be the correct style," he wrote. Tyler's insistence on claiming the title was a "direct violation both of the grammar and context of the Constitution." For Adams, this was no trivial matter. Only Congress could approve Tyler's receiving the president's pay or living in the White House, he argued. When Congress finally convened in May, a Pennsylvania Whig introduced legislation to establish his title as "Vice President Now Exercising the Office of President." It was quickly defeated, but denigrating nicknames such as "His Accidency" dogged Tyler throughout his administration. Letters addressed to "Acting President Tyler" were returned unopened.[16]

The most pressing question was whether Henry Clay would accept Tyler as president. Although the two had been friends, Clay remained wary and initially referred to him as "vice president." On April 15, he expressed his concern over the uncertainty caused by the transition. In the end, however, Clay believed Tyler would take direction from congressional Whigs in passing the party's legislative agenda. Indeed, Clay believed that this moment diminished the president's power. The new "administration will be in the nature of a regency" and although that would help Congress establish its dominance, it could also lead to dissension. Tyler's message to the nation persuaded Clay that the new president would "concur in the leading measures of the Whigs." Although Clay believed Tyler a second-rate man, he believed he would help champion the American System and refused to join any challenge to Tyler's claim to the presidency.[17]

On April 30, Tyler cautioned Clay about the upcoming congressional session. In the circumstances, the president insisted that he would not present "mature plans of public policy connected with deeply interesting and intricate subjects." On the matter of a new national bank, he urged a delay, since the "public mind is still in a state of great disquietude in regard to it." Clay believed the election was a mandate for Congress to address the nation's financial problems and that included a new bank. While Clay moved ahead with his plan, Tyler submitted his own bill that gave states the right to refuse the establishment of bank branches in their borders. The two men met to discuss a compromise, but nothing came of it. "Go you now then, Mr. Clay, to your end of the avenue, where stands the Capitol, and there perform your duty to the country as you shall think proper. So help me God, I shall do mine at the end of it as I shall think proper," Tyler said. Congress passed Clay's strong bank bill on August 6. The president decided to hold Congress in session with his constitutional right of ten days, hoping to calm tempers. The delay also allowed Tyler to consult the group of Virginia states' rights partisans, whom he had been calling on for advice. On August 16, he vetoed the bill, declaring that he was "against the exercise of any such power by this government." For Tyler, to sign a bill that he deemed unconstitutional meant "surrendering all claim to the respect of honorable men."[18]

Although many had expected the veto, it still managed to stun most Whigs. His advice to Congress was to produce a more amenable bill that addressed his concerns. Clay was infuriated that a mediocrity such as Tyler stood between him and his American System. From the Senate floor, he accused the president of thwarting the public will and suggested that if the bank bill offended the president's principles then he should resign—just as he had resigned from the Democratic Party in 1836. The Cabinet urged him to sign this second, more amenable, bill but the attacks by Clay's supporters angered him. He vetoed it as well. In a message to Congress, he answered the Whig charges that he purposefully thwarted the people's will. "Mere regard to the will of the majority must not in a constitutional republic like ours control this sacred and solemn duty of a sworn officer."[19]

This was a principled stand. Tyler staked the power of the presidency on the opposite ground of Jackson, who had claimed that the president represented the will of the people. For the republican Tyler, the president stood guard against the whim of the majority. Clay was at his wit's end, especially since Tyler's actions pleased the Democrats, a group of which paid a call on the president to thank him for his bank veto. On September 13 Clay condemned the president at a caucus meeting of the congressional Whigs. "[Tyler] will stand here, like [Benedict] Arnold in England, a monument of his own perfidy and disgrace," he argued. In the end, the Whigs read him out of the party. Tyler became a "President without a party." Clay even hoped to force the president's resignation. By September 11, the Senator had orchestrated the resignation of five of the six-member cabinet. Daniel Webster, a longtime interparty rival of Clay's, refused to resign—although it would damage his standing in the Whig Party.[20]

The resignations presented Tyler with the opportunity to establish the president's authority over his cabinet. He quickly appointed a Southern-dominated cabinet and, over Clay's objections, the Senate confirmed them in record time. Tyler ultimately nominated twenty-one people for six cabinet positions during his administrations, and the Senate consistently objected to most of them. In March 1842, the House of Representatives passed a resolution that called for the president to submit the names of any members of Congress who were seeking jobs in the executive branch. Tyler and his attorney general, Hugh Legaré, rejoined: "The appointing power, so far as it is bestowed on the President by the Constitution, is conferred without reserve or qualification." Throughout his term, he tried to establish his right to appoint and remove people from the cabinet, but the problem persisted.[21]

Isolated from his party, Tyler used his veto power to stop Whig legislation and protect his office. This infuriated Whigs who had made limiting presidential power the center of the 1840 campaign. For the first forty years of the republic, presidents had used the veto sparingly and only for the most serious reasons. Jackson had vetoed twelve bills, more than all his predecessors combined. Although his vetoes were nakedly political they were always based in constitutional logic. President Tyler issued ten vetoes during his term; they sparked continual debate.[22]

Clay argued that the president had used the veto to thwart the public's will on economic measures and threaten Congress's power. In early 1843 he proposed amending the Constitution to allow Congress to override presidential vetoes with a simple majority vote, instead of the two-thirds majority. The proposal touched off six months of intense debate. Remarkably, the most potent defense of the veto power came from arch-states' rights defender, John C. Calhoun, who argued that it provided protection for the rights of the minority. While the minority that concerned Calhoun was Southern slaveholders, this interpretation had far-reaching applications and helped kill the amendment.[23]

By mid-1842, a frustrated Henry Clay retired from the Senate and returned to Kentucky to plan his presidential run in 1844. Tyler's inflexibility and staunch defense of presidential prerogative left him little choice. Addressing the Senate before his departure, Clay lamented the failure of the Whigs to curb the president's power:

> Unfortunately, our chief magistrate possesses more power, in some respects, than a king or queen of England. The crown is never separated from the nation, but is obliged to conform to its will. If the ministry holds opinions adverse to the nation, and is thrown into the minority of the House of Commons, the crown is constrained to dismiss the ministry, and appoint one whose opinions coincide with the nation. This queen Victoria has recently been obliged to do: and not

> merely to change her ministry but to dismiss the official attendants upon her person. But here, if the president holds an opinion adverse to that of congress and the nation upon important public measures, there is no remedy but upon the periodical return of the rights of the ballot box.[24]

Clay's absence allowed Tyler to raise the stakes of the battle against the Whigs. He vetoed protectionist tariff legislation for policy reasons alone in the summer of 1842, citing no constitutional justification. The veto enraged Whigs and inspired a movement to impeach Tyler. From Kentucky, Clay insisted that the vetoes meant that the "inevitable tendency of events is to impeachment." In January 1843 Virginia Congressman John Minor Botts introduced impeachment measures to the House of Representatives. He accused the president of nine high crimes and misdemeanors, including "usurpation of power," "[w]icked and corrupt abuse of power," and an "arbitrary, despotic and corrupt use of the veto power." While Democrats did not welcome Tyler back into their ranks, he was their best weapon against the Whigs, and they prevented impeachment from going any further. Nevertheless, his congressional enemies continued to talk openly about it.[25]

The battle with the president had a devastating effect on the Whig Party. In Congress voting along sectional lines fractured the Whig coalition. Tyler made appeals to members of both parties who agreed with the constitutional interpretation of each decision, which drew enough support from Democrats and Southern Whigs to make it impossible to overturn his vetoes. His resistance to the Whigs' plans demoralized members and exacerbated sectional and policy differences. As the 1842 elections approached, demoralization turned into disorganization. In the end, Democrats soundly defeated the Whigs on all fronts. In the House, they lost over forty seats, giving the Democrats a substantial majority.[26]

Tyler's use of the veto power became the focus of public outrage. After vetoing the second bank bill, a group of pro-bank supporters threw rocks through White House windows. Whigs across the nation as well as in Washington burned Tyler in effigy. The party declared him an apostate. Late in his term, his enemies labeled a frightening epidemic of influenza as "Tyler's grippe." He received assassination threats, which continued throughout his tenure. An effort in Congress to establish a protective guard around the president met with resistance. In 1842, it allowed for only a four-man security detail referred to as "doormen," who were precursors to the Secret Service. Congress proved even stingier with Tyler's living situation. Although the White House had alarmingly deteriorated, Congress refused to allocate $20,000 for its repair, at least so long as he was its principal resident.[27]

Through the political and personal attacks, Tyler conducted his affairs with stoicism and grace but also demonstrated signs of losing his usual cool demeanor. In February 1842 a letter to some of his Philadelphia supporters revealed his frustrations and revealed his motivation behind his resistance to the Whigs. "Instead of being a leader he must be a follower of party, and he is required to be a piece of wax, to be moulded into any shape that others may please, or denunciations the loudest and boldest are in store from him," he wrote. The attempt by Clay and the Whigs to dominate and make him subservient to the party violated republican aversion to strict party loyalty. When Charles Dickens visited Tyler in the White House in 1842, the British author observed: "He looked somewhat worn and anxious, and well he might: being at war with everybody—but the expression of his face was mild and pleasant, and his manner remarkably unaffected, gentlemanly and agreeable. I thought that in his whole carriage and demeanor, he became his station singularly well."[28]

The lingering illness of his wife Letitia compounded President Tyler's worries. In 1839 a stroke had left her an invalid. At the White House, she remained confined to the second floor while her daughter-in-law, Priscilla, hosted White House events. In the midst of her husband's political travails, she suffered another stroke. On September 10, 1842, Letitia Tyler died, leaving her husband grief stricken. His stoicism and pleasant disposition led him through his period of mourning. Indeed, the president continued his battle with Congress and began planning for his future and building support for his own bid for election. His long public career had separated him from his family for long periods of time and had probably created distance between him and Letitia. In recent years, her illnesses became a great concern for him. A sense of relief that her suffering had ended probably allowed the genial-natured Tyler to prove even more emotionally resilient. Soon the fifty-three-year-old president met and fell in love with the twenty-three-year-old Julia Gardiner. Skeptics of the May-December marriage were answered by the couple's eighteen-year union, which produced seven children. In the long struggle between Tyler and Congress, the tragedy of death and burgeoning romance seemed never to have really distracted him.[29]

As with many presidents who endured stormy relations with Congress, Tyler turned to foreign policy to exercise his power and hoped to secure another term as president. For two years Daniel Webster proved the administration's most valuable member. The secretary of state negotiated the Webster-Ashburton Treaty, settling the disputed boundary along the American-Canadian border that had festered since the American Revolution. The treaty demonstrated how former enemies could peacefully compose such issues and also gave hope for settling the looming problem of Oregon. The treaty gave Tyler a brief boost in popularity and helped him pick up supporters from both parties. "The signs of the Tyler party are much stronger than I could have imagined," a puzzled John Quincy Adams wrote.[30]

President Tyler first raised the possibility of annexing the Republic of Texas after the Cabinet's resignation. Secretary Webster cautioned against it. Since Texas had won independence from Mexico in 1836, annexation had been a troubling issue in American politics. Northerners would never consent to the annexation of the large slaveholding nation. Even Andrew Jackson refused to attempt annexation. For a while, President Tyler heeded Webster's warning, rebuffing Texas President Sam Houston's efforts to begin a conversation about it. Tyler's desire for Texas came from his belief in the Jeffersonian idea of an empire of liberty, which advocated expansion as way to rejuvenate republicanism. Slavery in Texas failed to disturb the president. He clung to the Jeffersonian theory of diffusion, believing that expansion would draw slaves from the East and make emancipation more likely. To skeptical Northerners, Tyler tried to sell the benefits of annexation with the promise of new markets and expanded manufacturing.

The Democrats' congressional victory convinced him that he could achieve annexation. When he began pursuing the issue in 1843, Webster resigned. With no one to caution the president, he remained fixated on Texas, hoping it would bring glory to his presidency and advance his nomination as either the Democratic candidate or a third-party bid in the 1844 election.[31]

While domestic politics had prevented annexation, Great Britain moved closer to Texas and spurred rumors that it would use its power to encourage emancipation there. Tyler's new Secretary of State Abel Upshur, a fellow Virginian, used the fear of emancipation to force the president to allow secret negotiations with Sam Houston. The duplicitous Upshur, who secretly dismissed Tyler as an "obnoxious President," fought for annexation not for Tyler's political advantage but to preserve slavery and aid John C. Calhoun's quest for the presidency. The immediate annexation of Texas, a slave state, seemed the only way to thwart Great Britain and preserve slavery. On February 28, 1844, President Tyler, Secretary Upshur, and a large party of dignitaries boarded the USS *Princeton*. The iron warship had been Upshur's pet project when he was secretary of the navy. His investment in the vessel explains why he stood so close to the forty-two-pound cannonade during a demonstration. The gun exploded inward, killing the secretary and seven others. The president was unharmed.[32]

Tyler's appointment of John C. Calhoun as Upshur's successor made it clear that southern Democrats were now guiding the administration. With Calhoun dedicated to securing Texas annexation, Tyler hoped to secure the nomination for reelection from the Democratic Party with the platform, "Tyler and Texas." He also made peace with Andrew Jackson, who had been more than pleased with Tyler's vetoes of the banks bills. Yet most Democrats remained embittered over his role in the 1840 election. So Tyler moved ahead with his campaign as a third party candidate. Slavery complicated those plans. In April, after finding an outdated communication from British Minister Richard Pakenham that reaffirmed Britain's commitment to global emancipation, Secretary of State Calhoun wrote a terse reply. Calhoun insisted that Great Britain's abolition movement presented a direct threat to US interests, especially Texas. The threat would force the United States to act. On April 27, Tyler submitted the treaty for Texas annexation, with all the supporting documentation, to the Senate. Calhoun's Pakenham letter soon became public knowledge, and it caused considerable outrage among Northern supporters.

Tyler was now an independent candidate for reelection, complete with a convention to make his nomination official on May 27. On June 8, 1844, the Senate overwhelmingly rejected his treaty, 35 to 16. All Whigs, except John Henderson of Mississippi, voted against it. They were joined by eight Democrats, all Northerners but one. While Calhoun's letter enflamed the problem of slavery in the debate, Tyler's own ambition played a critical role in the defeat. "The truth is, this whole business is a fraud, a plan, with which John Tyler intends, if he can, to bamboozle the American people in the approaching election," one Whig senator insisted. Some Democrats also believed the issue had been rushed for Tyler's benefit. The president had agreed to drop out of the presidential race if congressional Democrats supported ratification of the treaty, but to no avail.[33]

In spite of the treaty's defeat, Tyler had injected Texas into the presidential campaign and forced both parties' presumptive candidates to address the issue. Those nominees, Martin Van Buren and Henry Clay opposed annexation as provocative and unwise. Unfortunately for Van Buren, his old mentor Andrew Jackson and many in the Democratic Party wanted Texas and secured the nomination for James K. Polk. The Democratic nominee made Texas the center of his campaign, but Tyler's presence in the race threatened to syphon votes. The president used this rare moment of political leverage to help many of his supporters and to force Democrats to end any remaining attacks upon him and his administration. On August 20, he officially ended his candidacy, in the hopes his withdrawal from the race would help achieve Texas annexation.[34]

But, Polk's victory over Clay fueled the president's desire to complete annexation himself. "[I]f the annexation of Texas shall crown off my public life, I shall neither retire ignominiously nor be soon forgotten," he wrote. In his final annual message to Congress, Tyler argued that Polk's election represented a mandate for annexation. "A controlling majority of the people and a large majority of the States have declared in favor of immediate annexation," he insisted. Realizing that he could not get the necessary two-thirds vote in the Senate, he asked Congress to pass a joint resolution to allow him to finalize and execute the treaty with Texas.

The resolution passed both houses by simple majority votes and Tyler signed the bill on March 1, 1845, just three days before leaving office. The joint resolution expanded the president's power by circumventing the Senate's role in approving treaties and strengthened the executive branch's control of foreign policy. With Texas within reach, the president celebrated. Throngs of visitors poured into the White House to send-off the president who had been so defiant. With satisfaction he looked at the crowd and declared: "They cannot now say that I am a president without a party." Many in Congress remained bitter at the president who had so solidified his office's power. The day before his term ended, Congress overturned one of his last vetoes—the first time the legislature had done so.[35]

The Tylers retreated to their Virginia plantation, where the former president oversaw the slaves who cultivated his wheat and corn as he tended to his young wife and their growing brood, the last of which he fathered at age seventy. Initially, Tyler received a cool reception from neighbors but eventually they warmed to him. While he certainly fell into obscurity, the issues that Tyler had confronted—separation of powers, the extent of executive power, and the crisis of sectionalism—would be consistently reargued. From his plantation, he watched as Texas annexation led to the Mexican War and the exacerbation of the nation's sectional crisis. As the issue of slavery inexorably divided the nation, Tyler gravitated back to the Democratic Party. He remained, as ever, a staunch defender of slavery. In February 1861, the elder statesman led a delegation to Washington for a peace convention, ostensibly to preserve the Union and avert war. The "Old Gentlemen's Convention" included 132 delegates representing twenty-one states, primarily Border States. As the head of the extra-constitutional peace convention, Tyler presented the resolutions to President-elect Lincoln, who recognized that the convention's goal was more to preserve slavery than save the Union. Lincoln rejected the resolutions. The realization that the demands of the slave states would not be met, soon led Tyler to declare his support for secession.[36]

Tyler's devotion to Virginia and slavery became apparent after the failure of the peace convention. The South's "connexions with the Northern hive of abolitionists," he wrote to his wife, was now broken, and Virginia would take "her stand as a sovereign and independent State." He became an impassioned advocate of disunion, driven as much by the desire to maintain white supremacy as to protect states' rights. After winning the battle for Virginia secession, Tyler negotiated the state's entrance into the Confederacy and the locating of the Confederate capital in Richmond. He was soon elected to the new House of Representatives of the Confederate States of America. He would not serve long, nor live long enough to see his home state ravaged by a war he did little to prevent. He died of a stroke on January 12, 1862, before taking his seat in the treasonous legislature in Richmond. Tyler's body lay in state in Virginia's capitol building in Richmond, his coffin draped not with the American flag under whose Constitution he had once vowed to preserve and protect against all enemies, but instead with the new colors of the Confederate flag. No services observing his passing were held in Washington: this was the only time in the nation's history that a president's death had gone officially unrecognized.[37]

For the second time, therefore, Tyler was branded a "traitor" by large portions of the American public. Although dead, his ignominy inspired violent reactions. In the spring of 1864, as General Ulysses S. Grant led Union forces in Virginia on a final push that would end the war, Tyler's plantation, Sherwood Forest, was surrounded by US troops. In April, US troops, including black soldiers, sacked the home Tyler had once ruled, freeing its slaves and bringing ruin to the Tyler family.[38]

What, ultimately, are we to make of the long crisis that was Tyler's entire presidency, a personal crisis if there ever was one, given its consequences for his very legitimacy in office? Long after his death, Tyler's presidential successors established many of his decisions as precedents. Most importantly, seven presidents followed his example of presidential succession. In the mid-twentieth century, many scholars insisted that Tyler's actions had actually violated the intentions of the framers, but the public now expected an orderly transfer of power upon a president's death. In 1967 the nation codified the succession plan as Tyler executed it with the Twenty-fifth Amendment to the Constitution. His belief that the veto gave presidents the power to block legislation for political or policy reasons became a standard part of American politics.

Furthermore, later presidents jealously guarded the power of the office over legislation and appointments much as Tyler had. The bitter feelings that he evoked and his ignominious leadership in the Confederate cause helped obscure how his tenure had protected the presidency.

In 1840 the Whig Party's victory gave it the power to carry out plans to weaken the office and make it subservient to Congress. The threat to presidential independence and the separation of powers turned the longtime republican who had fought the expansion of presidential power into its staunch defender. Even as he reverted to his strict states' rights doctrine, his presidential legacy lived on. Tyler's cause for states' rights, slavery, and republicanism ended at the hands of Abraham Lincoln, a former Henry Clay Whig, using those very powers that Tyler had been so instrumental in protecting. His response to crisis while in the White House, therefore, allowed the presidency not only to survive but to expand, affording a successor the means to deal with the greatest national crisis of all.[39]

NOTES

1. Robert J. Morgan, *A Whig Embattled: The Presidency under John Tyler* (Lincoln: University of Nebraska Press), 1954, 7; "Announcement to the Vice-President," April 4, 1841, James D. Richardson, ed. *A Compilation of the Messages and Papers of the Presidents 1789-1897* (Washington, DC: Government Printing Office, 1897), 4:22.
2. Fred Shelley, ed. "The Vice President Receives Bad News in Williamsburg," *Virginia Magazine of History and Biography* 76, No. 3 (July 1968): 337–39; *Hudson River Chronicle* quote from Alasdair Roberts, *America's First Great Depression: Economic Crisis and Political Disorder After the Panic of 1837* (Ithaca, NY: Cornell University Press, 2012), 93; Col. Charles S. Todd and Benjamin Drake, revised and enlarged by James Perkins. *Sketches of the Civil Military Services of William Henry Harrison* (Cincinnati: J.A. & U.P. James, 1847), 208. Todd and Drake published a letter from

Harrison's attending physicians to Secretary of State Daniel Webster, Dr. N.W. Worthington recounted the president's final words.

3. John Tyler, Sr. to Thomas Jefferson, May 12, 1810, *The Papers of Thomas Jefferson: Retirement Series, Volume 2, 16 November 1809 to 11 August 1810*, ed. J. Jefferson Looney, et al. (Princeton, NJ: Princeton University Press, 2005), 2:384; Lyon G. Tyler, ed., *The Letters and Times of the Tylers* (Richmond: Whittet & Sheppherson, 1884), 1:246. Dan Monroe, *The Republican Vision of John Tyler* (College Station: Texas A & M University Press, 2003), 10–14, 82; Kevin R.C. Gutzman, *Virginia's American Revolution: From Dominion to Republic, 1776- 1840* (Lanham, MD: Lexington Books, 2007), 151; Sylvan H. Kesilman, "John Tyler and the Presidency: Old Republicanism, Partisan Realignment, and Support for his Administration." (PhD diss., Ohio State University, 1973), 6–39.
4. Christopher Leahy, "Torn Between Family and Politics: John Tyler's Struggle for Balance" *Virginia Magazine of History and Biography*, Vol. 114, No. 3 (2006): 322–55; Seeger, *And Tyler Too*, 43, 57; Bertram Wyatt-Brown, *Southern Honor: Ethics and Behavior in the Old South* (New York: Oxford University Press, 1982), 74–87, 362–64.
5. Monroe, *Republican Vision of John Tyler*, 8–47; Daniel Feller, "Andrew Jackson versus the Senate," *Congress and the Emergence of Sectionalism: From the Missouri Compromise to the Age of Jackson*, eds., by Paul Finkelman and Donald R. Kennon (Athens: Ohio University Press, 2008), 266; Richard E. Ellis, *The Union at Risk: Jacksonian Democracy, States' Rights and the Nullification Crisis* (New York: Oxford University Press, 1987), 96, 167; Merrill D. Peterson, *Olive Branch and Sword: The Compromise of 1833* (Baton Rouge: Louisiana State University Press, 1982), 30, 66, 82.
6. Maurice G. Baxter, *Henry Clay and the American System* (Lexington: University Press of Kentucky), 1995, 205; Monroe, *Republican Vision of John Tyler*, 65–6, 73–5; Robert V. Remini, *Andrew Jackson and the Bank War* (New York: Norton, 1967), 61–65; Scott Reynolds Nelson, *A Nation of Deadbeats: An Uncommon History of America's Financial Disasters* (New York: Knopf, 2012), 123; William S. Stokes, "Whig Conceptions of Executive Power," *Presidential Studies Quarterly* 6, nos. 1 and 2 (Winter-Spring, 1976): 17; John Tyler to Dr. Henry Curtis, March 28, 1834, Tyler, ed., *The Letters and Times of the Tyler's*, 1:490–91.
7. Richard P. McCormick, "Was There a 'Whig Strategy' in 1836?" *Journal of the Early Republic* 4, no. 1 (Spring 1984): 47–70; William Nisbet Chambers, "Election of 1840," in *History of American Presidential Elections, 1789-1968*, eds. Arthur M. Schlesinger Jr. and Fred L. Israel (New York: Chelsea House, 1971), 1:640; Nelson, *A Nation of Deadbeats*, 123; Michael F. Holt, *The Rise and Fall of the American Whig Party* (New York: Oxford University Press, 1999), 62: Daniel Walker Howe, *The Political Culture of the American Whigs* (Chicago: University of Chicago Press, 1979), 123–25; Thomas Brown, *Politics and Statesmanship: Essays on the American Whig Party* (New York: Columbia University Press, 1985), 41; Robert Gray Gunderson, *The Log-Cabin Campaign* (Lexington: University Press of Kentucky, 1957), 74–5. The hard cider and log cabin insult appeared in the Baltimore *Republican*, December 11, 1839. Chambers, "Election of 1840," 677; Richard P. McCormick, *The Presidential*

Game: The Origins of American Presidential Politics (New York: Oxford University Press, 1982), 186.

8. Holt, *Rise and Fall of the American Whig Party*, 126; Abby L. Gilbert, "Of Banks and Politics: The Bank Issue and The Election of 1840," *West Virginia History* 34, no. 1 (1972): 37–39; Chambers, "Election of 1840," 677; Gunderson, *Log-Cabin Campaign*, 74–5, 121; McCormick, *Presidential Game*, 186.
9. William Henry Harrison to Nathaniel P. Tallmadge, February 22, 1840, quoted in Gunderson, *Log-Cabin Campaign*, 12; Jeffrey Bourdon, "Symbolism, Economic Depression, and the Specter of Slavery: William Henry Harrison's Speaking Tour for the Presidency," *Ohio History*, 188 (2011): 16–17; Holt, *Rise and Fall of the American Whig Party*, 110; McCormick, *Presidential Game*, 175, 177, 200–01.
10. Michael F. Holt, "The Election of 1840, Voter Mobilization, and the Emergence of the Second American Party System: A Reappraisal of Jacksonian Voting Behavior," in *A Master's Due: Essays in Honor of David Herbert Donald*, eds. William J. Cooper Jr., Michael F. Holt, and John McCardell. (Baton Rouge: Louisiana State University Press, 1985), 17–8; David S. Heidler and Jeanne T. Heidler. *Henry Clay: The Essential American* (New York: Random House, 2010), 339; Holt, *Rise and Fall of the American Whig Party*, 122–26; William Henry Harrison to Henry Clay, March 13, 1841, *The Papers of Henry Clay, Volume 9: The Whig Leader, January 1, 1837-December 31, 1843*, ed. Robert SeagerII, et al., (Lexington: University Press of Kentucky, 1988), 9: 515–16.
11. Freeman Cleaves, *Old Tippecanoe: William Henry Harrison and His Time* (New York: C. Scribner's Sons, 1939), 338; Richardson, ed., *Messages and Papers of the Presidents*, 4: 7; Jody C. Baumgartner, *The American Vice Presidency Reconsidered* (Westport, CT: Praeger, 2006), 7–23.
12. Article II, Section 1, of the Constitution states: "In Case of the Removal of the President from Office, or of his Death, Resignation, or Inability to discharge the Powers and Duties of the said Office, the Same shall devolve on the Vice President, and the Congress may by Law provide for the Case of Removal, Death, Resignation or Inability, both of the President and Vice President, declaring what Officer shall then act as President, and such Officer shall act accordingly, until the Disability be removed, or a President shall be elected." Philip Abbott, *Accidental Presidents: Death, Assassination, Resignation, and Democratic Succession* (New York: Palgrave Macmillan, 2008), 6–13; Samuel Tyler, *Memoir of Roger Brooke Taney*. The framers also gave Congress power in the succession process and hinted of a special election to elect a new president. In 1792, Congress passed a Succession Act; in 1804, upon ratification, the Twelfth Amendment addressed the complicated method of election and geographical issues, but neither clarified the succession.
13. Edward P. Crapol, *John Tyler: The Accidental President* (Chapel Hill: University of North Carolina Press, 2006), 9; Frank G. Carpenter, "A Talk with a President's Son," *Lippincott's Monthly Magazine* XLI, (1888), 448; Abbott, *Accidental Presidents*, 23; Kesilman, "John Tyler and the Presidency," 55.
14. Michael J. Gerhardt. *The Forgotten Presidents: Their Untold Constitutional Legacy* (New York: Oxford University Press, 2013), 34; Carpenter, "A Talk with A President's Son," 417–18.

15. Gerhardt, *Forgotten Presidents*, 34; Carpenter, "A Talk with A President's Son," 417–18; John Tyler, "Inaugural Address," April 9, 1841, Richardson, ed., *Messages and Papers of the Presidents*, 4: 37.
16. Allan Nevins, ed. *The Diary of John Quincy Adams, 1784-1845: American Political, Social and Intellectual Life from, Washington to Polk* (New York: Longmans, Green, and Co., 1928), 26, 520, 522; David P. Currie, *The Constitution in Congress: Democrats and Whigs, 1829-1861* (Chicago: University of Chicago Press, 2005), 178; Crapol, *John Tyler*, 10.
17. Henry Clay to Nathaniel Beverley Tucker, April 15, 1841, *Papers of Henry Clay*, 9:520; Henry Clay to John M. Berrien, April 20, 1841, *Papers of Henry Clay*, 9: 521; Heidler and Heidler, *Henry Clay*, 342; Stokes, "Whig Conceptions of Executive Power," 16–35; Holt, *Rise and Fall of the Whig Party*, 127.
18. John Tyler to Henry Clay, April 30, 1841, *Papers of Henry Clay*, 9: 527–28; Norma Lois Peterson, *The Presidencies of Harrison and Tyler* (Lawrence: University Press of Kansas, 1989), 60–70; Monroe, *Republican Vision of John Tyler*, 100–01; Tyler, ed., *Letters of the Tylers*, 2:33; Heidler and Heidler, *Henry Clay*, 344–46; Richard A. Gantz, "Henry Clay and the Harvest of Bitter Fruit: The Struggle with John Tyler, 1841-1842," (PhD diss., Indiana University, 1986); Robert J. Morgan *A Whig Embattled*, 40; Richardson, ed., *Messages and Papers of the Presidents*, 4: 64.
19. Gantz, "Henry Clay and the Harvest of Bitter Fruit," 161–203; Kesilman, "John Tyler and the Presidency," 71–93; Gerhardt, *Forgotten Presidents*, 44; "To the House of Representatives to the United States," September 9, 1841, Richardson, ed., *Messages and Papers of the Presidents*, 4:68; John Tyler, Jr. to Lyon Tyler, January 29, 1883, Tyler, ed., *Letters of the Tylers*, 2:122, note; Peterson, *Presidencies of Harrison and Tyler*, 79–81.
20. Gantz, "Henry Clay and the Harvest of Bitter Fruit," 161–203; Kesilman, "John Tyler and the Presidency," 71–93; Hugh Russell Fraser, *Democracy in the Making: The Jackson-Tyler Era* (Indianapolis: Bobbs-Merrill Co., 1938), 190; Gerhardt, *Forgotten Presidents*, 44; Henry Clay, "To the Whig Caucus," September 13, 1841, *Papers of Henry Clay*, 9:608–09; John Tyler Jr. to Lyon Tyler, January 29, 1883, Tyler, ed., *Letters of the Tylers*, 2:122, note; Peterson, *Presidencies of Harrison and Tyler*, 79–81.
21. Gerhardt, *Forgotten Presidents*, 48–58; "To the House of Representatives of the United States," March 23, 1842, Richardson, ed., *Messages and Papers of the Presidents*, 4:106.
22. Robert J. Spitzer. *The Presidential Veto: Touchstone of the American Presidency* (Albany: State University of New York, 1988), 33.
23. Spitzer, *Presidential Veto*, 33; William R. Brock, *Parties and Political Conscience: American Dilemmas, 1840-1850* (Millwood, NY: KTO Press, 1979), 108–12.
24. "On Retiring to Private Life," Lexington, June 9, 1842, Calvin Colton, ed., *The Works of Henry Clay, Comprising His Life, Correspondence and Speeches* (New York: G.P. Putnam's Sons, 1904), 10: 377.
25. Morgan, *A Whig Embattled*, 46; Spitzer, *Presidential Veto*, 44–47; Lonnie E. Maness and Richard D. Chesteen, "The First Attempt at Presidential Impeachment: Partisan Politics and Intra-Party Conflict at Loose," *Presidential Studies Quarterly* 10, no. 1,

(Winter, 1980): 56–7. Henry Clay to John J. Crittenden, July 16, 1842, *Papers of Henry Clay*, 9: 736.

26. Joel H. Silbey, *The Shrine of Party: Congressional Voting Behavior, 1841-1852* (Pittsburgh: University of Pittsburgh Press, 1967), 49–66; Peterson, *Presidencies of Harrison and Tyler*, 167; Holt, *Rise and Fall of the Whig Party*, 151; David Lee Amstutz, "John Tyler: Facing the Perils of a Politically Independent Presidency." (Master's Thesis, University of Nebraska at Kearney, 1993), 23.
27. Monroe, *Republican Vision of John Tyler*, 201–11; Seager, *And Tyler Too*, 159–160; Philip H. Melanson, PhD, with Peter F. Stevens, *The Secret Service: The Hidden History of an Enigmatic Agency* (New York: Carroll & Graf, 2002), 135–36; *Congressional Globe*, August 6, 1842, 27th Congress, 2nd session, 854; *The Medical Summary* 21, No. 1 (March 1899): 25.
28. John Tyler to Samuel Rush, James L. Tyson, James McHenry, Thomas B. Smith, and others on the committee, February 19, 1842, *National Intelligencer*, February 28, 1842; Charles Dickens, *American Notes and Pictures from Italy* (New York: Oxford University Press, 1957), 125.
29. Seager, *And Tyler Too*, 178–79; Elizabeth Tyler Coleman, *Priscilla Cooper Tyler and the American Scene, 1816-1889* (Tuscaloosa: University of Alabama Press, 1955), 84–99; Oliver Perry Chitwood, *John Tyler: Champion of the Old South* (New York: Appleton-Century Company, 1939), 403, 410; Henry A. Wise, *Seven Decades of the Union* (Philadelphia: J.B. Lippincott, 1871), 223.
30. Howard Jones, *To the Webster-Ashburton Treaty: A Study in Anglo-American Relations, 1783-1843* (Chapel Hill: University of North Carolina Press, 1977), xii, 161–62; Sam W. Haynes, *Unfinished Revolution: The Early American Republic in a British World* (Charlottesville: University of Virginia Press, 2010), 221; Charles Francis Adams, ed. *Memoirs of John Quincy Adams Comprising Portions of His Diary from 1795 to 1848, Vol. XI* (Philadelphia: J. B. Lippincott & Co., 1876), 256.
31. John Tyler to Daniel Webster, October 11, 1841, *Letters and Times of the Tylers*, 2:126; Sydney Nathan, *Daniel Webster and Jacksonian Democracy* (Baltimore: Johns Hopkins University Press, 1973), 206–07; Robert F. Dalzell, Jr., *Daniel Webster and the Trial of American Nationalism* (Boston: Houghton Mifflin, 1972), 84; Peterson, *Presidencies of Harrison and Tyler*, 79–81; Monroe, *Republican Vision of John Tyler*, 171; Frederick Merk, *Slavery and the Annexation of Texas* (New York: Knopf, 1972), 9–10; David M. Pletcher, *The Diplomacy of Annexation: Texas, Oregon, and the Mexican War* (Columbia: University of Missouri Press, 1973), 88.
32. Abel Upshur to Beverley Tucker, October 26, 1843, in Merk, *Slavery and Annexation*, 244; Peterson, *Presidencies of Harrison and Tyler*, 192–203; Steven E. Woodworth, *Manifest Destinies: America's Westward Expansion and the Road to the Civil War* (New York: Knopf, 2010), 112–14; Claude H. Hall, *Abel Parker Upshur: Conservative Virginian, 1790-1844* (Madison: State Historical Society of Wisconsin, 1964), 197–98.
33. Morgan, *A Whig Embattled*, 170–72; Charles M. Wiltse, *John C. Calhoun, Sectionalist, 1840-1850* (Indianapolis: Bobbs-Merrill, 1951), 167–170; John C. Calhoun to Richard Pakenham, April 18, 1844, *The Papers of John C. Calhoun* (Columbia: University of South Carolina, 1988), 18:273–78; Merrill D. Peterson,

The Great Triumverate: Webster, Clay, and Calhoun (New York: Oxford University Press, 1987), 346–48; Merk, *Slavery and the Annexation of Texas*, 76–81; Rachel A. Shelden, "Not So Strange Bedfellows: Northern and Southern Whigs in the Texas Annexation Controversy, 1844–1845," in *A Political Nation: New Directions in Mid-Nineteenth-Century American Political History*, ed., Gary W. Gallagher and Rachel A. Shelden (Charlottesville: University of Virginia Press, 2012), 19.

34. Monroe, *Republican Vision of John Tyler*, 177–179; Tyler's withdrawal letter to the *Madisonian*, August 20, 1844, Tyler, ed., *Letters and Times of the Tylers*, 2:343.
35. John Tyler to Alexander Gardiner, December 8, 1844, Tyler, ed., *Letters and Times of the Tylers*, 2: 359–61; "Fourth Annual Message," December 3, 1844, Richardson, ed., *Messages and Papers of the Presidents*, 4:344; Crapol, *John Tyler*, 220; Gerhardt, *Forgotten Presidents*, 61–64; Tyler, ed., *Letters and Times of the Tylers*, 2:361.
36. Eric H. Walther, *The Fire-Eaters* (Baton Rouge: Louisiana State University Press, 1992), 244; William J. Cooper, *We Have the War Upon Us: The Onset of the Civil War, November 1860-April 1861* (New York: Knopf, 2012), 173–84; Shearer Davis Bowman, *At the Precipice: Americans North and South during the Secession Crisis* (Chapel Hill: University of North Carolina Press, 2010), 134; Crapol, *John Tyler*, 262.
37. John Tyler to Julia Gardiner Tyler, April 17, 1861, Tyler, ed., *Letters and Times of the Tylers*, 2:641; Crapol, John Tyler, 262–63; 268; William A. Link, *Roots of Secession: Slavery and Politics in Antebellum Virginia* (Chapel Hill: University of North Carolina Press, 2003), 242–43.
38. Seager, *And Tyler Too*, 487–89.
39. Ruth C. Silva, "Presidential Succession and Disability," *Law and Contemporary Problems* 21, No. 4 (Autumn, 1956), 647–49; Edward S. Corwin, *The President: Office and Powers, 1787-1984*, 5th ed. (New York: New York University Press, 1984), 60.

A poignant photographic portrait of the frail Jane Pierce, the wife of President Franklin Pierce, and their son, Benny. The ten-year-old was killed in a train wreck two months before his father's inauguration. [Picturesnow.com]

3

Personal Loss and Franklin Pierce's Presidency

MICHAEL F. HOLT

What impact, if any, has grief stemming from family deaths had on the performance of American presidents? Absent documented evidence of depression and melancholia or uncharacteristic and seemingly irrational outbursts of anger, moreover, how can a historian or biographer begin to assess that impact? In such instances the historian must speculate based on facts about the president's character and behavior that can be documented. That is the approach this essay takes on Franklin Pierce, the famously affable president from New Hampshire who served in the White House from 1853 to 1857.[1] Such informed speculation suggests that a case can be made—to be sure, only by inference rather than direct evidence—that Pierce's grief over a son's death *may* have influenced the most important decision he made as president.

The son of a Revolutionary War hero named Benjamin Pierce, who later served a term as the state's governor, Franklin Pierce was born in Hillsborough, New Hampshire on November 23, 1804. He graduated from Bowdoin College, where in 1824 he formed a lifelong friendship with the novelist Nathaniel Hawthorne. He studied law in eminent attorneys' offices for a few years, opened a legal practice in Hillsborough, and then plunged into an astonishingly precocious political career. In March 1829, at the age of twenty-five, he was elected to the first of four one-year terms in the State House of Representatives, and in the last two of them his colleagues chose him as their speaker. Then, in March 1833 (New Hampshire held all but presidential elections in March and its congressional elections in odd-numbered years), he was elected to the US House of Representatives, to which he was reelected two years later. Finally in 1837 the state legislature sent Pierce to the single term he served in the US Senate. In all of these offices, as would be the case when he was later elected president, he was a fanatically loyal Jacksonian Democrat who shared that party's opposition to banks, paper money, corporate privilege, and almost all forms of positive governmental action.

In November 1834, during the break between the first and second sessions of Pierce's first term in Congress, he married Jane Means Appleton in her family's home in Amherst, New Hampshire. Franklin and Jane eventually had three sons. Pierce never saw the first, for he was in Washington when the unnamed infant died in New Hampshire three days after its birth. Pierce had retired from the Senate and returned to New Hampshire when the second son, Frank Robert, died at the age of four in 1843. Understandably, therefore, both Frank and Jane Pierce cherished their youngest son Benjamin, who was eleven when Pierce won the presidency in November 1852, three weeks before his forty-eighth birthday. At the time, he was the youngest man yet elected to the office.

In the weeks after his election, Pierce's top priority was trying to construct a cabinet that could keep the only recently reunited Democratic Party together. To Pierce, preserving the internal unity of the Democratic Party was an obsession, a fetish, a be-all-and-end-all. Only preserving the Union itself, he believed, was more important; yet, for him, Democratic Party unity was itself indispensable to preservation of the Union. Because Democratic factions in both Northern and Southern states had waged brutal warfare against their fellow state Democrats since 1850 over whether to embrace or reject the famous Compromise enacted that year, constructing a unifying cabinet proved far more difficult than the president-elect had initially anticipated. Even though the national Democratic Party platform on which he was elected now emphatically endorsed the Compromise, he was determined that Democrats who had opposed it as well as those who had supported it in 1850 and 1851 have representation in his cabinet. As a result of this intention, one name of a potential cabinet member after another was shot down when he broached them to fellow party members. Thus he had made little progress by late December when a death in the family intervened.[2]

Jane Pierce was an Appleton. In late December 1852, her uncle, the fabulously wealthy textile manufacturer Amos Lawrence, died. (The Appleton and Lawrence families were intermarried members of the renowned textile manufacturing syndicate, the Boston Associates. There is a reason, after all, why Lawrence University is located in Appleton, Wisconsin.) Because Lawrence had been especially fond of young Benny, the Pierces decided to take the eleven-year-old with them when they attended Lawrence's funeral in Boston. After the funeral, they planned to visit a few days with Jane's sister in Andover, Massachusetts, before returning to Concord, where Pierce had been trying to put together his cabinet. On January 6, 1853, two months before Pierce was to be inaugurated, the three of them left Andover on a one-car train for the short trip to Concord. Jane and Franklin sat beside each other on a bench with Benny alone behind them on a different bench. Little more than a mile outside the Andover station, this tiny train derailed. The lone passenger car plummeted into a twenty-foot culvert and landed on its roof. Both Franklin and Jane Pierce were badly bruised, but they survived. Benny did not. When the car capsized, he had the back of his head sheared off, and he died instantly. Both parents had to witness this ghastly sight, and both were badly shaken. Jane was so undone by the death of her lone remaining son that she remained in Andover rather than return to Concord for his funeral. It fell to Franklin Pierce to oversee the burial of Benny in a grave next to that of the son who had died ten years earlier.

Grief-ridden and hobbled by injuries, Pierce could not return to cabinet making until early February 1853, but with one important exception he had the entire Cabinet in place by March 4. On that day he gave his carefully prepared inaugural address, which, to the astonishment of the crowd, he delivered from memory without once consulting the text he held next to his thigh. An early sentence in that address, in fact, is the only public allusion, and an indirect one at that, he gave to his recent traumatic loss during his entire presidency. "It is a relief," Pierce announced, "to feel that no heart but my own can know the personal regret and bitter sorrow over which I have been borne to a position so suitable for others rather than desirable for myself."[3] The other signal Pierce gave of that deep sorrow was tacit. On all formal occasions where dress codes required him to wear gloves, he wore black rather than gray or white ones. When Abraham Lincoln later wore black gloves on such occasions, eastern Democratic newspapers hooted at his social gaucherie, but Pierce's habit was correctly interpreted as an emblem of his grief.

In any event, after his inauguration, Pierce plunged into his official duties, and as president he frequently entertained at the White House. Indeed, Pierce is renowned as one of the friendliest, most gregarious, and best-liked presidents the country has ever had. In short, he evinced no moody despondency while in the White House. Days before he left office in 1857, in fact, his entire cabinet which remained intact for his entire term signed a letter to him complimenting his unfailing politeness and good humor when interacting with them.

As historians of the 1850s know, Pierce made some serious blunders as president, but previous historians have not alleged any causal connection between those mistakes and the shocking death of his only remaining son. Nor, despite his reputation as an alcoholic, is there any evidence that the loss caused him to drink excessively while president. Indeed, he was quite abstemious while in the White House and drank toasts of wine or champagne only when public occasions outside of that building demanded it. Ostensibly, in sum, the personal loss had no impact on Pierce's public life. Peter A. Wallner, Pierce's most thorough and most admiring biographer, openly expresses his puzzlement that Pierce gave no outward manifestations of his inner suffering.[4] There can be no question that he felt this loss deeply. Pierce was not a callous, self-centered, ambitious political automaton. To the contrary, abundant testimony from others suggests that Pierce was a deeply sensitive, intensely feeling man with a genuine capacity for heartfelt human empathy.

Three examples of that testimony must suffice here. When he served in Congress in the late 1830s, Pierce visited his New Hampshire friend Benjamin Brown French in their boarding house after another congressman had died. Brown noted in his diary about Pierce's mood on that occasion. "He feels such things as sensibly as any man I ever saw, & were I about to leave this world I would have Frank Pierce at my pillow sooner than any other man I ever knew in whose veins flowed none of my own blood. I never—no never, shall forget his kind attentions to me when I was sick once in this city."[5] After he left the White House, Pierce and his wife visited his great friend Nathaniel Hawthorne and his wife Sophia in Rome, where both Hawthornes feared that their teenage daughter Una was dying. To relieve Hawthorne's mind, Pierce insisted that the novelist take him on walking tours of Rome, and after the daughter recovered Hawthorne wrote a friend about what Pierce had done for him. "Never having had any trouble before that pierced into my very vitals, I did not know what comfort there might be in the manly sympathy of a friend, but Pierce has undergone so great a sorrow of his own, and has so large and kindly a heart, and is so tender and strong that he really did us good, and I shall always love him better for the recollection of those dark days."[6] Finally, a few years later when Hawthorne knew he was dying, he wanted to see Pierce one more time. His wife sent him to Pierce with the following words: "I would not trust him in any hands now except such gentle and tender hands as yours."[7] Hawthorne in fact died when he and Pierce slept in adjoining rooms with an open door between them in a hotel in Plymouth, New Hampshire, where they had stopped on their way to the White Mountains.

As Hawthorne noted, Pierce was emotionally crushed by the death of his last son. The question is whether it is true that his emotional suffering had no impact on his performance as president, as the scholarly consensus holds. Yet the case can be made that grief over the death of Benny may well have influenced the biggest mistake Franklin Pierce made as president—his embrace and endorsement of the catastrophic Kansas-Nebraska Act of 1854. The grief that mattered in this case, however, was not Pierce's own but that of his wife Jane. And the key actor that linked her grief to the

Kansas-Nebraska disaster was Pierce's favorite cabinet member, whom he did not name until after his inauguration, the Mississippian Jefferson Davis, Pierce's secretary of war and the future president of the Confederate States of America. Or perhaps it's more accurate to say that the key link was Davis's young second wife, Varina Howell Davis, who befriended the distraught Jane Pierce.

Even before Amos Lawrence died, Pierce had asked Davis to consider serving in his cabinet; yet, as Davis's ablest biographer, William J. Cooper Jr. notes, Davis and Pierce were virtual strangers to each other.[8] The two men had met briefly in Washington in 1838 but had not seen each other or communicated since then. Both had served as officers in the Mexican-American War but Davis with Zachary Taylor, his former father-in-law, and Pierce with Winfield Scott, his opponent in the presidential election of 1852.[9] Pierce wanted Davis in his cabinet to facilitate the intra-party factional balance he sought, for Davis had been a prominent leader of anti-Compromise Southern Democrats. But the crucial fact is that the two of them became fast personal friends once in Washington. In the late 1850s, indeed, Davis, who, like Pierce, regarded the administration of Pierce's successor James Buchanan as an unmitigated disaster, pleaded with Pierce to seek the Democrats' 1860 presidential nomination. Pierce, in turn, urged Davis to do so. Neither man made the run, and the badly divided Democrats ended up running two rival presidential candidates that year.

The mutual admiration between Pierce and Davis survived the Civil War. Pierce, in his mid-50s, sat out that conflict in Concord, New Hampshire, while Davis presided over the Confederate government in Richmond. In 1867, after the Confederacy's defeat, Davis languished in a federal military prison awaiting a trial for treason that never took place. Pierce, who had privately condemned the war as a tragic mistake caused by Republicans' insulting vituperation against the South and who once, publicly, had denounced the Lincoln administration's military arrests of antiwar Democrats, visited Davis in prison and offered his legal help in preparing for the then-still-impending treason trial. Davis declined the help but gave him a note dated May 8, 1867, that said: "Given this day made bright by the visit of my beloved friend and ever honored chief."[10] Once Davis was released on bail, indeed, Pierce offered to let him and Varina stay in a house he had built on the shore in North Hampton, New Hampshire, but they declined his invitation.

Pierce and Davis had clearly bonded during the former's administration, even without considering the relationship between their respective wives. As noted above, however, the women may have been the key actors in linking Benny Pierce's death to Franklin Pierce's involvement with the Kansas-Nebraska Act. By all accounts, Franklin Pierce was an athletic, fun-loving, gregarious, charming extrovert. In contrast, Jane Pierce comes across in the same accounts as a sickly, morose, priggish, introverted hypochondriac—what one might call a sourpuss. She loathed smoking and drinking, and after marrying Pierce she quickly grew to loathe Washington and politics. Indeed, her reaction upon learning that Pierce had surprisingly won the Democratic Party's presidential nomination in 1852 was to faint dead away.

Still in deep mourning, Jane Pierce did not attend her husband's inauguration on March 4, 1853. She arrived in Washington with herfavorite cousin Abby Means eighteen days after that event, and Cousin Abby served as hostess at White House social events until the end of 1854. Jane herself, after having the White House's windows draped in black, remained largely out of the public eye. A visiting young woman from Boston described Jane at a White House dinner when she finally returned to presiding over them as follows. Jane, she carped, kept "the meanest table that has ever been kept at the White House. She is sordid, vain, selfish & egotistical. . . . She watches [her husband] it is said with the most contemptible jealousy. She makes him sit at table with his glass turned down as a constant advertisement that he has weaknesses that he could not mend & to let the world know she has a hard time taking care of him" while "placing him in a position degrading to his self-respect."[11]

However catty these remarks may strike us, Franklin Pierce almost surely suffered from alcoholism, but he was also quite conscious of his need to control his fondness for strong drink. As a young bachelor prior to his marriage and then during long absences from Jane after it as during the six months in 1847 when Pierce served as a brigadier-general in the Mexican-American War, he drank copiously on well-noted occasions. Indeed, during the 1852 campaign some Whigs joked that Pierce was "The Hero of Many a Well-Fought Bottle." After Pierce left the White House when away from Jane, and especially after her death in December 1863, he drank so heavily that liver failure ultimately caused his death in 1869. While in Jane's presence during their marriage and certainly while in the White House, however, Pierce did not drink wine or spirits. Aside from the hostile remark quoted above, moreover, there is scant, if any, evidence that it took his wife's censorious eye rather than his own self-discipline to keep him off demon drink.

Jane Pierce may not have been the controlling shrew described by the young Boston socialite, but virtually all students of Pierce have noted the mismatch between the couple and wondered what attracted Pierce to her. Pierce himself provided a very revealing answer. When a friend with whom he started drinking again after he left the White House bluntly asked him why he had wed such a woman, he instantly replied, "I could take better care of her than anyone else."[12] Many decisions that Pierce made during their marriage in fact testified to the sincerity of that solicitude. One reason he resigned from the US Senate in 1842 with a year left in his term was that both he and Jane feared that Washington's hard-drinking culture could tempt him to violate a temperance pledge he had recently taken at a public meeting in New Hampshire. In 1846 he declined an offer from President James K. Polk to serve as attorney general in his cabinet because he knew how much Jane hated Washington. Then in early 1852, after a Democratic state convention in New Hampshire plumped him for the party's presidential nomination, Pierce, with Jane's hatred of Washington life in mind, wrote a public letter to the convention's chairman announcing that the use of his name at the impending national convention would be "utterly repugnant to my tastes and wishes."[13] As long as Jane, who suffered repeated bouts of tuberculosis, lived after the Pierces left the White House in 1857, moreover, Pierce made repeated efforts to move her to warm climates during winters. Given Pierce's history of deep solicitude, if not outright pity, for Jane, it seems possible, indeed perhaps likely, that his empathy for her suffering in response to Benny's tragic death led to his involvement with the tragic Kansas-Nebraska Act.

So far as the public responsibilities of the First Lady went, Jane Pierce was mostly absent from March 1853 to December 1854; her cousin Abby Means handled those duties. But she was not a total recluse hiding away in the White House. She spoke with some visitors to that building, and it is clear that she treated young boys as surrogate sons to replace her beloved Benny. Henry Watterson, who would later become an influential newspaper editor in Louisville, Kentucky, and Democratic Party power-broker, was almost Benny's age when he encountered Jane Pierce while on a visit with his father to the White House in the summer of 1853. He recalled the incident in his autobiography as "one of the most vivid memories and altogether the saddest episode of my childhood." "A lady in black took me in her arms and convulsively held me there, weeping as if her heart would break."[14] Jane also occasionally left the White House that summer, and her favorite place to go, along with her husband, was to visit Jefferson and Varina Howell Davis in the house they rented a few blocks away. For the Davises had a one-year-old son named Sam who almost instantly became a surrogate for the three sons Jane had lost. Jane became so attached to Sam that the understanding Varina Davis allowed Jane to take him out on carriage rides as we today might allow her to walk him in a stroller. The devoted Franklin Pierce undoubtedly understood how much this connection to the Davis family brightened the spirits of his distraught wife.

Meanwhile, outside of Washington that summer and fall of 1853, the Democratic Party appeared to be on the verge of complete disintegration because of violent factional warfare over the administration's bungling distribution of federal patronage jobs. Democrats across the country pleaded with their leaders in Washington to come up with a concrete public policy that could reunite warring Democrats by provoking Whig opposition to it. Pierce, however, had no such domestic program that might revive interparty conflict and reunite feuding Democrats. As an ideologically rigid Democrat, Pierce opposed any actions by the national or state governments to foster economic development such as chartering banks or subsidizing railroad construction because all such actions, orthodox Democrats believed, created special privileges for some that violated others' equal rights. Pierce's term would in fact be punctuated by vetoes of various congressional initiatives on the domestic front.

Foreign policy was a totally different matter. Pierce dreamed of reviving the expansionist policies of his Democratic predecessor James K. Polk, who had added Texas, Oregon, and the enormous Mexican Cession that included ceding California to the United States. Thus Pierce announced in his inaugural address that "my Administration will not be controlled by any timid forebodings from expansion." [15] In 1854 this yen would help engender the notorious "Ostend Manifesto" in which three of Pierce's foreign ministers implied that the United States should seize the Spanish colony of Cuba by force if Spain refused to sell the island to the Americans. But during 1853 the upshot of Pierce's focus on foreign rather than domestic policy was the Gadsden Purchase from Mexico and a reciprocal trade agreement with Canada, neither of which, importantly, would be ratified until 1854. In any event, few people knew of the negotiations that had occurred in 1853. They hardly formed a program that could provoke Whig opposition and thereby force feuding Democrats to reunite.

In contrast to Pierce, Illinois Senator Stephen A. Douglas, who had been warned in December 1853 that the Democratic Party would be "shivered to atoms" unless Democratic congressmen devised a demonstrably Democratic program that Whigs would reflexively oppose, believed he had found a party-saving formula.[16] He sought a three-part program for the undeveloped West, which he correctly expected would prompt fierce Whig opposition: a homestead law; federal land grants to subsidize construction of a railroad to the Pacific Coast; and, indispensable to the feasibility of the first two, the establishment of a formal territorial government in the as-yet unorganized area of the old Louisiana Purchase Territory west of Missouri and Iowa.[17]

Yet Douglas encountered a substantial obstacle when he tried to prepare a bill in January 1854 to organize a new Nebraska Territory. According to the terms of the famous Missouri Compromise of 1820, slavery was to be "forever prohibited" from that area north of the thirty-six degrees-thirty-minutes line. Southern Democrats in the Senate had the votes to block any legislation they disliked, and they refused to allow any territorial bill to pass which heeded that prohibition of slavery. Thus Douglas searched for some formulation that would be acceptable to them without explicitly repealing the 1820 provision. Any such overt repeal, he knew, would infuriate Northerners who now regarded the thirty-four year-old promise that slavery would be excluded from the area as sacrosanct. Douglas had presented two versions of such a bill by mid-January, but southern Democrats deemed neither satisfactory. Then Philip Phillips, an Alabama Democrat in the House, and Archibald Dixon, a Kentucky Whig in the Senate, expressly demanded outright repeal; the key Southern Democratic Senators told Douglas he must include something like that or they would deep-six the bill. Douglas folded before that pressure even though he knew that outright repeal would raise what he called "a hell of a storm" in the North.

Douglas was scheduled to present the third version of the bill on Monday, January 23, but because it was bound to be so controversial he sought Pierce's blessing for this latest revision on Sunday, January 22. On the preceding Saturday, Pierce and the entire cabinet, who had been closely watching the proceedings in the Senate, had agreed that any outright repeal of the Missouri Compromise's language that slavery was "forever prohibited" from the area would decimate northern Democratic candidates in the impending congressional elections of 1854. Indeed, mass protest meetings against repeal had already emerged across the North.

The first problem for Douglas and the six southern Democrats who accompanied him to the White House on the morning of Sunday, January 22, however, was that the president normally refused to conduct official business on the Sabbath. Therefore, the group who were aware of the close relationship between Pierce and Davis, though not perhaps of how crucial that relationship was to Jane Pierce, stopped at Davis's house on their way to the White House. They persuaded Davis that it was crucial that they see Pierce that Sunday, and Davis interceded with him. No scintilla of evidence about what Davis and Pierce said to each other in their meeting exists; we only know that Pierce acceded to Davis's request. It would have been utterly out of character for Davis to play openly on the friendship between the Davis and Pierce families as a lever with Pierce. Besides, he was astute enough to know that he need not do so overtly. It is Pierce's reaction that requires speculation. It seems likely to this author that Pierce reluctantly agreed to see the delegation of congressional Democrats in part because he was unwilling to say no to a friend whose wife and little son had brought such consolation to his own grieving wife.

Thus he and Davis met with the delegation consisting of Douglas, the four most powerful Southern Democrats in the Senate, and two Southern Democratic members of the House of Representatives. In sum, Pierce and Douglas were the only Northerners in a room where they were outnumbered by seven slaveholding Southerners demanding that slavery be given a chance to go into the proposed Kansas and Nebraska Territories.[18]

Historians do not know what was said in that two-hour meeting. According to one memoir written years later by Philip Phillips, Pierce began the conversation by warning, "Gentlemen, you are entering a serious undertaking, and the ground should be well surveyed before the first step is taken."[19] If this recollection is roughly accurate, Pierce recognized the political risk at stake. Nonetheless, he was persuaded to commit himself and his administration to the Kansas-Nebraska bill. Indeed, Pierce himself wrote the key language that effected repeal of the Missouri Compromise's prohibition of slavery expansion into that area without overtly using the word "repeal." Pierce wrote instead that the Missouri Compromise had been "superseded by the principles of the legislation of 1850, commonly called the compromise measures and is hereby declared inoperative and void." Subsequently Pierce publicly declared that he expected all Democrats in Congress to back the bill, which he now identified as an administration measure.

What bears emphasis about this meeting is that Davis, the Mississippian, was the only member of the cabinet there. Had its northern members, who had presciently warned the preceding day against repealing the ban on slavery expansion, been there as well, Pierce more than likely would not have bent under the pressure the Southerners exerted on him. And the northern cabinet members—Secretary of State William L. Marcy,

Attorney General Caleb Cushing, and Secretary of the Interior Robert McClelland—were not present only because Jefferson Davis persuaded Pierce to meet with the congressmen and Davis by himself on a Sunday, the day, other cabinet members knew, on which he had hitherto refused to conduct official business. In fact, Pierce must have sensed their disapproval of what he had done, for he urged the delegation as they left him to go get the New Yorker Marcy's approval, something they had absolutely no intention of doing because they knew perfectly well that his reaction would be anything but approval.

The argument of this essay is that Franklin Pierce's empathy with his wife's grieving after the death of their son Benny helps explain why he acceded to Jefferson Davis's request that he meet with the congressional delegation on that Sunday in January 1854. The argument is *not* that his solicitude for his wife explains why he signed on to the Kansas-Nebraska bill once he did meet with that congressional delegation. Historians do not know what was said at the meeting; but they have offered a number of speculations about why he did so. Some say that Pierce was the quintessential proslavery, pro-Southern doughface. Hence he acquiesced to the Southerners' demands. Indeed, Pierce was always solicitous about preserving comity between the free and slave states, but this line of argument is not persuasive. Although Pierce had denounced abolitionists as a threat to the Union since the mid-1830s, he was never proslavery. New Hampshire's Democratic organization (which Pierce led) endorsed the Wilmot Proviso, which would bar slavery from the lands acquired from Mexico and was anathema to Southerners, in four consecutive state platforms between 1847 and 1850. Moreover, Pierce himself publicly denounced certain provisions of the Fugitive Slave Act of 1850. Pierce liked Southerners, and his pro-Southern bias would increase dramatically once he had committed himself to Douglas's measure, but there are compelling reasons to doubt that pleasing southern slaveholders explains the president's decision.

Three other considerations, however, appear to have moved him. Pierce hoped to make his administration's reputation in foreign, not domestic, policy. One of the slaveholders meeting with him that morning chaired the Senate's Foreign Relations Committee. We do not know if that Virginian,

James M. Mason, threatened to prevent ratification of Pierce's treaties with Mexico and Canada by never releasing them from his committee, but it seems likely that Pierce hoped to stay in his good graces. Second, Douglas had been making the case in the Senate for two weeks that the territorial provisions of the Compromise of 1850, which opened Utah and New Mexico territories to possible settlement by slaveholders, had already displaced the Missouri Compromise's ban on the extension of slavery. Given the language Pierce used, Douglas apparently convinced him of that utterly false claim. The Compromise of 1850 in fact had nothing to do with the area covered by the Missouri Compromise. Most important, Democratic Party unity remained a shibboleth for Pierce. It is very likely that Douglas prevailed with Pierce by arguing that only such a program as Douglas proposed could, by provoking Whig opposition, prevent the Democratic Party from being "shivered to atoms."

Signing on to the Nebraska bill was the biggest mistake of Franklin Pierce's political career, as subsequent events would show. Among other things, violent turmoil broke out between Northerners and Southerners in Kansas from early 1855 until August 1858 when residents of Kansas Territory voted overwhelmingly against entering the Union as a slave state. Then northern Democratic candidates suffered a rout in the congressional elections of 1854–55 when they lost sixty-six of the ninety-one northern House seats they held in 1854, and Pierce failed in his attempt to win another presidential nomination from the Democratic Party in 1856. Finally, the birth of the Republican Party rallied outraged Northerners against Pierce and his Democratic Party and the new party's victory in the presidential election of 1860 would prompt secession and a sanguinary Civil War.

For the remainder of his presidency, indeed for the remainder of his life, Pierce never admitted that he had made a mistake in embracing the Kansas-Nebraska bill or that he bore considerable responsibility for engendering the string of developments listed in the preceding paragraph. The worse the strife between Northerners and Southerners over the establishment of slavery in, or its prohibition from, Kansas became during his remaining two-and-a half years in the White House, the more obstreperously he defended the measure as an act of justice to the South.[20] In his annual message to Congress in December 1855 Pierce called the Nebraska Act "manly and ingenuous" and praised the repeal of the Missouri Compromise line, which so clearly infuriated a majority of Northerners, as "the final consummation and complete recognition of the principle that no portion of the United States [i.e., the North] shall undertake through assumption of the powers of the General Government to dictate the social institutions of any other portion."[21] A year later—after he had lost the Democratic presidential nomination, after residents of his hometown of Concord, New Hampshire, had burned him in effigy, and after Republicans had carried New Hampshire along with ten other of the sixteen free states in the presidential election of 1856 in large part because of events in what Republicans called "Bleeding Kansas"—Pierce was even more unapologetic. Sectional conflict over slavery in Kansas was "inevitable," he averred. "No human prudence, no form of legislation, no wisdom on the part of Congress could have prevented it." The Nebraska Act did not cause the troubles in Kansas. They were "inherent in the nature of things." [22] Thus did Franklin Pierce deny that he had any personal responsibility for the results of the decision he made on January 22, 1854, to endorse the Kansas-Nebraska bill and make it an administration measure.

In the end, it may be that Benny Pierce's tragic death had little or nothing to do with why Pierce made that decision. But it is seems reasonably clear that Pierce's empathetic concern with his wife's grieving over that death probably influenced his agreement to meet on a Sunday with the Democratic congressional delegation that somehow persuaded Pierce to make his fateful decision. Pierce and Jefferson Davis were so fond of each other that it is quite possible he would have succumbed to Davis's request even without invoking his always solicitous concern for his distraught wife as a causal factor. Nonetheless, it seems likely that Pierce agreed to this calamitous meeting in large part because he knew how important visits with little Sammy Davis were to his wife who was still devastated by Benny's death a year earlier. If that is so, the ultimate irony is that two weeks after Pierce signed the catastrophic Kansas-Nebraska Act into law on May 30, 1854, young Sammy Davis, the object of Jane Pierce's lavish affection, also died. But this death, in turn, seems only to have drawn the Pierce and Davis families even closer together. Jane Pierce could not bring herself to attend Sammy Davis' funeral, just as she had been absent from her own Benny's. But the president was there, attempting to console his friend. And Pierce would consider Davis a friend until he died in 1869, six years after his wife Jane Appleton Pierce had expired.

NOTES

1. In the second volume of his 1947 opus *Ordeal of the Union*, Allan Nevins entitles the first chapter "Enter the Pleasant Mr. Pierce," and other historians agree about the apparently unflappable congeniality of our fourteenth president. Allan Nevins, *Ordeal of the Union: House Dividing, 1852-57* (New York: Charles Scribner's Sons, 1947), 3–42.
2. See Michael Holt, *Franklin Pierce* (New York: Times Books, 2010), 48–52. For more in-depth treatments, see two older and longer biographies: Roy F. Nichols, *Franklin Pierce: Young Hickory of the Granite Hills* (revised edition; Philadelphia: University of Pennsylvania Press, 1958) and Peter A. Wallner, *Franklin Pierce: Martyr for the Union* (Concord, NH: Plaidswede, 2007).
3. James D. Richardson ed., *A Compilation of the Messages and Papers of the Presidents*, Volume V (Washington, DC: Government Printing Office, 1897), 197.
4. Wallner makes frequent comments about this in his chapters devoted to Pierce's presidency, but see, for example, Wallner, *Pierce*, 14 and 49.
5. *Witness to the Young Republic: A Yankee's Journal 1828-1870; Benjamin Brown French*, ed. Donald B. Cole and John J. McDonough (Hanover, NH: University Press of New England, 1989), 83.
6. As quoted in Wallner, *Pierce*, 322.
7. Sophia Hawthorne to Franklin Pierce, May 6, 1864, quoted ibid., 357.
8. William J. Cooper Jr., *Jefferson Davis: American* (New York: Alfred A. Knopf, 2000), 248.
9. Jefferson Davis's first wife was Zachary Taylor's daughter, Sarah Knox Taylor, who died a few months after she and Davis were wed.
10. Jefferson Davis to Franklin Pierce, May 8, 1867, quoted in Wallner, *Pierce*, 368.
11. Quoted ibid., 116.
12. Clement March in the unpublished memoirs of Sarah Parker Goodwin, quoted ibid., 355.
13. Holt, *Franklin Pierce*, 39.
14. Henry Watterson, *"Marse Henry": An Autobiography* (New York: George H. Daron, 1919), I, 32–33, quoted in Wallner, *Pierce*, 49.

15. Richardson, ed., *Messages and Papers of the Presidents*, V, 198.
16. Samuel Treat to Stephen A. Douglas, December 18, 1853, Stephen A. Douglas Papers (University of Chicago).
17. For this story, see Michael F. Holt, *The Political Crisis of the 1850s* (rev. edition; New York: W. W. Norton and Company, 1983), 141–46.
18. The new version of Douglas's bill called for two territories, not a single huge Nebraska Territory as the first two versions had.
19. Quoted in Wallner, *Pierce*, 96.
20. Entire books have been written about the turmoil in Kansas launched by the final passage of the Kansas-Nebraska Act on May 30, 1854, and this is hardly the place to recount that story. But for an able, brief summary, see the chapter "Two Wars in Kansas" in David M. Potter, *The Impending Crisis, 1848-1861*, edited and completed by Don E. Fehrenbacher (New York: Harper & Row, 1976), 199–224.
21. Richardson, ed., *Messages and Papers of the Presidents*, V, 348.
22. Ibid., 397–407.

A Lincoln family portrait. First Lady Mary Todd Lincoln, Willie, Robert, Tad, and the president. [Library of Congress Prints and Photographs Division.]

4

Abraham Lincoln and the Death of His Son Willie

MICHAEL BURLINGAME

During the Civil War, over 700,000 American soldiers died—more than the total who perished in all the other wars in US history combined. The population of the country in 1860 was 31 million. If proportionally similar casualties had been sustained during the twenty-first-century wars in Iraq and Afghanistan, over 7 million troops would have died.

The Union Army had fared badly in 1861, suffering defeats at Manassas, Virginia, in July, at Wilson's Creek in Missouri in August, and Ball's Bluff, Virginia, in October. Those agonizing setbacks caused President Lincoln to declare: "If Hell is [not] any worse than this, it has no terror for me."[1] In January 1862 he plaintively asked the quartermaster general of the army: "What shall I do? The people are impatient; [Treasury Secretary Salmon P.] Chase has no money, and he tells me he can raise no more; the general of the army [George B. McClellan] has typhoid fever. The bottom is out of the tub. What shall I do?"[2] The following month, a leading New York powerbroker groused that "most of the men trusted with the great responsibilities of the Government, either lack ability or fail to comprehend the magnitude of their trust. I am *sure* that [if] this war [had been] wisely entered upon and energetically carried on, [it] would have been virtually concluded now."[3] A resident of Cincinnati reported that Lincoln "is universally an admitted failure, has no will, no courage, no executive capacity . . . and his spirit necessarily infuses itself downwards through all departments."[4] Little wonder, then, that Lincoln was a "man of sorrows."

Few things did more to intensify his sorrow than the death of his favorite son, eleven-year-old Willie, in February 1862, less than a year into his presidency. That loss deprived Lincoln of an important source of comfort and relief from his heavy official burdens; exacerbated his tendency to suffer from depression; made it harder for him to deal with his mentally unbalanced wife; and caused him to reflect more profoundly on the ways of God and thus deepened his religious sensibility.

The Lincolns had four children: Robert, born in 1843; Edward, born in 1846; William, born in 1850 (the year Eddie died); and Thomas, better known as Tad, born in 1853. William H. Herndon, Lincoln's law partner from 1844 to 1861, recalled that Lincoln "worshipped his children and *what* they worshipped. . . . *disliked* what the[y] hated, which was everything that did not bend to their . . . whims." Lincoln, said Herndon, was "so blinded to his children's faults" that if "they s[h]it in Lincoln's hat and rubbed it on his boots, he would have laughed and thought it smart."[5] Herndon told an audience in Springfield shortly after the assassination of Lincoln that his partner had been "liberal—generous—affectionate to his children, loving them with his whole heart" and "as loving & tender as a nursing mother."[6] In 1866 Mary Todd Lincoln gave Herndon an interview in which she stated that her husband

> was the Kindest Man—Most tender Man & loving husband & father in the world: he gave us all unbounded liberty . . . he was very—indulgent to his children—chided or prais[ed them] for it—their acts —: he always said 'It [is my] pleasure that my children are free—happy & unrestrained by parental tyranny. Love is the chain whereby to Lock a child to its parents.[7]

A neighbor in Springfield remembered that at a dinner given by the Lincolns for several guests, "Mr. Lincoln was carving the chicken, and the first thing he did was to cut off the drumstick and give it to Tad . . ., and then he said, smiling at the rest of the company, 'Children have first place here, you know.' "[8]

In Illinois, Lincoln may have been an unusually indulgent father, but he was also an absent one, for his law practice kept him on the road for prolonged periods every fall and spring. Unlike other lawyers who practiced on the state's Eighth Judicial Circuit, Lincoln did not return home on weekends. His close friend and political ally, Judge David Davis, who presided over the circuit court's sessions, stated that "Lincoln was happy—as happy as *he* could be, when on this Circuit—and happy no other place. This was his place of Enjoyment. As a general rule when all the lawyers of a Saturday Evening would go home and see their families & friends at home Lincoln would refuse to go home." At first, Davis found this reluctance to return home to see his beloved children puzzling, but the judge and other attorneys on the circuit "soon learned to account for his strange disinclination to go home. Lincoln himself never had much to say about home, and we never felt free to comment on it. Most of us had pleasant, inviting homes, and as we struck out for them I'm sure each one of us down in our hearts had a mingled feeling of pity and sympathy for him." It seemed to Davis and to the others that Lincoln "was not domestically happy."[9]

Lincoln was notoriously "shut-mouthed" about his private life, sharing little about his domestic relations with anyone. An exception was his good friend and fellow attorney, Orville Hickman Browning, who during the Civil War regularly visited the White House. There, as he later recalled, the president often "used to talk to me about his domestic troubles. He has several times told me there that he was constantly under great apprehension lest his wife should do something which would bring him into disgrace." Browning added that on one occasion, when Lincoln was "in a state of deep melancholy" and talking "awhile about his sources of domestic sadness, he sent one of the boys to get a volume of [Thomas] Hood's poems and he read to me several of those sad pathetic pieces—I suppose because they were accurate pictures of his own experiences and feelings."[10]

Partly because of his long absences on the legal circuit, Lincoln did not bond closely with his first son, Robert. Weeks after his father's assassination, Robert told a biographer of the president:

> My Father's life was of a kind which gave me but little opportunity to learn the details of his early career. During my childhood and early youth he was almost constantly away from home, attending courts or making political speeches. In 1859 when I was sixteen and when he was beginning to devote himself more to practice in his own neighborhood, and when I would have had both the inclination and the means of gratifying my desire to become better acquainted with the history of his struggles, I went to New Hampshire to school and afterward to Harvard College, and he became President.[11]

Robert and his father were unlike in many ways. His son had little of Lincoln's sense of humor, idealism, magnanimity, generosity, warmth, or compassion. Ida Tarbell, who published a two-volume biography of Lincoln and interviewed Robert several times, said he was "all Todd."[12] Herndon agreed, stating that "Bob is not his 'daddy' nor like him in any respect whatever. Bob is little, proud, aristocratic, and haughty, is his mother's 'baby' all through."[13] As Ruth Painter Randall, author of *Lincoln's Son*, put it: "Robert seems to have been born with the Todd tastes, abilities, and inclinations. The Todd relatives had so much to offer in contrast to the modest household of his odd lawyer father.... The Todd kin whom Robert knew had the things he liked, high standards of social correctness, prosperity and the comfortable type of living that goes with it."[14] A Springfield neighbor of the Lincolns observed that Robert and his youngest brother, Tad, "were *Mama*, boys. They neither one had the slightest personal appearance or deliberate easy manner of Mr. Lincoln. They both resembled their mother in looks and actions."[15]

On the other hand, Willie (according to that same neighbor) "was the true picture of Mr. Lincoln, in every way, even to carrying his head slightly inclined toward his left shoulder. (This Mr. Lincoln always did while I knew him.)"[16] The poet Nathaniel Parker Willis, who befriended the Lincolns during the Civil War, believed that Willie "faithfully resembled his father" in many respects and "was his father's favorite. They were intimates—often seen hand in hand."[17] Ruth Painter Randall concluded that the lad "was his father over again both in magnetic personality and his gifts and tastes" and that "with Willie his father could get that special joy that comes to a parent when he recognizes that his child is mentally like him."[18]

Lincoln and Willie were so close that the father could almost read the son's mind. One day at breakfast in the White House, the president discovered his high-strung youngest son, Tad, awash in tears. Eager to console the little fellow, he hugged and kissed him while asking what was wrong. The boy sobbed that he had been ridiculed by soldiers to whom he had offered religious tracts. When presidential attempts to solace Tad proved unavailing, Willie "lapsed into a profound, absorbed silence," which his father would not allow anyone to interrupt. After a few minutes of intense concentration, with a smile the older lad looked up at the president, who exclaimed: "There! You have it now, my boy, have you not?" Lincoln told a fellow diner: "I know every step of the process by which that boy arrived at his satisfactory solution of the question before him, as it is by just such slow methods I attain results."[19]

Lincoln described Willie as "a very gentle & amiable boy."[20] A Springfield friend, the black barber William Florville, deemed Willie "a Smart boy for his age, So Considerate, So Manly: his Knowledge and good Sence, far exceeding most boys more advanced in years."[21] Others thought Willie was exceptionally self-possessed, frank, "studious and intellectual," as well as "sprightly, sweet tempered and mild mannered."[22] A White House secretary noted that he "was a child of great promise, and far more quiet and studious than his mercurial younger brother."[23] Horatio Nelson Taft, father of Willie's best friend in Washington, praised him as "an amiable good hearted boy," a "ceaseless talker, ambitious to *know* everything, always asking questions, always busy," one who "had more judgment and foresight than any boy of his age that I have ever known."[24] Taft's daughter Julia, who often played with Willie at the White House, thought Willie was "the most lovable boy I ever knew, bright, sensible, sweet-tempered and gentle mannered."[25] His manners were indeed gracious, as one eminent visitor to the White House discovered when he introduced some of his friends to the lad, who was playing in the driveway. In response, Willie said, pointing to the ground: "Gentlemen, I am very happy to see you. Pray be seated."[26] Alexander Williamson, who tutored Willie in Washington, reported that the lad "had only to con over once or twice a page of his speller and definer, and the impression became so fixed that he went through without hesitation or blundering, and his other studies in proportion."[27] Willie hoped to become a teacher or clergyman.[28] John Hay described Willie as a "bright, gentle, studious child," one "of great promise, capable of close application and study. He had a fancy for drawing up railway time tables, and would conduct an imaginary train from Chicago to New York with perfect precision. He wrote childish verses, which sometimes attained the unmerited honors of print."[29]

In early February 1862, the boy came down with a fever so serious that he grew delirious.[30] (It is not clear what disease he had. Perhaps it was typhoid, or smallpox, or tuberculosis. Some speculated that the source of his illness was the White House basement, which a presidential secretary described as "perennially overrun with rats, mildew and foul smells" and thus probably "the cause of the well-known mortality in the upper part of the building.)"[31] At that same time, eight-year-old Tad also became ill. The president became so preoccupied with the boys' health that he scarcely tended to public business.[32] On February 18 Attorney General Edward Bates confided in his diary that Lincoln was "nearly worn out, with grief and watching."[33] Regular White House receptions were called off. In time, Willie grew so weak that he resembled a shadow. Whatever disease he had finally killed him on February 20. When he died, his father chokingly announced to his principal White House secretary: "Well, Nicolay, my boy is gone—he is actually gone!" and burst into tears.[34] Over and over he cried out, "This is the hardest trial of my life. Why is it? Oh, why is it?"[35]

That day a Washington correspondent reported that "it would move the heart of his bitterest political enemy . . . to witness the marked change which grief has wrought upon him."[36] The following morning he looked "completely prostrated with grief" when speaking with an Illinois friend, who wrote that Lincoln "is one of the most tender-hearted of men and devotedly attached to his children."[37] He was so overcome that close friends worried about the effect that Willie's death would have on him. For the next two days he remained "in a stupor of grief" and took little interest in public affairs.[38]

Months later, to a friend Lincoln recited from Shakespeare's *King John* the lines of Constance, who bewailed the death of her dead child: "And, Father Cardinal, I have heard you say/ That we shall see and know our friends in heaven./If that be true, I shall see my boy again." He then asked: "Did you ever dream of some lost friend, and feel that you were having sweet communion with him, and yet have a consciousness that it was not a reality?" "I think we all have some such experiences," came the reply. "That is the way I dream of my lost boy, Willie," Lincoln said. He then "broke down in most compulsive weeping."[39]

On February 24 Phineas D. Gurley presided over Willie's funeral at the White House, a service that Orville H. Browning had arranged at the president's request. There, as Lincoln stood with his eyes brimming with tears and his lips quivering, a look of the utmost grief came over his face as he gazed at his boy's corpse. His body shook convulsively as he sobbed and buried his face in his hands. Weeping, he told Elizabeth Keckly, a black seamstress who befriended Mrs. Lincoln, that Willie "was too good for this earth . . . but then we loved him so. It is hard, hard to have him die!" Mrs. Keckly never observed a man so grief-stricken.[40]

A woman who attended the funeral complained that it "was in very bad taste, ostentatious & showy." She thought that "one needed only to look at the poor President, bowed over & sobbing audibly to see he had nothing to do with the pageant. The services by Dr Gurley were endlessly long and offensively fulsome. I felt glad that the poor Mother was ill in bed & so escaped the painful infliction."[41]

By the end of February, Lincoln had regained enough strength to resume his duties. On the twenty-sixth a journalist reported that he "is frequently called up three and four times in a night to receive important messages from the West. Since his late bereavement he looks sad and care-worn, but is in very good health again."[42]

But more time had to pass before the president recovered fully. At a general's funeral in early March, he appeared bowed down with extreme grief. "I certainly never saw a more impressive picture of sorrow," a fellow mourner recalled. Alluding to the success of Union arms in Tennessee (that February Grant won the first significant Union victories of the war at Forts Henry and Donelson in Tennessee), he wrote of Lincoln: "There seemed to be none of the light of the recent victories in his pale, cadaverous face." As the president climbed down from his carriage, he hesitated "as if about to stagger back into the carriage, and then seemed to collect himself for the duty at hand, with a fatigued air, which seemed to say, 'What will come next?' "[43] Willie died on a Thursday, and for weeks afterward Lincoln took time from work on Thursdays to mourn.[44]

In the brief period between Willie's death and the funeral, an office seeker entered the White House and loudly insisted on seeing Lincoln. When the president stepped from his office to see what was causing the commotion, the would-be postmaster brazenly demanded to speak with him. When he heard what the man wanted, Lincoln angrily asked: "When you came to the door here, didn't you see the crepe on it? Didn't you realize that meant somebody must be lying dead in this house?" "Yes, Mr. Lincoln, I did. But what I wanted to see you about was important." Heatedly, Lincoln exclaimed: "That crepe is hanging there for my son; his dead body at this moment is lying unburied in this house, and you come here, push yourself in with such a request! Couldn't you at least have the decency to wait until after we had buried him?"[45]

Compounding Lincoln's grief, just as Willie was wasting away Tad also developed a high fever and seemed in grave danger. Dorothea Dix, head of the Union Army nursing corps, detailed one of her nurses, Rebecca Pomroy, to minister to Tad and his overwrought mother. Mrs. Pomroy offered Lincoln the consolation that might be found in the prayers that many Northerners offered for Tad. "I am glad of that," he replied, then buried his face in his hands and cried. On February 24, he gazed at Tad and remarked to Mrs. Pomroy: "I hope you will pray for him, and if it is

God's will that he may be spared, and also for me, for I need the prayers of many."[46] She replied that her faith in God had helped her deal with the loss of her husband and two children. Calling her "one of the best women I ever knew," the president saw to it that her surviving son was granted a promotion.[47] Her piety may have strengthened Lincoln's faith.

In late March, a White House secretary reported that Lincoln had "recovered much of his old equanimity and cheerfulness; and certainly no one who saw his constant and eager application to his arduous duties, would imagine for a moment that the man carried so large a load of private grief, in addition to the cares of a nation."[48]

But Lincoln knew that it would take much longer for him to recover fully from Willie's death. He indirectly explained why in a letter of condolence he sent in late 1862 to Fanny McCullough, daughter of his friend, Lieutenant Colonel William McCullough. When the colonel, who had been sheriff and clerk of the courts in Bloomington, Illinois, died on December 5, his twenty-one-year-old daughter, "a guileless, truthful, warm hearted, noble girl" was devastated by the news.[49] On some days she paced back and forth violently, and on other days she sat listlessly mute.[50] When Lincoln heard about her condition, he offered her revealing advice: "It is with deep grief that I learn of the death of your kind and brave Father; and, especially, that it is affecting your young heart beyond what is common in such cases. In this sad world of ours, sorrow comes to all; and, to the young, it comes with bitterest agony, because it takes them unawares. The older have learned to ever expect it. I am anxious to afford some alleviation of your present distress. Perfect relief is not possible, except with time. You cannot now realize that you will ever feel better. Is not this so? And yet it is a mistake. You are sure to be happy again. To know this, which is certainly true, will make you some less miserable now. I have had experience enough to know what I say; and you need only to believe it, to feel better at once."[51]

But even with the passage of time, Lincoln never fully recovered from Willie's death. On his final day, he told his wife: "We must both be more cheerful in the future; between the war and the loss of our darling Willie, we have been very miserable."[52]

Indeed, Mary Lincoln was "very miserable." Like her husband, she was overcome with grief. But unlike Lincoln, she felt guilty, for two weeks prior to Willie's death she had given an elaborate, controversial White House party for hundreds of specially invited guests. She regarded her son's death as punishment for throwing the gala party while Willie and Tad both lay sick abed. In May 1862 she wrote a friend about her "crushing bereavement": "We have met with so overwhelming an affliction in the death of our beloved Willie a being too precious for earth, that I am so completely unnerved."[53] That same month she told an Illinois congressman that the White House seemed to her "like a tomb and that she could not bear to be in it." Willie, she said, "was the favorite child, so good, so obedient, so promising."[54] She steeped herself in mourning so deep that one day Lincoln escorted her to a White House window, pointed to a distant insane asylum, and said: "Mother, do you see that large white building on the hill yonder? Try and control your grief, or it will drive you mad, and we may have to send you there."[55]

Lincoln had good reason to fear that he might have to commit his wife to a mental hospital, for even before Willie died she had displayed alarming symptoms of psychological imbalance, including manic-depressive disorder.[56] Orville H. Browning called her "demented" and remembered that she "was a girl of much vivacity in conversation, but was subject to . . . spells of mental depression. . . . As we used familiarly to state it she was always 'either in the garret or cellar.' "[57] Similarly, a childhood friend of Mary reported that in her youth and adolescence she was "very highly strung, nervous, impulsive, excitable, having an emotional temperament much like an April day, sunning all over with laughter one moment, the next crying as though her heart would break."[58] Mary Lincoln also showed symptoms of narcissism and borderline personality disorder.[59] In 1875 an Illinois court adjudged her insane and had her confined in a mental hospital.[60] Lincoln's close friend and the executor of his estate, David Davis, reported that her behavior as First Lady indicated that she was "natural born thief" for whom "stealing was a sort of insanity."[61] He believed that she was deranged as early as the 1840s.[62]

In Springfield it was reported that her "mania was for shopping which she pitifully carried to the extreme of shop-lifting. Her family devised schemes to shield her and to protect or reimburse the merchants."[63] Her shopping mania led her as First Lady to purchase from the New York firm of Ball, Black & Company several thousand dollars worth of jewelry without her husband's knowledge.[64] From another jeweler she bought $3,200 worth of merchandise (including four clocks and two diamond-and-pearl bracelets) within three months. In a single month she purchased eighty-four pairs of gloves.[65] In March 1865 she spent $2,288 at the Galt & Brothers jewelry store in Washington.[66] A Democratic newspaper expressed astonishment at reports that she had bought a $5,000 shawl and $3,000 earrings. The editor wanted to know where "the money comes from that enables this very ordinary lawyer from Illinois . . . to live in this style, when the poor man can barely with the strictest economy after paying his taxes, get bread to eat?"[67]

After her husband's assassination, Mary Lincoln looted the White House, shipping many of its contents to Springfield. According to Alexander K. McClure, his friend Congressman Thaddeus Stevens of Pennsylvania, chairman of the House Ways and Means Committee, skillfully concealed the theft and got Congress to fund the refurnishing of the White House. McClure thought that "she was mentally unbalanced when she came to Washington and seemed to have been . . . all her life." McClure concluded that even though the First Lady "was a consuming sorrow to Mr. Lincoln," yet the president "bore it all with unflagging patience. She was sufficiently unbalanced to make any error possible and many probable but not sufficiently so as to dethrone her as mistress of the White House."[68] When William P. Wood, superintendant of the Old Capitol Prison, informed the president that his wife was involved in several unethical schemes, Lincoln replied: "The caprices of Mrs. Lincoln, I am satisfied, are the result of partial insanity."[69] (Mary Lincoln may have inherited her psychiatric problems, for many members of her family were mentally unbalanced.)[70]

Mrs. Lincoln's excessive grieving caused some popular resentment. Immediately after Willie's death she would not allow the Marine Band to give its popular weekly concerts on the White House lawn. When this ban persisted for months, public discontent grew strong. Navy Secretary Gideon Welles suggested a compromise—let the concerts be performed in Lafayette Park across the street from the White House—but she rejected it imperiously, using the royal *we*: "It is our especial desire that the Band, does not play in these grounds, this summer. We expect our wishes to be complied with."[71]

Mary Lincoln's sister Elizabeth Edwards came from Springfield to help calm the First Lady. Lincoln implored Mrs. Edwards to remain at the White House as long as she possibly could: "You have Such a power & control Such an influence over Mary—Come do Stay and Console me," he told her.[72] Elizabeth Edwards reported back to her family in Illinois that "my presence here, has tended very much to soothe, the excessive grief" of Mrs. Lincoln. In her agony, Mary Lincoln was unable to help care for her younger son, Tad, who also ran a dangerous fever. According to Elizabeth, Mary "has been but little with him, being utterly unable to control her feelings."[73]

When a woman friend visited the White House to offer condolences to the First Lady, she turned on her, asking accusingly: "Madam, why did you not call upon me before my ball? I sent you word I wished to know you."

"Because my country was in grief, as you now are, and I shunned all scenes of gayety."

"I thought so! Those who urged me to that heartless step (alluding to the party) now ridicule me for it, and not one of them has . . . come, to share my sorrow. *I have had evil counselors!*"[74]

When Elizabeth Edwards returned to Springfield, Mary Lincoln sought comfort from her friend, the black modiste Elizabeth Keckly, whose only son had died in battle the previous year. Because Mrs. Keckly had stoically accepted the death of her son, she was dismayed at the First Lady's excessive grieving. The dressmaker, however, strove as best she could to console her friend.[75] Mary Lincoln also visited spiritualists who claimed they could enable her to communicate with her dead son. At the White House, she held several séances, some of which her skeptical husband attended.

The death of Willie deprived Lincoln of an important source of comfort and relief from his heavy official burdens. His youngest son, the hyperactive, learning-disabled, effervescent Tad, was not a clone like Willie. Julia Taft recalled that he "had a quick, fiery temper," was "implacable in his dislikes," but could be "very affectionate when he chose."[76]

In the wake of Willie's death, the president's love for Tad grew stronger as he displaced onto him the powerful feeling he had harbored for the older boy. He explained to a friend that he wished to give Tad "everything he could no longer give Willie." The daughter of Lincoln's principal White House secretary wrote that after Willie died, Lincoln "was even more tender and indulgent toward [Tad] than before, if such a thing were possible. . . . The bond that had always been uncommonly close between them grew stronger after the older boy's death."[77] According to John Hay, after the death of Willie, Lincoln's "bereaved heart seemed . . . to pour its fulness on his youngest child." Hay described Tad as "a merry, warm-blooded, kindly little boy, perfectly flawless and full of odd fancies and inventions, the chartered libertine of the Executive Mansion." Tad "ran continually in and out of his father's cabinet, interrupting his gravest labors and conversations with his bright, rapid and very imperfect speech." The lad "would sit on his father's knee and sometimes even on his shoulder while the most weighty conferences were going on." Occasionally Tad "would take refuge in that sanctuary for the whole evening, dropping off to sleep at last on the floor, when the President would pick him up and carry him tenderly to bed."[78] Lincoln, Hay added, "took infinite comfort in the child's rude health, fresh fun, and uncontrollable boisterousness. He was pleased to see him growing up in ignorance of books, but with singularly accurate ideas of practical matters." Though the boy suffered from learning disabilities (he was unusually slow to learn to read) and a speech impediment that made him hard to understand, his indulgent father was unconcerned and often said: "Let him run; he has time enough left to learn his letters and get poky."[79]

Occasionally Lincoln tried to tame the lad but was forced to acknowledge that the effort was futile. One night when the White House staff found it impossible to get Tad to go to bed, Lincoln excused himself, explaining to his guests: "I must go and suppress Tad." On his return he said, "I don't know but I may succeed in governing the nation, but I do believe I shall fail in ruling my own household."[80]

A White House guard thought that Tad was "the best companion Mr. Lincoln ever had—one who always understood him, and whom he always understood."[81] Thus Tad became, to some degree, another Willie for his grief-stricken father. David Davis sympathized with Lincoln and feared that "if he should lose his other son, he would be overwhelmed with sorrow & grief."[82]

In 1866 Mrs. Lincoln told William H. Herndon that her husband took religion more seriously after Willie's death. She said her husband "was a religious man always, as I think: he first thought—to say think—about this subject was when Willie died."[83] She made a similar point about the death of their second son, three-year-old Eddie: her husband's "heart, was turned towards religion" following the lad's death in 1850, she wrote twenty years later.[84] Lincoln told a friend that if he "had twenty children he could never cease to sorrow for that one." The Rev. Dr. James Smith, pastor of the First Presbyterian Church in Springfield, conducted the lad's funeral and often visited the grief-stricken parents, offering what Lincoln called "loving and sympathetic ministrations."[85] Smith presented them a copy of his book, *The Christian's Defense*, which (Smith alleged) Lincoln found persuasive. Shortly after the funeral, the Lincolns rented a pew in Smith's church.[86] If the death of Willie deepened Lincoln's religious feeling, it may help account for two of the more remarkable documents that Lincoln ever wrote: the so-called Meditation on the Divine Will and his Second Inaugural Address. The former is a private memo, undated but probably composed in 1864:

> The will of God prevails. In great contests each party claims to act in accordance with the will of God. Both *may* be, and one *must* be wrong. God can not be *for*, and *against* the same thing at the same time. In the present civil war it is quite possible that God's purpose is something different from the purpose of either party—and yet the human instrumentalities, working just as they do, are of the best adaptation to effect His purpose. I am almost ready to say this is probably true—that God wills this contest, and wills that it shall not end yet. By his mere quiet power, on the minds of the now contestants,

> He could have either *saved* or *destroyed* the Union without a human contest. Yet the contest began. And having begun He could give the final victory to either side any day. Yet the contest proceeds.[87]

This document resembles a letter that Lincoln wrote in September 1864 to Mrs. Eliza P. Gurney, a Quaker, thanking her for her support: "It has been your purpose to strengthen my reliance on God. I am much indebted to the good christian people of the country for their constant prayers and consolations; and to no one of them, more than to yourself. The purposes of the Almighty are perfect, and must prevail, though we erring mortals may fail to accurately perceive them in advance. We hoped for a happy termination of this terrible war long before this; but God knows best, and has ruled otherwise. We shall yet acknowledge His wisdom and our own error therein. Meanwhile we must work earnestly in the best light He gives us, trusting that so working still conduces to the great ends He ordains. Surely He intends some great good to follow this mighty convulsion, which no mortal could make, and no mortal could stay."[88] Three years earlier, Lincoln amazed his friend Orville H. Browning, who was making his customary Sunday afternoon visit to the White House. When the president suggested that God might not favor the Union cause, Browning replied: "Mr. Lincoln, we can't hope for the blessing of God on the efforts of our armies, until we strike a decisive blow at the institution of slavery. This is the great curse of our land, and we must make an effort to remove it before we can hope to receive the help of the Almighty."

Lincoln, who had been reading the Bible that Sabbath, responded: "Browning, suppose God is against us in our view on the subject of slavery in this country, and our method of dealing with it." Browning was impressed by that remark, for as he later said, it "indicated to me for the first time that he was thinking deeply about the great events then transpiring."[89]

The private thoughts he shared with Browning and that he committed to paper in the "Meditation on the Divine Will" formed a prelude to the dramatic public airing of his views in the Second Inaugural Address. In that speech, widely regarded as his best, he speculated about God's reason for allowing the war to start and for permitting it to continue so long: "The Almighty has His own purposes. 'Woe unto the world because of offences! for it must needs be that offences come; but woe to that man by whom the offence cometh!' If we shall suppose that American Slavery is one of those offences which, in the providence of God, must needs come, but which, having continued through His appointed time, He now wills to remove, and that He gives to both North and South, this terrible war, as the woe due to those by whom the offence came, shall we discern therein any departure from those divine attributes which the believers in a Living God always ascribe to Him? Fondly do we hope---fervently do we pray---that this mighty scourge of war may speedily pass away. Yet, if God wills that it continue, until all the wealth piled by the bond-man's two hundred and fifty years of unrequited toil shall be sunk, and until every drop of blood drawn with the lash, shall be paid by another drawn with the sword, as was said three thousand years ago, so still it must be said 'the judgments of the Lord, are true and righteous altogether.' "[90]

NOTES

1. George P. Goff to Nicolay, Washington, February 9, 1889, John G. Nicolay Papers, Library of Congress.
2. M. C. Meigs, "The Relations of President Lincoln and Secretary Stanton to the Military Commanders in the Civil War," an article written in 1888, *American Historical Review* 26 (1921), 292.
3. Thurlow Weed to William M. Evarts, February 20, 1862, in Brainerd Dyer, *The Public Career of William M. Evarts* (Berkeley: University of California Press, 1933), 52.
4. W. M. Dickson to Friedrich Hassaurek, Cincinnati, September 27, 1861, Hassaurek Papers, Ohio Historical Society.
5. William Henry Herndon to Jesse W. Weik, Springfield, Illinois, February 18, 1887, Herndon-Weik Papers, Library of Congress.
6. William Henry Herndon, "Analysis of the Character of Abraham Lincoln," lecture delivered in Springfield, Illinois, December 26, 1865, *Abraham Lincoln Quarterly*, vol. 1 (December 1941), 417–418.
7. Mary Todd Lincoln, interview with William H. Herndon, [September 1866], in Douglas L. Wilson and Rodney O. Davis, eds., *Herndon's Informants: Letters, Interviews, and Statements about Abraham Lincoln* (Urbana: University of Illinois Press, 1998), 359.

8. Annie Lanphir Walters, daughter of the state printer, Captain William Walters of Springfield, Chicago *Examiner*, February 13, 1909.
9. David Davis, interview with William Henry Herndon, September 20, 1866, in Wilson and Davis, 49; William H. Herndon and Jesse W. Weik, *Herndon's Lincoln*, ed. Douglas L. Wilson and Rodney O. Davis (originally published in 1889 as *Herndon's Lincoln; The True Story of a Great Life: The History and Personal Recollections of Abraham Lincoln*; Urbana: University of Illinois Press, 2006), 194.
10. John G. Nicolay, "Conversation with Hon. O. H. Browning, Leland Hotel, Springfield, June 17, 1875," in Michael Burlingame, ed., *An Oral History of Abraham Lincoln: John G. Nicolay's Interviews and Essays* (Carbondale: Southern Illinois University Press, 1996), 3.
11. Robert Todd Lincoln to Josiah G. Holland, Springfield, June 6, 1865, in Rufus Rockwell Wilson, ed., *Intimate Memories of Lincoln* (Elmira: Primavera Press, 1945), 499.
12. Ida Tarbell, *All in the Day's Work: An Autobiography* (New York: Macmillan, 1939), 166.
13. William Henry Herndon to Jesse W. Weik, Springfield, Illinois, February 5, 1891, in Emanuel Hertz, ed., *The Hidden Lincoln: From the Letters and Papers of William H. Herndon* (New York: Viking, 1938), 291.
14. Randall, *Lincoln's Sons* (Boston: Little, Brown and Company, 1955), 26 and 177.
15. Joseph P. Kent, "Two Things Mr. Lincoln Would Not Loan," *Illinois State Journal* (Springfield), January 9, 1909, in Rufus Rockwell Wilson, ed., *Intimate Memories of Lincoln* (Elmira: Primavera Press, 1945), 136.
16. Ibid., 136–137.
17. N. P. Willis, "The President's Son," *The Home Journal*, n.d., reprinted *in Littell's Living Age*, Third Series, Vol. 17 (April-June 1862): 154.
18. Ruth Painter Randall, *Lincoln's Sons* (Boston: Little, Brown and Company, 1955), 51–52.
19. Elizabeth Todd Grimsley, "Six Months in the White House," *Journal of the Illinois State Historical Society*, vol. 19 (3 and 4), October 1926–January 1927 (joint issue), 53–54.
20. Owen Lovejoy to his children, Washington, February 23, 1862, Lovejoy Papers, William L. Clements Library, University of Michigan.
21. William Florville to Lincoln, Springfield, December 27, 1863, Lincoln Papers, Library of Congress.
22. Washington correspondence, February 21, Philadelphia *Inquirer*, February 22, 1862; Washington correspondence, February 24, New York *Herald*, February 26, 1862.
23. William O. Stoddard, "White House Sketches No. 2," New York *Citizen*, August 25, 1866, in Stoddard, *Inside the White House in War Times: Memoirs and Reports of Lincoln's Secretary*, ed. Michael Burlingame (Lincoln: University of Nebraska Press, 2000), 150.
24. Horatio Nelson Taft diary, Library of Congress (entries for January 13, February 20, 1862).
25. Julia Taft Bayne, *Tad Lincoln's Father* (Lincoln: University of Nebraska Press, 2001), 8.

26. Supreme Court Justice Noah Swayne told this to Seward's daughter Fanny. Diary of Fanny Seward, February 5, 1863, in Patricia Carley Johnson, ed., "Sensitivity and Civil War: The Selected Diaries and Papers, 1858–1868, of Frances Adeline Seward" (Ph.D. dissertation, University of Rochester, 1963), 647.
27. New York *World*, weekly edition, March 8, 1862.
28. Washington correspondence, February 21, Philadelphia *Inquirer*, February 22, 1862.
29. John Hay, "Life in the White House in the Time of Lincoln," 1890, in Michael Burlingame, ed., *At Lincoln's Side: John Hay's Civil War Correspondence and Selected Writings* (Carbondale: Southern Illinois University Press, 2000), 135.
30. Washington *Evening Star*, February 21, 1862.
31. William O. Stoddard, "White House Sketches No. 1," New York *Citizen*, August 18, 1861, in Stoddard, *Inside the White House in War Times: Memoirs and Reports of Lincoln's Secretary*, ed. Michael Burlingame (Lincoln: University of Nebraska Press, 2000), 145.
32. Edwin S. Stanton to Salmon P. Chase, Washington, February 16, 1862, Chase Papers, Historical Society of Pennsylvania; Washington correspondence, February 10 and 25, New York *Commercial Advertiser*, February 11 and 26, 1862; Washington correspondence, February 11, New York *World*, February 12, 1862.
33. Howard K. Beale, ed., *The Diary of Edward Bates, 1859-1866* (Washington: U.S. Government Printing Office, 1933), 233 (entry for February 18, 1862).
34. John G. Nicolay, journal entry for February 20, 1862, in Michael Burlingame, ed., *With Lincoln in the White House: Letters, Memoranda, and Other Writings of John G. Nicolay, 1860-1865* (Carbondale: Southern Illinois University Press, 2000), 71.
35. Anna L. Boyden, *War Reminiscences, or Echoes from Hospital and White House: A Record of Rebecca R. Pomroy's Experience in War-Times* (Boston: D. Lothrop, 1887), 56.
36. Washington correspondence, February 20, Philadelphia *Inquirer*, February 21, 1862.
37. Elihu Washburne to his wife, [Washington], February 21 [1862], Washburn Family Papers, Washburn Memorial Library, Norlands, Maine.
38. Washington correspondence by Van [D. W. Bartlett], 26 February, Springfield, Massachusetts, *Republican*, February 28, 1862.
39. This occurred on May 7, when the president was visiting Fort Monroe. LeGrande Cannon, *Personal Reminiscences of the Rebellion, 1861–1866* (New York: Burr Printing House, 1895), 173–174; LeGrande Cannon to Herndon, near Burlington, Vermont, October 7, [1889], Wilson and Davis, *Herndon's Informants*, 679; Francis B. Carpenter, *Six Months at the White House with Abraham Lincoln: The Story of a Picture* (New York: Hurd and Houghton, 1866), 39. The quoted passage appears in *King John*, act 3, scene 4, lines 79–81.
40. Elizabeth Keckley, *Behind the Scenes; or, Thirty Years a Slave, and Four Years in the White House* (New York: G. W. Carleton & Co., Publishers, 1868), 103.
41. Mrs. Henry A. Wise (nee Charlotte Everett) to her father, Edward Everett, Washington, March 2, 1862, Everett Papers, Massachusetts Historical Society.
42. Washington correspondence by Van [D. W. Bartlett], 26 February, Springfield (Massachusetts) *Republican*, February 28, 1862; Washington correspondence, February 27, New York *Evening Post*, February 28, 1862.

43. "Washington as it appeared in March, 1862," Brooklyn *Daily Eagle*, January 23, 1887.
44. Stoddard, *Inside the White House in War Times*, ed. Burlingame, 67.
45. Francis B. Fox to Ida Tarbell, New York, November 13, 1939, Tarbell Papers, Allegheny College.
46. Rebecca R. Pomroy, "What His Nurse Knew," *Magazine of History*, 32 (No. 1, extra number 150, 1932), 47.
47. Lincoln to Stanton, Washington, July 15, 1862, Roy P. Basler, ed.; Marion Delores Pratt and Lloyd A. Dunlap, assistant editors, *The Collected Works of Abraham Lincoln* (8 vols. plus index: New Brunswick, NJ: Rutgers University Press, 1953–55), 5:326.
48. Washington correspondence, 24 March, New York *Examiner*, 27 March 1862, in Michael Burlingame, ed., *Dispatches from Lincoln's White House: The Anonymous Civil War Journalism of Presidential Secretary William O. Stoddard* (Lincoln: University of Nebraska Press, 2002), 66.
49. David Davis to Laura Swett, Washington, December 21, 1862, David Davis Papers, Lincoln Presidential Library, Springfield. See also Leonard Swett to W. W. Orme, Bloomington, December 9, 1862, Orme Papers, Lincoln Presidential Library, Springfield.
50. Laura R. Swett to David Davis, Bloomington, December 13, 1862, David Davis Papers, Lincoln Presidential Library, Springfield.
51. Lincoln to Fanny McCullough, Washington, December 23, 1862, in Basler, *Collected Works*, 6:16–17.
52. Francis B. Carpenter, *Six Months at the White House with Abraham Lincoln: The Story of a Picture* (New York: Hurd and Houghton, 1866), 293.
53. Mary Lincoln to Julia Ann Sprigg, Washington, May 29, 1862, in Justin G. Turner and Linda Levitt Turner, eds., *Mary Todd Lincoln: Her Life and Letters* (New York: Alfred A. Knopf, 1972), 127.
54. Elihu Washburne to his wife, [Washington,] Tuesday [May 20, 1862], Washburn Family Papers, Washburn Memorial Library, Norlands, Maine. She said this on May 16.
55. Keckley, *Behind the Scenes*, 104–105.
56. Mary Lincoln's symptoms fit the description of manic-depressive illness as given in Kay Redfield Jamison, *Touched with Fire: Manic-Depressive Illness and the Artistic Temperament* (New York: Free Press, 1993). On her narcissism, see James A. Brussel, "Mary Todd Lincoln: A Psychiatric Study," *Psychiatric Quarterly*, vol. 15, supplement 1 (January 1941), 7–26, and Jean H. Baker, *Mary Todd Lincoln: A Biography* (New York: Norton, 1987), 330–32. Studies of her mental state have suffered from incomplete awareness of her symptoms and behavior. See John M. Suarez, "Mary Todd Lincoln: A Case Study," *American Journal of Psychiatry*, vol. 122 (1966), 816–19; Jennifer Bach, "Was Mary Todd Lincoln Bipolar?" *Journal of Illinois History*, vol. 8 (2005): 281–94; W. A. Evans, *Mrs. Abraham Lincoln: A Study of Her Personality and Her Influence on Lincoln* (New York: A. A. Knopf, 1932), passim.
57. John G. Nicolay, "Conversation with Hon. O. H. Browning, Leland Hotel, Springfield, 17 June 1875," in Burlingame, ed., *An Oral History of Abraham Lincoln*, 1.

58. Margaret Stuart in Katherine Helm, *The True Story of Mary, Wife of Lincoln* (New York: Harper, 1928), 32.
59. Baker, 330.
60. On May 19, 1875, she was adjudged insane. The following day she was taken to the Bellevue Place sanitarium in Batavia, Illinois, which advertised itself as a "Hospital for the Insane of the Private Class." She was released the following September. See Mark E. Neely Jr. and R. Gerald McMurtry, *The Insanity File: The Case of Mary Todd Lincoln* (Carbondale: Southern Illinois University Press, 1986), and Jason Emerson, *The Madness of Mary Lincoln* (Carbondale: Southern Illinois University Press, 2007).
61. Davis told this to Orville Hickman Browning in 1873. Browning diary, 3 July 1873, in Burlingame, ed., *At Lincoln's Side*, 187.
62. David Davis to Adeline E. Burr, Washington, July 19, 1882, Adeline Ellery Burr Davis Green Papers, Duke University.
63. Lulu Robinson, "Childhood and Girlhood Recollections about Lincoln," enclosed in Lulu Robinson to a Miss Warner, Bloomington, Indiana, October 17, 1950, Lincoln Collection, Indiana University.
64. Michael Burlingame, *The Inner World of Abraham Lincoln* (Urbana: University of Illinois Press, 1994), 312.
65. Willard King, *Lincoln's Manager, David Davis* (Cambridge: Harvard University Press, 1960), 235–36.
66. Records of the company as summarized in Gayle T. Harris, "Mary Lincoln's Shopping Spree," *The Lincolnian* 13 (1995): 3.
67. Columbus *Crisis*, July 20, 1864.
68. A. K. McClure to Alonzo Rothschild, Philadelphia, May 9, 1907, Lincoln Contemporaries Collection, Lincoln Financial Foundation Research Collection, Allen County Public Library, Fort Wayne, Indiana.
69. Washington *Sunday Gazette*, January 16, 1887.
70. Stephen Berry, *House of Abraham: Lincoln and the Todds, A Family Divided by War* (Boston: Houghton Mifflin, 2007), passim.
71. Mary Lincoln to John Hay, Washington, May 22, 1862, Hay Papers, Library of Congress.
72. Elizabeth Todd Edwards, interviewed by Herndon, [1865–66], Wilson and Davis, *Herndon's Informants*, 444–45.
73. Elizabeth Edwards to her daughter, Washington, March 2 and 12, 1862, Ruth Painter Randall, *Mary Todd Lincoln: Biography of a Marriage* (Boston: Little, Brown, 1953), 287.
74. Randall, *Mary Todd Lincoln*, 289.
75. Jennifer Fleischner, *Mrs. Lincoln and Mrs. Keckly: The Remarkable Story of the Friendship between a First Lady and a Former Slave* (New York: Broadway Books, 2003), 231; Keckley, *Behind the Scenes*, 105–6.
76. Bayne, *Tad Lincoln's Father*, 3.

77. Helen Nicolay, *Lincoln's Secretary: A Biography of John G. Nicolay* (New York: Longmans, Green, 1949), 133.
78. John Hay, "Life in the White House in the Time of Lincoln," 1890, in Burlingame, ed., *At Lincoln's Side*, 135–136.
79. John Hay, "Tad Lincoln," New York *Tribune*, 19 July 1871, in Michael Burlingame, ed., *At Lincoln's Side*, 112.
80. "Death of Tad Lincoln," unidentified clipping, John Hay scrapbook, Hay Papers, Brown University.
81. Margarita Spalding Gerry, ed., *Through Five Administrations: Reminiscences of William H. Crook, Body-Guard to President Lincoln* (New York: Harper and Brothers, 1910), 23.
82. Davis to his wife Sarah, St. Louis, 23 February 1862, Davis Papers, Lincoln Presidential Library, Springfield.
83. Mary Todd Lincoln, interviewed by Herndon, [September 1866], Wilson and Davis, eds., *Herndon's Informants*, 360.
84. Mary Todd Lincoln to James Smith, Marienbad, 8 June 1870, Justin G. Turner and Linda Levitt Turner, eds., *Mary Todd Lincoln: Her Life and Letters* (New York: Alfred A. Knopf, 1972), 567–68.
85. Lucy Harmon McPherson, *Life and Letters of Oscar Fitzalan Harmon* (Trenton, N.J: MacCrellish & Quigley, 1914), 11.
86. James Smith to William Henry Herndon, Dundee, Scotland, 24 January 1867, in Douglas and Davis, eds., *Herndon's Informants* 549; Wayne C. Temple, *Abraham Lincoln: From Skeptic to Prophet* (Mahoment, IL: Mayhaven, 1995), 37–44.
87. Basler, *The Collected Works of Abraham Lincoln*, 5:403–404. The editors date this September 1862, but it was probably written in 1864. Douglas L. Wilson, *Lincoln's Sword: The Presidency and the Power of Words* (New York: Alfred A. Knopf, 2006), 255–56, 329–30.
88. Lincoln to Eliza P. Gurney, Washington, 4 September 1864, Basler, *The Collected Works of Abraham Lincoln*, 7:535.
89. Nicolay, "Conversation with Hon. O. H. Browning, Leland Hotel, Springfield, 17 June 1875," in Burlingame, ed., *An Oral History of Abraham Lincoln*, 4.
90. Basler, *The Collected Works of Abraham Lincoln*, 8:333.

A much-doctored photograph of Woodrow and Edith Wilson during the president's convalescence, first published in Edith's *My Memoir* in 1938. [Courtesy Princeton University Library.]

5

"One Long Wilderness of Despair"

Woodrow Wilson's Stroke and the League of Nations

THOMAS J. KNOCK

Woodrow Wilson is neither fondly remembered nor well understood by most Americans. Even so, he occupies a secure position within the exclusive pantheon of great presidents. The domestic legislation that he signed into law and the new directions he charted in foreign policy during World War I shaped the politics and diplomacy of the United States throughout the twentieth century and beyond. Among all presidents, only Franklin Roosevelt and Lyndon Johnson have matched Wilson's record in enacting a significant legislative program. Like FDR's and LBJ's, much of Wilson's program, known as the "New Freedom," is still with us today. It included the creation of the Federal Reserve System and the Federal Trade Commission, tariff reform, and the first federal laws to establish the eight-hour day (for railroad workers) and to restrict child labor. In appraising Johnson's Great Society in 1965 the commentator Tom Wicker suggested that the early New Deal was not a sufficient measure; rather, he observed that one had "to go all the way back to Woodrow Wilson's first year to find a congressional session of equal importance." As for the realm in which he carved out his most monumental legacy, no chief executive has ever communicated more effectively to the peoples of the world the ideals of democracy or, through the Covenant of the League of Nations, set in motion a more original idea for reducing the risk of war than the twenty-eighth president. According to Senator J. William Fulbright, this was "the one great new idea of the 20th century in the field of international relations, the idea of international organization with permanent processes for the peaceful settlement of disputes."[1]

Yet few presidents, after accomplishing so much, experienced a reversal of fortunes as tragic as the one that happened to Wilson in his second term. The stroke that he suffered in October 1919 engendered a political crisis without precedent—the first, and arguably the worst, instance of presidential disability in US history. This was not only an illness literally of constitutional magnitude; it also occurred at a crucial moment in world history when the Great War had come to an end and ratification of the Treaty of Versailles and American membership in the League of Nations hung in the balance.

The postwar peacekeeping organization that Wilson had designed at the Paris Peace Conference was no slender proposal. The Covenant of the League included provisions for settling disputes between nations through arbitration, for the reduction of armaments among the great powers, and for the imposition of collective economic and military sanctions against any nation that attacked another. Because League membership held serious implications for national sovereignty and unilateral action, however, many Senators (chiefly Republicans, though not exclusively) would agree to the treaty only if it included certain reservations that limited American obligations to the international organization. The president demurred. He believed that these reservations would "change the entire meaning of the Treaty," that if the United States joined only on conditions of its own choosing then the league would be undermined from the start.[2]

Faced with the prospect of the Senate's rejection, Wilson came to a fateful decision. Against the advice of his personal physician, Cary M. Grayson, and the protests of his wife, Edith, he embarked upon a strenuous speaking tour in order to shore up popular support for the treaty. For three weeks in September 1919, he traveled ten thousand miles by train throughout the

Middle and Far West, making some forty speeches to hundreds of thousands of people. From the standpoint of public education on the League, Wilson performed well, often brilliantly, in arguing why the United States could not exempt itself "from all responsibility for the preservation of the peace." On occasion the emotional appeal eclipsed the intellectual. If the League were crippled by reservations, he said in St. Louis, he would feel obliged to stand "in mortification and shame" before the boys who went across the seas to fight the war to end all wars and say to them, "You are betrayed. You fought for something that you did not get." And there would come, "sometime in the vengeful Providence of God, another struggle in which, not a few hundred thousand fine men from America will have to die, but as many millions as are necessary to accomplish for the final freedom of the peoples of the world."[3] (Americans would recall this and similar prophetic remarks by Wilson as World War II drew to a close.)

But as the throngs grew larger and the cheers louder, Wilson looked more haggard and worn out at the end of each day. In city after city, he endured endless parades, shook hands with hundreds of well wishers, and spoke to gigantic crowds without the aid of an electronic public address system. Coughing spells plagued him at night. Excruciating headaches recurred. At Cheyenne, Wyoming, a reporter noticed "a look of inexpressible weariness" pass over his face. At Pueblo, Colorado, he stumbled and needed assistance in mounting the speaker's platform. The following morning, he awakened nauseated, his cheek muscles twitching uncontrollably. "I have never been in a condition like this, and I just feel as if I am going to pieces," he said to Joe Tumulty, his personal secretary. At last, Dr. Grayson, sustained by Mrs. Wilson and Tumulty, called a halt to the tour and rushed him back to Washington. On October 2, four days after his return, the president suffered a stroke that paralyzed his whole left side. From that point onward he would be but a frail husk of his former self, a tragic recluse in the White House shielded by his wife and doctor.[4]

Not until the opening of Dr. Grayson's papers in 1987 and 1990 did we have reliable details (much less a complete picture) on Wilson's medical condition during his presidency. It is now reasonably well established that the president suffered from progressive hypertension and arteriosclerosis since middle age—a worrying condition, but one that was not so severe as to prevent him from working effectively most of the time, at least until the late summer of 1919. During the previous six months at the peace conference he had kept up a killing pace, often working twelve and fourteen hours a day. The president's labors at Paris had rendered him medically much older than his sixty-two years when he set out on his speaking tour and the strain probably accelerated the onset of stroke.[5] According to Dr. Francis Dercum, the distinguished Philadelphia neurologist that Dr. Grayson called in to examine Wilson, the stroke, affecting the right side of the brain, was ischemic in nature—that is, one brought on by clotting and that develops gradually, is rarely fatal, and does not affect speech or intellectual function. This sort of stroke nonetheless causes physical impairment and often has an impact on the patient's judgment and ability to concentrate. (Wilson was never at risk of death by stroke; but a few days later, he developed a life-threatening prostate infection and a urinary blockage. Though it receded within a week, the blockage gravely complicated his condition.)[6]

For an entire month after the stroke the president of the United States was utterly incapable of performing the duties of office. Not until mid-November did he see anyone other than family members and his doctors. (Even the loyal Tumulty was kept at bay for a while.) Not until December could he work at all and then only for a few minutes a day. Dr. Grayson, in accordance with Mrs. Wilson's wishes, made no mention of paralysis or stroke to the press. Instead he issued only vague reports that the president was suffering from extreme fatigue and "nervous exhaustion" and that his mind was clear.[7] Despite Wilson's obvious paralysis, Dr. Dercum acceded to the misleading diagnosis that was released for public consumption. On his behalf, however, it should be said that Grayson had planned to make a full disclosure about the extent of the president's incapacity, but Mrs. Wilson overruled him. Inexorably, then, Wilson would become the subject of conjecture and wild rumor in the weeks and months ahead, although it eventually became common knowledge that he was the victim of "cerebral thrombosis." The First Lady also firmly vetoed Grayson's recommendation that her husband resign from office even when, during two brief interludes, Wilson himself thought he ought to step down. (In an undated memo, Grayson made the notation: "President Wilson's intention to go to the Senate in a wheel chair for the purpose of resigning.")[8]

Since their wedding in December 1915 (seventeen months after Wilson's beloved first wife had died), Edith had been her husband's most important confidant, passionately dedicated to what she considered his best interests.* In explaining herself in her best-selling memoir in 1938, she claimed that Dr. Dercum advised her of the importance of the president *not* resigning. "If he resigns," Dercum allegedly said, "the greatest incentive to recovery is gone." What the president needed was rest and release from every disturbing problem; in the meantime, she should act as his steward. The neurologist supposedly further advised that, while consulting with members of the cabinet, she should have everything of an official nature come to her and "weigh the importance of each matter" as to whether it should be put before the president or could be left to others. In this, she would be doing him and the nation a great service.[9]

The account was fanciful; the conversation almost certainly never took place. But for sixteen months she served as a sort of self-appointed White House chief of staff, the arbiter of what and whom the president should, or should not, see. Contrary to popular invention, however, Edith Wilson was not the first woman president, and she did not run the executive branch of the government. For all practical purposes, the departmental heads managed their own agencies to the end of Wilson's term. Things ran fairly smoothly in the president's absence largely due to the considerable autonomy he had usually allowed his cabinet members. The State Department was the single exception (albeit a major one). More so than most presidents before him, Wilson had always conducted his own foreign

* Wilson had been married to Ellen Axson Wilson for twenty-nine years. An accomplished artist who had studied at the Art Students League of New York, the mother of three daughters, and the creator of the White House Rose Garden, Ellen had always been Wilson's closest political adviser. When Bright's disease struck her down in August 1914 (the week war broke out in Europe), he was devastated. In March 1915, he met Edith Bolling Galt, a widow fifteen years his junior. The president was immediately smitten. They were married nine months later. Like Ellen, Edith became his singularly devoted mate.

policy. As the journalist Ray Stannard Baker recorded in February 1920, after a visit with the frustrated, chain-smoking secretary of state, Robert Lansing, "The real foreign secretary lies ill in the White House."[10]

That the president should have resigned there can be no doubt. Until the Twenty-fifth Amendment went into in effect in 1967, however, the Constitution contained but a single convoluted sentence referring to disability or removal from office.* In 1919 there was no precedent for invoking it. Four successions had occurred up until that time, but they took place upon the death of a president. No one knew what to do, and no one wanted to take action. Vice President Thomas R. Marshall had never desired to hold the office—indeed, the possibility frightened him—and he declined to take part in any initiative that might lead to his succeeding Wilson unless Congress or the White House formally addressed the issue. Within the administration, only Secretary Lansing had the temerity to do that—at a cabinet meeting four days after Wilson was stricken. Dr. Grayson was there and he assured the cabinet "that the President's mind was not only clear but very active . . . and that he wanted to know by whose authority the meeting had been called."[11]

Public apprehensions about his condition actually subsided in December, after two senators on the Foreign Relations Committee—the Democrat Gilbert Hitchcock of Nebraska (who had met with Wilson twice in November to discuss the League of Nations) and Albert Fall, a Republican from New Mexico—were granted a carefully orchestrated bedside interview for forty minutes. Their host was in cheerful good form and, he said, "feeling fit." Senator Fall, an irreconcilable foe of the League, told reporters, "He seemed to me to be in excellent trim, both mentally and physically, for a man who has been in bed for ten weeks." Indeed, Wilson was recovering somewhat—enough so into 1920 to take rides in his touring

* Article II, Section 1 reads as follows: "In case of removal of the President from office, or of his death, resignation, or inability to discharge the powers and duties of the said office, the same shall devolve on the Vice President, and the Congress may by law provide for the case of removal, death, resignation or inability, both of the President and the Vice President, declaring what officer shall then act as President, and such officer shall act accordingly, until the disability be removed, or a President shall be elected."

car, to converse, to write or dictate letters, and otherwise intermittently to assert himself. (He fired Lansing for insubordination in February and held a few cabinet meetings in April and May.) Yet he would continue to fade in and out and truly ceased to function any longer as president. The palace guard—chiefly Mrs. Wilson, Dr. Grayson, and Tumulty—in essence "practiced a deception upon the American people," Ike Hoover, chief usher at the White House, wrote in a draft of his memoirs. "Never was a conspiracy so pointedly or artistically formed."[12]

Between November 1919 and March 1920, the Senate voted on the Treaty of Versailles three times. But efforts at compromise never got very far. Whether on a motion to approve the treaty unconditionally or with fourteen reservations attached to it (to match Wilson's Fourteen Points), the tally always fell short of the required two-thirds majority. As the next electoral cycle approached, the fortunes of the Democratic Party plummeted. In November 1920, Warren G. Harding, the Republican presidential candidate, ran on an anti-League platform and won a resounding victory over the pro-League Democrat, James M. Cox. Republicans were happy to interpret the returns as the "great and solemn referendum" that Wilson had said he wanted for his Covenant. "So far as the United States is concerned," Senator Henry Cabot Lodge, his arch nemesis, affirmed, "that League is dead." The following month Wilson was awarded the Nobel Peace Prize for his part in founding the League of Nations.[13]

* * *

Not without good reason, much of the literature on the ratification fight has focused on a persistent controversy—that is, on the degree to which Wilson's stroke determined the outcome. Whereas the debate during the interwar years often stressed cultural and some psychological factors, in more recent decades historians who have surveyed the ruins locate the primary responsibility for the debacle in the White House sickroom.[14] They argue that a healthy Wilson would have grasped the situation and found some middle ground on the question of reservations. Yet other historians have contended that his refusal to compromise was consistent with his behavior throughout his life—that his psychological makeup would never have permitted him to yield to the Republicans or to Henry Cabot Lodge, who chaired the Foreign Relations Committee.

In 1956, in their pioneering *Woodrow Wilson and Colonel House: A Personality Study*, Alexander and Juliette George suggested that the president's apparent inflexibility on the League was a function of feelings of inadequacy ingrained in him in his youth by an overly demanding father, the Reverend Joseph Ruggles Wilson. They hypothesize, for example, that the boy's delay in learning to read until the age of ten was a manifestation of unconscious resentment toward his father. Furthermore, Wilson found compensation through "his quest for political power," and it was "his manner of exercising it"—his urge to dominate—that had sometimes brought on failure. To illustrate their case, the Georges cite the battles that Wilson lost when he was president of Princeton (such as the bitter disputes over the university's eating clubs and the location of the Graduate College). While not utterly dismissing the impact of the stroke, they maintain that Wilson "did not *want* to reach a compromise agreement with the Senate. He wanted to defeat the Senate, and especially Lodge."[15]

Serious analysis of the stroke and Wilson's health in general was catapulted to the forefront of the historiography in 1981 when Dr. Edwin Weinstein published *Woodrow Wilson: A Medical and Psychological Biography*. Weinstein, a distinguished neurologist, asserted that, in addition to the catastrophic stroke of 1919, Wilson had experienced a series of smaller, undetected strokes starting in his forties, in 1896, 1900, and possibly 1907, and a major one in 1906. According to Weinstein, these afflictions not only coincided with but also accounted for Wilson's adverse behavior in his earlier clashes at Princeton: the ones that the Georges had subjected to Freudian interpretation. He took exception as well to the Georges' psychoanalysis of the boyhood reading difficulty and argued that Wilson likely had developmental dyslexia. He also diagnosed as a minor stroke or virus encephalopathy the flu-like illness and fever that had put the President in bed for several days in April 1919 in Paris. Weinstein believed that this explained his lamentable decisions, during that critical month of the peace conference, to accede to reparations and the infamous war guilt clause that the Allies imposed on Germany. Illness supposedly also set off Wilson's suspicions that his French maids and butlers were reporting his conversations back to their government and his crackdown on his staff against using the limousines for their personal recreation. Finally, it was Weinstein's view "that the cerebral dysfunction which resulted from Wilson's devastating strokes prevented the ratification of the Treaty. It is almost certain that had Wilson not been so afflicted, his political skills and his facility with language would have bridged the gap between the Hitchcock and Lodge resolutions."[16]

Many of Weinstein's findings did not stand up to scrutiny. In some instances, the president's seemingly odd behavior could be explained without recourse to physiological circumstances or strokes. Of far greater importance, however, Weinstein had very little hard evidence to support his diagnosis of dyslexia and the presumption of a series of strokes. Yet he offered his conclusions, not hypothetically, as one skeptic noted, but "as unequivocal fact." Indeed, medical records for Wilson prior to the presidency are virtually nonexistent, and those from October 1919 onward are scant, in part because he was never hospitalized.[17]

It was perhaps inevitable that Arthur S. Link, the author of a five-volume biography of Wilson and editor of the sixty-nine-volume project, *The Papers of Woodrow Wilson*, would find a trained neurologist's interpretation of the treaty fight compelling. Before Weinstein published his book, the two of them had collaborated on an article that called into question the Georges' findings as well as their research and methodology. Once Link began to incorporate Weinstein's suppositions into the annotations and appendices of *The Papers of Woodrow Wilson*, however, the Georges took them both severely to task. Among other refutations, they noted that in April 1919 Wilson had restricted the use of automobiles to official business (and only temporarily) because one day when he was sick he was annoyed to discover that every member of his staff had gone out joyriding. Moreover, Dr. Grayson, Mrs. Wilson, and several members of the American peace commission (including Colonel House) recorded their own wariness about the eavesdropping of French attendants, and some of them complained that their phones had been tapped. As for why Wilson was slow in learning to read, neither Weinstein nor the Georges ever acknowledged that this was ultimately unknowable. (John Milton Cooper Jr., who had accepted Weinstein's diagnosis years earlier, raised questions about it in his exemplary biography, *Woodrow Wilson*, in 2009. Once Wilson learned to read, Cooper observes, "he never made the grammar and spelling mistakes that often plague dyslexics," and he mastered three foreign languages.)[18]

On the heels of the Georges, several eminent neurologists and ophthalmologists at leading universities also cast grave doubt on major parts of Weinstein's work. In articles in historical, medical, and political science journals, these critics all found value in some of his insights, but they pointed out that Weinstein had either omitted or overlooked factors that contradicted his hypotheses, or that he had made much too much out of inconclusive evidence. "It is inconceivable that Wilson suffered from a major stroke in 1906," declared Dr. Jerrold Post, a major expert in the field of political psychology and psychiatry, while Dr. Michael Marmor, in *The New England Journal of Medicine*, invoked the old medical school adage about the perils of seizing upon the least likely of possible diagnoses, "When you hear hoof beats, don't think of zebras."[19]

It was a point well taken. In the wake of these disputations, Arthur Link brought onboard his Editorial Advisory Committee Dr. Bert E. Park, a well-regarded neurologist and author of *The Impact of Illness on World Leaders* (1986). Based on a fresh review of all the then extant materials, Park wrote five substantive appendices between 1988 and 1991 for the volumes of *The Papers of Woodrow Wilson* covering 1919 and 1920. In the first essay, he praised Weinstein for directing attention to the impact of "neurologic illness on the President's capacity to lead." But he also determined that "some revisions are required in Weinstein's synthesis." Park, like Marmor and Post, saw no grounds for the claim that a stroke had occurred in 1906. Indeed, high blood pressure was no doubt the cause of the ocular hemorrhage (as Wilson's own doctors had told him) "and not a stroke from the carotid artery of the neck." He believes that the proposition that the president had had a stroke or encephalitis at Paris "is untenable" as well. And although Wilson "most likely suffered significant ischemic injury over the years," he doubts, too, the supposition that his condition "impacted negatively on what was agreed to at Paris." Nonetheless, the president was "seriously ill" when he set out on his speaking tour, and it made his condition worse. The October 1919 stroke was probably "a hypertension-related occlusion or bursting of a small perforating vessel within the right side of the brain," Park posits. It is his opinion that "illness was *one* of the prime causes of the defeat of the Treaty of Versailles."[20]

The historiography on Wilson's illness and his personality has been fraught with contention for many years. Yet, whereas they are of obvious relevance to the subject of the treaty's defeat, it may be that neither the state of his health or the nature of his personality presents an entirely correct or complete explanation. The focus of the foregoing debate, as important as it is, tends to sidetrack and rob the larger issue of its significance. It provides few, if any, insights into the evolution of the idea of the league, the intensity of the struggle over it, or its domestic political origins, which had predated the stroke by at least three years. Nor does illness shed light on the ideological gulf that had always separated the contending sides. There was, not incidentally, a pretty stubborn refusal to compromise in both camps. The crisis of the stroke may have been the key factor in the failure to ratify; but it does not automatically follow that the absence of the stroke would have produced a better outcome. Let us, then, explore in brief compass some of the hard issues that meant so much to both Wilson and his adversaries and, of course, to the future of the United States in world politics.

Wilson had first begun to champion the league idea during his reelection campaign in 1916, a bitterly fought match that the Republicans had expected to win. In 1912, the Democrats, then the country's minority party, had come to power only because the GOP was split wide open between the incumbent, William Howard Taft, and his predecessor, Theodore Roosevelt, while the Socialist Party candidate, Eugene Debs, pulled 6 percent of the vote. By 1916 common enmity for Wilson had enabled Roosevelt to reconcile with his party's conservative leadership as the Republicans united behind Charles Evans Hughes. Even so, Wilson narrowly won because he was able to swell the normal Democratic vote on Election Day by attracting to his side independent progressives who had voted for Roosevelt and socialists who had rallied to Debs in 1912. This remarkable left-of-center coalition was built on two main pillars. First, in 1916, Wilson pushed through Congress a raft of social justice legislation (the eight-hour day, curbs on child labor, workmen's compensation) along with a progressive income tax that placed almost the entire revenue burden on corporations and the wealthy. Second, regarding foreign policy and the terrible conflict in Europe, the party ran on the slogan, "He Kept Us Out of War" and he advocated American membership in a postwar league to keep the peace. One progressive editorialist interpreted the meaning of his victory this way: "The president we just reelected has raised a flag that no other president has thought or perhaps dared to raise. It is the flag of internationalism." Yet, leading Republicans had castigated Wilson for his progressive legislation, and Roosevelt and Lodge had thwarted former president Taft's efforts to secure a vague endorsement of the Lidea in the party's platform. Thus the issue already had begun to take on a partisan complexion.[21]

The Great War had raged in Europe and elsewhere since 1914. Long before the United States entered the conflict in April 1917, Wilson had sketched out a rudimentary plan for an international peacekeeping organization. Its most far-reaching provision was for so-called collective security, or the mutual guarantee of political independence and territorial integrity as against aggression, as manifested in Article 10 of the Covenant of the League of Nations. Yet, at every turn, Wilson put the heavier stress on the crucial machinery for avoiding war before it started—for facilitating disarmament and settling international disputes peacefully through the process of arbitration. Wilson did not think that military sanctions would come into play often in the postwar period—in part because of the deterrent value of the threat of such sanctions, but especially because disarmament and the "cooling off" features entailed in arbitration would defuse most problems before they could explode into war. Wilson once said the League "must grow and not be made," that it would evolve by stages, on a case-by-case basis. He admitted that it probably would not prevent conflict in every instance. But it could provide a shelter after the storm, a measure of tranquility for a few years to explore the potential for rationality and enlightened self-interest in the conduct of international relations. In January 1918, when the changing circumstances of the war and the Russian Revolution compelled him to iterate a set of progressive war aims—that is, his celebrated Fourteen Points address—he made the league its capstone. This manifesto would become the ideological cement that held the Allied coalition together at a critical juncture in the war; among most of the war-weary people of Europe it would acquire the status of sacred text.[22]

In all of this, the concept of the League was in a constant state of metamorphosis, and Wilson was by no means the sole author. He had drawn most of his ideas from a new internationalist movement that had come into being in the United States in 1915–1916. Thousands of progressives and conservatives alike composed this broad-gauged movement in the conviction that something had to be done to avoid future catastrophes like the current one—but they held divergent views on just what the League ought, or ought not, to do. As Senator Hitchcock said near the beginning of the parliamentary debate in 1919, "Internationalism has come, and we must choose what form the internationalism is to take." No one ever put the matter more astutely. That is how most people at the time understood it—as a struggle between Wilson's and a more conservative form of internationalism. (To appreciate it fully, one also must reckon with the fact that the contention between progressive and conservative internationalists was heightened by their conflicting, respective visions for the future of American society as well.)[23]

Wilson's supreme ambition seemed on the threshold of accomplishment when, on October 6, 1918, the German government appealed to the president to take steps leading to negotiations with the Allies on the basis of the Fourteen Points. The Armistice was signed on November 11. Yet the domestic political circumstances in which the war ended—specifically, the coincidence of the midterm congressional elections—greatly complicated his task. Indeed, the rancor and ugliness of the 1918 campaign to control the Congress exceeded by far that of 1916's contest to control the White House. To begin, the unprecedented centralization of the nation's wartime economy, alongside the core of Wilson's foreign policy, placed him far enough to the left to make all Democrats vulnerable to charges that they somehow were "unAmerican." In a typical exposition of its fiercely partisan, ultra-conservative platform, Chairman Will Hays of the Republican Party decried the "bolshevik principles" and "socialistic tendencies of the present government." Senator Lodge, too, railed against Wilson and "the socialists and Bolsheviks among his advisers" and worried that he would pursue "peace at any price." As the armistice negotiations proceeded the ever-apoplectic Theodore Roosevelt declared "against the adoption in their entirety" of the Fourteen Points, which, he said, were admired only by the "professional pacifist and the professional internationalist" who were "equally undesirable citizens." Taft, a leading conservative internationalist, asked in his weekly column, "Do we need during the life of the next Congress an absolute dictator?"[24]

Subjected to tremendous pressure from fellow Democrats to respond to these attacks, Wilson, most historians say, committed the worst blunder of his presidency. He issued (albeit reluctantly) an appeal to the American people to sustain the Democratic congressional majorities. Even though, unlike his opponents, he impugned no one's patriotism, the Republicans cried foul against the partisan interposition. Six days before the signing of the Armistice, they captured both houses—the Senate by a majority of two—and claimed that the president had been repudiated. Interestingly, many senatorial races were extremely close; the addition of ten thousand Democratic votes appropriately allocated among five states would have given the Democrats a Senate majority of three. Nonetheless, for the first time Wilson faced a Republican Congress—the first tangible sign of the depletion of the political environment essential both to ratification and American leadership in a *Wilsonian* league. This, then, was the intensely ideological and partisan atmosphere in which the great struggle was about to unfold. The situation is an important consideration not only in its own right, but also because it is where, chronologically, speculative questions in the writings about the president's health and behavior begin to intrude—regarding his appeal to the electorate and, right after the election, his decision not to appoint any Republicans to the peace commission. Yet, however Wilson may have erred, the explanation seems not to lie in the state of his health. His adversaries already had declared war on his peace program in toto; what is more, they would persist in their efforts, almost bordering on treason, to discredit him (particularly in the eyes of his European counterparts), further eliminating any realistic basis for cooperation.[25]

The forces of political reaction suffused the League controversy in other ways. One of the chief reasons why the Democrats had lost their majorities was because Wilson had sorely failed to nurture the left-of-center coalition that had elected him to a second term. He had begun to lose important elements in his base of support as the tidal wave of anti-Germanism and "One Hundred Percent Americanism" swept across the country in 1917–18. Caught up in the jingoistic spirit of war (which the Wilson administration had abetted) citizens committed acts of political repression practically everywhere against pacifists and radicals, not just German Americans. Eugene Debs, to cite but one of countless examples, was sentenced to ten years in prison for making a speech against the war. Grievously, Wilson acquiesced in the suppression of such civil liberties and of the radical press. As a consequence, tens of thousands of progressive internationalists, who had put him over the mark in 1916, stayed home in 1918. Thus Wilson contributed to the gradual unraveling of the coalition that he very badly needed to sustain him.[26]

In contrast to his troubles at home, the president's arrival in France in mid-December was triumphal. Buoyed by the ending of the carnage on the Western Front, two million people turned out to greet "Wilson the Just" in Paris. Fully as many choked the streets when he entered Milan and Rome. The scenes were repeated in London, Carlisle, and Manchester. Never before in modern European history had demonstrations of such magnitude taken place to honor any statesman or general, nor had cheering throngs held up such banners that read "Welcome to the God of Peace," "Hail the Champion of the Rights of Man," and "Honor to the Founder of the Society of Nations." These outpourings strengthened his hand during the early phases of the peace conference, especially in seeing to the inclusion of the Covenant of the League in the Treaty of Versailles. Yet they also generated some resentment among his fellow peacemakers—David Lloyd

George, Georges Clemenceau, and Vittorio Orlando—who were aware of the new arithmetic in the Senate. They would leverage their acceptance of the Covenant to gain concessions from Wilson on other issues. (As Clemenceau quipped: "God gave us the Ten Commandments, and we broke them. Wilson gives us fourteen points. We shall see.") In some cases, however, he was able to moderate the Allies' more extreme demands against Germany. In others in which he went along, his rationale was that eventually the League would be able to rectify injustices contained in the treaty itself.

Still, Wilson paid a heavy price in terms of support among his natural constituency. By the summer of 1919 the punitive features of the treaty had become apparent. Regardless of his motives, it began to look like he had compromised on too many of his Fourteen Points. In a special edition, the *New Republic*, usually a pro-Wilson magazine, editorialized: "THIS IS NOT PEACE." Soon greater numbers of progressive internationalists withdrew their support for him in the conviction that, in the present circumstance, the League of Nations could serve only reactionary interests and that it might be best to stay out of it.[27] (In a sense, Wilson would ultimately come to the same conclusion himself.)

* * *

As for the Senate, partisanship motivated a lot of the opposition. One of the goals of Senator Lodge, frankly, was to deny Wilson his crowning glory. (The two men loathed each other personally.) At the same time, though, many of the objections (including Lodge's) were grounded in authentic differences separating two competing forms of internationalism. Only a few of Wilson's adversaries were isolationists, per se. The majority of Republicans, like Lodge, were conservative internationalists. As such, they could accept a world parliament, but they thought the United States also should expand its army and navy, resist any diminution of sovereignty, and reserve the right at all times to exercise force independently. To be sure, Wilson did try to accommodate some of their concerns. For instance, he had agreed to provide for withdrawal from the League and to exempt immigration policy and the Monroe Doctrine from its jurisdiction. But his conservative critics believed that he had consigned (or would consign) too many vital national interests to the will of an international authority.[28]

Ratification foundered on the shoals of sovereignty. To quote Lodge, the Republicans' concerns about collective security and arbitration settled upon not just "releas[ing] us from obligations which might not be kept," but preserving "rights which ought not to be infringed."[29] Yet Wilson had frankly acknowledged, "Some of our sovereignty would be surrendered," when he met with thirty-four members of the House and Senate at the White House during a ten-day visit back home in February 1919. "[It is] inconceivable that any concert of action of the nations . . . [of] the world could be taken without some sacrifice." Although he reminded them that the League's Executive Council must reach unanimity before military force (or economic sanctions) could be set in motion under Article 10, he still emphasized that the League would fail "if the objection of sovereignty is insisted upon by the Senate." He also believed the country "would willingly relinquish some of its sovereignty . . . for the good of the world."[30]

This was something of a leitmotif. In campaigning for reelection in October 1916, he had told Chicagoans: "There is coming a time, unless I am very much mistaken, when nation shall agree with nation that the rights of humanity are greater than the rights of sovereignty." Three years later in Billings, Montana, he addressed objections to Article 10 and arbitration this way: "The only way you are going to get impartial determinations in the world is by consenting to something you do not want to do." The corollary to this, then, was to refrain from doing something that you want to do. There might be times "when we lose in court . . . [and] we will take our medicine."[31]

The Lodge Reservations, as they often were called, came out just as the president embarked on his speaking tour. They were intended to impose a distinctly conservative construction on Wilson's internationalism. The two most important reservations would render Article 10 optional and arbitration voluntary rather than mandatory. Two others would nullify restrictions on the right to increase the size of the armed forces without consulting the League and rejected membership in the International Labor Organization. Still another asserted the right, in the face of a League boycott, to continue trading a state that broke the Covenant. Perhaps the most telling one was the reservation that cast doubt on whether the United States would contribute its fair share to the league's expenses. In substance and in tone the fourteen reservations constituted a frontal assault.[32]

If Americans accepted such reservations, Wilson warned in response throughout the tour, they would have to go it alone. They would have to maintain a large standing army and to levy exorbitant, never-ending taxation to pay for it. In time the United States would become a "militaristic organization of government" with "secret agencies planted everywhere." In short, they would always have to be "ready to fight the world." Some months later, after his stroke and also after the political gridlock had spread over Washington, he wrote to Senator Hitchcock, "The imperialist wants no League of Nations, but if . . . there is to be one, he is interested to secure one suited to his own purpose." The missive, dated March 6, 1920, was intended for publication just before the Senate rendered its final verdict.* For Wilson, international security involved the acceptance of constraints and obligations, or "a renunciation of wrong ambition on the part of powerful nations," including the United States. Article 10 constituted "the only bulwark . . . of the rising democracy of the world against the forces of imperialism and reaction." If his stroke made the President less amenable to compromise, then it had rendered him no less consistent in his convictions about progressive internationalist principles. And so, in the end, if he permitted the United States to go in under the Lodge reservations, then the nature of the League would no longer be in doubt. It would be a reactionary league, a Lodgian league. And perhaps no league would be better than one that would "venture to take part in reviving the old order."[33]

* * *

One can admire and appreciate Wilson's case on behalf of progressive internationalism while acknowledging that he had reached the point

* This time, on March 19, 1920, the roll was called on the treaty with the Lodge reservations. With eighty-four senators present, the vote was forty-nine for and thirty-five against, or seven votes short of ratification.

where he was no longer capable of advancing membership in the League untrammeled by explicit reservations. "Perhaps it was providential that I was stricken down when I was," he remarked in retirement in September 1923, five months before he died. "Had I kept my health I should have carried the League. Events have shown that the world was not ready for it." Yet, even if Wilson had never suffered a severe stroke, it is probable that the changed political conditions of 1918–19—the Republicans' parliamentary restoration on one hand and the unraveling of Wilson's once-ascendant progressive-left coalition on the other—had already made ratification of a *Wilsonian* league nearly impossible. If this was so, then the crisis of the stroke did not matter quite as much as one might have reasonably assumed. In the actual circumstances, the only realistic hope for salvaging something may, indeed, have been the president's resignation or removal from office. But there were many obstacles to the latter path: first and foremost, the Constitution's defect; second, Mrs. Wilson's capacity to prevent disclosure of the extent of the president's disability against the better judgment of Dr. Grayson and one or two other counselors; and, third, Vice President Marshall's disinclination to pursue the matter actively.* In his memoir, Marshall left fairly clear markers to suggest that he would have moved to compromise had he become president. Had Wilson resigned willingly, upon making the dramatic appearance in the Senate he once had mused about to Grayson, the vice president might have taken on the hero's

* The Twenty-fifth Amendment is an improvement over Article II, Section 1, but no guarantee against the recurrence of comparable crises. In addition to establishing succession, the amendment provides for a president to declare himself unable to discharge his duties and for the vice president to act in his stead. Another section permits the vice president and a majority of the cabinet also to declare the president thus unfit; and "when the President transmits . . . that no inability exists, he shall resume his powers" unless the Vice President and Cabinet declare within four days "that [he] is unable to discharge the powers and duties of his office." Medical and political dilemmas abound herein. Bert Park has written that the amendment begs the question of how these parties should go about ascertaining the medical facts to make such decisions. He has recommended the establishment of a Presidential Impairment Panel for advisory purposes. Jerrold Post has asked what are the president's rights to privacy in such circumstances. He has raised issues as well about confidentiality and ethical requirements regarding whom a president's physician serves, and whether or not presidential candidates should be required to open their medical records to public scrutiny. See the special issue of *Political Psychology* (Vol. 16, No. 4, 1995), edited by Dr. Post, for an introduction to these and related problems.

part.[34] But one is then borne back to the question of what difference such an uncertain party to the League would have made.

On his last day in office Wilson was not well enough to attend his successor's inauguration. Instead he went to the President's Room in the capitol to sign last-minute bills and to say farewell to his cabinet. Just before noon, an official delegation led by Senator Lodge entered to say that Congress stood ready to adjourn unless he had "any further communications." The two statesmen studied each other briefly for the last time, then Wilson broke the silence. "I have no further communication to make. I would be glad if you would inform both Houses and thank them for their courtesy." A moment later, clutching Edith's arm, he walked out of the room and into history.

History was ironic, and Wilson could not have been more wrong in telling Lodge he had "no further communication to make." In the 1920s and 1930s assessments of his legacy were unfavorable. Many Americans came to believe that intervention in World War I had been a mistake, and criticisms of the Treaty of Versailles multiplied as another European conflict loomed. After 1941, however, Wilson's reputation soared. A new wisdom took hold that World War II might have been averted if America had joined the League. Thus the United States would play the chief role creating the United Nations in 1945. Even so, in the 1950s and 1960s, most practitioners of American foreign policy condemned his ideas as unsound in a bipolar world overwhelmed by the Soviet-American confrontation. But in the aftermath of victory in the Cold War and well into the twenty-first century, the architects of American foreign policy still had yet to come to grips with the main tenets of Wilsonianism—disarmament, multilateral peacekeeping and enforcement of international law, and the notion of a community of nations.

As for Wilson himself, whatever the central cause of his historic failure, his conservative and partisan detractors believed that his was a dangerously radical vision, a new world order alien to their own understanding of how the world worked. His severest critics among his fellow progressives believed he had not done enough to resist the forces of reaction either in America or at the peace conference. "What more could I have done?" he asked historian William E. Dodd shortly before he left the White House. Of the "receding ideals" of the previous year, Dodd observed, it had all been "one long wilderness of despair and betrayal, even by good men." But it was Ray Stannard Baker who commented on Wilson's fate more perceptively than anyone: "He can escape no responsibility & must go to his punishment not only for his own mistakes and weaknesses of temperament but for the greed and selfishness of the world."[35]

NOTES

1. Speaking at the Center for the Study of Democratic Institutions in 1973, quoted in Randall Bennett Woods, *Fulbright, A Biography* (New York: Cambridge University Press, 1995), 647.
2. As he said in Cheyenne on his speaking tour; see Arthur S. Link *et al.* (eds.) *The Papers of Woodrow Wilson*, 69 vols. (Princeton, NJ: Princeton University Press, 1966–1996), LXIII, 480 (hereafter cited as *PWW*).
3. Ibid., 42.
4. News report, Sept. 25, and Grayson diary, Sept. 26, 1919, in ibid., 487 and 42; and Thomas J. Knock, *To End All Wars: Woodrow Wilson and the Quest for a New World Order* (New York: Oxford University Press, 1992), 259–263.
5. Bert E. Park, M. D., M. A., "Wilson's Neurologic Illness During the Summer of 1919," *PWW*, LXII, 628–38.
6. See "Dr. Dercum's Memoranda," detailing his first examination of the President, on October 2, and his subsequent exams on October 4, 11, 18, which he sent to Dr. Grayson on Oct. 20, 1919, in *PWW*, LXIV, 500–05. See also Dr. Park's 1991 commentary on Dercum's finding in ibid., 506–07, as well as in "Woodrow Wilson's Stroke of October 2, 1919," (*PWW*, LXIII, 639–46). See also John Milton Cooper Jr., *Woodrow Wilson* (New York: Alfred Knopf, 2009), 532–34.
7. See two *Washington Post* reports (Oct. 3, 1919) conveying statements by Grayson and Dercum in *PWW*, LXIII, 543–47, and Park, "Wilson's Stroke," ibid., 642–43.
8. Knock, *To End All Wars*, 263, and Cooper, *Woodrow Wilson*, 552; see also, Ray Stannard Baker diary, Feb. 4, 1920, *PWW*, LXIV, 362–63n1, and Nov. 28, 1920, ibid., LXVI, 436.
9. Edith Bolling Wilson, *My Memoir* (New York: Bobbs Merrill, 1938, 1939) 288–89; see also Cooper, *Woodrow Wilson*, 535–37.
10. Ibid., 204; Knock, *To End All Wars*, 263; Baker Diary, Feb. 5, 1920, *PWW*, LXIV, 365.
11. Grayson memorandum, Oct. 6, 1919, printed out of sequence in *PWW*, LXIV, 496 (quoted in Cooper, *Woodrow Wilson*, 538).

12. Two reports in the *New York Times*, Dec. 6, 1919, *PWW*, LXIV, 129–33; Hoover, "The Facts about President Wilson's Illness," undated, ibid., LXIII, 634; and Cooper *Woodrow Wilson*, 561–63.
13. Knock, *To End All Wars*, 269.
14. The best works include Lloyd Ambrosius, *Woodrow Wilson and the American Diplomatic Tradition* (New York: Cambridge University Press, 1987); Kendrick Clements, *Woodrow Wilson, World Statesman* (Boston: Twayne Publishers, 1987) and *The Presidency of Woodrow Wilson* (Lawrence: University of Kansas Press, 1992); Arthur S. Link, *Woodrow Wilson: Revolution War and Peace* (Arlington Hts, IL: Harlan Davidson, 1979); Robert Ferrell, *Woodrow Wilson and World War I* (New York: Harper, 1985); and especially John Milton Cooper Jr., *Breaking the Heart of the World: Woodrow Wilson and the Fight for the League of Nations* (New York: Cambridge University Press, 2001), and *Woodrow Wilson*.
15. Alexander L. and Juliette L. George, *Woodrow Wilson and Colonel House: A Personality Study* (New York, 1956), 6–8, 40–43, 114, 117, and 311. See also the scathing *Thomas Woodrow Wilson, Twenty-eighth President of the United States: A Psychological Study* (New York, 1967), by Sigmund Freud and William C. Bullitt. Publication of this book was held up for thirty-five years out of respect to Mrs. Wilson, who died in December 1961. It was principally the work of Bullitt, a disgruntled former member of the US peace commission to Paris, who had made Freud's acquaintance in the 1930s. Freud's family disowned the book and claimed that the father of modern psychoanalysis had little or nothing to do with its composition.
16. Edwin Weinstein, *Woodrow Wilson, A Medical and Psychological Biography* (Princeton, NJ: Princeton University Press, 1981), 13–21, 165–80, 195–216, 336–41, and 363 (emphasis added); see also Weinstein, "Woodrow Wilson's Neurological Illness," *Journal of American History*, 57 (September 1970), 324–51; and Weinstein, Arthur S. Link, and James W. Anderson, "Woodrow Wilson's Political Personality: A Reappraisal," *Political Science Quarterly*, 93 (Winter 1978), 585–598.
17. Michael F. Marmor, "Wilson, Strokes, and Zebras," *The New England Journal of Medicine*, Vol. 307, No. 9 (August 1982), 528–35 (quote 533).
18. One of a number of examples that the Georges cite is as follows: "Years of excessive work take their toll in May 1906 when Wilson suffers a major stroke that seems for a moment to threaten his life" (*PWW*, XVI, vii). See "Woodrow Wilson and Colonel House: A Reply to Weinstein, Anderson, and Link," *Political Science Quarterly*, Vol. 96, No. 4 (Winter 1981–82), 641–65 (646–50 and 657–59); and Juliette George, Michael Marmor, and Alexander George, "Issues in Wilson Scholarship: Reference to Early 'Strokes' in the Papers of Woodrow Wilson," *Journal of American History*, Vol. 70, No. 4 (March 1984), 845–53. Link replies in the same issue in a letter to the editor of the *JAH*, 945–55. Compare Cooper's *Woodrow Wilson*, 19–20, with his *The Warrior and the Priest, and Woodrow Wilson and Theodore Roosevelt* (Cambridge, MA: Harvard University Press, 1983), 20–21.
19. Jerrold M. Post, "Woodrow Wilson Re-examined: The Mind-Body Controversy and Other Disputations," *Political Psychology*, Vol. 4, No. 2, (1983), 289–306 (quote 301), and Marmor, "Wilson, Strokes, and Zebras," 533. Weinstein had

declared that Wilson had suffered a "major stroke" in May 1906 on the basis of suddenly impaired vision and the appearance of blood in his left eye, the result, it turned out, of a burst retinal blood vessel. Yet Weinstein employed the term "blood clot" and asserted that the cause was a transient blockage of the carotid artery, an unmistakable sign of carotid artery disease—even though both the famous ophthalmologist and the internist who examined Wilson left behind no records. As Marmor, Post, the Georges, and other critics point out, Weinstein ignored the more logical explanation, as revealed in at least one letter about the incident written by Wilson, another by his internist, and two by Ellen—"a hemorrhage of one of the blood vessels of my left eye," as Wilson described it. No one mentioned "stroke" or "blood clot," and the blood in Wilson's eye was quickly absorbed. Crucially, though, the incident did reveal that Wilson had "a very moderate grade of arterial trouble," his internist wrote. "You were fortunate in having the local (ocular) trouble because it called attention to the general condition which would otherwise have passed unnoticed. I feel entirely confident that a rest of three months will restore you fully." Wilson followed his doctors' orders regarding changes in his diet, more exercise, and a full summer of rest, and that was that. Weinstein based his diagnosis of a stroke in 1896 on Wilson's complaints of recurrent writer's cramp and a sore arm, which both Marmor and Post suggest was far more likely some form of carpal tunnel syndrome. "To fit Wilson's chronic hand and arm pain into a stroke syndrome," Marmor states, "is to struggle unreasonably against the evidence" (ibid., 533). These and other matters are explored also in responses to Post from Weinstein and the Georges in the special issue of *Political Psychology* cited above.

20. Bert E. Park, *The Impact of Illness on World Leaders* (Philadelphia: University of Pennsylvania Press, 1986), 3–76; "The Impact of Wilson's Neurologic Disease During the Paris Peace Conference," *PWW*, LVIII, 611–30 (quotes, 611, 615, 612, and 630); commentary on Dr. Dercum's memorandum, ibid., LXIV, 506; "Woodrow Wilson's Stroke of October 2, 1919," ibid., LXIII, 639–46 (quote, 639 and 644); "The Aftermath of Wilson's Stroke," ibid., LXIV, 525–28 (quote, 528, emphasis added). See also Park's "Wilson's Neurologic Illness During the Summer of 1919," ibid., LXII, 628–38; and, in ibid., LVIII, Weinstein's "Woodrow Wilson's Neuropsychological Impairment and the Paris Peace Conference," 630–35, and James F. Toole, M.D., "Some Observations on Wilson's Neurologic Illness," 635–38.
21. On Wilson's coalition and the 1916 campaign, see Knock, *To End All Wars*, 85–104 (Amos Pinchot quote, 104).
22. The Covenant and Wilson's presentation are printed in *PWW*, LV, 164–78; for the writing of it, see Knock, *To End All Wars*, 210–26 (esp., 224–26), and 127; for the Fourteen Points, see ibid., 142–47.
23. Ibid., 48–69, for the origins and evolution of the two forms; 229 for Hitchcock quote.
24. For the Republican attacks on the administration, see ibid., 167–69, 176, and 180.
25. See ibid., 178–80, 184–85, and 189–91.
26. Ibid., 132–37, 158–60, and 185–87.
27. Ibid., 252–57.

28. For his efforts to compromise, see ibid., 240–42 and 247–48.
29. Quoted in William C. Widenor, *Henry Cabot Lodge and the Search for an American Foreign Policy* (Berkeley: University of California Press, 1980), 321.
30. A news account of the meeting is printed in *PWW*, LV, 268–76.
31. For the 1916 Chicago speech see ibid., XXXVIII, 488; for 1919 in Billings, ibid., LXIII, 177.
32. For an excellent analysis of his antagonist's perspective, see Widenor, *Henry Cabot Lodge*, 338–48 and also 319–21 and 328–30.
33. See Wilson's speeches in St. Louis, Kansas City, Sioux Falls, Portland, and Billings, *PWW*, LXIII, 46–47, 69, 112, 279, and 173; and Wilson to Hitchcock, March 8, 1920, ibid., LXV, 67–71.
34. Lord Riddell's Diary, Sept. 10, 1923, *PWW*, LXVIII, 422; *Recollections of Thomas R. Marshall* (Indianapolis, 1925), 363; Cooper, *Breaking the Heart of the World*, 201–11.
35. William E. Dodd, *Woodrow Wilson and His Work* (New York: P. Smith, 1932), 434; Baker Diary, April 3, 1919, *PWW*, LVI, 577–78.

A man of few words, President Calvin Coolidge found even less to say—but more to do—following the untimely death of his beloved son, who passed away in the same White House bedroom as Lincoln's son. [Courtesy Calvin Coolidge Presidential Foundation.]

6

Calvin Coolidge

"When he went the power and the glory of the Presidency went with him"

AMITY SHLAES

In July 1924, death came to the East Room once more. A navy orchestra played a funeral march at the bier of sixteen-year-old Calvin Coolidge Jr.[1] "Calvin," as the boy was called, had been the light of the White House, in sharp contrast to his somber father, "Cal," "Mr. President," or "The President." Like Willie Lincoln, whose funeral service had taken place in the same room, Calvin was especially beloved of his father. And like Willie, Calvin went unexpectedly. Playing tennis on the White House South Grounds, the high schooler developed a blister on a toe. The blister led to sepsis, which took the boy in a week.

When the Coolidges and their sons John and Calvin had arrived in the bubbly, loquacious Washington of 1921, the press had noted the new vice president's reluctance to chatter. "A well of silence. A center of stillness," commented the journalist Edward Lowry of Coolidge. With the death of President Warren Harding in 1923, Coolidge became president, and the habit of reticence remained. The thirtieth president differed from the twenty-ninth, Secretary of State Charles Evans Hughes noticed.[2] Whereas Harding had kept people about him, Coolidge worked alone. And when a visitor came to ask something of President Coolidge, the answer was usually "no."

The press noted that Calvin's death hit his father hard. Nearly all photos taken after that July show a president not merely reticent but dark, whether or not he was alone or accompanied by First Lady and his remaining son, the older John. The president slept a lot, people noted, perhaps more than in the old days.[3] Not only his son's but his own mortality hung over Coolidge: after all, the presidency had left Woodrow Wilson incapacitated and Harding had died in office. Lincoln had also lain in the East Room. Night and day, Coolidge insisted doctors check his pulse and blood pressure.[4] Grief made the president sour: White House staff noted that Coolidge could be hard on John, forbidding dancing at the White House or sending scolding letters to his son at Amherst. The president dosed himself with strange medicines.[5] Coolidge was so often depicted as frozen the image became stereotype. When Coolidge did die in 1933, the *New Yorker* commentator Dorothy Parker asked: "How could they tell?"

More recently, researchers have gone so far as to suggest that the death of his second son incapacitated Coolidge and therefore limited execution of his work. "It certainly affected Coolidge's campaign and probably his remaining years in the White House," writes one of Coolidge's early biographers, Donald R. McCoy.[6] The most thorough of these scholars is Robert Gilbert, who in his biography *The Tormented President* contends that "Coolidge's presidency died when his son died, and he served out his remaining years in office as a mere shadow of his former self."[7]

Some authors have even hinted that Coolidge's depression caused him to make policy errors that in turn set the stage for the Great Depression. In the *Atlantic* magazine, for example, commentator Jack Beatty writes that "[T]hanks to Gilbert, historians of the 1920s can better understand how depression reinforced Coolidge's principled aversion to active government and his political fear of the costs of tampering with the speculation-driven dynamics of "Coolidge prosperity."[8] This thought might be rendered as: (Mental) depression = (Economic) depression.

His son's death did indeed weigh upon Coolidge. To this, the president himself testified, writing in his autobiography of his son: "When he went, the power and the glory of the presidency went with him." But the more significant contention, that bereavement rendered Coolidge unfit for office, is harder to prove. With the band of mourning still on his left arm, Coolidge competed in presidential contest in 1924 and won a stunning mandate: an absolute majority in a three-way race. Following that 1924 election, Coolidge achieved many of the policy goals set out by his party in 1920 and 1924. It is, however, possible to argue that the death of young Calvin affected presidential policy in one way. Sorrow at loss of life may have driven the president to emphasize a policy aimed at preventing carnage generally. The evidence of this is the quiet but definite Coolidge stewardship of the Kellogg-Briand Pact to outlaw war, an initiative taken late in 1927 and 1928, after Coolidge had lost his father as well.

To drag the Great Depression into the argument over Coolidge's performance is to stretch the argument into true distortion. Many economists and authors have provided evidence unrelated to Coolidge for the decade-long downturn. But what matters in this article in any case is whether Coolidge succeeded by his own terms. This is not a story of "yes, but." This is a story of "but, yes."

What enabled the glum Coolidge to execute his tasks? A feature that the president also identified in his autobiography: perseverance. "If I had permitted my failures or what seemed to me at the time a lack of success to discourage me," Coolidge wrote, "I cannot see any way in which I would ever have made progress. If we keep our faith in ourselves and what is even more important keep our faith in regular and persistent application to hard work, we need not worry about the outcome."[9] Though Coolidge may have lost his son, he could not forget what he had promised Harding or his party. Like Lyndon Johnson after John Kennedy so many years later, the thirtieth president took up his turn in the presidential relay with near-martial determination, vowing to execute his predecessor's plans "to perfection." Other forces we would also recognize today, such as family and religious faith, drove Coolidge forward.

Yet other factors sustaining the mourner are less obvious to the modern eye: a community of fellow mourners to comfort the president, for example. A final clue to Coolidge's work after his younger son's death can be found in the melancholy coincidence of the memorials in the East Room: Abraham Lincoln. All Republicans publicly claim some connection to Lincoln, for association with their party's founder burnishes their own reputation. But Coolidge studied, emulated, and derived consolation from Lincoln even when no one was looking. Like Lincoln before him, Coolidge as president believed that the work he had undertaken warranted the tremendous effort it took to suspend even the greatest grief. Lincoln suppressed his grief because he believed he must fulfill the Republican coalition's goals to prosecute the Civil War. Coolidge suppressed his own sorrow because he believed he must fulfill the Republican promise of that decade: to restore the country to "normalcy" and smaller government after the disruption of World War I.

This analogy may startle. A bloody military campaign does not resemble a peacetime budget-and-tax campaign. Coolidge, who as governor of Massachusetts had motored out into Boston Harbor to greet the ragged returning veterans of World War I knew this full well. Still, it can be said that Coolidge and, for that matter, Harding before him deemed their government rollback work a moral imperative to be carried out, as Harding put it, with "resolute devotion to duty."[10] Coolidge for his part actually labeled budgeting, the process for cutting the government back, his "obsession."[11] Whereas Lincoln spoke of freedom from slavery, Coolidge spoke of freedom for the American people in economic terms: "I want them to have the rewards of their own industry. This is the chief meaning of freedom."[12]

Many readers may disapprove of Coolidge's emphases, but doing so is not the same as proving that Coolidge failed. In any case, such disapproval tends to distract from the genuine drama of the Coolidge story: that from his life's beginning, our thirtieth president did very often come close to failing.

From his birth in rural Plymouth Notch, Vermont, the red-haired quiet child was considered delicate. His mother Victoria died when he was twelve, very likely from tuberculosis. This loss was, as he later recalled "the greatest grief that can come to a boy."[13] Those around him wondered whether the boy would succumb, too: after all, tuberculosis was then so common it was known as the "New England disease." Coolidge's grandmother, Sarah Coolidge, took over much of the childrearing.

As would become the pattern, Coolidge found early that learning distracted from sorrow. The chance to attend a nearby boarding school, Black River Academy in Ludlow, ten miles down the road, made him brighten again. "[O]ne of the greatest adventures of my life," was how Coolidge described the day of his departure. At school came another blow: his only sibling, his sister Abigail, died suddenly, probably of appendicitis. The lanky high school senior Calvin delivered his father's report of the death and funeral to the editor of the Ludlow Tribune for publication himself.[14] And the youth became ill while sitting the entrance exam for Amherst College in 1890. The young Coolidge returned home, requiring half a year to recover, and managed to enter college only the following autumn.

At Amherst, failure loomed again. The young man from Vermont expected to gain entrance to one of Amherst's numerous fraternities. Yet during rush no one knocked on his door. Indeed, Coolidge was blackballed by the only fraternity that seriously considered him. The names of other undergraduates filled the college newspaper, the *Student*—but not Coolidge's. His peers from Boston and New York perceived him as a bumpkin, "a sandy haired boy with freckles and trousers which do not come down to his shoes."[15]

Again, it was a combination of work and family that heartened him. Two lecturers, Charles Morse and Charles Edward Garman, captured Coolidge's attention, as did the victory of Democrat Grover Cleveland in 1892. Like all young men, he drew inspiration from past leaders, among them Lincoln. In a moment of bravado, the undergraduate sent his father a little survey of the nineteenth century, including a line about the sixteenth president: "Our own Lincoln finished his life's work when he struck the shackles from four millions of slaves and saw the surrender of General Lee."[16] His father, John Coolidge, remarried and the relief at having a mother—that was what Coolidge called his stepmother—can be read in his letters: "I have just a few moments and so will send you a line as you may get some lonesome if Mother is gone."[17] In another letter Coolidge confessed to his father, "I am only trying to get some discipline now." Indifferent to football, Coolidge desultorily turned to the attorney's sport: debate. Arguing the roots of American Revolution, or the merits of parliaments over the American presidential system—even trying humor—the upperclassman finally earned the respect of his peers. Turning disadvantage to advantage, Coolidge even argued, and won, the case against college football. It was as if the undergraduates had encountered, one later wrote, "a new and gifted man."[18] In his senior year Coolidge was finally tapped by a fraternity, albeit one new to campus, Phi Gamma Delta.

Coming out of college, Coolidge hoped to attend law school along with many of his classmates, but his father resisted, probably because of the cost. In the end Coolidge found a place not at Harvard or Columbia, where other Amherst men went, but at a Northampton, Massachusetts law firm led by two Amherst alumni, John Hammond and Henry Field. He would not study law but rather prepare to sit the bar by clerking—an old-fashioned training. At night in the town's Forbes Library, or in the day at the clerk's desk, Coolidge took consolation in the fact the young Lincoln had followed a similar course. Much later, as clerking became yet rarer, Coolidge would derive pride in having learned as Lincoln has, even going so far as to explain the educational track to others. "In the strict sense of the old phrase," Coolidge later wrote of Abe, "he read law."[19] The partners at Hammond and Field approvingly described him as "a hog for work."[20]

From the beginning of the young lawyer's career, two things were clear. The first was that that work would include politics: the young Coolidge put in so much time helping out the local Republican Party that he could quickly move from ward officer to city representative to city solicitor, state representative, mayor, and state senator. The second was that Coolidge was a business lawyer, the kind who easily handled writs and deeds, or served as counsel to firms. His focus on trade proved intense enough to amuse his peers. "One June evening we went trolley riding," a friend from his college period, Alfred Pearce Dennis, later recalled. The trolley line was new and fast. Its ticket costs were being debated in the newspaper. As the train raced, the young men took in the evening, and Dennis fell to thinking of a girl, "clothed in filmy white raiment with roses in her hands . . ." Dennis's reverie was interrupted by Coolidge, who let him know that he had used the same free minutes to count up the costs of the trolley line, labor, rails, poles, copper wire, crossties and all, and that he concluded that the trolley line was entitled to charge what fares it liked.[21]

To the astonishment of friends and perhaps his father, Coolidge did eventually look up from business—to court one of most popular women in town. A lively teacher of the deaf, a fellow Vermonter named Grace Goodhue espied the lawyer through a window (the future president was shaving) and requested an introduction. By 1905 Coolidge and Miss Goodhue, as he addressed her, were married in Burlington at her parents' house. The Coolidges settled soon in a modest half of a two-family house on Northampton's Massasoit Street. By 1906, when their first son was born, Coolidge was finally indulging himself in moments of reverie. As the proud father wrote later of the arrival of his first son, "The fragrance of the clematis which covered the bay window filled the room like a benediction, where the other lay with her baby." He also wrote, "We called him John in honor of my father. It was all very wonderful to us." And, "we liked the house where our children came to us and the neighbors were so kind." The second son, Calvin Jr., came soon after. Coolidge meanwhile collected experience in the law, handling the standard country cases. His colleagues noticed he was more solicitor than barrister, and he preferred settling in offices to litigation.

Coolidge's entry into politics was likewise modest. As he rose from state representative to Northampton mayor or state senator, what struck others about him was his modesty. Progressive ideas had been around for a long time: the first great antitrust law, the Sherman Act, had passed the year Coolidge finished high school. But under presidents Theodore Roosevelt, William Howard Taft, and Woodrow Wilson, progressives advocating state and federal intervention in areas from business (aggressive antitrust law) to health (food or drug legislation) were taking the lead. Many experienced politicians were having trouble finding where they fit into the transformation. How progressive should they be? Some lawmakers favored minimum wage and reform at the state level only. Others preferred that reform come from Washington.

In his twenties and early thirties, the young lawmaker did not hurry to establish his own positions. He went along with the party, endorsing antitrust legislation at times, but sometimes holding back. After negotiating a strike in Lawrence, Massachusetts, Coolidge found himself siding more with employers than strikers, writing impulsively to his stepmother: "The leaders there are and they do not want anyone to work for wages. The trouble is not about the amount of wages, it is a small attempt to destroy all authority, whether of any church or government."[22]But publicly, he was not ready to take a stand, and so simply focused on honoring the law and representing his constituents well. This attitude of lawyerly professionalism comes clear again in a brief address he made to Massachusetts senate when he became its president in 1914:

> Do the day's work. If it to be protect the rights of the weak, whoever objects, do it. If it be to help a powerful corporation better to serve the people, whatever the opposition, do that. Expect to be called a stand patter, but don't be a stand patter . . . don't hesitate to be as revolutionary as science. Don't hesitate to be as reactionary as the multiplication table. Don't expect to build up the weak by pulling down the strong. Don't hurry to legislate.

Coolidge's colleagues rewarded this respectful pragmatism with their own respect. Part of professionalism was avoiding corruption. When colleagues used state funds to travel to a fair on the West Coast, Coolidge stayed back, pointedly setting an example. The Coolidges were known for their upright abhorrence of political favors. Unlike some colleagues, Coolidge chose to practice law rather than take political contributions. Indeed, as he would conclude later, it was only because of that income stream that "I could be independent and serve the public without ever thinking that I could not maintain my position if I lost my office . . . This left me free to make my own decisions in accordance with what I thought was the public good."[23]

Coolidge rose and rose again but always and only with the support of his family. Grace Coolidge, popular and bright, defined her own career as providing stability for Coolidge. The house on Massasoit Street featured not only boys but also toy trains, a radio, a phonograph and, numerous pets. "Any man who does not like dogs and want them about does not deserve to be in the White House," Coolidge later said. Coolidge vented his temper at home and at times Grace even called herself a "safety valve." His children were also "safety valves," or comforts, to whom Coolidge returned after a work week as a bachelor lawmaker at the Adams House Hotel on Washington Street in Boston. Quickly people observed that Coolidge felt especially close to Calvin. Early on, the boy demonstrated a sense of humor and an understanding of service. The only time his colleagues ever saw the phlegmatic Coolidge turn emotional was during one of his second son's illnesses. When Calvin entered the hospital with pneumonia in 1913, the young politician even told a doctor that his political friends could pay high medical fees to help the boy. "I am a poor man, but I could command considerable money if you need it." [24] This rare slip in the upright Coolidge's carriage betrays the extent of his desperation.

As the years passed in state politics, Coolidge grew more confident in his conservatism. Half a year after becoming US Senate president, for example, he actually showcased his positions when he used his special status as Senate president to kill a new stock tax by creating a tie. [25] Elected governor in 1918, he vetoed spending to improve city ferries and then a pay increase to $1500 from $1000 for fellow lawmakers, commenting that "service in the general court is not obligatory but optional."[26]

The year 1919 brought challenges on a scale Coolidge had not encountered and for which he seemed no match. As governor it was his job to greet the returning ships of veterans, which meant he came eye to eye with the consequences of war. Many of the men were wounded and stood or sat on Boston's streets. Employment was difficult to find, and prices were rising faster than they had in decades, in part because the young Fed and the Treasury had inflated.[27] The great influenza epidemic raged, especially in port cities like Boston. The intense demobilization work separated him more than ever from his family at home in Northampton. One of his few comforts were the visits of Grace, his father, and his sons John and Calvin to Boston. Father Coolidge, safe in green Vermont, received a letter from the Massachusetts governor's office signed "Calvin Coolidge." Upon close inspection one could see the signature wobbled. The governor had risked bringing his son into the city and the office, and Calvin jr. had signed for his father.

Another source of consolation was Lincoln. Early in that first year as governor, Coolidge penned the state's annual Lincoln Day proclamation, so flamboyant in its admiration it bordered on blasphemy: "Five score and ten years ago," Coolidge wrote, referring to Lincoln's birth, "that divine providence which infinite repetition has made only the more a miracle sent into the world a new life destined to save a nation. No star, no sign, foretold his coming." Doubtless thinking of his own mother, Coolidge described the death of Lincoln's: "About his cradle all was poor and mean save only the source of all great men, the love of a wonderful woman. When she faded away in his tender years, from her deathbed in humbled poverty, she dowered her son with greatness. There can be no proper observance of a birthday which forgets the mother."[28]

A dramatic event in September of that year did finally force Coolidge to take a public stand on policy. Early in the month Boston policemen joined a union and walked off the job, expecting the governor (who had negotiated with labor groups before) to negotiate this time or send a representative.[29] The policemen were not radicals; they had affiliated with the mild American Federation of Labor, whose leader, Samuel Gompers, had aided President Wilson in France. What's more, Boston's bobbies were, as Coolidge himself conceded, underpaid. Finally, many of the police were Irish, an ethnic group upon whose support Coolidge relied. When the police left their posts, riots broke out in Boston. Coolidge did not ask for talks or negotiation. The governor called out the National Guard to preserve law and order. He also supported the decision by Boston's police commissioner to fire the strikers as deserters. In staccato the telegraph machines rattled out a line of Coolidge's still quoted today: "There is no right to strike against the public safety by anyone, anywhere, anytime."

The firing of the policemen pleased many conservatives. But among the general population the move was so controversial Coolidge feared his step would cost him not only an election but a career. "People applaud me a great deal but I am not sure they will vote for me," he wrote his father. "This was a service that had to be done. And I have been glad to do it."[30] The tradeoff was an incredibly difficult one: order and the rule of law against the needs of the police officers. Enervated after the crisis, Coolidge fell ill with a cold so thick it kept him down for two weeks. Also weighing upon him was a difficult burden less discussed: the state had tasked the governor with cutting back departments: Coolidge had to lay off more than a hundred peers, work he later said to his friends was as tough as the strike challenge. Finally, once again, personal sorrow further weighed him down. Coolidge's stepmother Carrie suffered from cancer. In the same letter where he discussed the consequences of his strike position, Coolidge also wrote: "I had a letter from Mother last night. I know she has a very hard time and it seems impossible to find any relief for her."[31] Carrie Coolidge died shortly thereafter.

Yet as it happened, President Wilson backed up the Massachusetts governor in the strike decision. So too the voters, who reelected him come November.[32] Suddenly he seemed presidential material. Coolidge's friends, most notably Amherst classmate Dwight Morrow, thought to teach Coolidge, shipping him material on all areas of economics to read. (Morrow, a J. P. Morgan executive, sent Coolidge material on protectionism in the hopes that the governor would lose his enthusiasm for the policy, but Coolidge could not see his way to endorsing free trade. Responding to the Wall Streeter in a dry letter, Coolidge wrote that theory was all right, but in his experience (by now some twenty years of politics) protectionism worked better. Others, too, found that it was too late to teach: Coolidge suddenly knew what he thought. Unions were all right, but more important was what he called "the reign of law." And for a government to manage supply and demand through laws was folly. To make the last point to a visitor, the advertising man Bruce Barton, Coolidge drew an old Revolutionary-era document describing the failure of price controls in Belchertown. "Isn't it a strange thing that in every period of social unrest men have the notion they can pass a law and suspend the operations of economic law?"[33]

Coolidge's personal confidence rose as well. If there were any contradictions in his own policies (and there were of course) he was now comfortable with them. A politician must be taken by the people flaws and all. Around this time Coolidge was asked to supply a forward to a new publication of Carl Schurz's biography of Lincoln. This time, Coolidge's tone in describing Lincoln shifted away from hagiography and toward humility. He used the opportunity to underscore the point that politicians could be imperfect. "He does not need to be glorified," Coolidge wrote of Lincoln, "That but degrades. To idealize him destroys him. . . . Leave him as he is."[34]

The challenges left by World War I hit not only Coolidge but also the nation. The first was a federal debt unparalleled in living politicians' experience, amounting to the equivalent of 42 percent of the economy.[35] The top rates of the income tax, a fiscal tool originally designed almost as an afterthought, had risen to high rates in the 70 percent range.[36] A wartime levy of up to 60 percent, the excess profits tax, weighed on business. A leading banker, John S. Bache, led other bankers in warning of a "strike by capital."[37] While the average man did not even pay the income tax in this period, employers argued, they could not hire with such heavy levies. Money that would have flowed to new companies instead flowed to the largest tax haven available: municipal bonds. Liberty Bonds had paid for a great share of the war but might not be counted on to fund the government in peacetime.

The Wilson administration began the rollbacks, cutting tax rates and commencing to pare back the wartime state. The Republicans, however, campaigned on the premise that they were the more likely party to restore the nation to prewar patterns. "Normalcy" was therefore the motto chosen by Warren Harding, the Ohio senator whom the 1920 Chicago convention nominated as candidate. As the vice presidential candidate selected at Chicago, Coolidge received a mandate: his job was to represent law and order.[38] That suited his record as the strikebreaker governor and his general lawyerly orientation. But Coolidge also saw his own job as one of simple loyalty: backing up Harding in promoting "normalcy." The argument behind the phrase was simple. Two forces, the war and progressive experiment, had tilted the country dangerously far to the left. Harding and Coolidge promised to recenter the country and to offer, rather than radical change, what Harding would call "efficient administration of our proven system." Harding hammered especially hard on the effects of Wilson's hasty nationalization and denationalization of the railroad, calling nationalization a blunder of "surpassing proportions."[39] (In the case of the railroads. such suspicions would prove out in the long run. The railroad was supplanted by the largely unregulated trucking industry.[40]) In Harding's view, "government ought to strike the shackles from industry." Harding also believed "we need vastly more freedom than we do regulation."[41]

The Republicans identified their normalcy specifics: the budget that had increased by more than ten times must shrink. Wartime debts were at $27 billion, thirteen times the level just a few years earlier before the war.[42] The numbers had to come down. The old resort to "Liberty Bonds" must not become a habit, and a proposal to give bonds to former soldiers would be, as Harding put it "the worst thing possible."[43] Income taxes would have to descend rapidly, farther than Democrats might take them. Coolidge railed especially against the then-in-force excess profits tax. The tax had been established both for revenue purposes and with the justification that corporations were indeed pulling in enormous profits during the war. Now that the war was over, however, the tax must also go: in his August 1920 speech accepting the vice presidential nomination, Coolidge called the tax "that great breeder of public and private extravagance."[44] Progressive incursion into new areas, such as a permanent pension for veterans, the bonus, must be vetoed. Farmers might seek permanent subsidy, but Harding and Coolidge promised to block that as well. A new budget law must be promulgated to strengthen the authority of the executive to cut spending. The Harding-Coolidge program was ambitious, for the progressive wing of the Republican Party remained strong. Progressives sought not retrenchment but expansion of government: the peacetime nationalization of the new industry of utilities, for example. Robert La Follette, the senior senator from Wisconsin, threatened to lead a departure from the party.[45] Nonetheless, Harding-Coolidge and normalcy did prevail, and handsomely, in November 1920.

To serve as vice president, Coolidge mustered not only energy but friends and family. The vice president to precede Coolidge, Thomas Marshall, might have come from the opposing party, but he and Coolidge early on had struck up a friendship: both men had been members of the same fraternity, Phi Gamma Delta.[46] When Coolidge was elected, Marshall sent him a humorous note: "Please accept my sincere sympathy."[47] The Marshalls helped the Coolidges set up in the Willard Hotel, where the Marshalls had also lived while Marshall was vice president. Grace joined Coolidge at every social event: "I do not know what I would do without her," Coolidge wrote of Grace to his father. Son Calvin, especially, caught the spirit. A Massachusetts newspaper asked the boy to provide a guest column and Calvin produced a column of palpable goodwill: "I felt very sorry to see Mr. Marshall go out of office. I was very proud of my father. I liked to look at the ministers of other countries . . . When I went out on the platform I saw the crowd extending way down the street. They looked very nice."[48] In summer, Calvin, worked in the tobacco fields of Hatfield, Massachusetts. Someone, a reporter perhaps, told the boy that if his father were vice president, he would not work in the fields. "If my father were your father, you would," Calvin replied. Exciting at first, all the Coolidges enjoyed Washington. Calvin taught his mother to swim at the pool of one of Washington's wealthy families.

Harding succeeded in executing some of the tasks on the Republican agenda. 1921 saw the passage of the Budget and Accounting Act, which gave the executive stronger authority to oversee spending and, crucially, the power to impound money. In addition, Harding pushed through a tax cut but hardly the dramatic one they had all envisioned: top rates still stood in the 50 percent range. The new treasury secretary, Andrew Mellon, was one of the greatest and wealthiest businessmen of the era. Mellon was developing a theory about lower tax rates. On paper, lowering rates meant receiving lower revenues from taxpayers. But taxes were like tolls or prices. In railroading, Mellon had noted, sometimes lines with lower rates or tolls drew more trains. That in turn brought in greater revenues. This was what we would now call the Wal-Mart Principle: cut price and make up profits on volume. Mellon of course put the principle in his own terms: when it came to taxes, the government ought to charge "what the traffic will bear." He wagered that the same rule that held in business would hold in the case of taxation. Harding backed up Mellon. Harding also vetoed a bonus. Harding aimed to privatize excess oil reserves.

Nonetheless Washington proved a kind of purgatory for the vice presidential family. Much had improved since Lincoln's day, but New Englanders rightly suspected the still damp city as a trap for disease. In an era of influenza, exposing teen boys to thousands of visitors seemed unwise. As tuberculosis had become to New England, influenza was to the District of Columbia. Within a year, Grace and Calvin shipped their boys to a boarding school in the more healthful countryside of Mercersburg, Pennsylvania. Grace languished in the apartment at the Willard, there being no vice presidential residence in the era. Denied pets for the time, she amused herself feeding the mice that crossed the carpet. In the Senate, the vice president officially presided, but the senior senator from his own state, Henry Cabot Lodge, made Coolidge's new rank feel like a demotion. At school or not, their sons picked up the tension. It was Calvin again, who expressed the family mood, and this time in a poem he ironically titled "Success." "Men slave for you and with life pay/If they can clutch you for one day . . . Men say untruths for you alone/And by foul means you're called their own."[49]

Part of the trouble was the mounting embarrassment of Harding. Rather than continue the budget and tax-cut plan, the president became mired in challenges to his veterans' compromise, a hospital project. Suspicions of corruption surrounded the Veterans Bureau administrator he had named, Charles Forbes. The privatization of government oil reserves, which had sounded worthy, was now also receiving scrutiny as perhaps untoward: Harding crowd friends, rather than regular bidders, had won concessions. Coolidge knew little of the detail of what would emerge as the Veterans Bureau scandal and Teapot Dome, but the very whiff of corruption proved terrifying to a politician who had always staked his reputation on clean government. The prospect of scandal kept him awake at night. When a cannon sounded in the morning at Fort Myer, across the Potomac, Coolidge muttered, "How I hate that sunrise gun."[50]

The obligation of a presidential administration to finish what it started dominated Coolidge's thoughts, as became clear when Coolidge made a trip to Springfield, Illinois, to mark the anniversary of Lincoln's birth. He was alone, for Grace had gone to visit their sons, and gave a thoughtful speech about Lincoln's determination. "The place which Lincoln holds in the history of the nation is that of the man who finished what others had begun," Coolidge said. "He never halted. He never turned aside. He was no opportunist. He had no lack of tact. He had a mighty sense of what was timely. He was wise as a serpent. But he did not stop part way. He followed truth through to the end."

Coolidge seemed destined to endure an unsatisfying turn as vice president when, without warning, Harding died in the summer of 1923. Too much a friend and gentleman to be elated, Coolidge nonetheless was energized. Just as Theodore Roosevelt had at William McKinley's death, he hurried to Washington by train. "I think I can swing it," he told a reporter. What seized Coolidge was not merely ambition but also a sense of obligation, the need to deliver on the party's 1920 promises, and those, for that matter, of presidents before him. The Coolidges all drew consolation from the Lincolns. A picture of Lincoln that Theodore Roosevelt had placed there hung in Coolidge's office. The Coolidges moved the famous rosewood Lincoln Bed, in which Willie had died, to the Master Bedroom, so that the Coolidge family might be closer to the great president. It was at this point that Coolidge vowed to execute where Harding had failed, to deliver on their promises "to perfection."

Some observers considered President Coolidge a lame duck, "the accident of an accident," as one put it. To their surprise, he moved with firmness and focus. As always, his primary concentration was economic. Observers noticed quickly that Coolidge and Treasury Secretary Mellon made a powerful pair: Mellon saw instantly that Coolidge, the small-town lawyer who had tried so hard to figure out the economics of a trolley system, shared Mellon's intuitive focus on what was then called "commerce." Observers humorously commented that Silent Cal and the inscrutable, also taciturn Mellon "conversed almost entirely in pauses."[51] Coolidge and Mellon committed to bringing the top income tax rate down to the 30 or even the 20 percent range. Extraordinarily for a treasury secretary in that period, the quiet Mellon published a book on the virtue of tax cuts, 1924's "Taxation: The People's Business." Harding had vetoed farm subsidies, but the farmers were back, their case for help backed by a recent dramatic drop in commodity prices. Coolidge let them know he would veto again. Meanwhile, corruption emerging at the federal veterans' hospitals strengthened the case for a pension, a direct cash payment, to the vets. Republicans abhorred the precedent such a pension would set.

With considerable acumen, Coolidge hired a southern conservative, Congressman C. Bascom Slemp, as his advisor. Slemp noted of Coolidge that he "concentrated more intensely than any man I have ever known. He was always thinking, thinking, thinking."[52] In his first year Coolidge vetoed a bill that offered pensions for soldiers. He also, for a time, became more talkative. In his press conferences, reporters noted, he could give and take. (Silent Cal's first "State of the Union" address, delivered in December 1924, clocked in at over ten thousand words.) By June 1924, when Coolidge's sons came home for the holidays, there was a sense of pride in the Coolidge household and the Grand Old Party. Coolidge was ready to run for president himself. Son Calvin was especially excited. He followed the Democratic convention on the radio, stopping only to play tennis with his brother, a secret service man, or a White House doctor, Joel Boone.

That same June brought the catastrophe. By the time the doctors saw the bister, red lines streaked the boy's leg, which was an ominous sign. Charles Dawes, who would become Coolidge's running mate in 1924, visited in this period. Dawes himself had lost his own son Rufus years before when the Princeton undergrad drowned in Lake Geneva, Illinois. So desperate had Dawes been that he had vainly hoped for a miracle, sending a new invention, a "pulmotor," out from Chicago to Geneva to see if the apparatus might revive the young man. Now Dawes saw the president similarly desperate, holding the boy's hand and praying. Fever shook him and Calvin was shortly removed to Walter Reed, the veterans' hospital. There doctors tried one legitimate or experimental antidote or another. Those who attended the boy's bedside remarked again on the president's agitation. Into Calvin's hand he pressed his mother's locket, not once, but several times. The most dramatic and troubling description of Calvin's last hours came from Albert Kolmer, a University of Pennsylvania doctor called in by desperate colleagues: "The President sprang from his chair and took his dying son in his arms, shouting hysterically into his ears that he would soon join him in the great beyond and requesting that Calvin so inform his grandmother (the mother of the president)."[53]

On the evening of July 7, a week into Calvin's illness, the Democratic convention leader, Joe Walsh, interrupted the raucous crowd at Madison Square Garden. Something about Walsh's demeanor impressed the delegates, and they fell into something like silence. Then Walsh spoke a few words into the microphone.[54] What happened next was later reported by the *New York Times*. A low moan lasting many seconds filled the hall.[55] The sound of the grief as it traveled around the great space, a reporter noted, suggested the "nearness of the White House to every American home and the solicitous regard in which all people hold their president." A country exhausted by politics suddenly saw the presidency, and Coolidge, in a new light. Wrote the newspaper: "Their sorrows are his, as he often testifies, but in an especial sense his grief is also theirs." Calvin was gone.

In the days that followed none of the Coolidges even dared to think of the future. The train from Union Station headed north with its sad cargo. Friends waited for them at Northampton, their home, and then later in Vermont. The boy was buried in the little cemetery close to his grandmother and the young Abbie. At the last minute Grace rushed to place Calvin's Bible on his coffin before the dirt fell over it. While in Plymouth the family repeated a ritual: marking the height of their children on a post. The president carefully asked John and Grace how tall Calvin had been. "J.C., 1924," Coolidge marked. And then, guessing, Coolidge made a second mark: "C.C., 1924" and then added "if he had lived." Mrs. Coolidge and the secret service men dug up a spruce from the Coolidge sugar lot; they would replant it in Washington. In Washington, Mrs. Coolidge wore white, her own choice for mourning, for a year. The year before the Coolidges had established a new tradition of a national Christmas tree; a forty-eight-foot fir had been cut and brought to Washington.[56] This year, perhaps sensitive to their first family's state, authorities would order the transplant of a living tree, a Norway spruce from New York this time. Watching the Coolidges grieve, it was hard for many to see how Coolidge would serve competently the remaining months of his term of office, let alone campaign for another four years.

As it turned out, Coolidge did both. Signs that Coolidge would move forward emanated at first from Plymouth Notch. Mourn they might, but the Coolidges also used the quaint village as stage set for hosting the single most important donors and backers for the Republican campaign that year, Henry Ford and Thomas Edison. Photos of the pair and a third magnate, Harvey Firestone, visiting with the Coolidge family were shipped across the land. Ford loudly endorsed the Grand Old Party ticket of Coolidge and Charles Dawes. Though the president did not give traditional public speeches, with the strong encouragement of his backers, he did launch a Coolidge motorcade to cross the country on the Lincoln Highway, a famous road predating the modern interstate. Coolidge also quickly returned to his most pressing work, reducing debt and cutting taxes—and displayed at times an enthusiasm or interest impossible in a fatally depressed personality.

The level of Coolidge concentration in the fiscal area comes clear in a Phonofilm video, one of the first outdoor talkies of a politician ever, and made in August 1924, just a month after Calvin's death. Dressed in a suit, and with no armband evident this time, Coolidge delivered an original lecture he had prepared for the film,[57] In 1924 only higher earners paid the income tax directly, so Coolidge sought to explain that such a tax must eventually hit all voters. "The costs of government are all assessed upon the people," explained Coolidge, and then elaborated: "The wage earner makes his contribution perhaps not directly but indirectly in the advanced costs of things he buys." He followed up with a detailed series of example of tax payments that would be due if government expanded: "If the government should add one hundred million dollars of expense, it should represent four days of more work for the wage earners." Coolidge closed with vehemence: "Until we can reestablish a condition under which the earnings of the people can be kept by the people we are bound to suffer a severe and distinct curtailment of our liberty."[58] To endorse low taxes for top earners was not merely to help plutocrats; Coolidge backed up Mellon in the wager that lighter burdens for top earners would result in benefits for lower earners.[59] Coolidge also believed that if he did not continue to cut the budget, the US might lose the pride of place in the world economy it had enjoyed since the war.

Another example of this financial preoccupation shows up in a conference call Coolidge held with Jewish leaders that October, toward the end of the 1924 presidential campaign. Rather than simply reading something aloud, he confided in his listeners over the wire:

> The budget idea, I may admit, is a sort of obsession with me. I believe in budgets. I want other people to believe in them. I have had a small one to run my own home; and besides that, I am the head of the organization that makes the greatest of all budgets, that of the United States Government. Do you wonder, then, that at times I dream of balance sheets and sinking funds, and deficits, and tax rates, and all the rest?[60]

More and more Americans were beginning to see value in this approach. After all, joblessness had come down since the postwar period, and interest rates were dropping. What's more, inflation had abated. One area of the economy, farming, was performing poorly. But the rest of the economy, led by the private sector, was faring well. Even many workers believed that business, rather than unions, offered the best hope of prosperity: union membership dropped.[61] Coolidge clearly was a minimalist president: he led by cutting and not doing. The Grand Old Party picked a motto that captured this ethos: "Keep Cool with Coolidge." The tone accorded perfectly with the times, so much so that the Democratic opponent, John Davis, ended up campaigning conservatively as well. Coolidge, the quiet emblem of this new normalcy, won the election, and handily. Republicans had feared that a third party, the Progressives, might cause the defeat of the Republicans. That after all had been what Theodore Roosevelt and the Bull Moose Party did in 1912, thereby handing victory to the Democrat candidate Wilson of New Jersey. Coolidge and his Republicans, however, took an absolute majority, beating both Democrats and Progressives.

In the new term Coolidge showed no sign of flagging. He and Mellon continued their great battle, cutting taxes further and shrinking the government. To their frustration, they were not able to pass the new tax law they sought in 1925. But they continued to cut spending, thanks in part to Coolidge's rigorous attention and extensive work with the budget director, General Herbert Mayhew Lord. Data collected from the president's diary, or White House calendar, shows Coolidge meeting 55 times with Lord in 1924, the year of Calvin's death, 52 times in 1925, 63 times in 1926, and 51 times in 1927.[62] These meetings were key to budget cutting, because they came before cabinet sessions, and they achieved their result. The federal budget dropped.

The level of attention Coolidge paid to fiscal questions even became the butt of jokes. In other words, he came off as cheap. This did not bother Coolidge. Indeed, sometimes he played on his own stereotype. The White House received a gift of pet lion cubs from South Africa, for example. They were twins but did not receive the usual animal names: Rex, or Spot, for example. Instead the White House named the lions "Budget Bureau" and "Tax Reduction" and kept them an even weight. The point was clear: without budget cuts, no tax cut.

By the winter of 1925-1926, Coolidge and Mellon smelled victory in their tax campaign: they were close to gaining congressional support for lowering the top tax rates even further, and getting agreement that the very top rate, the so-called top marginal rate, would be 25 percent. This was Coolidge's and Mellon's final contest, and they waged it well, scarcely leaving their desks. Around the same period, however, the health of Coolidge's father began to fail. Coolidge hoped to make it up to Vermont. As soon as the tax bill passed, however, other matters pressed. By the time Coolidge did reach Plymouth, the men were already clearing the snow-covered path to the cemetery for his father's grave. It was a tough blow, and, as Coolidge later wrote, reminded him that "it costs a great deal to be president." Still, after the funeral, Coolidge was back in Washington, cutting some more.

By 1928 Coolidge could report what Harding had only hoped to: one-third of the national debt had been paid off. The tax data vindicated both Mellon and Coolidge on nearly every point, even the point about growing tax revenues. The US Treasury's official report, the Statistics of Income, showed that income tax revenues increased from $19.6 billion in the year the Mellon tax experiment commenced, to $25.7 billion in 1924, and, though dropping slowly, never went below $20 billion and, by 1928, returned to $25.2 billion. The rate cuts had permitted more economic activity.[63] The rates had not caused the wealthy to pay a smaller share of taxes, now they in fact paid a larger share. Mellon had predicted money would move from municipal bonds into the general economy when the bonds became less attractive. That appeared to have happened. In 1928 earners over $100,000 paid more than half the personal income taxes, whereas in 1920 they had paid just over 30 percent.[64] Coolidge had said in 1925 that "the chief business of the American people is business."[65] But he had also said, in the same speech, that "the chief ideal of the American people is idealism." Many Americans were coming to believe the two went together as well. The average family also fared better, getting a car, electricity, and new appliances. Birth rates rose in the 1920s, and infant mortality dropped. Death from infection of the sort that had taken Calvin also dropped with new hygiene measures. Coolidge's silence and emphasis on saving seem unattractive to our modern culture with its own emphasis on compassion. But what seemed evident to most in the 1920s was a reality: the grieving Scrooge, Coolidge, had begot a period of plenty.

Coolidge's final great policy move also reflects the determination of a man who believed he, and the country, had seen too much death. Whatever he might do to reduce the chances of another great war, he would do. Woodrow Wilson had failed to win ratification of the League of Nations. The World Court, which Coolidge did favor, did not win approval in the Senate. So, late in the game, in partnership with his Secretary of State Frank Kellogg, Coolidge tried again. An astute politician, Coolidge understood that another kind of pact, one to outlaw war, stood a better chance of passage. Such a pact was favored both by progressives and many Europeans, especially the French leader, Aristide Briand. Coolidge, an attorney, also understood that such a law could not prevent war: such a pact could be a "swordless sheath," as one critic put it. Nonetheless the symbolic value seemed important. Coolidge's own default mode in any case, dating back to the days of the Boston strike and his vice presidential campaign, was to turn to "the reign of law," or "law and order." In his second term the young regent of Ethiopia sent the president a gem-studded gold shield as a bid for favor. In reply Coolidge sent back not another weapon but a gift that reflected his own approach to international relations: a leather-bound copy of *Moore's International Law Digest*.[66]

Coolidge backed up Kellogg first in the arduous task of collecting foreign governments' assent to the treaty.[67] With his boss supporting him, Kellogg had by summer assembled an astonishing sixty-two signatures.[68] Coolidge, risking humiliation, campaigned for the treaty, arguing that it represented "a new and important barrier, reasonable and honorable" to war. The agreement represented, he said, "a revolutionary policy among nations. If promulgated, he said, the Pact's provisions "will prove one of the greatest blessings ever bestowed on humanity."[69]

That autumn and early winter of 1928, Coolidge and Kellogg undertook the yet tougher task of gaining the support of the US Senate, the same Senate that had rejected Wilson's League of Nations and, more recently, the concept of a World Court. By January of 1929, only months before he left office, Coolidge and Kellogg prevailed. The vote for Kellogg-Briand went eighty-five to one, with only John Blaine of Wisconsin going against. In other words, Coolidge had succeeded, albeit in a more modest way, where other presidents had failed. He had stewarded a peace treaty.

That family made Coolidge's perseverance possible is again clear. Grace, as much as Coolidge, suffered at her son's death. But her religious faith lifted her and then Coolidge as well. For by now he was "church-y" as the Lindbergh anecdote suggests: even in South Dakota at the summer White House, the Coolidges could be seen on Sunday at Congregationalist churches. Together, the pair made all the decisions of the bereavement, determining that, for example, Grace would not wear black but rather white for the period. Coolidge's father John did not like to come to Washington but had done so without hesitation, traveling down in the summer of 1924 to comfort his son. After the presidency, Coolidge and his wife came together again. Coolidge even urged Grace to write her own memoirs.

As bitter as Coolidge was over the loss of Calvin, he also found consolation in the community of mourners. Not only Plymouth, but all towns in New England had their winter hearse: death was simply known to them. Today the parent who has lost a child or a spouse is rare but in Coolidge's time one was an exception if one had not lost someone. Among Coolidge's professional peers, this was also the case. The Coolidges were friendly with General John Pershing, and knew well the horrible story: Pershing's wife and three daughters had perished in a fire at the Presidio in San Francisco. Mrs. Coolidge discussed this with the general early on, shortly after Coolidge became vice president.[70] In those very days in 1921 when the Coolidges had gotten to know vice president and Mrs. Marshall, tragedy struck their family, whose adopted son Morrison died. John W. Davis, Coolidge's opponent in 1924, had lost his wife Julia young. Coolidge's running mate, Charles Dawes, had of course lost his son.[71] When Edward Hall, a father who had also lost a son, asked Coolidge for his signature, Coolidge wrote: "In recollection of his son and my son, who had the privilege by God to be boys through eternity."[72]

And, of course, in the background there hung those presidents before him who had lost their own children, including Lincoln. Late in his administration, after the death of both his son and father, the frugal Coolidge finally permitted a federal purchase that some might deem extravagant: he signed off on the $50,000 acquisition of the Oldroyd Collection, a great assemblage of Lincoln curios including the walnut cradle in which Mary and Abe had rocked their sons.[73] This small cost the federal government could now afford.

Why then do we not know of Coolidge's drive and the record of his second term? The evidence suggests two reasons. The first involves presidential style. In modern times, indeed since the 1930s, both parties have favored not only compassionate but active presidents who drive policy. Coolidge was not, as his early biographer, Claude Fuess, noted, "a great constructive president."[74] He preferred to work in the shadows, not because he was sly or underhanded, but because he deemed the office more important than the man. Coolidge's intense commitment to the principle of delegation has therefore often been interpreted by others as lassitude, as per the hostile "how could they tell?" line of Dorothy Parker.

A second reason for misunderstanding Coolidge is our general interpretation of history. The Progressive movement of Theodore Roosevelt and Woodrow Wilson that Coolidge sought to stave off did prevail in the presidency of Herbert Hoover, a different kind of Republican, and later, of course, in the presidency of Franklin Roosevelt. Standard postwar texts generally favor progressive ideas: the action-packed New Deal earns positive description as "progress." Coolidge's economic achievements, which represent the antithesis of action, therefore receive scant appreciation. The tax cuts, or the budget cuts, are either ignored or treated as suspicious, perhaps even as poor policy causing the stock market crash and Great Depression that followed. By the same token Coolidge's failings, and they existed, are amplified in modern texts. Tariffs contributed to the severity of the Great Depression. The tariffs signed by Warren Harding and Herbert Hoover did damage the economy and, as commentators legitimately point out, were not reversed by Coolidge. Not only Beatty but also before him Arthur Schlesinger and William Leuchtenburg have suggested Coolidge is to blame for the 1929 market crash or more. Schlesinger treats Coolidge's unwillingness to intervene as incompetence.[75] Leuchtenberg treats Coolidge's passivity as apocalyptic: "The administration took the narrow interest of business groups to be the national interest and the result was catastrophe."[76] Yet some of us have found evidence for a different argument: Coolidge's pro-business attitude did not cause the Great Depression. It was government intervention, first by President Herbert Hoover and Congress, and then by President Roosevelt and Congress, that prolonged the Depression and made it "great."[77] Yet in the 1920s, many Americans, including Democrats, could not imagine that the president would be called to manage the stock market: at that time the Securities and Exchange Commission did not yet exist.

And to debate this is to force too much of the 1930s into the 1920s. The most accurate way to analyze Coolidge is to judge him in the context of his time. Looking at the 1920s, we can see that what Coolidge said of Lincoln holds also for Coolidge himself: "He did not stop part way."

NOTES

1. "Simple Service for Calvin, Jr.," *Cleveland Plain Dealer*, July 10, 1924, p. 2.
2. 'Amity Shlaes, *Coolidge* (New York: HarperCollins, 2013), 263.
3. Robert Gilbert, *The Tormented President: Calvin Coolidge, Death and Clinical Depression* (Westport, CT: Prager, 2003), 213.
4. Ibid., 222.
5. Ibid., 220.
6. Donald McCoy, *Calvin Coolidge: The Quiet President*, (Lawrence, KS: University Press of Kansas, 1968), , 251.
7. Gilbert, 3.
8. Jack Beatty, "President Coolidge's Burden: Review of Robert Gilbert's "The Tormented President," Atlantic online," December 2003. https://www.theatlantic.com/past/docs/unbound/polipro/pp2003-12-31.htm
9. Calvin Coolidge, *The Autobiography of Calvin Coolidge* (New York: Cosmopolitan Books, 1929), 59.
10. "Harding in Person Asks Senate for Delay in Bonus Bill: President Performs 'Thankless Task' Made Imperative by National Finances," *Philadelphia Inquirer*, July 13, 1921, 1.
11. Coolidge, Telephone Remarks to the Federation of Jewish Philanthropic Societies of New York, October 26, 1924.
12. DeForest Phonofilms. 1927. Phonofilm Phonofilm video: https://www.youtube.com/watch?v=5puwTrLRhmw
13. Coolidge, *Autobiography*, 13.
14. Hendrik V. Booraem, *The Provincial* (Lewisburg, PA: Bucknell University Press, 2004), 97.
15. Harold Nicholson, *Dwight Morrow* (New York, Harcourt Brace, 1935), 34.
16. Edward Connery Lathem, ed., *Your Son, Calvin Coolidge*, (Montpelier, VT Historical Society, 1968), 61.
17. Lathem, 56.
18. Booraem, 170.
19. Calvin Coolidge, *The Place of Lincoln*, Speech at Springfield, Illinois, February 12, 1922.
20. Gilbert, 40.
21. Lathem, 15.
22. Shlaes, 116.
23. Coolidge, *Autobiography*, 95.
24. Gilbert, 55.
25. "Coolidge Kills Stock Tax Bill," *Boston Journal*, July 2 1914, 6.

26. Coolidge, "Have Faith in Massachusetts."
27. Hugh Rockoff, "Until It's Over, Over There: The U.S. Economy in World War I," National Bureau of Research Working Paper 10580, June 2004.
28. *Addresses and Messages to the General Court, Official Addresses, Proclamations and State Papers* (Boston: 1920), 36.
29. Francis Russell, *A City in Terror, 1919: The Boston Police Strike* (New York: Viking Press, 1975). See also *Fourteenth Annual Report of the Police Commissioner City of Boston, Year Ending November 30, 1919* (Boston: Wright & Potter Printing Co., 1920).
30. Gilbert, 89.
31. Ibid.
32. Shlaes, 168.
33. Shlaes, 191.
34. Carl Schurz, *Lincoln* (Boston: Houghton Mifflin, 1920), iv.
35. Hugh Rockoff, U.S. *Economy in World War I*, Economic History Association, eh.net. See also Hugh Rockoff, *America's Economic Way of War: War and the U.S. Economy from the Spanish American War to the Persian Gulf War* (Cambridge: Cambridge University Press, 2012).
36. Ibid. The historical tax rates, "normal tax" and "supertax" are all also charted at "Taxfoundation.org," and United States Bureau of the Census, (1975), *Historical Statistics of the United States: Colonial Times to 1970*, Volume 3, p. 1095.
37. "Strike by Capital Predicted by Bache," *New York Times*, June 30, 1920.
38. "Give Coolidge Formal Notice," *Idaho Statesman*, July 27, 1920, 1.
39. "Harding Declares Country is Adrift: Senator Tells Brooklyn Meeting that Natyiona Suffers from Too Much Regulation; Rail Control A Blunder," *New York Times*, Feb. 11, 1920, 11.
40. Albro Martin, *Railroads Triumphant, The Growth, Rejection and Rebirth of a Vital American Force* (New York: Oxford University Press, 1992), 360.
41. Robert Murray, *The Harding Era* (Minneapolis: University of Minnesota Press, 1969), 171.
42. For federal debt levels, see http://www.treasurydirect.gov/govt/reports/pd/histdebt/histdebt_histo3.htm, Accessed June 1, 2015. For general discussion of the debt level, see Gary Walton and Hugh Rockoff, *History of the American Economy*, (Mason, OH: Cengage, 2012).
43. "Harding Opposes New Bond Issues: Says Giving Bonds to Former Soldiers would be 'The worst thing possible," *Harrisburg Patriot*, March 12, 1920, 10. See also Paul Dickson and Thomas B. Allen, *The Bonus Army: An American Epic* (New York: Walker and Company, 2004), 37.
44. "Harding and Coolidge, The American Economist," *American Protective Tariff League*, Vol. 66, Aug. 6, 1920, 44.
45. "Convention Wanders from Crag to Crag," *Seattle Daily Times*, July 15, 1920, 15.
46. Towner Blackstock, "Phi Gamma Delta: The First Seventy Five Years," online archive of the fraternity, www.phigam.org/early
47. Robert Sobel, *Coolidge: An American Enigma* (Washington, DC: Regnery, 2012), 188.

48. Shlaes, 212.
49. Margaret Jane Fischer, *Calvin Coolidge, Jr.* (Plymouth, VT: Calvin Coolidge Memorial Foundation, 1981), 16.
50. Shlaes, 245.
51. David Cannadine, *Mellon: An American Life* (New York: Knopf, 2006), 213.
52. Gilbert, *The Tormented President*, 124.
53. Ibid., 156.
54. Bates, Leonard, *Senator Thomas J. Walsh of Montana* (Champaign: University of Illinois Press, 1999), 245.
55. "The President's Son," *New York Times*, July 9, 1924, 18.
56. National Park Service history of the national Christmas tree, www.nps.gov.
57. "Coolidge Talks to Phonofilms," *Boston Herald*, August 24, 1924.
58. Phonofilm video is at: https://www.youtube.com/watch?v=5puwTrLRhmw
59. Cannadine, *Mellon: An American Life*, 313.
60. Coolidge Telephone Remarks to the Federation of Jewish Philanthropic Societies of New York City, October 26, 1924.
61. Data on union membership and unemployment, as well as other factors in the 1920s are summarized neatly in Gene Smiley, "The U.S. Economy in the 1920s," Gene Smiley, Economic History Association, http://eh.net/encyclopedia/the-u-s-economy-in-the-1920s/, accessed June 1, 2015.
62. Coolidge Papers, Library of Congress, Diary of the President, White House. Appointments Books of the President, 1923–1929.
63. Gene Smiley and Richard H. Keehn, "Federal Personal Income Tax in the 1920s," *The Journal of Economic History*, 55(2), June 1995, 295.
64. Ibid. See also http://www.irs.gov/pub/irs-soi/28soirepar.pdf, accessed June 1, 2015.
65. *Address to the American Society of Newspaper Editors*, Washington, DC, January 17, 1925.
66. Shlaes, 416.
67. Robert Ferrell, *Peace in Their Time: The Origins of the Kellogg-Briand Pact* (New Haven, CT: Yale University Press, 1952).
68. John Earl Haynes, ed., *Calvin Coolidge and the Coolidge Era: Essays on the History of the 1920s* (Washington, DC: Library of Congress, 1998), 292.
69. "Pact to Outlaw War Lauded by Coolidge: The President's Speech," *Omaha World Herald*, August 15, 1928, 6.
70. Lewis L. Gould, *American First Ladies: Their Lives and Their Legacy* (New York: Routledge, 2014), 262.
71. "Banker C.G. Dawes's Son is Drowned," *Daily Register Gazette*, Rockford, Il., Sept. 6, 1912.
72. Ishbel Ross, *Grace Coolidge and her Era* (New York: Dodd, Mead and Company, 1962), 276.

73. "Purchase By U.S. of Oldroyd Collection Now Up to Coolidge," *Daily Illinois State Journal*, May 3, 1926, 20; "U.S. to Buy Lincoln Relics for $50,000," *Illinois State Journal*, July 4, 1926, 32.
74. Claude Fuess, *Calvin Coolidge* (Hamden, CT: Archon Books, 1965), 499.
75. Arthur M. Schlesinger, *The Crisis of the Old Older Order, 1919–1933* (New York: Houghton Mifflin, 1957), 70.
76. David Greenberg, *Calvin Coolidge* (New York, Times Books, 2006), 147.
77. This is the thesis of the author's own book, *The Forgotten Man*, but also discussed in the work of many others, including Lee Ohanian and Harold Cole, "New Deal Policies and the Persistence of the Great Depression: A General Equilibrium Analysis," *Journal of Political Economy*, 112(4), August 2004, 770–816.

President Franklin D. Roosevelt flanked by British Prime Minister Winston Churchill and Soviet Premier Joseph Stalin during their historic meeting at Yalta, February 4 to 11, 1945, near the end of World War II and near the end of Roosevelt's life. [Courtesy Franklin D. Roosevelt Presidential Library and Museum.]

7

The Splendid Deception of "Doctor" Roosevelt

FRANK COSTIGLIOLA

To some degree, paralysis afflicts every president of the United States. His or her hands are tied by the limited powers of the office and the demands of securing both reelection and a legacy.[1] Even the triumph of a second electoral victory can hobble a president's power so that he or she is reduced to a "lame duck." Franklin D. Roosevelt, however, actually aspired to having Americans see him as lame—rather than as paralyzed. The polio that he contracted in 1921 at age thirty-nine had left him with almost no functioning leg muscles. In response, Roosevelt, his aides, and sympathetic reporters practiced a "splendid deception" to make it appear that he could walk despite his handicap.[2]

Roosevelt was unique in another way as well. For most afflicted presidents, their disabilities and illnesses weaken and often impose grave limitations on their leadership; but in the remarkable case of FDR, his paralysis rendered him a more empathetic, effective leader and contributed to his historic greatness. As Americans struggled with their own crises in the Great Depression and in World War II, many found Roosevelt's fortitude inspiring and reassuring. Here was a leader who understood. He had defied his misfortune and had triumphed just as they had to do in their own lives. In his inaugural address on March 4, 1933, he suggested that the American people, through no fault of their own, had been struck by an economic paralysis: "The means of exchange are frozen in the currents of trade; the withered leaves of industrial enterprise lie on every side; farmers find no markets for their produce; the savings of many years in thousands of families are gone."[3]

Roosevelt aimed to combat that broad national paralysis with the New Deal. Over the next four years the Works Progress Administration and similar jobs programs cut the nation's 25 percent unemployment in half. By 1940–41, workers in these projects had constructed literally tens of thousands of bridges and public buildings (including schools, hospitals, courthouses, and airports), nearly 500,000 miles of roadways, and a network of dams and improved harbors—all of which exerted a palpable salutary effect on virtually every area of the economy. Moreover, the New Deal stabilized the banking system by insuring individual savings accounts, protected workers' rights through the Wagner Act, and helped to keep older folks from falling on harder times through Social Security. Most important of all, both FDR and the New Deal fostered an atmosphere of hope and progress.

But Roosevelt's paralysis created a permanent crisis in his presidency. He and his aides knew, or at least believed, that his effectiveness would be diminished if the public realized the extent of his disability. Whenever and wherever the president traveled, there was the need to camouflage his inability to walk unaided and to head off the danger that he could injure his health and image by falling in public. This was a crisis that Roosevelt, his family, his staff, and the press managed magnificently. He and his aides practiced how to prevent a fall and, if necessary, hide it. The secret service oversaw the construction of ramps and perfected techniques for getting the president in and out of buildings. Like his stripped-down wheelchair, FDR's Ford convertible with hand controls, his personalized train, and his airplane with an elevator enabled him to move about easily despite his nearly useless legs. In sum, the personal crisis of Roosevelt's paralysis failed to cripple his presidency.

Instead, the ordeal of polio spurred FDR to develop the personality, empathy, charisma, and techniques of leadership that would make him the most talented and successful president of twentieth-century America. The cruel lesson of the paralysis was that, despite his privileged upbringing as a Hudson River aristocrat, he remained fallible; things could go terribly wrong, and he had to make the best of bad situations. A corollary instruction was that appearances and emotions could prove as important as substance and reasoning. In winning six straight electoral victories and in carrying out his executive duties as governor and president, Roosevelt had to sustain a "splendid deception." He had to tamp down the public's primordial fear of the lame and the sick while spurring confidence in his ability, as a self-styled physician, to heal the nation, as he supposedly cured his paralysis. What he learned from his struggle with polio would prove invaluable in the White House. In the aftermath of the closing of the banks in 1933 and the attack on Pearl Harbor in 1941, FDR's calm, confident, and determined leadership inspired Americans to mobilize their strength amidst fears that the Depression would never end and that the Axis would prove unbeatable.

As an executive, FDR operated as an empathetic yet no-nonsense healer, a practical-minded solver of problems willing to entertain fresh ideas. Calling himself "Dr. Roosevelt," he had pioneered physical rehabilitation for polio at a center he established at Warm Springs, Georgia, in the 1920s. There he honed leadership skills he would later deploy as president. In 1943 he explained that he had prescribed the New Deal in the 1930s because "there was an awfully sick patient called the United States of America . . . . and they sent for the doctor." And then at Pearl Harbor, the "patient" suffered "a pretty bad smash up." "Old Doctor New Deal" enlisted his partner, "Dr. Win-the-War," and "the result is that the patient is back on his feet." In a reference reflecting his own struggle, FDR described the comeback after Pearl Harbor as the patient "giv[ing] up his crutches."[4]

In tackling and, to an impressive degree, mastering his challenges as president, Roosevelt was unfortunately strengthened in his conceit that he was a man of destiny. Even as his health deteriorated in 1944–45, he continued to believe that he would survive a fourth term and lead the United States and its major allies—Britain, the Soviet Union, and China—into a collaborative postwar order that would secure the peace. Assuming that

God would surely allow him to finish this work, FDR paid insufficient attention to whom the Democratic convention chose as his vice president for the 1944 election. Compounding this error, he neglected to inform Vice President Harry S. Truman of his ideas about how to navigate the difficult transition from war to peace. With this last failure, FDR's ebullient confidence devolved into dangerous hubris.

Yet this error was still decades away when Roosevelt first entered politics as a New York State senator in 1910. He dazzled many with his charismatic good looks and his seemingly boundless energy. Frances Perkins, who would serve as labor secretary during FDR's presidency, was perhaps speaking also for herself when she recalled how presidential kingmaker Louis M. Howe had first been drawn to the young Roosevelt: "Louis really fell in love with him because he was so beautiful. His first view of Franklin Roosevelt was of a beautiful, strong, vigorous Greek god-king." An avid sailor, hiker, and sportsman, Roosevelt in his pre-polio years epitomized physical mobility. At the 1920 Democratic national convention, he "was always rising," Perkins would later remember. "He was always having something to say." At one point when the convention chairman refused to recognize his waving hand, Roosevelt, sitting well back from the front, "put his hands on the back of the chair in front of him and he vaulted—a regular gymnasium vault—over at least four or five rows of chairs." He then scrambled onto the platform. Such athletic self-propulsion helped secure the vice presidential nomination for the ambitious thirty-eight year-old.[5]

FDR's snaring of that plum fit his plan to follow the path into the White House blazed by his fifth cousin, Theodore Roosevelt. The younger man had already served in the New York State legislature; he had married TR's favorite niece, Eleanor Roosevelt; and, after Woodrow Wilson appointed him Assistant Secretary of the Navy, he had helped prepare for World War I. Although the Democrats lost the 1920 election badly, Roosevelt had won friends and recognition as he campaigned vigorously across the nation. Reflecting this easy rise to the top, plus his good looks and old-money background, Roosevelt before the onset of polio remained a self-centered, shallow aristocrat cosseted from the harsher aspects of life.

That privileged existence ended after he contracted infantile paralysis. In the early twentieth-century polio loomed as a menace that could inflict mental and moral as well as physical disability. A "cripple," warned a leading medical textbook, was often "destestable in character," a flawed being who could descend easily into "the mendicant and criminal classes."[6] FDR's agony was aggravated when caregivers, following the doctors' mistaken diagnosis, kneaded his withering muscles with deep massage. The treatment felt like torture and aggravated the paralysis. "I don't know what is the matter with me, Louis, I just don't know," Roosevelt moaned to his friend.[7] Further torment ensued when shriveling muscles pulled his legs backward, tugging his heels up toward his hips. Doctors arrested the deformity by placing his legs in plaster casts and then, day after painful day, hammering ever wider wedges in the casts behind his knees so as to force his legs to straighten. While resolving never to complain, he could snap. "One night he was out of his head" with despair, Eleanor acknowledged years later.[8] FDR and his family and supporters mobilized not only against the disease and its aftereffects but also against any public perception that he was paralyzed. When they could no longer put off announcing to the press the diagnosis of polio, the Roosevelts made sure that the newspaper story included the line: "He will definitely not be crippled."[9] But he was precisely that. An observer listed only some of the joys that were stolen from him by the disease. Never again could the former outdoorsman "take a hike, kick a football, dance, climb a fence, skate, or play with his toes in the sand."[10]

Nevetheless, Roosevelt *had* to walk in order to reach the presidency. In a sense, the crisis of his presidency began long before his election. If he was going to persuade skeptics that he was not a "cripple," that he was physically fit to bear the burdens of the presidency, the parapalegic had to demonstrate that he could indeed move about without a wheelchair. Roosevelt had to devise, somehow, a technique for advancing across the stage of an arena to the podium and then standing erect while he spoke. If the gaping thousands should see him fall, his credibility and probably his career would be shattered. (Indeed, Roosevelt as president would tumble in public on at least three occasions. Each time, aides immediately flocked around him to block the humiliating spectacle, and the press cooperated by not reporting the mishap.) Once at the lecturn, FDR's beaming smile, inflected voice, and knack for turning a phrase could work their magic. But first he had to get there. Devising a technique for walking, or appearing to walk, remained a focus of Roosevelt's rehabilitation from the stabilization of his disease in late 1921 to his run for the governorship of New York State in 1928.

Learning how to crawl came even before trying to walk. Roosevelt suffered a lifelong phobia of dying in a fire, a fear aggravated by his witnessing a cousin burn to death. Even while living in the White House, he would practice lowering himself to the floor and crawling backward, dragging his legs behind him to reach the stairs, and then inching himself downward. With only family and close friends present, he sometimes moved about by crawling backward, all the while bantering so as to divert attention from his otherwise humiliating mode of locomotion.

By the time of the 1924 Democratic convention in New York City, the chair-vaulter of 1920 had suffered through three years of painful therapy. Despite this effort, he could not stand without braces or walk without crutches. Delegates had heard that Roosevelt "had polio and he was dead, so far they knew."[11] His supporters had inveigled an invitation for him to nominate for president New York governor Al Smith. The speech offered an opportunity for political resurrection. The challenge lay in negotiating the fine line between displaying courage and evoking pity. Roosevelt devised for the event a way to "walk." He had his son, James, stand to his left so that the father could grasp the young man's arm while placing most of his weight on a crutch under his right arm. Roosevelt could jerk forward by pivoting his body alternately right and left with his shoulders. So as not to " 'scare everybody half to death,' " father and son joked and smiled as they moved forward. James later recalled that while his father's face was "beaming . . . his fingers dug into my arm like pincers—I doubt that he knew how hard he was gripping me. His face was covered with perspiration." The final fifteen feet to the podium Roosevelt shuffled forward alone, using two crutches.[12]

Whether he was "fit" for high office remained open to interpretation because the evidence was so ambiguous and the emotions so wrenching.

As the once-spry forty-two-year-old labored his way toward the podium, "There was a hush and everybody was holding their breath," Perkins later recounted. "The old-line politicians remembered him as a very vigorous young man at the previous convention. Here was this terribly crippled person . . . it was a surprise . . . to see that his voice was strong and true and vigorous." Sitting close to the stage, she could see that the hand on the paper of his address "was literally shaking, because of the extreme pain and tenseness with which he held himself up to make that speech." But from a distance, "he looked well. . . . The man in the street just assumed, 'Isn't that wonderful. This fine fellow we thought dead still lives.'"[13]

If potential supporters were to sustain such faith, Roosevelt and his aides had to camouflage his disability. Perkins realized that after his convention speech—and the magic of his voice—had wound down, the man with the paralyzed legs would be stuck up on that stage. In front of gawking thousands he would have to make an awkward, painful shift: from leaning on the podium to grasping his crutches and hobbling away on them. As the applause was fading, Perkins and another woman rushed up to the stage to stand "in front of him so he didn't show." She later explained, "I realized somebody must do it. I saw all these fat slob politicians—men—around and I knew they wouldn't think of it." At subsequent public events supporters perfected "the trick of shielding him. Women could shield him better than men because we had skirts and coats. You could sort of lift your hand to fix your hat and that would make the coat hang like a large screen."[14] The concerted effort succeeded. The audience erupted in seventy-five minutes of applause, a record for Madison Square Garden.

The dual spectacles of the laborious "walk" and the inspiring talk cut both ways. On the one hand, Roosevelt beguiled many delegates who, in the deadlocked national convention of 1924, eyed him as an attractive dark-horse candidate for president. Yet the assumption persisted that a man burdened by polio simply could not take on the responsibilities of the White House. The *Los Angeles Times* concluded, "He is hopelessly an invalid, his legs paralyzed."[15] That description did not, however, factor in the force of charisma. Tom Pendergast, the Kansas City political boss who would later launch the career of Harry Truman, remarked: "You know, I am seldom carried away . . . but I want to tell you that had Mr. Roosevelt . . . been physically able to withstand the campaign, he would have been named by acclamation. . . . He has the most magnetic personality of any individual I have ever met."[16]

Nevertheless, as Roosevelt realized, no personality, however magnetic, could blot out perceptions of disability. Unless he lost the crutches, he could not win the presidency. Between the 1924 and 1928 elections, FDR redoubled efforts to restore physical capability to himself as well as to the increasing number of other polios attracted to Warm Springs by publicity about the healing potential of the naturally heated, mineral-rich waters. Ignoring the skepticism of his wife and mother, FDR had used much of his personal fortune to buy a falling-down hotel in Warm Springs and considerable acreage surrounding it. Meanwhile, Howe and other supporters helped keep him in the public eye. From 1921 to 1928, his name appeared in over two hundred front-page stories in the *New York Times*.

Roosevelt continued to spend freely and invest in the current and future needs of Warm Springs while he tried different strategies for rebuilding wasted muscles and compensating for those forever gone. The therapist-in-chief mastered the physiology of muscles and prescribed exercises and daily regimens, many of which he had himself developed. He inspired, cajoled, and manipulated others to do what he wanted. While working with other therapists, he remained in charge. He cultivated a network of confidants with himself at the center and apprised himself of the small details as well as the big picture.

Parallels abounded also in the ways he pursued his missions at Warm Springs and in the White House. Roosevelt focused not only on the physical but also on the social and emotional needs of the people looking to him for leadership and succor. Though dedicated to hard work at Warm Springs, he also encouraged a happy atmosphere with frequent parties, picnics, and poker games. Years later, a former resident reminisced with Toi Bachelder, a Warm Springs polio sufferer who had gone on to become a White House secretary: "Oh Toi, "*wasn't it fun!*"[17] As a historian of Warm Springs notes, "There was flirting, falling in love, sexual hanky-panky—and much gossip about it all."[18] The White House would similarly ring with chatter about the flirtations of the president, his family and aides, and visiting actresses and celebrities.

Despite the gaiety at Warm Springs, FDR remained focused on rehabilitation and in particular on walking. For all his hard work, he made little progress in actually recovering the muscle function of his lower body. What he did develop was a technique for utilizing his robust upper torso and the strength of an aide to make it appear that he was walking. The inspiration for this approach came to Roosevelt in 1928, when adroit politicking had again secured a chance to nominate Al Smith at the Democratic national convention. Although the 1924 audience had cheered his courage in stumping across the stage in crutches, crutches remained a symbol of disability that evoked pity and even revulsion.

Roosevelt knew that his political future would be quashed unless he could display evidence of dramatic progress. He wanted to show voters that he was a "cured cripple."[19] With his legs in braces, he had Elliott, one of his husky sons, stand on his left with the boy's right arm flexed at a ninety-degree angle. While leaning his arm heavily, though casually, on Elliott's arm, Roosevelt grasped in his right hand a cane "with his index finger pressed firmly straight down along the line of the cane." The finger would transfer much of his weight to the walking stick. In this manner he could "walk" by "hitching up first one leg with the aid of the muscles along the side of his trunk, then placing his weight upon that leg, then using the muscles along his other side, and hitching the other leg forward," and so on. Elliott had to match his stride, step by step. It looked awkward, but it also looked like walking. "Don't forget," a therapist reportedly warned Elliott, "if he loses his balance, he'll crash down like a tree."[20] At the 1928 Democratic convention, as in the White House, deception was essential. "Don't look at me, son," FDR reportedly admonished Elliott. "Keep your head up, smiling, watching the eyes of people. Keep them from noticing what we're doing."[21]

The walking technique enabled Roosevelt to make a hit at the convention. Upon reaching the podium, he beamed, his "head held high this time, braced legs spread wide apart to provide balance, one arm free now to wave and gesture."[22] His voice boomed. Will Durant, the journalist and writer of popular history, saw in this body the evidence of past torment and future promise. Here was "a figure tall and proud even in suffering; a face of classic profile; pale with years of struggle against paralysis; a frame nervous and yet self-controlled . . . most obviously a gentleman and a scholar. A man softened and cleansed and illumined with pain." An old friend had another reaction to Roosevelt's muscular upper torso: "Frank, you look like a gorilla!" The fighter Jack Dempsey remarked that FDR had the best developed set of shoulder muscles he had ever seen.[23] Nevertheless, fear and loathing of sickness, and especially of polio, persisted.[24] Al Smith, the party's standard bearer in 1928 whose personal feelings about Roosevelt would turn poisonous in future years, assured a friend that the younger man would never become a rival; indeed "he won't live a year."[25] FDR not only survived; he would be reelected governor by a huge margin in 1930 and shove Smith aside to secure the Democratic nomination for president in 1932.

In his 1928 campaign for governor, Roosevelt combated doubts about his health with relentless campaigning. He drew attention to his body's ability to endure the rigors of his crisscrossing the state. FDR's strategy, scholars have noted, was "not to deny his disability but to modify its appearance, to argue its temporary nature, and to dialectically deflect the most severe accusations with sarcasm and irony—and with his own apparently healthy body."[26] "It seems to me that I am pretty husky," the candidate boasted to a crowd.[27] By highlighting his infectious charm, good looks, and upper body strength, Roosevelt obscured the paralysis in his legs. This was the strategy he would use in besting the crisis of his presidency.

* * *

By 1932, the fourth year of the Great Depression, the United States itself was suffering economic and political paralysis. Many commentators used the metaphor of bodily sickness in referring to the hard times. In this discursive context, "Doctor" Roosevelt enjoyed an advantage over his opponent, Herbert Hoover. Like the economy, FDR had to face paralysis. And he knew, or so he claimed, what it required to regain full health.

After receiving news of his nomination for president, Roosevelt stunned the nation by announcing that he would flout the tradition of waiting at home to receive formal notification. Instead he would fly from Albany to the convention in Chicago to accept the nomination in person and so jumpstart his election campaign. Elliott Roosevelt, who was on that flight, later recalled that his father "wanted to demonstrate by this gesture that he was a man of vigorous action, not the semi-invalid depicted without fail by his enemies in both parties."[28] (FDR no doubt knew about the dramatic air campaign waged by a future foe, Adolf Hitler, who had recently barnstormed around Germany in seeking the presidency.)[29]

Flying so far was risky. Knute Rockne, the beloved football coach, had recently died in a plane crash. Roosevelt had never flown before; indeed he would come to hate flying, and he would refuse to travel by airplane again until wartime conferences made it imperative. With his paralyzed legs unable to brace him, his body jerked helplessly as the plane pitched up and down. Flying also aggravated his chronic sinus troubles and his phobia about fire. He realized that if he did survive a plane crash, he would have to crawl away from the burning wreck. Planes of that era, with their underpowered engines and primitive navigation aids, remained dangerous—indeed passengers in 1932 were two hundred times more likely to die in a crash than were those flying in postwar decades. The plane was buffeted by winds "like a balloon," the pilot later reported.[30] After the eight-hour ordeal the candidate landed in Chicago.

The *New York Times* interpreted the journey as a symbol of the candidate's manner and message. His "appearance and address" embodied "something of the breeziness that went naturally with his flight through the air. The dash and vigor which he had shown by setting out for Chicago in an airplane also marked his speech."[31] A story in the Republican-leaning *Chicago Daily Tribune,* titled "The Nominee in Action," suggests that while Roosevelt's disability was apparent, so was his success at surmounting it. The reporter concluded that while "many may think of [Roosevelt] as a patient invalid, he goes strong." For a nation with an "invalid" economy, a leader who could "go strong" commanded emotional appeal.[32] Borrowing from what had worked so well in his campaigns for governor, Roosevelt displayed himself. His train would stop wherever there was a gathering. The candidate, leaning on a cane and on the arm of one of his sons, would "walk" to the rear railing, enabling the crowd to see his robust upper torso. As a reporter observed, "The whole idea of the Governor's managers is to let the people see him during the day and hear him at night over the radios while the vision of his large, handsome features and broad shoulders is still in their minds."[33]

Part of the reason Roosevelt's splendid deception succeeded is that so many wanted to believe that the paralysis would not prevent him from exercising national power. As a campaign staffer observed, "The women are also saying that he appeared in splendid physical condition and that he must be a remarkable man to have overcome his unfortunate physical disabilities in such a complete manner."[34] As president, FDR was both praised and pilloried, but he was almost never depicted as paralyzed. The ubiquitous political cartoons often pictured him walking, running, or jumping. Indeed, the hit film *Yankee Doodle Dandy* (1942) featured James Cagney playing a tap-dancing President Roosevelt.[35] Moreover, the president's handlers had the aid of the secret service in obscuring the disability. Husky secret service agents prohibited photographing the president as he was being carried into a building or a car.[36] Journalists, many of whom rooted for Roosevelt despite the Republican bias of their editors and publishers, would assist by "accidentally" knocking to the ground any cameras that violated the rule. One of the reasons FDR loved being president was that it simplified his getting around. The White House had wide corridors, ramps, elevators, and large bathrooms. Secret Service agents and other aides were available to wheel his chair or carry him to and from an automobile. Agents also built ramped entrances to the capitol and other buildings he frequented. Stages were modified so that he had to "walk" only short distances to the podium. Unable to prowl around Washington, FDR nurtured an unsurpassed network of friends and confidants. He encouraged key ambassadors to report directly to him. At the wartime summits, he shut out the state department and relied almost wholly on hand-picked advisers. That limitation proved unfortunate when some of his closest aides, such as Louie Howe, Harry Hopkins, and Missy LeHand took sick or died.

Roosevelt also compensated for his paralysis by driving—dangerously fast—his beloved Ford Phaeton equipped with hand controls. He criss-crossed the nation by train, traveling more than a half-million miles during his presidency. Lest rounding a curve throw him off balance, he limited the presidential train to thirty-five miles an hour. (The train speeded up while he slept.) Rail travel also enabled him to see, and be seen by, the American people as the train stopped at small towns and road crossings. As the train approached a station, he would put on his painful braces and "walk," leaning on the arm of a son, onto a specially constructed back platform of the train. There he would banter for a few minutes with the assembled crowd.

Despite the upturned-cigarette-holder exuberance for which FDR became famous, he often looked, and felt, worn out. These down periods hit not only in 1944–45 when he was combating heart disease and wartime pressures, but throughout his presidency. Even before he took office in 1933, an aide found him looking "worn and tired. His color was bad." In 1938 a parishioner encountering him in church "really was shocked when I saw his face—he looked almost ghastly." What FDR needed at such junctures was a week or more of rest and relaxation—time away from the cares of office when he could fish, arrange his stamps, play cards, and tell old stories. Some of his vacations proved a physical work out. He once landed a 237-pound shark after a two-hour fight.[37]

No amount of rest, however, could remove Roosevelt's susceptibility to a fall. As Mike Reilly, his bodyguard, put it, "No infant was ever as helpless as this 180 pound giant with useless legs."[38] In this pre-television era, the president was able to preserve the fiction that he had recovered almost totally from polio and that he had only minor problems in walking. Roosevelt's image as a mobile, robust, and vigorous leader buttressed the substance of his presidential power. He sustained that power through his exertions and his adaptability, and by enlisting the cooperation of others, including journalists, photographers—and, on some implicit level, the American people. At a time when most Americans were struggling to survive the Great Depression, having a president who had struggled against his own tribulations, and who remained a bit hampered by them, probably seemed reassuring.

FDR's combination of confident strength and embarrassing weakness was dramatically illustrated when, just moments before a highpoint of his presidency, he tumbled nearly to the ground. The near disaster and his brilliant recovery from it constitute a synecdoche of Roosevelt's presidency. FDR had mounted a stage to accept renomination at the 1936 Democratic national convention in Philadelphia. Developments were going his way. He had gotten the party platform he wanted. He had also pushed through a game-changing rules modification that would prove crucial in the 1940 convention. At his behest the Democratic Party abandoned its century-long tradition of requiring presidential nominees to secure the votes of two-thirds of the delegates. Still another reason to celebrate was his going into the election with a winning record. National income had doubled since "Dr. New Deal" began practicing in March 1933. Unemployment had fallen by half, while the stock market had soared 80 percent.[39] Despite setbacks from the Supreme Court and the still lagging economy, his program had revived hope. As the convention reached its climax on the evening of June 27, FDR prepared to deliver a triumphant acceptance speech. Over 100,000 supporters wedged into Franklin Field stadium, eager to see and hear their champion. Suddenly, trumpets blared and an excited call rang out: "The President is here!" Roosevelt's car drove up onto the rear of a huge platform.

As the band launched into "Hail to the Chief," klieg lights lit up the stage, and the curtain swooshed open to reveal a beaming FDR, his arm raised high. The crowd gasped, then exploded into a roar that sounded "like the surf breaking," a journalist recorded. Even the "police, who have been ordering everybody off chairs, now [got] on rails and chairs themselves."[40] Roosevelt, leaning heavily on the arm of James walked stiffly toward the podium, shaking hands and chatting as he went. As Democratic bigwigs surged forward, someone accidentally pushed James, who fell against his father. The brace supporting Roosevelt's right leg unsnapped, and he toppled over. Reilly, the bodyguard, dove down and caught the president just before he hit the ground. The pages of the speech scattered under the shoes of the milling crowd. Roosevelt's tallest aides immediately positioned themselves so as to block the still cheering thousands from seeing their leader's near helplessness.

FDR's celebratory mood dissolved into fear and anger. He was "badly shaken," Reilly later recalled.[41] "I was the damnedest, maddest white man . . . you ever saw," Roosevelt later said, admitting, "it was the most frightful five minutes of my life." As aides raised him to his feet, he barked: "Clean me up," and "Keep your feet off those damned sheets."[42] Once FDR recovered his presidential bearing and the pages of the speech, the circle of aides dispersed. With his arm again raised in greeting to the crowd and with a smile pasted on his face, the "Boss" stumped to the podium. There he faced a further problem: "When I put the speech on the stand, it was smudged and dirty, and the first half dozen pages were terribly mixed up," he later recounted. He took advantage of the vice president's address to smooth out and order the crumpled sheets.

It had been a close call. His collapsing body had put such tension on the braces that one had given way. That tension could also have broken his leg bone, weakened by fifteen years of paralysis. Roosevelt fell in public at least two others times during his presidency. After each mishap, he and his staff remained calm, adapted their practiced response to the particular layout of their location (in this case the stage) and drew on the help of close by supporters. The team also counted on moral suasion. If reporters and photographers learned what had happened, they kept the secret.

Evidence hints that the Roosevelt machine perhaps even co-opted a reporter from the enemy camp. In a front page story of the anti-Roosevelt *Chicago Daily Tribune*, journalist Philip Kinsley noted, without any further comment, that subsequent to the president's arrival there elapsed "several moments before the crowd" could catch more than the initial "glimpse of him." When again visible, the president displayed a "pale" face. Did Kinsley discern what had really happened? Did he then decide to give the president and his image a break? Despite the tough politics of this era, the press generally regarded private lives as off limits. Kinsley might also have been solicitous of presidential dignity, regardless of his feelings about the current president. Finally, many a reporter sympathized privately with FDR even while working for a Roosevelt-hating publisher.

As usual, FDR bounced back with verve. According to Raymond Clapper, a journalist who knew him well, the president's voice was "never more confident, never more commanding, never warmer in its sympathy" than it was that evening at Franklin Field.[43] The acceptance speech of course had been written well before the mishap; nevertheless, its tone and substance underscored Roosevelt's eagerness to tackle big challenges. Indeed, the address ranks as one of the most radical speeches ever given by a sitting US president. FDR began by recalling the national crisis on the eve of his inauguration in March 1933 and his pledge back then: "The only fear we have to fear is fear itself." In again reciting those words, FDR may have flashed back to his personal mishap only moments before and his long-term battle with paralysis. "We have fought fear," he now insisted, and "we have conquered fear."

He then launched an assault on the unequal distribution of wealth in the United States and on the excessive privileges of the rich. Picking up on Philadelphia's history as the birthplace of the 1776 revolt against the royal despotism of King George III, Roosevelt depicted wealthy enemies of the New Deal as "economic royalists," the "privileged princes" of the contemporary era, who were bent on creating "new dynasties" with their riches. Calling, at least rhetorically, for change more radical than mere reform, Roosevelt declared: "Our allegiance to American institutions requires the overthrow of this kind of power." The essence of American democracy was threatened by "this new industrial dictatorship." As Eleanor noted, Roosevelt's paralysis heightened his sympathy with others who suffered.

With similarly hard-hitting language, Roosevelt shifted his focus to overseas. He denounced the dictatorships in Nazi Germany and elsewhere. Though aware that most Americans opposed entering yet another foreign war, he dared an explicitly martial metaphor. "We are waging a great . . . war for the survival of democracy . . . for ourselves and for the world," Roosevelt insisted. He promised: "I am enlisted for the duration of [that] war." In what would become the most memorable line of the 1936 speech, he declared: "This generation of Americans has a rendezvous with destiny."[44]

These last words were drowned out by the roar of the adoring crowd. Reilly singled it out as "the greatest ovation I ever heard" in my ten years with Roosevelt.[45] It was to be expected that pro-Roosevelt observers would praise the speech. But there was evidently also something "over the top," something really unusual in both the delivery and the substance of the speech. We can surmise that for FDR, getting "badly shaken up" in the fall set his adrenaline flowing. Pumped up, the president, with an unknowable degree of intentionality, turned the personal crisis to political advantage. He poured his physical, psychic, and intellectual resources into making an extraordinarily intense connection with the 100,000 people in the stadium and with the additional millions listening on the radio. Clapper judged the performance "one of the most skillful political addresses of our time. It was more than a feat of showmanship. It was a work of art."[46] Also reaching for superlatives was Secretary of the Interior Harold Ickes, who declared it "the greatest political speech I have ever heard."[47] Once the applause died down, the orchestra struck up "Auld Lang Syne." Roosevelt began singing the melody. The orchestra played it again, and then thousands in the stadium joined in, "as old friends who had fought through the crisis together."[48] The president then returned to his limousine. With the paralysis of his legs effectively hidden, he stood erect in the car, waving to the cheering crowd as the vehicle took a victory lap around the stadium track.[49]

A master at tugging people's heartstrings, Roosevelt usually kept his own emotions under wraps. Arguably it was the feelings aroused by those frightening moments in the stadium that infused his speech with that discernible extra jolt of force. FDR was a master also at adapting to difficult unavoidable circumstances—whether it was trying to "walk" without the use of his leg muscles, run a vigorous campaign when he had to deceive the public about the extent of his paralysis, or combat the Depression and the dictators when he had only a limited understanding of economics himself—and he led a nation strongly adverse to fighting another world war.

* * *

Even before the Japanese attack on Pearl Harbor on December 7, 1941, brought America into World War II, Roosevelt realized that the United States needed powerful allies. He aimed to build an effective alliance linking imperial Britain, Soviet Russia, and democratic-capitalist America.

Not only did these three nations have divergent ideologies and institutions, but their respective leaders remained strangers to one another. Roosevelt and Prime Minister Winston S. Churchill believed that personal meetings could help bridge the gap. After the November-December 1943 Tehran summit of the Big Three, Soviet leader Joseph Stalin would agree. Long distance journeys, however, remained especially arduous for Roosevelt, whose paralysis made it flying particularly arduous. The war thus rendered FDR's paralysis a crisis of global import.

At the Atlantic Conference of August 1941, Roosevelt met with Churchill aboard US and British battleships anchored off the coast of Newfoundland. Despite an "extremely cold and violent wind" blowing across the deck of the battleship *Prince of Wales*, Churchill spent hours directing rehearsals for the joint religious service that was planned as the emotional centerpiece of the upcoming conference. The prime minister expected that FDR, because of his paralysis, would be compelled to stand in place as British officers filed past him.[50] Shortly before the Sunday service, Roosevelt sent word that he would walk, not just stand. He boarded the *Prince of Wales* "leaning on a stick and linking his [other] arm" with his son, Elliot. Churchill's aide observed: "It is a very great effort for the President to walk, and it took him a long time to get from the gangway to his chair." On the one hand, FDR was trying to obscure what was obvious: "His legs are evidently rather wasted and he has not much control over them."[51] On the other hand, he was demonstrating—as he had at the Democratic conventions—that he *could* walk. Roosevelt was defying the jibes of the dictators and upending the considerate though patronizing assumptions of Churchill; the president wanted his prospective ally to judge him, and the nation he led, as courageous and fit.

FDR tried to lure Stalin to a summit of their own. He believed that a meeting *a deux* would enable him to work his charm while offering the suspicious dictator assurance of a lasting entente. Roosevelt envisioned a postwar order run by the "Four Policeman"—the United States, Britain, Russia, and China—each patrolling its part of the world and collaborating to keep the peace. Stalin appreciated this implicit recognition of Soviet dominance in Eastern Europe. In May 1943, FDR sent an old friend to

Moscow to invite Stalin to a meeting, without Churchill, in either Alaska or Siberia. Stalin assured the emissary, "Your President is a great man. I will be very glad to meet with him." As to whether the conference would take place in Siberia, the Kremlin boss, flashing apparent empathy, said: "No. The President has difficulty in walking, as I understand. It is difficult for me, physically, to come by air, but I will be glad to meet him at Nome or Fairbanks, whichever he prefers. This will make it easier for him."[52] Within days, however, Stalin was probably cursing the very notion of a cozy meeting. He learned that Churchill for the third time since mid-1942 had convinced Roosevelt to postpone the second front desperately needed by the Soviets to relieve the pressure of the German invaders.

Roosevelt's meeting with Stalin did not take place until late November 1943 in Tehran, and then only in the company of Churchill. Nevertheless, the president still aimed for accord with the dictator. To avoid a transatlantic flight, FDR boarded the battleship *USS Iowa*. An escort vessel accidentally fired a live torpedo at the president's ship. As the captain ordered, "Right full rudder—all engines ahead full" and the ship swerved, Roosevelt flung out his arm to grab hold.[53] His powerful upper body could not have stabilized him so easily in an airplane. In Tehran Roosevelt learned that German agents were plotting assassination. Traveling the distance from the US legation could prove deadly. Stalin invited him into the Soviet embassy while he moved to a building nearby. Roosevelt later explained that accepting this hospitality "was a small thing to do to please them. "If we could woo them"—the phrase was suggestive of FDR's strategy—"in this way, perhaps it was the cheapest thing we could do." He added, "It was a matter of exhibiting my trust in them, my complete confidence in them. And it did please them. No question about it."[54]

One reason it pleased the Soviets was that they had bugged Roosevelt's quarters.[55] Just as FDR had tried to lure the Kremlin chief to Alaska, now Stalin was seeking closer relations—Kremlin style. He assigned agents to transcribe everything FDR said. Attitudes seemed important: Stalin demanded to know "how Roosevelt said something—even what his intonation was."[56] FDR apparently seized the chance to foster trust and intimacy. The transcriber got "the impression that sometimes Roosevelt quite simply said things [into the microphones] he couldn't say to Stalin officially. That he conveyed a whole lot of information to him which it was impossible to convey at a state level."[57]

The president welcomed the Soviet leader to his quarters. "With a most engaging grin on his face," Stalin ambled over to Roosevelt, who, sitting in his wheelchair, said, "I am glad to see you. I have tried for a long time to bring this about."[58] Stalin and his interpreter began stopping by his suite unannounced for chats. The dictator, who could lavish extraordinary courtesy on favorites—including some he later had executed—would ask Roosevelt, did he need anything? Was he comfortable? . . . all the while smiling and showing great deference for his guest." Stalin "showed genuine liking for Roosevelt," an aide would recall.[59]

Although Tehran outlined a rough schema for postwar cooperation, the meeting and its follow-up were limited by frailties of the body. After the flight into Tehran, Stalin appeared "exhausted and for that reason not in the best of humor."[60] Churchill arrived with a head cold. "He is not fit and not in the best of moods," observed his military adviser.[61] Though excited about meeting Stalin, FDR had dreaded going "to Tehran, which is full of disease" and lay across mountains requiring, after the *Iowa* docked, a high-altitude flight.[62] Earl Miller, a bodyguard and family friend, later wrote that the "Boss" "contracted an intestinal bug" and that "most of the Secret Service was ill most of the time while [in Tehran]—water, food or whatever."[63]

After returning to the States, FDR came down with influenza. In March 1944 he would be diagnosed with congestive heart failure. No longer confident that he was the only "doctor" needed in the White House, the president accepted the supervision of a navy cardiologist, Dr. Howard Bruenn. Heart disease alone did not account for all of FDR's ills. His intermittent slack jaw, blank stare, hand tremor, and forgetfulness probably arose from encephalopathy (reduced supply of oxygen to the brain) which resulted from heart and obstructive pulmonary disease and the phenobarbital he took.[64] Yet, despite these and other physical problems, Roosevelt remained mentally fit.

By February 1945, as the summit at Yalta approached, Roosevelt was torn between his presidential duty and the needs of his weakening body. "He doesn't relish this trip at all," his close friend, Margaret ("Daisy") Suckley, recorded, "Thinks it will be very wearing, & feels that he will have to be so much on the alert, in his conversations with Uncle Joe [Stalin] & W[inston] S. C[hurchill]."[65]

After weathering the strains of traveling to far-off Russian Crimea, Roosevelt, as usual, bounced back. A British official acknowledged that FDR "looks rather better."[66] Charles E. ("Chip") Bohlen, who interpreted for the president, remembered that whereas his "physical state was certainly not up to normal, his mental and psychological state was certainly not affected." He remained "mentally sharp" and "effective."[67] Valentin Berezhkov, one of Stalin's interpreters, later testified that "everybody who watched [FDR] said that in spite of his frail appearance, his mental potential was high." He emphasized that "those who say that Roosevelt did not quite grasp what was going on in Yalta are wrong."[68] Dr. Bruenn later recalled that at Yalta Roosevelt's "mental clarity was truly remarkable." His "recollection of detail" outshone "associates ten and twenty years younger than himself."[69]

Such testimony gives the lie to a subsequent fabrications, promoted in the 1950s by Republicans such as Senator Joseph McCarthy and others that Roosevelt, the supposed "sick man at Yalta," had naively and weakly given away Eastern Europe to Stalin. Despite his physical frailty at the conference, FDR remained mentally astute and effective. With the Red Army occupying most of Eastern Europe, that region simply was not Roosevelt's to give away. Acting on this reality, FDR tried to win Stalin to lasting postwar cooperation.[70]

Part of Roosevelt's strategy was paying homage to the prickly dictator with a dramatic gesture—traveling thousands of miles to meet on his doorstep. Sublimely self-confident, FDR had little compunction about demonstrating such respect, even at the cost of his own physical suffering, if he could secure his postwar aims. He bravely refused to let the crisis of his paralysis wreck chances for a lasting peace. A close observer later reflected that Stalin seemed to "realize that Roosevelt had shortened his life in order to come meet with him because he cared so much about the future of the world."[71] The dictator responded to Roosevelt's show of respect and regard. He arranged for the Americans to live in the conference headquarters, the fifty-room summer home of the czar, Livadia Palace, while he resided six miles away. Churchill, by contrast, was housed ten miles distant. A special shop had been set up to produce for the floors marble smooth enough for a wheelchair.

Stalin, abandoning his customary harshness, seemed genuinely to care for Roosevelt. After leaving the president's room, he reportedly stopped, turned to his aides, asking, "Why did nature have to punish him so? Is he any worse than other people?" The head of the secret police marveled "how full of consideration he is where Roosevelt is concerned, when, as a rule, he is dreadfully rude."[72] A presidential aide later recalled that Stalin "deferred to [Roosevelt] and his whole expression softened when he addressed the President directly."[73] Indeed, Churchill complained that on issue after issue, "Stalin made it plain at once that if this was the President's wish, he would accept it."[74] Years later, the dictator would remark, with apparent sadness that "President Roosevelt had a great sense of duty, but he did not save his strength. If he had, he would probably be alive today."[75] FDR's successor, Harry S. Truman, would never develop the personal/political ties with Stalin that FDR had so carefully cultivated.

Once Roosevelt was back home, Daisy rejoiced "that F[ranklin] looks so much better than anyone can expect—his color is good & his blood pressure is pretty good.[76] Walter Lippmann, who before the 1944 election had called FDR a tired old man, agreed that he had returned "manifestly" in "good health and much refreshed."[77] On 1 March, Dr. Bruenn recorded: "Patient has rested well. Cough has disappeared. No cardiac symptoms."[78] But wasn't FDR's death imminent?

Nearly all histories of Roosevelt's last year track an irresistible story line: Great Leader Dies on Eve of Triumph. Pervasive cultural memories—of Moses dying as he approached the Promised Land and of Abraham Lincoln being assassinated just after the Confederacy surrendered—add emotional resonance to this grand narrative. Accounts of Roosevelt's demise have clinched the sentimental script. The drama of the fallen war hero seduces us into underplaying the contingency of FDR's death weeks before V-E Day. He continued his strategy for cheating death—and for cheating those who calculated on his dying in office. Believing he was a man of destiny, he did not prepare any of his vice presidents. He may well have been deluding himself about his own mortality. But Roosevelt also could point to aides who had accomplished much after others had given them up for dead; moreover, his father survived a decade after his heart attack and died at seventy-two, and his mother thrived until the age of eighty-six.

After returning from Yalta, FDR focused on issue number one—overall cooperation with Moscow and sustaining the Grand Alliance into the postwar era. He resisted pressure from Churchill and others to break with Stalin.[79] He looked forward instead to another meeting of the Big Three—now institutionalized as the United Nations Security Council—in a cozy getaway, possibly the Azores. He personally authored the last telegram he sent Churchill before his death: "I would minimize the general Soviet problem as much as possible.... We must be firm, however, and our course thus far is correct."[80] Despite his failing energy, Roosevelt was working late into the night. By late March he looked "very badly," Bruenn recorded. "Color is poor (grey). Very tired."[81]

Even so, within days of arriving at Warm Springs on March 30, the president showed "decided improvement."[82] His blood pressure levels, however, fluctuated. By April 10, he was eating double helpings, and his face had regained color. He was taking it easy while also working through baskets of papers. He looked like he was recovering, yet again. Then, on Thursday, April 12, he was signing documents when he suddenly slumped forward and complained of a terrible headache and soon lost consciousness. He died at 3:30 p.m.

In projecting the image of a charming, vigorous man on the move, Roosevelt deployed camouflage, a phalanx of aides, emotional control, and jaw-clenching exertion. He loved secrets, and on some level he probably enjoyed hiding the extent of his paralysis. His body politics underscored that he was a man for his time, a symbol for the nation. For a people unsure how to escape the crippling Depression, he embodied confidence that recovery was possible, and that he could lead the way. To a world wondering whether the United States would assume the burdens of helping defeat the Axis and engaging in the postwar world, he demonstrated that America had grit and would venture abroad, however painful the steps. Roosevelt bested the crisis of his presidency. He remains the only leader in world history who could not walk but who nevertheless attained a commanding position. Attuned to emotional reactions, FDR probably understood that the spectacle of his intense effort as well as the appeal of his flirtatious charm—whether at the Democratic conventions, on the deck of the *Prince of Wales*, or in intimate meetings with Stalin and Churchill—could sway and perhaps even transform others. An observer later recalled the unifying emotions that flowed from watching Roosevelt's stumping walk: The "slow procession became extremely impressive." Onlookers seemed "hypnotized. . . . An audience of strangers had become a group of friends."[83]

Despite his status as America's indispensable leader in the 1930s and 1940s, FDR could not have pulled off his "splendid deception" in a less forgiving era of nonstop television news, YouTube, and "gotcha" journalism. Then again, more enlightened attitudes about supposed "disablility" might have enabled a latter-day Roosevelt to rise to the presidency even if she or he could not walk to the inaugural stand unaided. How to fit his paralysis into the narrative of his presidency remained controversial for decades after his death. In the 1990s, when the Roosevelt Memorial at last was built on the National Mall in Washington, DC., its designers decided, in effect, to sustain the deception. The principal statue has him sitting with a cloak covering his lap, thereby obscuring that he was in a wheelchair. When some historians and disability rights advocates protested, the sculptor added small casters visible only from behind the chair. Finally, a rights organization raised funds for a second statue depicting Roosevelt in the kind of simple wheelchair that he actually used. FDR, who loved intrigue, probably would have been both pleased and a bit disappointed that no longer did he have to persist in his "splendid deception."

NOTES

1. Portions of this essay were previously published in Frank Costigliola, *Roosevelt's Lost Alliances: How Personal Politics Helped Start the Cold War* (Princeton, NJ: Princeton University Press, 2012) and in "Roosevelt's Body and National Power" in Emily Rosenberg and Shanon Fitzpatrick (ed.), *Body and Nation: The Global Realm of U.S. Body Politics in the Twentieth Century* (Durham, NC: Duke University Press, 2014).
2. Hugh Gregory Gallagher, *FDR's Splendid Deception* (New York: Dodd, Mead and Company, 1985).
3. http://www.inaugural.senate.gov/swearing-in/address/address-by-franklin-d-roosevelt-1933
4. Franklin D. Roosevelt Press Conference, December 28, 1943, http://www.presidency.ucsb.edu/ws/?pid=16358 (accessed August 3, 2014).
5. Reminiscences of Frances Perkins (1955), Columbia University Oral History Research Office Collection (hereafter CUOHRC), vol. 4, 457; vol. 2, 68–70.
6. Gallagher, *Splendid Deception*, 30–31.
7. Kenneth S. Davis, *F.D.R. The Beckoning of Destiny, 1882-1928* (New York: Putnam, 1972), 651.
8. Bernard Asbell, *The F.D.R. Memoirs* (Garden City, NY: Doubleday, 1973), 259.
9. Gallagher, *Splendid Deception*, 19.
10. John Gunther, *Roosevelt in Retrospect* (New York: Harper & Brothers, 1950), 235.
11. Reminiscences of Perkins (1955), CUOHRC, vol. 2, 547.
12. Geoffrey C. Ward, *A First Class Temperament: The Emergence of Franklin Roosevelt* (New York: Harper & Row, 1989), 695–96.
13. Reminiscences of Perkins (1955), CUOHRC, vol. 2, 325, 548.
14. Ibid., 325–26, and 565.
15. David W. Houck and Amos Kiewe, *FDR's Body Politics: The Rhetoric of Disability* (College Station: Texas A&M Press, 2003), 31.
16. Frank Freidel, *Franklin D. Roosevelt The Ordeal* (Boston: Little, Brown and Company, 1956), 180.
17. Gallagher, *Splendid Deception*, 58 (emphasis in the original).
18. Ibid., 57.
19. Ibid., 55.
20. Ibid., 65–66.
21. Turnley Walker, *Roosevelt and the Warm Springs Story* (New York: A. A. Wyn, 1953), 149–50. Though Walker most likely fabricated many of the conversations he quotes without attribution, he also interviewed former residents of Warm Springs who had worked with Roosevelt.
22. Jean Edward Smith, *FDR* (New York: Random House, 2007), 785.
23. Gunther, *Roosevelt in Retrospect*, 241.
24. See, for instance, Susan Curell and Christina Cogdell, *Popular Eugenics: National Efficiency and American Mass Culture in the 1930s* (Athens, Ohio: Ohio University Press, 2006).

25. Ward, *A First-Class Temperament*, 785, 789, and 788.
26. Houck and Kiewe, *FDR's Body Politics*, 50.
27. Ibid., 47.
28. Ibid., 84.
29. Smith, *FDR*, 710 n.117.
30. Ibid., 276.
31. Houck and Kiewe, *FDR's Body Politics*, 92.
32. James O'Donnell Bennett, "The Nominee in Action," *Chicago Daily Tribune*, July 3, 1932, p. 3.
33. Houck and Kiewe, *FDR's Body Politics*, 98.
34. Ibid., 107.
35. http://www.youtube.com/watch?v=bV-U1DJxsAM
36. For one instance of such enforcement by the secret service, see http://www.youtube.com/watch?v=qWYR3eC3hQw
37. Sumner Welles journal, January 11, 1933, box 265, Sumner Welles papers, Franklin D. Roosevelt Presidential Library (hereafter FDRL); Ruby Nelle to Folks, February 14, 1938, Small Collections, FDRL.
38. Michael F. Reilly, *Reilly of the White House*, as told to William J. Slocum (New York: Simon and Schuster, 1947), 104.
39. Arthur M. Schlesinger Jr., *The Politics of Upheaval, 1935-1936* (Boston: Houghton Mifflin, 1966), 571.
40. Philip Kinsley, "Crowd Laughs in Rain, Waiting for President," *Chicago Daily Tribune*, June 28, 1936, 1, 4.
41. Reilly, *Reilly of the White House*, 99.
42. Schlesinger, *Politics of Upheaval*, 582–84; William D. Hassett, "The President Was My Boss," *Saturday Evening Post*, October 10, 1953.
43. Raymond Clapper, *Watching the World* (New York: McGraw-Hill, 1944), 87.
44. Franklin D. Roosevelt: "Acceptance Speech for the Renomination for the Presidency, Philadelphia, Pa.," June 27, 1936. Online by Gerhard Peters and John T. Woolley, The American Presidency Project. http://www.presidency.ucsb.edu/ws/?pid=15314.
45. Reilly, *Reilly of the White House*, 101.
46. Clapper, *Watching the World*, 87.
47. Schlesinger, *Politics of Upheaval*, 585.
48. Clapper, *Watching the World*, 88.
49. Schlesinger, *Politics of Upheaval*, 585.
50. H. V. Morton, *Atlantic Meeting* (London: Methuen, 1943), 78.
51. Ian Jacob diary, August 10, 1941, Churchill Archive, University of Cambridge.
52. Joseph E. Davies, "Meetings with Stalin and Molotov," May 20, 1943, box 13, Joseph E. Davies papers, Library of Congress, Washington, DC.
53. Captain John L. McCrea, "History of the *USS Iowa*," box 11, John L. McCrea papers, Library of Congress.
54. Reminiscences of Perkins, v. 8, p. 312, CUOHRC.
55. Foreign Relations of the United States, The Conferences At Cairo and Tehran (Washington: Government Printing Office, 1961), *Tehran*: 461–63; Valentin Berezhkov, *History in the Making. Memoirs of World War II Diplomacy* (Moscow: Progress Publishers, 1982), 249–52; Reilly, *Reilly of the White House*, 175–78.

56. CNN interview with Sergo Beria [1996] http://www.cnn.com/SPECIALS/cold.war/episodes/01/interviews/beria/ (accessed January 27, 2008).
57. Ibid.
58. *FRUS Tehran*: 483; Reilly, *Reilly of the White House*, 179.
59. William M. Rigdon, *White House Sailor* (Garden City, NY: Doubleday, 1962), 81–82.
60. *FRUS Tehran*, 838.
61. Alex Danchev and Daniel Todman (ed.), *War Diaries 1939-1945* (Berkeley: University of California Press, 2001), 482; David Dilks (ed.), *The Diaries of Alexander Cadogan* (New York: G. P. Putnam's Sons, 1972), 578.
62. Geoffrey C. Ward (ed.), *Closest Companion* (Boston: Houghton Mifflin, 1995), 252, 250.
63. Earl Miller to Joseph P. Lash [1968], box 44, Joseph P. Lash papers, FDRL.
64. Bruenn, "Clinical Notes," April 23, 1944; September 20, 1944; March 1, 1945, Howard G. Bruenn papers, Small Collections, FDRL.
65. Ward (ed.), *Closest Companion*, 390.
66. Dilks (ed.), *Cadogan Diaries*, 704.
67. Charles E. Bohlen, *Witness to History* (New York: Norton, 1973), 172.
68. Valentin Berezhkov to Arthur Schlesinger Jr. [no date, but probably 1970s], box 2, Miscellaneous Documents, Small Collections, FDRL.
69. Bruenn to Ross McIntire, August 1, 1946, Bruenn papers, FDRL.
70. See Russell D. Buhite, *Decisions at Yalta: An Appraisal of Summit Diplomacy* (Wilmington, DE: Scholarly Resources, 1976); John Lewis Gaddis, *We Now Know* (New York: Oxford University Press, 1997); Costigliola, *Roosevelt's Lost Alliances*.
71. Kathleen Harriman, interview with Abramson, #4, December 9, 1987, Rudy Abramson papers, in private possession.
72. Sergo Beria, *Beria, My Father* (London: Duckworth, 2001), 106.
73. Wilson Brown, unpublished memoir, Wilson Brown papers, FDRL, 186.
74. Lord Moran, *Churchill at War 1940-45* (New York: Carroll & Graf, 2002), 279.
75. Gunther, *Roosevelt in Retrospect*, 367.
76. Ward (ed.), *Closest Companion*, 398.
77. Lippmann, *Today and Tomorrow*, March 3, 1945.
78. Bruenn, "Clinical Notes," March 1, 1945, Bruenn papers.
79. Warren F. Kimball (ed.), *Churchill and Roosevelt* (London: Collins, 1984), 3: 588.
80. Ibid., 3:630; Mary E. Glantz, *FDR and the Soviet Union* (Lawrence: University Press of Kansas, 2005), 161–62.
81. Bruenn, "Clinical Notes," March 16, 28, 1945, Bruenn papers.
82. Bruenn, "Clinical Notes," April 6, 1945, Bruenn papers.
83. Philip Hamburger, "Talk of the Town," *The New Yorker* November 17, 1962.

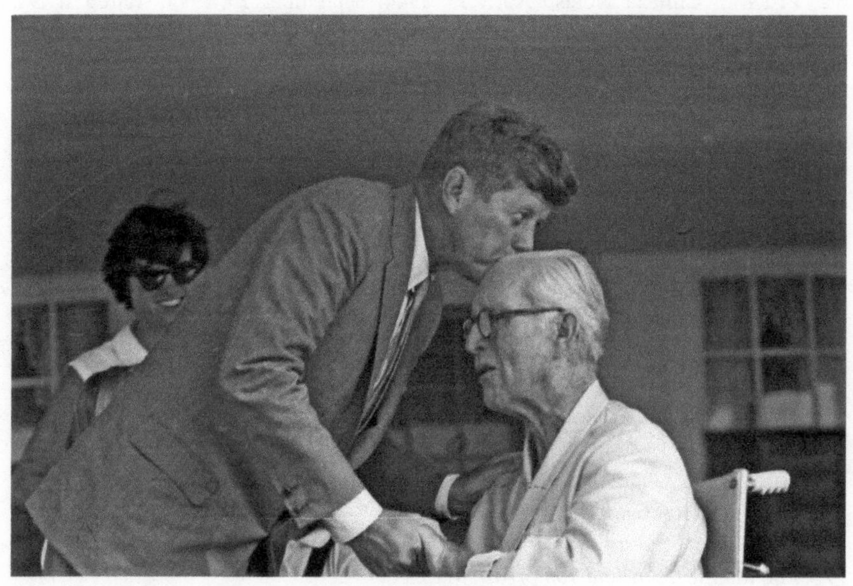

President John F. Kennedy shows his abiding affection for his father, Joseph, who suffered a debilitating stroke in December 1961, during JFK's first year in office. [Courtesy John F. Kennedy Library and Museum.]

8

The Kennedy Family through Sickness and Death

DAVID NASAW

The Kennedy family was plagued by loss, illness, and untimely death. By the time John Fitzgerald Kennedy was elected to the presidency, two of his siblings had suffered violent deaths in plane crashes and a third had been institutionalized after a horribly botched operation. Less than a year into his presidency, his father, at age seventy-three, would be felled by a near-fatal and debilitating stroke that robbed him of his ability to communicate in speech or writing. Twenty months later, the president's infant son, Patrick Bouvier Kennedy, would die two days after his premature birth.

But pain, suffering, and untimely death were not and would not be part of the Kennedy family narrative. Trim, hearty, tanned, their photographs had from the mid-1950s appeared often in the daily press and glossy magazines, as they sailed their yachts, swung their golf clubs and tennis rackets, ran down and out and across the front yard in touch football games, and rode fast horses over open fields. Of the Kennedy brothers, Jack looked the fittest. Ted was taller, more classically handsome, but prone to put on weight. Bobby was an inch or two shorter but seemed smaller still because he tended to slouch. The Kennedy women—mother Rose, sisters Jean, Eunice, and Patricia, sisters-in-law Ethel, Joan, and Jackie—were as fit as the men, boyishly thin and athletic.

The parents, too, were specimens of good health. Exercise was part of their daily regimen. Seventy-two when his son was elected president, Joseph P. Kennedy played golf and swam nearly every day and, when in Hyannis Port, went horseback riding in the morning. Rose Fitzgerald Kennedy was a manic golfer who preferred to play by herself and literally raced from hole to hole. She also swam regularly and went for long walks on the beach.

As individuals and as a family, the Kennedys took pride in their physical well-being and good looks and willfully refused to acknowledge frailty, infirmities, or weakness of any sort. Other people took ill, complained, slacked off, rested until they felt better; Kennedys did not. They carefully, artfully hid their infirmities and their pain from the public.

Rosemary, the third child and first daughter, had health problems almost from the moment she was born. "She crawled, stood, took her first steps, said her first words late; she had problems managing a baby spoon and porringer," her mother recalled in her memoirs. "She was slow in everything, and some things she seemed unable to learn how to do, or do well or with consistency. . . . She went to kindergarten and first grade at the usual ages, but her lack of coordination was apparent and as time went on I realized she could not keep up with the work."[1] In her mid-twenties, after the unsuccessful lobotomy that robbed her not only of her Kennedy good looks but her cognitive capacities, Rosemary was moved to a convent school in Jefferson, Wisconsin, where she lived out her life, watched over, cared for, and protected by the Sisters of St. Francis of Assisi. Rosemary's childhood problems had been serious but not life-threatening. The same could not be said of her brother Jack who was struck by every childhood illness imaginable and nearly died from scarlet fever before he was three years old. Eunice also had more than her share of illnesses, as a child, a teenager, and an adult. She, like her brother Jack, would later be diagnosed with Addison's disease.

The entire family suffered from stomach problems. In her interviews with historian and family adviser Arthur M. Schlesinger Jr., Jacqueline Kennedy recalled that her husband had been troubled by "stomach trouble, which gave him a lot of pain . . . But all his family have it. It's just a Kennedy stomach."[2] Joseph P. Kennedy, on several occasions, and for long periods when he was ambassador to London, was nearly incapacitated by them. He and his wife Rose, a finicky eater, watched their diets, stayed away from heavy or rich foods, and drank lightly or not at all. They preferred to eat at home where their cooks could prepare their food—often fresh fish—according to their instructions. Perhaps, because of their own weak stomachs, and certainly because they expected their children to look as trim and healthy as they were, they paid close, sometimes near obsessive, attention to their diets. Joseph P. Kennedy was insistent that his daughters not carry a surplus ounce on them. In nearly every phone call and letter to his daughter Rosemary before her lobotomy, he had cautioned her about her weight.

To Rose was delegated the task of monitoring the children's eating habits. "I used to weigh them every week and keep track and then give them more nourishment if they were losing weight, give them an extra glass of milk or cream in their milk. Jack, who was always thin, used to get the extra juice from the steak when it was carved, or the roast beef juice, which was an idea I had to build up his health."[3] All nine of them, she was convinced, required individualized attention, some to lose weight, others to put on a few pounds. "Almost go mad listening to discussion of diets," she wrote in her diary during a family vacation in the south of France, "as Jack is fattening, Joe Jr. is slimming, Pat is on or off, and Rosemary (who has gained about eight pounds) and Kathleen and Eunice are all trying to lose."[4] When Eunice, in her early twenties, decided that she wanted to relocate to California and attend classes at Stanford, Rose moved in with her, in large part, she told her husband, because she had to make sure Eunice was eating right.[5]

Rose watched and worried over the children's weight and health and kept careful track, on index cards, of their illnesses, inoculations, and doctor's visits. When, however, serious illness struck, as it first did when Jack, three months shy of his third birthday, caught scarlet fever, it was Joseph P. Kennedy who was called on to play the lead role. Now virtually disappeared from the land, this childhood illness was, in 1920, "a dreaded disease," Rose recalled in her memoirs, "fairly often fatal, quite often crippling in aftereffects; heart, eyes, ears; there were various possibilities that were awful to think about."[6] The mortality rate was 15 to 20 percent, the risk of complications higher. Because there were two infants, Joe Jr. and Rosemary, and a newborn, Kathleen, at the Kennedy home in Brookline, and because scarlet fever was acutely contagious, the first priority was getting baby Jack away from his siblings. Fortunately, for the Kennedys, Boston City Hospital had a special unit, the South Department, for infectious childhood diseases; the physician in charge, Dr. Edward Place, was perhaps the nation's leading expert on measles and scarlet fever. Unfortunately, the Kennedys did not live in Boston, but in Brookline. Joseph Kennedy, ever resourceful, especially when it came to his family, used his contacts with his father-in-law, former mayor John Fitzgerald, known as "Honey Fitz," and with the current mayor, Andrew Peters, to get Boston City to violate its own rules and admit a non-Boston resident, John Fitzgerald Kennedy.

"By the time he got there," Rose later remembered, "Jack was a very, very sick little boy."[7] Worried that she might get infected and bring the illness home to her infants, Rose Kennedy did not visit her son Jack for the two months he was in the hospital and the three weeks afterward that he spent, still in isolation, at a hotel in Poland Spring, Maine.

Joseph P. Kennedy took over the care of the infant, consulted with the doctors, spent every afternoon and early evening at the hospital, and pledged to himself that if the boy survived, he would give half his fortune to the church (which he did). After the danger had passed, he confessed in a letter to Dr. Place that he had "little realized what an effect such a happening could possibly have on me. During the darkest days I felt that nothing else mattered except his recovery."[8]

Jack recovered from his scarlet fever but would spend the rest of his childhood suffering from one illness or another: bronchitis, chicken pox, ear infections, German measles, measles, mumps, whooping cough. He was no healthier as an adolescent. At age fourteen, he was incapacitated by abdominal pains so severe a surgeon was called in. His appendix was removed, but the pains continued, landing Jack in the hospital several more times. At age eighteen, while at the London School of Economics for a year of preparation before college, he was taken ill, hospitalized, then brought back to the United States and enrolled at Princeton so that, should he be struck down again, he would at least be close to his regular doctors. "Jack is far from being a well boy," Joseph Kennedy wrote the British ambassador Robert Bingham, whom he had hoped to visit in London. "As a result I am afraid my time for the next six months will be devoted to trying to help him regain his health."[9] In December, Jack left Princeton, his second abrupt withdrawal in four months. After the Christmas holidays which he spent recuperating with his father in Palm Beach, he checked into the Peter Bent Brigham Hospital for two months of tests and then returned to Palm Beach for another round of rehabilitation.

This was to be an ongoing experience. For the next twenty years, Jack's problems with his back and stomach, his sudden high fevers, and his difficulties keeping his weight up, would land him in the hospital for lengthy stays, followed by periods of recovery in Palm Beach. His father was at his side through every illness. It was he who signed Jack into the clinics and the hospitals, chose and then consulted with the doctors on courses of treatment and medication, and repeatedly oversaw his recuperation.

Despite a childhood and adolescence marked by ill-health or perhaps because of it, Jack Kennedy insisted not only on enlisting in the navy but on volunteering for physically arduous service on a PT (patrol torpedo) boat. In March of 1943 Jack boarded a troopship on the first leg of his long journey to the Solomon Islands where he was to be stationed. Five months later, on August 2, 1943, PT 109, which he commanded, was rammed by a Japanese destroyer while on patrol in the Blackett Strait in the mid-Solomons. The boat's plywood hull ripped in two. Its gasoline tanks exploded, killing two crew members and injuring others. Jack and his crew stayed afloat in the water for hours, holding on to the only intact piece of the hull. They then swam four hours to the nearest island, Kennedy towing a badly injured sailor behind him. They were marooned there for several days with nothing to eat or drink until the rescue crews located them.

Lieutenant Kennedy returned to the United States five months later, "having lost about twenty odd pounds, with his stomach in pretty poor shape," his father wrote Joe, Jr.[10] He suffered as well from a duodenal ulcer, malaria, and the now chronic back pains which had plagued him for years, but had been sorely aggravated by the physical stress he had endured on duty in the Solomons. In June of 1944, he was admitted to the Chelsea Naval Hospital, then transferred to New England Baptist to be operated on. The surgery, which removed some soft tissue from his back, did nothing to alleviate the now constant back pain.

It would take months in the hospital before Jack could rebuild his health to the point where he could consider what to do with the rest of his life. The family had never envisioned a political career for him, in large part, because he had always seemed too sick, frail, and weak to survive the rigors of a campaign. But when his oldest brother, Joseph P. Kennedy Jr., the family's most likely future candidate, died after his plane crashed and burned during a bombing run in June 1944, Jack and his family began to reconsider his future. In the summer of 1945, still far from fully recovered from his wartime injuries, he decided to run for election to Congress from his grandfather's old district. Photos taken at the time reveal a painfully thin, frail young man.[11] Despite several near collapses and constant stomach and back pain, Jack never slowed down or complained. He outcampaigned and outspent his rivals and won his first election.[12]

In the fall of 1947, a year after his election, he was taken ill again, as ill as he had ever been. Visiting his sister in Ireland prior to a congressional investigative trip with, of all people, Richard M. Nixon, Congressman Kennedy was rushed to a London hospital where he was diagnosed with Addison's disease. The doctor who treated him confided to family friend Pamela Churchill (later Pamela Harriman) that the young man would probably not last another year. On the voyage back to the United States, he was given the last rites. As he had done at every such moment in the past, Joseph P. Kennedy intervened, arranged for his son's medical care, and to protect his political future put out the erroneous news that he had suffered a recurrence of his wartime malaria.[13]

Having served three rather uninspiring terms in the US House of Representatives, Jack Kennedy, still suffering from constant back pain, but now taking steroids to treat his Addison's disease, consulted with his father and his brothers and then decided that the time had come for him to run for the Senate in 1952 against the incumbent and quite popular Henry Cabot Lodge II. Though the Republicans would regain the White House and control of Congress that year—and Dwight D. Eisenhower would outpoll Adlai Stevenson in the presidential race by 208,800 in Massachusetts—Kennedy stunned the political world by defeating Lodge by 70,000 votes.[14]

The physical stress of the campaign took its toll on Jack's health. He recovered sufficiently to take his place in the Senate and, in September of 1953, marry Jacqueline Bouvier, but within less than a year, his back pains had become so unbearable that he was forced to rely on crutches to propel himself from one place to another. In the summer of 1954 his doctors recommended that he have surgery to fuse his spinal disks. They warned that if he did not do so, there was a strong possibility that he would be confined to a wheelchair for the rest of his life. If, on the other hand, he went ahead, there was a high risk of infection because of his Addison's disease.

In most families, as children become adults, their parents take a step back. But that did not happen in the Kennedy family, where Joseph Kennedy continued to manage his children's health care. Having virtually lost one child, Rosemary, to an operation that had gone bad, the patriarch did everything he could to dissuade his son from submitting to major back surgery. "Joe first tried to convince Jack that even confined to a wheelchair he could lead a full and rich life," Rose recalled years later. "After all, he argued, one need only look at the incredible life FDR had managed to lead despite his physical incapacity."[15] But, this time, probably for the first time, Joseph Kennedy was overruled by his son who told his father he could no longer live with the incessant pain from his back and was prepared to take whatever risks were necessary and undergo the surgery.

The surgery was performed on October 21, 1954, at the Hospital for Special Surgery in New York City. Afterward, as the doctors had warned, Jack developed a urinary tract infection, his temperature spiked, and he fell into a coma. Once more, a priest was summoned to administer the last rites. But Jack, as he had so many, many times in the past, recovered and, on December 21, 1954, two months after the surgery, was flown to Palm Beach to begin another round of recuperation at his parents' home.[16]

Joseph P. Kennedy converted the ground floor into a makeshift hospital and hired rotating shifts of doctors and nurses to look after his son. But the wound in Jack's back would not heal. And he was unable to walk. Worried that something was wrong, very wrong, Joseph Kennedy took matters into his own hands and flew to New York City to consult with Jack's doctors who recommended a second surgery to remove the metal plate that had been inserted with three screws to stabilize his lower back.[17] After the second operation, Jack spent another three months at his parents' home in Palm Beach, again with his father supervising his rehabilitation. He did not return to the Senate until late May, 1955.[18]

As the senator resumed his political career, the Kennedys carefully structured the narrative about his medical history and prognosis they gave to the press and the public. They attributed his back problems to a war injury and claimed that he was now cured. What was not disclosed was that from May of 1955 to October 1957, he would suffer not only from intense back pain but from recurring bouts of colitis, intense diarrhea, prostatitis, and throat, respiratory, and urinary-tract infections that landed him in the hospital on nine different occasions, including a nineteen-day and two-week-long stays. He was now regularly treated with dozens of different medications, including large doses of antibiotics, steroids for his Addison's disease, Nembutol to help him sleep, testosterone to keep up his weight, anti-spasmodics for his colitis, injections of procaine for his back pain, and assorted pain killers.[19]

Those who voted for or against John Kennedy, read about him in the glossy magazines and newspapers, heard him on the radio or saw him in person or on television as he campaigned for office in Massachusetts and began his run for the presidency, largely knew nothing of his illnesses and chronic pain. They were instead presented with the portrait of a superbly healthy young man, an athlete, a veteran, a smiling, affable, dynamic, energetic, youthful, handsome American with a smiling, healthy, athletic wife, parents, brothers, and sisters. The medical condition of Rosemary, was also covered over with lies. When, on September 7, 1957, the *Saturday Evening Post* published a glowing, glossy puff piece on "The Amazing Kennedys," it was reported that Rosemary who was not present in any of the photos was teaching "exceptional" children in a Catholic school near Milwaukee.

There comes a time in the history of most families when children and parents reverse roles—when the children become the caregivers and the parents the cared-for. That did not occur in the Kennedy family. Joseph Kennedy had suffered all his life from what his doctors diagnosed as chronic gastritis, but he did not at any time burden his children with his complaints, seek their sympathy, or solicit their advice. His pain and illness were his concern, not theirs. And, fortunately, it was not life-threatening. He was hospitalized only once in adult life, at age sixty-eight, for prostate and perhaps abdominal problems; but there were no complications and, other than having to delay his trip to Florida until after Christmas, no change in family routines.

While his children continued to take their father's good health for granted, Joseph Kennedy never stopped worrying about or offering advice on their medical problems. When Jack, nearing forty now, considered whether or not to seek the vice presidential nomination in 1956, his father counseled him not to. He was sure Adlai Stevenson, the Democratic candidate for president, would lose and he did not want anyone attributing the defeat to his having chosen a young Catholic for his running mate. As importantly, as he told Charles Wyzanski, chairman of the Harvard Board of Overseers during lunch at the Tavern Club in Boston, "If Jack were . . . to run for vice president it was not clear that he had the stamina to withstand the strain, and even if he did, people would contend that his health was not good enough to bear the rigors of the presidency if the office devolved upon him."[20]

In 1958, when Jack campaigned for reelection to the Senate, his father insisted on reviewing and approving his schedule. "It's crazy," he exploded at campaign managers Larry O'Brien and Kenny O'Donnell. "You're going to kill him. You don't have to run him all over the state, just put him on television. . . . You'll wind up with a dead candidate on your hands and you'll be responsible."[21] He demanded that time be built into the schedule for Jack to rest and take a leisurely lunch. Fearful that neither the candidate nor his aides were going to follow the rules he had set for them, Joe

Kennedy enlisted Frank Morrissey, his spy on his son's staff, to call him daily with a report on Jack's health.

Jack was easily reelected to the Senate in 1958 and almost immediately began campaigning for the presidential nomination in 1960. Through sheer will power and with the help of dozens of medications administered orally and by injection, the senator from Massachusetts was able to work longer and harder than his opponents. The energy that went into his relentless campaigning, his youthful good looks, and his permanent tan (a byproduct of his heavy use of cortisones) effectively disguised his health deficits.

Although his father had worried that his son's health might become a campaign issue, it did not. Lyndon Johnson, the last man standing between Kennedy and the nomination, having himself suffered from a near-fatal heart attack, was reluctant to introduce the question of health into the campaign, fearful that doing so might prompt a reexamination of his own recent illness. Only when it became apparent that Kennedy had the nomination nearly locked up did Johnson, in an act of desperation, direct India Edwards, former vice chairman of the Democratic National Committee, to announce at a press conference that not only did Jack Kennedy have Addison's disease, but "would not be alive if not for cortisone." The Kennedys sidestepped the issues by claiming that Jack did not have the "ailment described classically as Addison's Disease" and did not take cortisone. Technically, this was true, as "classical" Addison's disease was caused by tuberculosis, which Jack had never had, and he was treated with a cortisone derivative, not cortisone itself.[22] On the campaign trail, John Kennedy hid his health problems rather brilliantly. During the critical first debate with Richard Nixon, it was he who appeared most "fit" to be president: athletically thin, tanned, tall, with perfect posture. His opponent, on the other hand, looked almost ill—pale, sweating, slumped over. In a remarkably close contest, Kennedy prevailed.

As president-elect, then as president, John Fitzgerald Kennedy continued to disguise his health problems by projecting an image of vigor, athleticism, and physical well-being. The month before his inauguration, *Sports Illustrated*, owned by Henry Luce who had supported Nixon but remained a friend of the Kennedy family, put on its cover a smiling president-elect in his boat with the First Lady–elect alongside, two vibrant examples of American vigor. In the accompanying article entitled "The Soft American," the president-elect who had campaigned and won as a hardline Cold Warrior, warned the nation that good health and fitness was not simply a personal preference but a national security issue. "In a very real and immediate sense, our growing softness, our increasing lack of physical fitness, is a menace to our security. . . . We face in the Soviet Union a powerful and implacable adversary determined to show the world that only the Communist system possesses the vigor and determination necessary to satisfy awakening aspirations for progress and the elimination of poverty and want. To meet the challenge of this enemy will require determination and effort on the part of all Americans. Only if our citizens are physically fit will they be fully capable of such an effort." On taking office, Kennedy declared that he was going to "establish a White House Committee on Health and Fitness to formulate and carry out a program to improve the physical condition of the nation," invite the governor of each state "to attend an annual National Youth Fitness Congress [and] make it clearly understood that the promotion of sports participation and physical fitness is a basic and continuing policy of the United States."[23]

On January 20, 1961, John Fitzgerald Kennedy was inaugurated as the nation's thirty-fifth president. For Americans who had experienced the successive presidencies of Franklin Roosevelt, Harry Truman, and Dwight David Eisenhower, none of them (or, for that matter, their First Ladies) known for health, vigor, or good looks, a new era had dawned. The nation now had a First Family who exuded glamour and athleticism, and they were young enough to have toddlers in the White House. In hindsight, we can look back at the portraits and videos of the president and see that there is something amiss, that the president stands too erect, winces ever so slightly when he departs from his airplane or exits his car, appears too bronzed, even in winter. At the time, most of us bought the story we were presented with and asked few questions about his health.

As he had all his life, John Kennedy, in the White House, pushed forward through the pain without complaint; his father was perhaps the only one who knew how ill he had been and how much he continued to suffer. Though Joseph P. Kennedy refused to visit the White House for fear his son's opponents would make too much of his influence on policy matters, he saw his children and grandchildren regularly in Hyannis Port and Palm Beach. And he talked to them often on the telephone. Even with a son as president, another as attorney general, and a third on his way toward the Senate, the patriarch remained the unquestioned anchor of the family, the unchanging constant, his children's principal advisor on most matters, especially on their health and their finances, the fixed point around which the other Kennedys swirled in motion, the family cheerleader. He also provided his sons with his ongoing commentary—complete with political advice—on domestic and foreign affairs, knowing full well, of course, that they were going to reject most of what he said, but only after listening intently.

The administration's first major crisis occurred within months of the inauguration. In April 1961, Cuban exiles trained on American soil invaded the Bay of Pigs, with disastrous results. One hundred were killed, a thousand captured, and the Kennedy administration, which had tried to deny American involvement, was caught up in a series of lies. The president was as distraught, Jackie recalled, as she had ever seen him. Robert Kennedy suggested that they "call Dad, maybe he can cheer us up." Though the senior Kennedy agreed that the events in Cuba had been an unmitigated disaster, he insisted there was a silver lining. Because the Bay of Pigs debacle had occurred in the early months of the administration, there was plenty of time to restore the president's reputation, and Jack had, by accepting responsibility for the disaster, taken a giant step in this direction. "Americans," the father reassured his sons, "love those who admit their mistakes." He predicted that the president's approval ratings would climb quickly, and they did.[24]

There was nothing new in this dynamic. All their lives, the father had been his children's chief booster and cheerleader; and the children, even those in high places in Washington, counted on this. When they sat down to talk with him on the porch, at poolside, or at meals, when they followed him around on the golf course or went sailing with him or called from Washington or wherever they might happen to be, they filled him in on their news and their concerns. He would offer his suggestions, sometimes in stronger language than they appreciated, then advise them, caution them, assure him that he would stand behind them, and that he was confident that everything was going to be okay. No matter how dire the crisis appeared at the moment, there was a way out of it, and, as Kennedys, they would find it.

"The Ambassador," as Joseph P. Kennedy preferred to be called, did not allow the change in his sons' status to disrupt his daily activities or his seasonal schedule. He was older now, but he still played golf and swam every day, traveled with the seasons from Palm Beach in winter, to Washington and New York, and Hyannis Port in early spring, his villa in the south of France for the summer, then back to Hyannis in the fall.

In September 1961, eight months into his son's presidency, he celebrated his seventy-third birthday with his children and grandchildren in Hyannis Port. "My own children," he wrote publisher Walter Annenberg,

> seem to feel a sense of obligation to their father for permitting their children to ruin the carpets, spoil the lawn, mess up the house in good style, and so forth and so forth. So the least they can do is to bring them all to the birthday party, and hope and pray that at least their children will look good in the picture.[25]

The ambassador remained at Hyannis Port through the Thanksgiving holidays. There were thirty-three Kennedys at Thanksgiving dinner, which the patriarch, as always, presided over. But there was something different this year. "For the first time, I have noticed he has grown old," Rose wrote in her diary. "Doctor [Janet] Travell here with Jack & says cold wind & air bad for Joe but he keeps going out." On his flight back to Washington, Jack "expressed his concern" for his father's health to Ted Sorensen.[26]

In mid-December, Joseph Kennedy flew to Florida for the winter, as he did every year. On December 19, 1961, he drove his son, the president, to the airport after a brief visit and then went directly to the Palm Beach Country Club to play nine holes of golf. After playing seven of them, however, he felt faint, he told Rose's niece, Ann Gargan, who now lived with the family in Palm Beach. He had trouble walking off the course. Gargan called for a golf cart to take him to his car. By the time they got home, he felt better and announced that he was going upstairs to change into his bathing suit and go for a swim with Jackie and Caroline who were visiting. He was persuaded to rest for a bit. Five minutes later, he awoke choking, unable to speak, paralyzed on his right side. He had suffered "an 'intracranial thrombosis,'" a blood clot in the artery in the brain which triggered a massive stroke. The doctors transferred him at once to the hospital. The president who had just returned from his flight from Palm Beach was informed by phone during a meeting of the National Security Council. He contacted his brother, Bobby, and flew with him and sister Jean to Palm Beach. By the time they arrived at the hospital, their father had contracted pneumonia, was in a coma, and had had the last rites performed. By the next morning, Joseph P. Kennedy was out of mortal danger, but he could not move the right side of his body or speak. He would spend the rest of his life in a wheelchair unable to walk or communicate in speech or writing.

The Kennedys had succeeded rather miraculously, until now, in keeping their medical problems out of the press. That would no longer be possible. Reporters, photographers, and television cameramen had trailed the president from Washington to the Palm Beach hospital where his father had been taken and stayed on the story from that moment forward. The White House provided briefings on Joseph P. Kennedy's condition, with constant reminders that the father's illness would have no impact on the president's plans or priorities. On December 20, the day after the ambassador's stroke, press secretary Pierre Salinger announced that the president would depart on the next morning, as scheduled, for his summit meeting in Bermuda with Prime Minister Harold Macmillan. When he decided to remain in Palm Beach with his father through the Christmas holidays, his press office made it clear that he was, in addition to visiting the hospital, conferring with his aides on budget plans and his State of the Union message, as he would have were he in the White House. On December 27, lest anyone even subliminally connect the father's physical ailments to any debility on the part of the son, the White House announced that Dr. Preston Wade of the New York Hospital-Cornell Medical Center examined the president in Palm Beach and found his health excellent.

All their lives, Joseph Kennedy had taken care of every medical crisis. In his absence, the family floundered. Rose, who had been left out of the decision-making process for half a century, was not prepared to step in now. When hit with a problem she could not solve, no matter how minor, she reached out to her eldest child for help. In November of 1962, just after the midterm elections, she wrote the president in the White House to ask his help in finding a "good man for your father, instead of two female nurses."[27] Major decisions were made in committee, with everyone in the family, including the in-laws, joining in.

Each of the Kennedy children, including the one in the White House, would, over the months and years to come, visit the ambassador regularly in Palm Beach, Hyannis Port, and Washington. So that he might move with the seasons as he had before his stroke, they outfitted the president's former campaign plane, the "Caroline," to transport him in his wheelchair wherever he wanted to go. Though he was unable to communicate over the phone, they called, as they always had, and carried on what were now one-way conversations, interrupted occasionally by gibberish or grunts on the other end. Rose, worried that the constant calls were tiring the old man, felt obligated to intervene. "The best time to call is during the cocktail hour . . . I might suggest that the boys telephone Monday, Tuesday, and Wednesday, and the girls Thursday, Friday, and Saturday, although this is optional."[28]

Now that no one could claim that he might exert undue influence on his son, the patriarch was free to visit the White House, which he did on several occasions. Ben Bradlee, one of Jack's closest friends in Washington and managing editor of the *Washington Post*, recalled in his memoirs dining with the president, his father, and other members of the family. "The evening," Bradlee recalled, "was movingly gay . . . His children involve him in their every thought and action. They talk to him all the time. They ask him 'Don't you think so, Dad?' or 'Isn't that right, Dad?' And before he has a chance to embarrass himself or his guests by not being able to answer, they are off on the next subject."[29] There was never the slightest hint of pity in anyone's voice or gaze, nor any reference to his diminished capacities. Only Jackie refrained from denying the reality of the situation. "While the others pretended not to notice the side of his body that was affected by the paralysis," Rita Dallas, his nurse, later observed, Jackie "always held his deformed hand and kissed the affected side of his face."[30]

On a private level, Jack Kennedy and his family were profoundly sorrowed—and changed—by their patriarch's sudden but lasting debilities. But they did not grieve publicly, they did not let the world into their suffering, and they did not comment on the loss they had suffered and the pain they felt every time they visited or tried to speak with their father on the telephone. Jack especially had learned early to compartmentalize his public and private lives, to screen out personal hurts, pains, and crises, to smile for the cameras when he was so exhausted he could barely stand. He would not allow this tragedy, as he had refused to permit other family tragedies, to enter his public life, to affect his decision making, to alter his schedule of activities.

In the aftermath of the patriarch's stroke and the very public pictures of the now-crippled, twisted old man, the family began to let down its guard, if only slightly. In September of 1962, Eunice Kennedy Shriver published a *Saturday Evening Post* article, "Hope for Retarded Children," in which she stated plainly that "Rosemary was mentally retarded."[31] The term carried none of the stigma in 1962 that it does today. Still, the Kennedys had never before acknowledged their sister's condition and, in fact, had done everything possible to hide it from the public. Privately, without mentioning their sister, but in direct homage to Rosemary, Joseph Kennedy had donated millions of dollars through the family foundation to support institutions that cared for the retarded and did research on the causes and treatments for retardation. When Jack was elected president, Eunice, who had perhaps been closest to Rosemary among the siblings and had taken the lead in steering the family foundation, asked him to do something for the "retarded." The president-elect, after long discussions with his father and Eunice, agreed to establish a presidential panel on mental retardation, which he charged with preparing a "National

Plan to Combat Mental Retardation." In announcing the initiative, he had referenced Rosemary, but as a victim of "cerebral palsy," not mental retardation.[32] The panel was appointed on October 17, 1961, and given a year to present its "recommendations concerning research and manpower, treatment and care, education and preparation for employment, legal protection and development of federal, state and local programs" for the mentally retarded.[33]

Eunice Kennedy Shriver's declaration that sister Rosemary was "mentally retarded" appeared weeks before the recommendations were made public. The decision to cross the boundary between the family's private and public lives was motivated by political as well as by personal necessities. Letting the world know that there was a Kennedy who was less than perfect humanized the family and took it a step down from its pedestal—and that might have made good political sense. More importantly, it brought home the fierce reality that mental retardation could strike anyone. There were, the president's sister emphasized

> approximately 5,400,00 retarded children and adults in the United States. . . . Like diabetes, deafness, polio or any other misfortune, mental retardation can happen in any family. It has happened in the family of the poor and the rich, of governors, senators, Nobel prizewinners, doctors, lawyers, writers, men of genius, presidents of corporations—the President of the United States.[34]

The president's intervention to secure federal funding and direct public attention to the problem of the mentally retarded was, arguably, his most successful venture into the historically vexed area of national health care. He would not fare nearly as well with his other major health initiative—his plan to broaden Social Security benefits to include hospitalization insurance for the elderly. In his first state of the union address, President Kennedy had made it clear that securing hospitalization insurance for the elderly would be a priority of his administration. Nine days later, he sent Congress a message proposing such legislation. When his first attempt at a health-care bill failed to garner the support it needed, he put it aside, only to pick it up again after pollster Lou Harris recommended that he make it the centerpiece of domestic policy for 1962.

Between the president's first and second campaigns for health-care legislation, his father suffered his stroke. Although Kennedy had been committed to the legislation before his father took ill—he had in fact pushed for it while in the Senate—he moved forward with more urgency now, having experienced firsthand the effects of an elder's illness on an entire family. In his first book about the Kennedy administration, Ted Sorensen recalled how the president told legislators at a breakfast meeting that "the cost of his own father's hospitalization . . . made him all the more aware of how impossible it was for those less wealthy to bear such a burden."[35]

Whereas in most other areas of domestic policy, Kennedy, according to Larry O'Brien, his special assistant for congressional relations, "chose a strategy of conciliation . . . Medicare became an exception."[36] As part of his campaign to counter congressional opposition and create a groundswell of support for his program, the president flew to New York in May of 1962 to address a pro-Medicare rally at Madison Square Garden. On his arrival, he visited his father at the Rusk Institute of Physical Medicine and Rehabilitation where, six months after his stroke, he was being attended to. On Saturday, May 19, after another visit to his father, the president attended a fund-raising birthday party at Madison Square Garden. Dozens of performers participated, but it was Marilyn Monroe's rendition of "Happy Birthday Mr. President" that stopped the show. On Sunday, he returned to Madison Square Garden for the health-care rally. Seats had been sold for $1 and the house was packed with 17,500 mostly elderly supporters inside and another 2,500 outside on Forty-ninth Street. The president's address—at 4:30—was broadcast nationally and, like the birthday party festivities, delivered by closed-circuit television to Joseph P. Kennedy's room at the Rusk Institute.

His father's condition was clearly on his mind that weekend—as it was often now. Like every other member of the Kennedy family, the patriarch's inability to communicate had left a void in his life, an absence that affected him deeply. He grieved his loss, but grieved even more for his father, once the most independent and vital of men, now reduced to invalid status, unable to speak, walk, or to care for himself. In response to the criticism that his health-care bill would "sap the individual self-reliance of Americans," he departed from his prepared text to declare that he couldn't imagine anything more likely "to sap someone's self-reliance than to be sick, alone, broke." His father, he reported, was neither "alone" nor "broke," but he was now entirely dependent on others. "I visited twice, yesterday and today, in hospital, where doctors labor for a long time, to visit my father. It's isn't easy—it isn't easy." He hadn't asked his speechwriters to include any reference to his father's condition, nor had he planned to do so himself. But after departing from his script to speak of his father and, in doing so, displaying an uncharacteristic flash of sentiment that might be mistaken for weakness, he pushed forward to hammer home his point, but gently, with a joke. His father, he reminded his audience, "can pay his bills, but otherwise I would be. And I am not as well off as he is. But what happens to him and to others when they put their lives' savings in, in a short time?"[37]

In referring to his father's illness, the president, much as Eunice had in her reference to her "retarded" sister, crossed the otherwise impermeable boundary between the private and the public—but only for a fleeting moment before retreating again. Never again would he make reference to his father's condition or the pain he, the son, suffered because of it. Nor would he ever make public mention of the death of his second son, Patrick Bouvier Kennedy, in August of 1963.

To succeed in politics or in public life, certainly in the mid-twentieth century, arguably a bit less today, a president has to scrupulously compartmentalize one's private and public lives. For the Kennedys, this was both more necessary and more difficult than for others. They had myriad secrets to hide: infidelities, illnesses, the effect on all of them of the premature and violent deaths of Joe Jr. and Kathleen, and Rosemary's botched lobotomy. The most carefully guarded secret, even more so than Rosemary's condition, was Jack Kennedy's precarious health and the myriad drugs, treatments, and hospitalizations he required to stay on his feet and functioning.

While we may admire the skill with which the Kennedys managed to shield so much and to present a family narrative that privileged health over illness, joy over suffering, triumph over tragedy, it is difficult to avoid the conclusion, albeit arrived at in retrospect, that voters—and the nation—may have been ill-served by the withholding of vital information about Jack Kennedy's health. There was, for the Kennedy family, nothing remiss in keeping so much of their private lives hidden from public view. They truly believed that their illnesses, their pain, and their tragedies did not and would never affect their performance in the political arena. And they may have been correct. But the decision of what to disclose to voters and what to hide should not have been theirs alone to make.

John Fitzgerald Kennedy was not the only president in the twentieth century to suffer from personal tragedies, near calamitous bouts of illness, and treatment by multiple and powerful medicating agents, the effects of which were never made known to the public. Questions have also been raised about the role of ill health on the performance in office of Woodrow Wilson, Warren Harding, Calvin Coolidge, Franklin Roosevelt, Dwight Eisenhower, and Ronald Reagan. It is not the task of the historian to make policy recommendations for the future based on the interpretation of the past. Still, it is incumbent on us to ask, based on our investigations and interpretations, how a democracy can and should balance the rights of privacy for aspiring and elected officials with the public's need to know enough about their mental and physical well-being to make decisions on their fitness for office. The Kennedys, it must be said, denied the public that discussion.

NOTES

1. Rose Elizabeth Fitzgerald Kennedy, *Times to Remember* (New York: Doubleday, 1974), 132.
2. Jacqueline Bouvier Kennedy, *Jacqueline Kennedy: Historic Conversations on Life with John F. Kennedy* (New York: Hyperion, 2011), 21
3. Rose Kennedy, 70.
4. Rose Kennedy, 204.
5. Coughlin interview in Barbara A. Perry, *Rose Kennedy: The Life and Times of a Political Matriarch* (New York: Norton, 2013), 49.

6. Rose Kennedy, 73–4.
7. Ibid.
8. Amanda Smith, *Hostage to Fortune: The Letters of Joseph P. Kennedy* (New York: Viking, 2001), 24.
9. David Nasaw, *The Patriarch: The Remarkable Life and Turbulent Times of Joseph P. Kennedy* (New York: Penguin, 2012), 239.
10. Nasaw, 560.
11. Nasaw, 594
12. James MacGregor Burns, *John Kennedy: A Political Profile* (New York: Avon, 1961), 76–8
13. Nasaw, 617.
14. Burns, 118.
15. Doris Kearns Goodwin, *The Fitzgeralds and the Kennedys* (New York: Simon & Schuster, 1987), 774–5.
16. Nasaw, 684–5.
17. Goodwin, 776.
18. Burns, 164.
19. Robert Dallek, "The Medical Ordeals of JFK," *Atlantic Monthly* (December 2002), 49–52, 54, 56, 58, 60–61.
20. Wyzanski memo, Oct. 20, 1964, Box 498, folder 11, Arthur M. Schlesinger Jr. papers, New York Public Library.
21. Lawrence O'Brien, *No Final Victories* (Garden City, NY: Doubleday, 1954), 54–5.
22. Robert A. Caro, *The Passage of Power* (New York: Alfred A. Knopf, 2012), 96–7.
23. John F. Kennedy, "The Soft American," *Sports Illustrated,* December 26, 1960, in *SI VAULT, http://sportsillustrated.cnn.com/vault/article/magazine/MAG1134750/.*
24. Nasaw, 768.
25. Joseph P. Kennedy to Walter Annenberg, Sept. 14, 1961, Box 213, Joseph P. Kennedy Papers, John F. Kennedy Presidential Library (hereafter JFKPL), Boston, Mass.
26. Rose Fitzgerald Kennedy Diary, "Thanksgiving '61," Box 4, Rose Elizabeth Fitzgerald Kennedy Papers, JFKPL.
27. Perry, 267.
28. Rose Kennedy to children, September, 1962, in Edward Moore Kennedy, ed., *Her Grace Above Gold: In Loving Remembrance of Rose Fitzgerald Kennedy* (Joseph P. Kennedy Jr. Foundation, 1997), 54.
29. Benjamin C. Bradlee, *Conversations with Kennedy* (New York: Norton, 1975), 167–9.
30. Rita Dallas and Jeanira Ratcliffe, *The Kennedy Case* (New York: G.P. Putnam's Sons, 1973), 87.
31. Eunice Kennedy Shriver, "Hope for Retarded Children," *Saturday Evening Post,* vol. 235, no. 33, September 22, 1962, 71.
32. *New York Times*, Oct. 19, 1961, 24.
33. President's Panel on Mental Retardation, "Foreword" to "Report of the Taskforce on Law," January, 1963, http://mn.gov/mnddc/parallels2/pdf/60s/63/63-ROT-PPMR.pdf.
34. Shriver, 72.
35. Theodore C. Sorensen, *Kennedy* (New York: Harper & Row, 1965), 342–3.
36. Lawrence F. O'Brien, *No Final Victories* (Garden City, NY: Doubleday, 1973), 133
37. *New York Times*, May 20, 1962, 20.

President Lyndon B. Johnson during a tense and weary moment in the White House. Vice President Hubert Humphrey is to his right. [Courtesy Lyndon B. Johnson Library and Museum.]

9

Lyndon Johnson at Home and Abroad

RANDALL B. WOODS

Lyndon Johnson, master politician and architect of both the Great Society and the war in Vietnam, was a tormented man. He had a good deal to be tormented about, and his insecurities—and his particular personal demons—sometimes affected his public policies behavior. Two in particular stand out: the first was Johnson's decision to have the FBI illegally wiretap members of the Mississippi Freedom Democratic Party (MFDP) as they sought to unseat the regular, all-white Mississippi delegation to the 1964 Democratic National Convention in Atlantic City where he was nominated for president in his own right. The second was his decision to justify intervention in the Dominican Republic in June 1965 as a necessary step to prevent the island nation from falling under the sway of Fidel Castro and the forces of international communism. Both were overreactions fraught with dangerous implications. Both decisions grew directly from his own personal crises and led to unfortunate consequences. The manner in which Johnson handled the MFDP affair gave J. Edgar Hoover a hold over him that would allow the FBI director to continue to demonize Martin Luther King and paint the civil rights movement as a communist conspiracy. The terms in which the president chose to justify the Dominican intervention helped perpetuate a simple-minded anti-communism that would make a negotiated settlement of the Vietnam conflict increasingly difficult, if not impossible. In addition, the way in which Johnson handled both episodes created "credibility gaps," as they were then called, the first with activists of the Student Nonviolent Coordinating Committee (SNCC) and the Congress on Racial Equality (CORE) who were convinced that LBJ had betrayed them at Atlantic City; and the second with authentic internationalists like J. William Fulbright and other liberals who were convinced that Johnson had been captured by hardline anti-communists.

* * *

Lyndon was the eldest son of Rebekah Baines and Sam Ely Johnson. His parents shared a common interest in and commitment to politics and public service—but little else. Rebekah was a devout Southern Baptist, an aspiring intellectual, and a cultural maven, insofar as the Hill Country of Central Texas had cultural mavens. She did not drink, dance, or consort with people who did—except for her husband. Sam Johnson was a religious free thinker, a backwoods schoolteacher turned state legislator who liked nothing better than to drink and dance. Except when they were discussing their children or politics, Sam and Rebekah lived apart even as they occupied two ends of the family home in Johnson City. In her half, Rebekah would provide elocution lessons to local children, have her friends to tea parties, and dream of a better, more cultured world. On his porch, Sam would harangue local attorneys, politicians, farmers, and ranchers as they drank corn whiskey.[1]

Lyndon was initially closer to his mother. He bought into her image of herself as a cultured woman being destroyed by a frontier environment that was beneath her. But that would change. Rebekah Johnson was a master of conditional love. If she became displeased with her son, or if he disappointed her, she refused to touch him, talk to him, to acknowledge his existence. She saddled her eldest with a lifetime sense of inadequacy. In 1955 after LBJ suffered a near-fatal heart attack, Rebekah descended upon the family ranch in the Hill Country to "nurse" her son. In truth she reproached him continually for not immediately returning to public life. "She was so damn mean to him," observed George Reedy, a longtime LBJ aide. "She had all these impossible standards for him."[2] In his early adolescence, Lyndon began accompanying his father as he campaigned in and around Johnson City and then during some of his stays in Austin when the legislature was in session. "I wanted to copy my father always, emulate him, do the things he did," LBJ later observed.[3] But his father's behavior became increasingly erratic; one of Lyndon's contemporaries recalled that Sam, scheduled to give an address in the upstairs auditorium at the Johnson High School, was so drunk that he fell repeatedly while ascending the stairs.[4] Alcohol became even more of a problem after he failed in business in 1919. His mother's tears of frustration and loneliness and his father's bouts with both the bottle and the market provoked defiance and rebelliousness in young Lyndon.

Johnson was nonetheless driven to succeed. He worked his way through Southwest Texas State Teachers College in San Marcos. In his junior year he served as principal of the segregated school for Mexican children in Cotulla, an experience that accentuated a natural impulse to uplift the downtrodden. Following graduation he taught high school debate in Houston. As Congressman Richard Kleberg's secretary in Washington during the early 1930s, he worked seven days a week and drove the office staff like a plantation overseer, a trait that would persist. Indeed, the young pol from Texas was at times manic, even in his courtship of Lady Bird. Lyndon met his future wife in 1934 in Austin over drinks with friends. He invited her to breakfast the next morning, which was a meal followed by an automobile tour of Austin. Throughout the day Johnson talked nonstop, mostly about himself and his ambitions. "It was just like finding yourself in the middle of a whirlwind," Lady Bird later recalled.[5] At the end of the day, to her astonishment, Lyndon asked her to marry him. Several months later, as she waited in her San Antonio hotel room for her marriage ceremony to begin, she told her bridesmaid that, for a quarter, she would jump out the window.[6]

After heading up the National Youth Administration in Texas, Johnson was elected to Congress from the Tenth Congressional District in 1937. A faithful servant of his constituents and an avowed disciple of Franklin Roosevelt and the New Deal, LBJ, on his second try, won election to the Senate in 1948. His rise in the upper chamber was meteoric: first minority leader and then, beginning in 1954, majority leader, a post he used to establish a competitive partnership with the Eisenhower administration. To a superficial observer LBJ seemed a man who moved inexorably from strength to strength.

But then there were also fits of depression. When the "black dog" visited, Lyndon would withdraw, sometimes for days on end. As he confronted the monumental task of defeating Coke Stevenson in his 1948 campaign for the Senate, LBJ was wracked with anxiety. In February of that year, Johnson had hired as his speechwriter Horace Busby, a University of Texas graduate and former *Daily Texan* editor, who was working as a journalist in Washington. When Busby arrived in Austin he went immediately to campaign headquarters. No Johnson. Where was he? Lyndon had not made an appearance in two days, another staffer said, so Busby drove out to the candidate's apartment. There he found Johnson chain-smoking with blinds drawn. "Do you think we have a chance?" Johnson asked Busby. "No, not really," Busby replied. The phone began to ring. It rang a dozen times, stopped, and rang some more. Johnson eyed it suspiciously. "He whispered to me as though the phone could hear us," Busby remembered. "He said, 'that's them . . . I mouthed back to him, 'Who? Who is them?' And he said, whispering, "Headquarters.' "[7]

There were intimations of a split personality. Joe Phipps, a campaign aide who worked for Johnson during the 1948 campaign recalled that his boss constantly alternated between the refined and the crude. Obsessively clean, immaculately dressed by day, "but in the privacy of an overnight hotel room on the road, he almost seemed to take pleasure in shocking the more protected of our little cadre," Phipps wrote, "presenting himself as a hunk of lumpen flesh born with low animal circulatory, nervous, respiratory and digestive systems; belching, breaking wind, stalking into an adjoining bathroom to urinate or defecate without even bothering to close the door." But then he would launch into a description of some future utopia, with himself as creator and director.[8] The only person really capable of writing a biography of LBJ, George Reedy observed, was the Italian playwright Luigi Pirandello, whose best-known plays, *Six Characters in Search of an Author* (1921) and *Henry IV* (1922), exploited the notions of multiple personality and the relativity of reality.[9]

Charles Marsh, the media mogul and oilman, who was Johnson's sponsor and cuckold, thought LBJ was bipolar. Marsh knew from experience, having himself been treated several times for manic depression. LBJ's physician, J. Willis Hurst, later speculated on the possibility that the president suffered from a bipolar disorder: "Extremely interesting people do display many emotions, ranging from anger, to humor to unpredictability, to all kinds of things; up to a point this of course is entirely normal. Now, whether or not you want to say that his swings in all of this, his emotional swings, reached the abnormal state, would be a very debatable issue."[10]

Except on a very few occasions, LBJ failed to exhibit the ironic detachment that characterized his predecessor, Jack Kennedy. He took everything personally and was at times absurdly literal minded. His thin skin, his inability to satisfy his expectations of himself, led to subpar health. Not only was there the near-fatal 1955 heart attack but no fewer than six cases of pneumonia, recurrent kidney stones, and two hernia operations.

Despite his shortcomings and idiosyncrasies, LBJ was a master politician and social visionary determined not only to fulfill the promise of the New Deal but also to move beyond and create a "Great Society" that would realize the nation's material and aesthetic potential. Capitalizing on Kennedy's martyrdom, the Texan pushed through Congress the Kennedy tax cut and the 1964 Civil Rights Bill enacted in June. He named Sargent Shriver, Kennedy's Peace Corps Director, to head the War on Poverty, a program that would reduce the hardcore poor from 21 percent of the population to 11 percent by the end of the decade. By summer, Johnson's attention was focused completely on winning the forthcoming presidential election, deflecting charges that he was nothing more than an accidental president and earning a mandate for the ambitious reform program he had in mind. But the road to the Democratic nomination, much less the presidency, was hardly clear.

By the summer of 1964, Mississippi had become the principal battleground in the struggle over civil rights. The black population there was the most disfranchised in the nation. "Only 5 percent of black Mississippians [who made up 45 percent of the state's population] were registered to vote, the lowest rate in the United States," Juan Williams of the *Washington Post* reported.[11] Denied access to the all-white regular Democratic Party, black Mississippians assembled in April in Jackson and voted to establish the Mississippi Freedom Democratic Party. During the ensuing Freedom Summer of 1964, local activists joined with volunteers from the Congress for Racial Equality (CORE) and the student Non-violent Coordinating Committee (SNCC) to try to register the disfranchised. Rebuffed at every turn, they announced a "freedom registration" campaign. On August 6, 2,500 people jammed the Masonic Temple for the MFDP State Convention. There they selected sixty-four blacks and four whites as the MFDP delegation to the Democratic Convention in Atlantic City. The plan was to challenge the regular all-white Mississippi delegation on two grounds: that it had racially discriminated and that its members had refused to sign a loyalty oath committing them to support the Democratic ticket.[12]

The revolt among Mississippi's black voters terrified Johnson. He desperately wanted to be elected president in his own right, and was already convinced that JFK's followers were planning to hijack the convention and throw the nomination to Robert Kennedy. As his protégé, Governor John Connally of Texas indelicately put it to LBJ, "If you seat those black jigaboos, the whole South will walk out."[13] Governor Carl Sanders of Georgia echoed Connally's warning. Whereas Mississippi and Alabama were probably going to withdraw anyway if a loyalty oath was required, this was not likely to precipitate a bolt by the entire South. But seating the MFDP would. The stakes were considerable: Texas and Georgia alone accounted for thirty-seven electoral votes. And then there were the border states. "I know this," LBJ told Hubert Humphrey, his future running mate. "If we mess with the group of Negros . . . who said we want you to recognize us and throw out the governor and the elected officials of the state . . . we will lose 15 states without campaigning. . . . I don't want to do anything in Mississippi to lose Oklahoma for me and I don't want to do anything in Mississippi to lose Kentucky for me."[14]

On August 19 the president met with a delegation from the MFDP as well as representatives from CORE and SNCC. He pled with them to listen to reason. If the MFDP tried and failed, there were liable to be massive, and probably violent, demonstrations across the country. The ensuing white backlash could well undermine what he was trying to do in the area of civil rights. Law and order would be the bedrock of the fall campaign; it had to be the base on which the administration would build its case in the South for obedience to the Civil Rights Act. His pleas fell on deaf ears.[15]

The MFDP delegation arrived by bus in Atlantic City on August 21. The next day David Lawrence gaveled the Credentials Committee to order and spokespersons for the MFDP and the regular, all-white delegation proceeded to make their cases before a bank of television cameras. Heading the regular contingent was Governor Paul Johnson, who had once joked that NAACP stood for "niggers, alligators, apes, coons, and possums."[16] Speaking for the MFDP was Mrs. Fannie Lou Hamer, a black sharecropper from Ruleville who had been driven off her farm, jailed, and finally beaten, all for merely attempting to vote.

In truth LBJ knew what the MFDP was going to do before it did it. So agitated had he become over the issue that in late July he had issued an order to put in place an unprecedented program of illegal political espionage designed to protect his presidential candidacy. On August 1 Johnson had his aide, Walter Jenkins, call Deke DeLoach, the FBI's liaison to the White House. "Deke," Jenkins said, "the President is very concerned about his personal safety and that of his staff while they're at the convention. Would you head a team to keep us advised of any potential threats?"[17] Jenkins subsequently spelled out exactly what the White House expected, namely all the information the FBI could gather about the MFDP, its sixty-eight delegates to Atlantic City, and its allies in SNCC, CORE, and the SCLC. The president wanted to know every detail of the Freedom Democrats' strategy and tactics as they presented their case to the convention's credentials committee. "Lyndon is way out of line," Hoover commented when DeLoach told him. Nonetheless, he instructed his assistant to "tell Walter [Jenkins]we will give him whatever help he wants."[18]

Over dinner at the White House on August 20, Johnson complained to his close friend, Senator Richard Russell of Georgia, that it took him "hours each night" to read all the wiretap reports he was receiving, including those of Martin Luther King speaking with Joseph Rauh. (Rauh, co-founder of the Americans for Democratic Action and general counsel to the MFDP and the United Auto Workers, was one of the nation's most prominent liberals.) "Hoover apparently has been turned loose and is tapping everything," Russell noted in his diary.[19] Indeed, the Director fed LBJ's ever-present sense that conspiracies were forming against him.

As the president became more anxious about his ability to control the outcome of the Mississippi imbroglio, he became depressed, pessimistic, and paranoid. For months Hoover had been bombarding the White House with raw data allegedly proving that MLK was in bed with the Communist Party of the United States. "Those communists are moving in on King, and King's moving in on Rauh," Johnson complained to Secretary of Labor Willard Wirtz. When Mayor Richard Daley of Chicago questioned whether there was "someone behind" the MFDP challenge, Johnson replied, "Oh, yes, Dick. The Communist Party is the leader."[20]

The Democratic Convention's Credentials Committee was divided, but Rauh had enough votes to lead a floor fight. If the dispute spilled over onto the floor, the deep schism in the party would be revealed on television for all to see. The president was as frustrated by the regular all-white Mississippi delegation—which refused to compromise even on a loyalty oath—as he was with the MFDP. He demanded of Senator James Eastland to know whether the Mississippi regulars had come to the convention "as traitors to the party—or are they going to try to be helpful?" On Sunday evening he warned Eastland that he "might cut out your goddamn [agricultural] subsidies and cut out your $6 billion cotton program."[21]

Then King cabled LBJ at one o'clock on the morning of the twenty-fourth to urge him to throw his lot behind the seating of the MFDP. Johnson called Richard Russell. "What do you do when they [King and the Freedom Democrats] are getting ready to take charge of the convention . . . and they run over you—which they will—then what do you do?" Sensing that Johnson was overreacting, Russell said, "You don't do a thing, but say you're sorry. You think they are ill-advised. And let it go." But LBJ would not, could not. The president then speculated that King's telegram was part of a plot hatched by Robert Kennedy, the attorney general. "This is Bobby's trap," he insisted.[22]

On the following morning, August 25, a depressed Johnson called his Texas friend and business partner, A.W. Moursund. He informed Moursund he was leaning toward announcing later in the day that he was withdrawing as candidate for the Democratic presidential nomination and retiring to Texas.[23] "I am absolutely positive that I cannot lead the South and the North," he told George Reedy later that day. "And I don't want to lead the nation without my own state and without my own section. I am very convinced that the Negros will not listen to me. They're not going to follow a white Southerner."[24] Johnson then called Senator Russell again at his home in Winder, Georgia. He was going to Atlantic City at about 7:30 that night, and there he would serve notice that he had incurred "too many scars and could not unite the country . . . He would tell the convention "to get some fresh figure to nominate and elect." Russell listened patiently until his friend exclaimed that he had "only accepted the vice presidential nomination in 1960 to avoid dropping dead on the Senate floor as majority leader." He had been "looking for the peace and quiet of the vice president's job." That was too much for Russell, who had endured Johnson's overweening ambition for sixteen years. He was "speaking like a child—and a spoiled one at that," he told the president and advised him to "take a tranquilizer and get a few hours' sleep."[25]

With the Credentials committee deadlocked, the White House proposed a compromise on the afternoon of the twenty-fifth: two MFDP delegates would be seated as delegates-at-large; only those members of the regular Mississippi contingent who signed a loyalty oath would be seated; and the Democratic Party would prohibit racial discrimination in the selection of delegates to all future conventions. The committee was deeply divided but in the end announced at a televised press conference that it had voted to accept the two-seat compromise. Despite the pleadings of Bayard Rustin, Martin Luther King, and others, the MFDP would have none of it. "We didn't come all this way for no two seats," Fannie Lou Hamer famously exclaimed.[26] The all-white Mississippi delegation, most of whose members immediately departed Atlantic City, were just as disgruntled. On Tuesday evening, twenty-one MFDP delegates, furnished credentials by friendly delegates from other states, pushed their way into the seats vacated by the regular delegation. After an unsuccessful effort to evict Hamer and her colleagues, the sergeant-at-arms and his men simply ignored them, and the convention proceeded with its business.[27]

Johnson went on to win in a landslide in 1964, of course, as Russell had told him he would. There was never really any chance he would lose to Barry Goldwater, the ultra-conservative Republican nominee, no matter what transpired at Atlantic City. But the MFDP episode had ironic consequences. The president would continue his crusade on behalf of civil rights for African Americans, including passage of the Voting Rights Act of 1965, the Fair Housing Act of 1968, and executive branch initiatives to desegregate hospitals and schools that received federal aid. In the long run, those initiatives changed the nature of the party, leading to the emergence of Jesse Jackson's Rainbow Coalition. But in the short run, the way the MFDP was treated at the convention alienated SNCC and CORE; it caused them to question the wisdom of working within the Democratic Party and created the first of several credibility gaps. Perhaps most significant for the Johnson presidency, the MFDP controversy made LBJ and Hoover allies whether the president wanted it or not. In the months that followed, the FBI director worked tirelessly to convince the White House that all of the administration's problems were the result of a communist conspiracy. And Johnson proved increasingly willing to listen to the Hoover's siren song. Indeed, Johnson's insecurities and paranoia as well as his and Hoover's tendency to see a Red under every bed would play out again in the Dominican crisis of 1965.

* * *

At 4:40 in the afternoon of April 28, 1965, Lyndon Johnson sat down with his foreign policy team—Secretary of State Dean Rusk, his deputy George Ball, Defense Secretary Robert McNamara, National Security Adviser McGeorge Bundy, and presidential aide Bill Moyers—to discuss the perilous situation in Vietnam. An hour into the meeting President Johnson was handed a cable marked "critic" (critical) from Ambassador W. Tapley Bennett in Santo Domingo. The Dominican military had split into at least two factions, and one was arming the populace in an effort to seize power. "Regret report situation deteriorating rapidly," it stated. "Country team unanimously of opinion that time has come to land the marines . . . American lives are in danger." After conferring with his advisers, all of whom approved intervention, Johnson ordered four hundred marines to proceed to the Dominican capital at once to protect the embassy.[28]

The causes of the Dominican Republic's many troubles were varied, but most were rooted in the thirty-year dictatorship of Rafael Leonidas Trujillo Molina. Trujillo had brutally suppressed all opposition, turned the army into his personal palace guard, and ravaged his country's fragile economy. Then, in the summer of 1961, assassins shot him in the head. His family tried to perpetuate his tyranny without him but failed and fled into exile. In December 1962 Dominicans elected the liberal intellectual, Juan Bosch, to the presidency. Seven months later, a military coup overthrew him, its leaders charging that he was too tolerant of communists and Marxism. Despite support from the Johnson administration for the new government of Donald Reid Cabral and the presence of some 2,500 Americans on the island, stability eluded the Dominicans. Drought, widespread unemployment, strikes, sabotage, and continuing opposition from dissidents kept the country in constant turmoil. From exile in Puerto Rico, where he was a college professor, Juan Bosch directed the disruptive activities of the Dominican Revolutionary Party (PRD).[29]

The spring of 1965 found the Dominican military deeply divided. A minority was devoted to Bosch's return, but the majority regarded him as a dangerous revolutionary who would "open the door to the communists" and, more to the point, do away with the military's privileges. When officers loyal to Reid Cabral attempted to arrest some of Bosch's fellows for plotting against the government on his behalf, the PRD declared a general uprising and surrounded the presidential palace. At this point, the anti-Bosch military, led by the pious and reactionary General Elias Wessin y Wessin, issued an ultimatum to the PRD, demanding that it cease its insurrection and turn over power to the army. Wessin had become convinced that Bosch and the PRD were encouraging the "14th of June Movement," similar to the insurrection led by Fidel Castro that took control in Cuba only years before. When the rebels ignored his demand, air force planes began bombing and strafing the palace, as well as the slums of Santo Domingo, which were Bosch strongholds and, in the minds of the military, seedbeds of communist agitation. The brutal attacks inflamed the general population, which flooded into the streets in response to calls from the PRD. At this point, Santo Domingo teetered on the edge of chaos. Under the auspices of Ambassador Bennett, who decided that the embassy could no longer remain aloof, the anti-Bosch military put together a junta headed by Colonel Pedro Bartolome Benoit. The primary purpose of this government was to request armed intervention by the United States.[30]

On the afternoon of April 28, while President Johnson met with his advisers on Vietnam, Undersecretary of State Robert Mann and Ambassador Bennett exchanged a flurry of telegrams. Bennett managed to convince the State Department that, given General Wessin and Colonel Benoit's inability to control the situation in Santo Domingo, there was a very real danger of a communist, Castro-controlled takeover in the Dominican Republic. All "responsible" elements agreed that US Marines should be dispatched at once, and he agreed with them, Bennett declared. Mann then advised the ambassador that he must compel Benoit to base his request for American intervention on the need to protect American lives. "We did instruct our Ambassador to go back to Benoit . . . and in order to improve our juridical base asked him to specifically say that he could not protect the lives of American citizens," Mann subsequently admitted to the Senate Foreign Relations Committee (SFRC). Following instructions, Bennett insisted in his later cables that the large number of Americans residing at the Hotel Embajador were in danger of being killed or wounded as the crisis escalated.[31]

The Latin Americanists within the State Department urged Johnson to work through the Organization of American States (OAS). On the twenty-eighth the president had appealed to the OAS to authorize a joint military operation to restore peace in the Dominican Republic. To his intense frustration, the head of the inter-American body informed the White House that it would take some time just to get the delegates together, much less agree on the wording of a statement. For the president, any delay was out of the question.[32]

There was nothing in Johnson's background to indicate that he was a knee-jerk anticommunist. The Texan was in basic agreement with the foreign policies of the Kennedy administration: military preparedness and realistic diplomacy, he believed, would contain communism within its existing bounds. To keep up morale among America's allies and satisfy hardline anticommunists at home, the United States must continue to hold fast in Berlin, oppose the admission of the People's Republic of China to the United Nations, and continue to confront and blockade Cuba. He was aware of the split growing between Red China and the Soviet Union and of the possibilities for dividing the communist world. He had taken a flexible, even hopeful, view of the Soviet Union and Nikita Khrushchev until his ouster the previous October. It was just possible, LBJ believed, that the USSR was becoming a status quo power and as such would be a force for stability rather than chaos in international relations. In the developing world, the United States must continue its "flexible response" of military aid, economic assistance, and technical/political advice in response to the threat of Communism in international relations. However, there was nothing wrong with negotiating with the Soviets at the same time in an effort to reduce tensions. Insofar as Latin America was concerned, Johnson was an enthusiastic supporter of the Alliance for Progress; and, as a progressive, he was drawn to the notion of seeking openings to the democratic left.

But then, in the midst of the Dominican crisis, the president began to panic. Late in the morning of the 30th, he called Abe Fortas, his long-time adviser who had agreed to trouble-shoot in Santo Domingo. Suffering from a terrible cold, his voice harsh and shrill, the President was barely comprehensible:

> They're killing our people. They've captured tanks now and they've taken over the police, and they're marching them down the street and they're saying they're going to shoot them if they don't take over. Now, our CIA says this is a completely led, operated, dominated–they've

> got men on the inside of it–Castro operation. That it started out as a Bosch operation, but he's been moved completely out of the picture.... They are moving other places in the hemisphere. It may be a part of a whole Communist pattern tied in with Vietnam. I don't think that God Almighty is going to excuse me for sitting with adequate forces and letting them murder human beings.[33]

Johnson's version of events was largely a product of his fevered imagination and Hoover's memos, rather than any hard evidence from the CIA.

That afternoon, the president and his advisers hit on the idea of dispatching several battalions of regular army troops to establish an "international safety zone" in Santo Domingo, the Dominican capital. Nationals of all countries seeking safety from the fighting could congregate there, and it would give the United States cover with the international community for intervening militarily in what was clearly a civil war.[34]

With Johnson scheduled to go on nationwide television that night at 8:40 to inform the country of his decision, a nasty argument broke out among his advisers as to what justification should be used. Undersecretary Mann and the CIA wanted Castroism and the threat of another communist regime in the hemisphere to be front and center. LBJ wholeheartedly agreed. Both hardliners like Russell and liberals like Mike Mansfield and Wayne Morse were telling him that it was on these grounds, and these grounds alone, that Congress and the public would accept massive armed intervention in a civil conflict.

McNamara, however, was of the opinion that the Red card ought to be played but that the president's advisers, and not the president, ought to do it. "I think you have got a pretty tough job to prove that [they] have got a handful of people there but you don't know that Castro is trying to do anything," the Secretary of Defense cautioned him. "I think it puts your own status and prestige too much on the line." LBJ then asked him if the CIA would be able to document the fact of communist domination of the insurgency. McNamara said he did not think so.[35]

By six o'clock, Johnson was nearly beside himself. "While we were talking yesterday, we ought to have been acting," he told McGeorge Bundy, his national security adviser. "I think they're going to have that island in another twenty-four hours. We've run under the table and hid." When Bundy said that some in the State Department were afraid that the OAS might construe claims of communist domination of the insurgency in the Dominican Republic as an effort to stampede the membership, LBJ blew his top. "All right," he screamed at Bundy, "Let's see if we can satisfy that bunch of damn sissies over there on that question! Let's cut it [the possibility of communist influence] and say they're 'great statesmen.'"[36]

In the end, LBJ could not resist the temptation to invoke the communist bogeyman. In his address on the evening of April 30 and at press conference two days later, he declared that without the insertion of US forces into the Dominican Republic, "men and women–American and those of other lands—will die in the streets." In the midst of the unrest, he continued, events

> took a tragic turn . . . Communist leaders, many of them trained in Cuba, took increasing control. And what began as a popular democratic revolution was taken over and really seized and placed into the hands of a band of Communist conspirators. The American nations cannot, must not, and will not permit the establishment of another Communist government in the Western Hemisphere.[37]

During the hectic days in late April, when the president was coming to his decision to intervene and subsequently to his rationalization for it, he had asked the FBI to join the CIA in hunting for card-carrying Reds in the Dominican Republic. Hoover had been more than happy to oblige; from the beginning he was convinced, he said, that "this so-called Bosch fellow and his stooge down there [Colonel Francisco Alberto Caamano Deno, leader of dissident troops loyal to Bosch] were either communists or fellow travelers." There was no doubt, Hoover told LBJ over and over, that "the communists are holding and directing the principal policy of the rebel forces."[38]

In the first week in May reporters flooded into the Dominican Republic determined to check out the administration's version of events. They quickly discovered that no American civilian had been killed or even wounded at the Hotel Embajador or anywhere else on the island. And where were the Castroites? When pressed, anonymous sources in the American embassy declared that they had in their possession the names of fifty-eight communists who had led the uprising against Reid Cabral. Editorials in the *New York Times*, the *New York Herald Tribune*, and the *Washington Post* began to question the administration's reasoning and veracity. The notion that fifty-eight insurgents posed a massive threat in any Latin American country, even one as small as the Dominican Republic, seemed ludicrous. J. William Fulbright, chair of the Senate Foreign Relations Committee, led a chorus of critics inside and outside the United States. There was no communist menace in the Dominican Republic, the Arkansan declared. Instead, professional anti-communists in the State Department had formed a tacit alliance with "Latin American oligarchs who are engaged in a vain attempt to preserve the status quo–reactionaries who habitually use the term communist very loosely." Various Latin American nations pointed out that the interjection of troops violated the charter of the OAS which stipulated that "no State or group of States had the right to intervene, directly or indirectly, for any reason whatever, in the internal or external affairs of any other State."[39]

Despite Fulbright's broadside, the OAS soon agreed to send delegates to a gathering in Washington, DC, in May 1965. There the attendees narrowly voted to send an inter-American peacekeeping force to the unsettled island. Under cover of this multinational army, US forces withdrew. In June 1966 Joaquin Balaguer, a moderate rightist, defeated Bosch in the presidential election. The new president quieted the island by taking a few of Bosch's followers into the Cabinet, but Bosch remained unreconciled. For his part, Johnson remained committed to his rationale unapologetically. "What can we do in Vietnam if we can't clean up the Dominican Republic?" he remarked to an adviser.[40]

As with the Mississippi Freedom Democratic Party, LBJ had overreacted during the Dominican crisis of 1965. Bill Moyers, his special assistant and White House press secretary, noted that the CIA reported that the developments in Santo Domingo had actually taken Havana by surprise. Castro and communism were bogeymen. The president's linkage of Vietnam with the Dominican Republic—defending his actions in both places as interventions necessary to halt the spread of Sino-Soviet imperialism— would, moreover, come back to haunt him. Even if he had wanted to pursue a more moderate course in Southeast Asia, he could not do so, having thus rhetorically and psychologically straitjacketed himself. And the Texan had driven yet another wedge into his credibility, a gap that Fulbright and other opponents of the war in Vietnam would labor relentlessly to widen in the years to come.

Notwithstanding these two instructive examples, Lyndon Johnson's decisions in regard to both domestic and foreign policy were not always made in the midst of an ongoing hysterical fit. The decision to escalate the war in Vietnam taken in the spring and summer of 1965 was exhaustively debated and almost entirely so on strategic and pragmatic grounds. Indeed, the old debate teacher from Texas put his foreign policy team through the wringer before he acceded to their recommendations. And he remained skeptical throughout. Then, too, the thousand pieces of legislation that comprised the Great Society could not have made their way through Congress without LBJ's cold, calculating guidance and his shrewd and artful appeals to public opinion. The presidency is a scourge, especially in times of war, and the Johnson presidency was no less fraught than those of Lincoln, Wilson, and Roosevelt. Yet, despite his bipolar tendencies—his uncontrollable outbursts and overreaction that were so apparent in the MFDP and Dominican episodes—the president's judgment was not on the whole impaired by mental illness. The Texan, though extremely intelligent, was intellectually limited, and those limitations led at times to his intense frustration. Johnson had little or no appreciation of irony, little familiarity with the imp of the perverse. When the civil rights movement shifted to the North and the ghettoes began to burn, and when the very youth for whom he had been building the Great Society turned on him, the president, with his deep and abiding faith in the American political system and his own vision of reform, could do no other than to believe that forces outside the American social and political system were responsible.

In assessing Lyndon Johnson's performance in the light of the recurrent crises of his mental health, it is important to note that that issue may also be overshadowed by questions regarding his physical well-being. His decision to announce, on March 31, 1968, that he would neither seek nor accept his party's nomination for another term as president stemmed in part from his perception that he had expended all of his political capital; that further domestic reform was impossible, given the urban violence and white backlash that gripped the nation; and that removing himself from the national politics might lead to a more reasonable public discourse on the war in Vietnam. But his abdication was prompted as well by his personal physician's dire warning that he would most certainly not live to see the end of another term. Johnson's 1955 heart attack had nearly killed him, and heart failure would cause his demise in 1972. Indeed, so sure that the stresses of the job would kill her husband, Lady Bird purchased a black dress for the funeral in the fall of 1967. The counterfactual question most often asked about presidents of the Cold War era is what might have happened if Kennedy had lived? But an equally intriguing question is what if LBJ had been healthy enough to keep Richard Nixon out of the Oval Office?

NOTES

1. Biographies of Lyndon Baines Johnson are legion. For starters see Robert Dallek, *Lyndon B. Johnson: Portrait of a President* (New York, 2004); Randall B. Woods, *LBJ: Architect of American Ambition* (New York, 2006); and Mark K. Updegrove, *Indomitable Will: LBJ in the Presidency* (New York, 2014). For the latest scholarship on the Johnson presidency see Mitchell B. Lerner, *A Companion to Lyndon B. Johnson* (Boston, 2012).
2. George Reedy Oral History, VIII, Aug. 16, 1983, Lyndon Baines Johnson Library (hereinafter LBJL).
3. Doris Kearns Goodwin, *Lyndon Johnson and the American Dream* (New York, 1977), 39.
4. John Brooks Casparis Oral History, Jan. 7, 1982, LBJL.
5. Lady Bird Johnson Interview, Mar. 29–Apr. 2, 1993, National Park Service Oral Histories.
6. Jan Jarboe Russell, *Lady Bird: A Biography of Mrs. Johnson* (New York, 1999), 20.

7. Horace Busby Oral History, II, Mar. 4, 1982, LBJL.
8. Joe Phipps, *Summer Stock: Behind the Scenes with LBJ in '48* (New York, 1992), 21.
9. George Reedy Oral History, III, June 7, 1975, LBJL.
10. J. Willis Hurst Oral History, II, Oct. 31, 1970, LBJL.
11. Quoted in Ronald Radosh, *Divided They Fell: The Demise of the Democratic Party, 1964-1996* (New York, 1996), 2.
12. Joseph Rauh Oral History, III, Aug. 8, 1969, LBJL.
13. Quoted in John Dittmer, *Local People: The Struggle for Civil Rights in Mississippi* (Urbana, IL, 1994), 290.
14. LBJ and HHH Conversation, Aug.14, 1964, WH Tapes, WH6408.18, LBJL.
15. Lee White to President, August 19, 1964, Diary Backup, Box 8, LBJL.
16. Quoted in Adam Cohen and Elizabeth Taylor, *American Pharaoh: Mayor Richard J. Daley; His Battle for Chicago and the Nation* (Boston, 2001), 321.
17. Nick Kotz, *Judgment Days: Lyndon Baines Johnson, Martin Luther King Jr., and the Laws that Changed America* (New York, 2005), 199.
18. Ibid.
19. Ibid., 200.
20. Ibid., 196.
21. Ibid., 209.
22. Ibid., 210.
23. Michael Beschloss, *Taking Charge: The Johnson White House Tapes, 1963–1964* (New York, 1997), 527.
24. LBJ and George Reedy Conversation, Aug. 25, 1964, in Beschloss, *Taking Charge*, 527–532.
25. Kotz, *Judgment Days*, 213.
26. Quoted in Dittmer, *Local People*, 92.
27. See ibid., 287–302; Joseph Rauh Oral History, III, LBJL; and Radosh, *Divided They Fell*, 1–15.
28. Chronology of Pertinent Events in the Dominican Republic Situation, n.d., National Security File, Box 8, LBJL.
29. Eric Thomas Chester, *Rag Tags, Scum, Riff-raff, and Commies: The U.S. Intervention in the Dominican Republic, 1965–66* (New York, 2001), 17–18.
30. US Senate Committee on Foreign Relations, *Executive Sessions of the SFRC*, Vol. 17, 1965 (Washington, DC, 1990), 491.
31. Ibid., 492 ff.
32. LBJ and Abe Fortas Conversation, Apr. 28, 1965 in Michael Beschloss, *Reaching for Glory: Lyndon Johnson's Secret White House Tapes, 1964–1965* (New York, 2001), 289.
33. LBJ and Fortas Conversation, April 29, 1965 in Beschloss, *Reaching for Glory*, 297–300.
34. LBJ-Rusk-McNamara Conversation, Apr. 29, 1965, WH Tapes, 7389a, LBJL.
35. LBJ and McNamara Conversation, Apr. 29, 1965, WH Tapes, Transcripts of Telephone Conversations, LBJL.
36. President Johnson's Notes on Conversation with M. Bundy, Apr. 30, 1965, WH Tapes, Transcripts of Telephone Conversations, 7432, LBJL.

37. "Radio and Television Report to the American People on the Situation in the Dominican Republic," May 2, 1965, *Public Papers of the Presidents: LBJ*, Vol. I (Washington, DC, 1967), 469–473.
38. LBJ and J. Edgar Hoover Conversation, Sept. 10, 1965, WH Tapes, WH6509.03, LBJL.
39. Quoted in Randall B. Woods, *Quest for Identity: America Since 1945* (New York, 2005), 240.
40. Quoted in John Bartlow Martin, *Overtaken by Events: The Dominican Crisis from the Fall of Trujillo to the Civil War* (New York, 1966), 661.

President Nixon speaks at the Lincoln Memorial with Barbara Hirsch from Cleveland, Ohio, and Lauree Moss from Detroit, Michigan. Note the early morning fatigue on all the faces. Note also the civility of this unlikely encounter. [Photograph by Bettmann/ Corbis.]

10

A Depressed and Self-Destructive President

Richard Nixon in the White House

JEREMI SURI

One of the most bizarre moments in the history of the American presidency occurred in the early morning hours of May 9, 1970. During the course of three hours—beginning after 4:00am—an isolated, sleepless, and famously reclusive President Richard Nixon left the White House accompanied by his butler, doctor, and four perplexed Secret Service agents to visit the Lincoln Memorial. The beautiful monument stood illuminated against a dark sky, but it was filled with hundreds of angry young men and women who had traveled to Washington to protest the president's policies in Southeast Asia. The protesters came from cities and college campuses across the country, and hoped to "take back" the government from the "war mongers" whom they perceived controlled daily policies.[1]

Two years after the assassinations of Martin Luther King Jr. and Robert Kennedy, Nixon thus entered a potentially hostile setting without planning or preparation. He was exposed to immediate harm. He walked, largely unprotected, into a chamber filled with young people who hated him. This event never should have occurred. No one—including the president, his bodyguards, and the students—was prepared. In an era when most political encounters are carefully stage managed, the serendipity of the Lincoln Memorial visit was almost unparalleled.[2]

A similar meeting will probably never occur again. And that is what makes the events of May 9, 1970, so revealing. The spontaneity of that moment provides a valuable window into the feelings, aspirations, and demons of a president who was besieged and vengeful but also desperate for support—or at least for some understanding—from his most vocal critics. Nixon acted out his fears and hopes that morning, without the filtering that typically accompanies the routines, the handlers, and the scripting of normal presidential behavior. The abnormality of the moment opens fascinating insights about what hides behind the daily appearance of rational policymaking. This observation is particularly true for Richard Nixon, whose anxieties and hatreds dominated his days in the White House.

A sense of crisis pervaded the Nixon presidency. He and his closest advisors felt attacked and mistreated from their first days in office, and this feeling only grew from year to year. The controversy surrounding the Vietnam War, which Nixon inherited from his predecessor, was a primary source of crisis. Domestic racial tensions, manifest in widespread urban violence, were another. Most of all, the crisis of the Nixon presidency grew out of his own personal depression. Nixon was deeply analytical, politically savvy, and driven to achieve big things for American society. He was also a troubled, insecure, and brooding man who often expected the worst and acted in ways that brought on those dreaded consequences. The political scandal known as Watergate, which ultimately eroded his presidency, was a result of Nixon's depression and so were other distortions of domestic and foreign policy.

President Nixon confronted a double-barreled set of challenges: a stalemated war in Vietnam and growing anger about the war at home. He entered the White House with a fragile ego and acute sensitivity to the insults he had long endured from leading figures in American society. Nixon blamed the political establishment, especially in the Democratic Party, for the failures and frustrations of the war. Public agreement with these criticisms helped to elect him president over his Democratic rival, Vice President Hubert Humphrey. Nixon's claims, however, exposed him to even greater public condemnation, especially from his longtime political enemies, if he could not deliver immediate change in the war. This proved an insurmountable task for the new administration.[3]

During his presidential campaign in 1968, Nixon claimed to possess "secret plan" to end the Vietnam War and preserve the dignity of the United States. Just one year into his presidency, however, it became clear that he could not win the war, despite improved battlefield tactics by American military forces. At the same time, public manifestations of American anger with the war continued to grow. Americans disagreed on their preferred policies, but generally agreed that the conditions of the conflict were not improving, as soldiers continued to die, and the fighting and the bombing escalated. Nixon had to find a way to convince Americans that he was ending the war while preserving the dignity of the United States. He needed to negotiate enough to produce a settlement with North Vietnam but fight enough to show that Americans were still strong and determined to defeat communism.[4]

The weight of these challenges and Nixon's isolation from the public, partially self-imposed, contributed to the president's evident bouts of depression. Nixon functioned reasonably well in most public settings, but descended into self-pity, paranoia, and vengeance during private meetings and personal musings. His fears of his enemies multiplied, his sense of victimhood deepened, and his premonitions of failure grew. To escape his depression and restore hope, Nixon frequently lashed out at his advisers and adversaries alike. He valorized extraordinary, often illegal, behavior as a source of empowerment. He looked to "win big" because he feared losing it all very quickly. Nixon's depression infected all elements of his Vietnam policies, including his visit to the students at the Lincoln Memorial.

On the evening of April 30, 1970, President Nixon announced that American forces in South Vietnam were invading the neighboring country of Cambodia to interdict North Vietnamese supply lines. This announcement ignited convulsive protests on college campuses and in cities across the United States. Despite pledges by the administration to end the draft and limit American military deployments in Vietnam, young citizens feared the escalation meant they would have to participate in a pointless but still deadly war.[5] They expressed an extreme and widely shared frustration with a conflict that was now expanding rather than diminishing as the new president had promised. Even the defenders of American anticommunist efforts in Southeast Asia, including Secretary of State William Rogers and Secretary of Defense Melvin Laird, doubted the wisdom of bringing yet another country into this terrible war.[6]

American society seemed to be coming apart. Antiwar demonstrations dominated public life in much of the country and often turned violent. After three years of rising public unrest against the Vietnam War—what Nixon called the "war at home"—the angry protests of early May 1970 marked a new, dangerous peak. On May 4, 1970, panicked National Guardsmen fired upon demonstrating students at Kent State University in Ohio, killing four of them, to the shock of the entire nation, including President Nixon. Eleven days later, this tragedy repeated itself when National Guardsmen again fired upon students, allegedly throwing rocks and bricks at police, from a dormitory at Jackson State College in Mississippi. Firing repeatedly into the building, the National Guardsmen killed two students and wounded twelve others.[7]

The images of armed soldiers occupying American college campuses, with dead young bodies lying on the ground, and horrified onlookers grieving over the deaths, circulated around the world. It seemed absurd that a conflict so far from the United States could spark such violence in Ohio and Mississippi, along with other parts of the country. Tens of thousands of American citizens—despite their political differences—demanded that the madness inspired by the Vietnam War must stop.[8]

Everyone had a different explanation, but no one doubted that American society had entered a new period of turmoil, greater even than the disruptions of 1968. Many universities shut down, canceling classes and end-of-year commencements. Others operated as war zones, with armed soldiers and police officers deployed around buildings and public gathering points. Nixon and his wife, Pat, had to cancel their planned attendance at the graduations of their daughter, Julie, from Smith College, and their son-in-law, David Eisenhower, from Amherst.[9]

These absences were personally painful for the Nixon family, and were symbolic of how hated and isolated the president had become. The announcement of America's invasion of Cambodia turned the vocal minority who despised Nixon into an apparent mass movement committed to his demise. The president accurately assessed the common enmity directed at him, especially from the nation's most educated citizens. Even if there was a "silent majority" of Nixon supporters, as the president claimed, the country's most prominent, articulate, and youthful figures disdained him. The majesty of the American presidency could not confer on Nixon the public respectability that he had craved for so long. Nixon revered President Dwight Eisenhower, under whom he had served as vice president, but recognized that he could never command the same authority among America's most influential elites. Nixon was a diminished president.[10]

The emotional toll on Nixon was evident to all who worked with him. He could not sleep. He was preoccupied. He displayed the dark and depressive elements of his personality that often appeared in moments of greatest stress.[11] As soldiers from the US Third Army entered Washington DC to control growing crowds of protesters in the wake of Cambodia and Kent State, the Secret Service parked empty buses around the White House to protect the building, and the most powerful man in the world showed signs of coming unhinged. His chief of staff, H. R. Haldeman, commented in his diary that Nixon was dejected, tired, and terribly in need of rest. The president's national security adviser, Henry Kissinger, expressed similar sentiments, registering "deep concern" about Nixon's attitude and his health. Secretary of State William Rogers agreed with Kissinger, which was rare. Rogers and Kissinger both believed that Nixon needed relief from the extreme pressures of the office.[12]

As he often did in difficult moments, Nixon looked to acquaintances and staff for validation. (He had few real friends.) On the night of May 8, 1970, following a hostile press conference, he called more than fifty people to solicit praise and affirmation. He telephoned Henry Kissinger eight separate times. His calls continued beyond midnight and into the earliest hours of May 9. Then, after no more than two hours of sleep, the president was awake again, on his way to the Lincoln Memorial. For a man who prided himself on his leadership experience and strategic planning, his actions displayed confusion and desperation.[13]

When he arrived at the Lincoln Memorial and encountered hundreds of young protestors camping out, Nixon did not know what to say. Neither did they. The president and his detractors viewed each other as mortal enemies, but they had always assumed a spatial distance that facilitated mutual vilification. Now, the mutual adversaries were real in-the-flesh human beings: scared, disoriented, and staring one another in the eyes. There was evident humanity in the awkward figure of Richard Nixon and in the innocence of the students that night. The moment was, nonetheless, deeply uncertain.

Nixon mumbled unintelligibly at times. He tried to convince the students that he shared their opposition to war. He argued that he was fighting to preserve American power so that the country could withdraw from Vietnam and avoid conflicts like that again. He claimed as well that he wanted to preserve American democracy, and sought to identify with the aspirations of young men and women.

The bleary-eyed students listened politely, by all accounts. They showed a sincere desire to hear the president. They also expressed disbelief about his main claims. They did not see any justification for expanding a terrible war; nor did they believe that the president was pursuing peace or that preserving existing American institutions was necessarily the right thing to do. The protesters at the Lincoln Memorial were not revolutionaries, but they had adopted a popular radical critique of American imperialism and an imperial presidency. They wanted to curtail the war-making power of the White House. Nothing Nixon said changed that.[14]

The president and the students were standing in the same space but operating in separate rhetorical universes. They were talking past one another. They were unable to find common meanings for shared references—particularly the Vietnam War—that provoked fundamentally different judgments. The students assumed the war was unjust, unnecessary, and irredeemable; Nixon believed the war was well intentioned, unavoidable, and worthy of redemption in a withdrawal without defeat.

These assumptions made their words incomprehensible to one another. The students could not understand why Nixon wanted to expand a self-defeating war; Nixon could not understand why the students did not see the value to the United States in standing up against foreign adversaries. Nixon and the students held different "faiths" about the war, and direct dialogue only clarified that divergence. There was little common ground for conversation. That was the central political and social divide of the era. Nixon could not accept his inability to change his listeners' opinions, even when they respectfully heard him out. He could not accept the power of the students' alternative understanding of the Vietnam War, American society, and his presidency.[15]

The political crisis that motivated Nixon's visit to the Lincoln Memorial became an even deeper personal crisis when he returned to his normal routine, knowing that his extraordinary act of outreach had produced no results other than to open him to further ridicule. Accounts of the incident made him sound desperate and confused, and they recorded a failure of persuasion. He did not sound or look like a strong commander-in-chief in his early morning discussion with the students.[16]

Nixon tried to turn the event into an exercise of statesmanship, but even his closest advisors could not accept that interpretation. In his private reflections, recorded four days later, the president criticized both the media's coverage and his own staff's understanding of this strange event. He complained to Haldeman that his advisors cared too much about "material things" and "what we accomplish in our record." They did not appreciate the "infinitely more important qualities of spirit, of emotion, of depth and mystery of life, which this whole visit was really all about."[17]

The events of May 9, 1970, were historically significant. Nixon was honest about that. What he tried to cover up, however, was how the inner motivations for his actions revealed his personal weaknesses and difficulties at a time of supreme stress. Nixon was in a psychologically unstable state, as most people around him recognized, and his erratic behavior (as well as his later efforts to disguise it) grew out of that personal condition. The visit was about *him*, not about the students or anyone else.

What did Nixon mean by the "qualities of spirit, of emotion, of depth and mystery of life" in his recorded reflections on his visit? Why did he travel at 4:30 a.m. to the Lincoln Memorial and talk so informally with his young detractors? He was not drunk, as some have alleged, and he was not deranged. He seemed fully functional, if a little disoriented, to all who interacted with him that strange morning. Did the president really think he could convince the young people he had met? Did he really believe that his visit would accomplish anything, other than endanger and subject himself to ridicule?

The most persuasive explanation for the events at the Lincoln Memorial and Nixon's subsequent impulsive and self-destructive acts is that he suffered from intermittent but acute bouts of depression. When he felt helpless, as he did in early May 1970 (and in many other moments before and after) Nixon became convinced that the world was out to get him, with powerful forces committed to his failure. Even as president, he often perceived himself as a victim, as an outsider (from Whittier, California) suffering from unfair treatment by powerful insiders (Ivy League graduates, Jews, Kennedys, and Rockefellers). Nixon felt failure was almost unavoidable, he expressed self-pity, he lost sleep, and he pushed people away, including family and his wife, Pat. The protests of May 1970 imprisoned the president in the White House, and thus reinforced his own self-isolating tendencies in times of trouble.[18]

Nixon surrounded himself with other brooding figures—Chief of Staff H. R. Haldeman, White House Counsel John Ehrlichman, and National Security Advisor Henry Kissinger, among others. They shared his sense of victimhood, and they endured his depressive and self-destructive moments. More than advisors, these men were facilitators, therapists, and protectors for the president when he fell into depressive moods. Each of them has described listening to the president's diatribes and outlandish requests, pledging to follow his demands, and then waiting for him to calm down while stalling on any action. Thus they filtered his most dangerous tantrums.[19]

The peril, of course, was that Nixon's demands often had serious consequences, especially when they involved his targeting of real and perceived enemies. The wire-tappings, break-ins, and cover-ups that began in Nixon's first months in office, in 1969, were facilitated by Haldeman, Ehrlichman, Kissinger, and others. Nixon's depressive justifications for illegal activities against elites allegedly out to get him confirmed his advisors' own feelings of inadequacy. The president's angry requests often brought out the worst in his close, dependent circle.[20]

In February 1971 Nixon began taping his Oval Office conversations, primarily so he could remember the details of his discussions for current policy and posterity. He continued recording, with a voice-activated system, until July 1973. The Nixon tapes, including also many of his telephone conversations, are particularly insightful because they penetrate the public image of banal stability that Nixon had created to hide his personal demons. On the tapes he frequently becomes unhinged, issuing rambling tirades about critics and self-justifying soliloquies about his "toughness," his "will," and his "balls." Nixon repeatedly seeks validation from his advisors, but he never gets enough. The more they praise him, the more of it he demands. His efforts to gain validation only reinforce his feelings of inferiority and his lonely isolation.[21]

The tapes recount more than just stray salacious comments that Nixon's defenders want to dismiss. The tapes show a powerful man paralyzed by a self-defeating personality. The pattern of rhetoric and rant is one of a man who is filled with hate and self-doubt, and scared of hostile forces. There is almost no optimism, little self-confidence, and never any grace about his detractors. The portrait of Nixon on the tapes is not just the president against the world, but the world closing-in on the president who must fight to forestall his nightmares.

As the evidence of presidential involvement with the June 17, 1972 break-in at Democratic Party headquarters in the Watergate office complex mounted, Nixon's comments on May 11, 1973, to his press secretary, Ron Ziegler, were hardly unique:

> NIXON: Ron, let's be quite candid [about] the media or the left . . . Don't you really think that what they're trying to do is to destroy not so much the [Administration?] but what I stand for?

ZIEGLER: They would be—from their standpoint, their motive...

NIXON: Is destruction.

NIXON: Every campaign they've opposed. Well, in any event, if that is the case, isn't that what the larger battle is about? The larger battle is really we're just trying to kill the President. [Loud exhale.] That's very, very tough. That's what we must not let them do.[22]

These words, repeated in similar forms on countless occasions in the Nixon tapes, are the ruminations of a powerful man who is filled with rage about his perceived victimization. Nixon repeatedly calls upon his aides to use all their resources to "fix" his adversaries so they can never threaten him again:

NIXON: Espionage and Sabotage. Do you understand? That's the point that I'm making . . . [E]spionage and sabotage is illegal only if against the government. Hell, you can espionage and sabotage all you want, unless you use illegal means . . . Can I get away with it?

JOHN DEAN: "I don't think we'll get away with it forever.[23]

John Dean served as legal counsel to the president, and Nixon anticipated his answer. The president believed he was the victim of abuse and attack from all directions, but he also understood that his defenses were extreme, illegal, and ultimately self-defeating. That was the fundamental root of his depression. He had to fight to save himself and he knew that he could not win because his fighting would elicit more attacks from those who sought to destroy him. Nixon felt trapped in a spiral he could not escape. He was self-righteous, but he was also deeply pessimistic about his options. He saw himself stuck in a corner from which he lashed out and dug in for a long winless struggle.[24]

Careful to conceal this private darkness, Nixon made it a point to limit his public appearances as much as possible. He claimed his isolation was a choice to maximize his opportunities for "big" thinking, but the taped conversations reveal few strategic reflections or deep policy analyses. The same is true for his frequent memos to staff. The president's dialogues with Haldeman, Ehrlichman, and Kissinger focused overwhelmingly on personal politics: who was against the administration, and who was trying to hurt them. The president and his advisors spent most of their time together brooding about their vulnerabilities and plotting to take action. They wanted, in Nixon's words, to "get out front," "to hit them hard" before suffering additional blows. There was no distinction between high policy and personal politics for the Nixon administration.[25]

There was also no break between the president's national goals and his individual vendettas. Nixon's depression empowered his advisors to break the rules of civility and democracy. He encouraged this atmosphere in the White House when he charged his staff, following the release of the "Pentagon Papers," the Department of Defense history of the Vietnam War: "You can't fight this with gentlemanly gloves."[26]

Calling on his advisors to use the Internal Revenue Service (IRS) as a mechanism for pressuring and discrediting adversaries, Nixon made his intentions clear:

> We have all this power and we aren't using it. Now, what the Christ is the matter? . . . You've got the facts. Did they check the other side of the facts? What is being done? Who is doing this full-time? That's what I'd like to know. Who is running IRS? Who is running over at Justice Department?[27]

The insecure and hyper-aggressive atmosphere created by the president within his inner circle encouraged ever-escalating attacks on detractors. This began in the first months of the new administration. The lead came directly from the president who demanded the destruction of his enemies in the State Department, the Defense Department, and other parts of government.[28]

In March 1969 Nixon formed a personal White House intelligence group, acting outside the purview of Congress, the courts, the FBI, and the CIA. He had no statutory or constitutional basis for this radical extension of presidential power, which he hid from all but his closest advisors. On the president's order, White House Counsel John Ehrlichman hired New York City police detective John Caulfield to investigate Nixon's critics. Caulfield was officially a "liaison" with federal law enforcement agencies. He hired an assistant named Anthony Ulasewicz, also from New York. Ulasewicz was paid illegally from contributions left over after the 1968 presidential campaign.[29]

Forming a personal intelligence office in the White House was one of the president's first priorities; adhering to the rule of law and basic ethical principles was not. Nixon began his presidency by devoting his time and energy to activities that did not contribute to productive policymaking. He created, at the center of his administration, a group of illegal actors. He also set a tone of illegality, or at least cavalier disregard for the law, among those closest to him. Nixon was smart enough to understand the dangers, but he could not keep his fears and animosities under control.[30]

The president's personal intelligence office and its rag-tag group of zealots and mercenaries became known as "The Plumbers" for their use of a basement space in the Executive Office Building, next to the White House. Nixon ordered the Plumbers to wiretap a large roster of State Department, National Security Council, and Defense Department figures whom he accused of leaking information critical of the White House. His advisors also initiated a series of wiretaps on newspaper reporters who printed negative stories about the administration. Beyond the media, the Plumbers collected information on domestic critics, civil rights activists, and other groups deemed threatening to the president's policies, especially the conduct of the war in Vietnam. Covert efforts to undermine critics and harass their families followed from the collection of information.[31]

The White House flaunted laws protecting privacy and due process. National security concerns were a false rationalization for what were almost exclusively personal and political considerations. In 1971 Daniel Ellsberg's release of the Pentagon Papers, which detailed earlier administration's rationales for engaging in Southeast Asia, elicited more of the patterned behavior that had begun around the president months before. The Nixon tapes are filled with the president's obsessive condemnations of

Ellsberg and his supporters, especially the editors of the *New York Times*, who courageously published the secret documents.

On June 29, 1971, for instance, Nixon told his aide, Charles Colson, to "get him [Ellsberg] tied in with some communist groups." The next day Nixon demanded that Attorney General John Mitchell and Henry Kissinger "get everything out. Try him in the press. Everything, John, that there is on the investigation, get it out, leak it out. We want to destroy him [Ellsberg] in the press. Press. Is that clear?"[32]

The president followed up these vengeful comments with orders for his aides to slander and discredit Ellsberg, his supporters, the *New York Times*, and other mainstream media. By the summer of 1971 the Plumbers were already actively undermining democratic rule of law, following the explicit instructions of an unhinged president. Nixon created an early and enduring pattern of executive aggression without legal limits.

The president felt threatened by the critical treatment of the Vietnam War, even though the Pentagon Papers focused on US policies before 1969. Nixon perceived a conspiracy against him. He feared that his enemies would, once again, circle together to bring him down. In anticipation of this outcome, he mobilized the Plumbers and others to break into the offices of Ellsberg's psychiatrist, the Brookings Institution, the RAND Corporation, and the Council on Foreign Relations to gather information that might discredit opponents of the Vietnam War. Nixon repeatedly made it clear in taped conversations that he would stop at nothing to undermine those who attacked him.[33]

The same pattern of behavior motivated the incompetent break-ins by Nixon administration operatives at Democratic Party offices, on June 17, 1972. This was the infamous Watergate incident, named for the large multiuse building complex in Washington DC where it occurred. The break-in was poorly planned, but it fit the logic of White House behavior since 1969. The Nixon tapes show that the effort to obtain damaging information about opponents had become standard operating procedure for the staff of a president who always feared the worst of his enemies. The Nixon tapes also show without a doubt that the president knew about the break-in soon after it occurred.[34] Nixon acted consistently, often desperately, to cover-up his involvement. The more he tried to erase his tracks, divert attention, and minimize the misdeeds, the more critical scrutiny he faced. The cover-up exposed the president in ways that deepened his depressive moods and furthered his urge to lash out.

Nixon tried to imagine that the public would rally to him, but his explanations rang hollow, even to his own ears. On June 21, 1972, just four days after the Watergate break-in, he acknowledged his guilt and expressed empty hopes that exposed his cornered position:

> My view is, and I still hold with this view, that in terms of the reaction of people, the reaction is going to be primarily Washington and not the country, because I think the country doesn't give much of a shit about it other than the ones we've already bugged. Now, somebody else, you see—now, everybody around here is all mortified by it. It is a horrible thing to rebut. And the answer of course is that most people around the country think that this is routine, that everybody's trying to bug everybody else, it's politics. That's my view. The purists probably won't agree with that, but I don't think they're going to see a great uproar in the country about the Republican committee trying to bug the Democratic headquarters.[35]

Pushed by his own staff about his tortured logic and unlikely diminishment of the crime, Nixon tried again to convince himself and others that the damage could be ignored:

> Look, breaking and entering and so forth, without accomplishing it, is not a hell of a lot of crime. The point is that this is not—that only thing I'd say if somebody was going to ask me about, do you agree with [Press Secretary Ron] Ziegler's cut calling it a third-rate burglary, I'd say: No, I disagree, it was a third-rate *attempted* burglary.[36]

The president used his personal intelligence staff to set up a series of denials, prevarications, and diversions, but all of these actions only drew more attention to the crime and the responsibility of the White House.

Like other depressed people, Nixon found that his efforts to conceal his vulnerability only contributed to greater exposure. He could not come clean about his misdeeds—as he should have for self-preservation—because of the larger pattern of illegal White House behavior. Confession to the Watergate break-in would reveal greater crimes that multiplied with each passing day and each effort at a cover-up.

More fundamentally, Nixon could not come clean because he feared showing weakness and vulnerability to his enemies. He anticipated that an admission of mistake would open a wound that his detractors would exploit to bleed him to death. The president tried desperately to reinforce his armor, as the body of his administration rapidly decayed from what an aid aptly called a "cancer" of illegal behavior.[37]

The most striking element of the Watergate scandal is not only how unnecessary it was but also how dark and brooding the president became with each passing month. At every step, he feared the worst from any admission of error. At every step, he saw himself as more of a victim, attacked by those who, in his mind, had done similar things. Nixon recognized that he had broken the law, but he did not believe that someone with all of his disadvantages had to abide by the law. He had suffered, and he had been excluded. He had been disrespected by the high and mighty. Why did he have to play by rules that benefited them? Why did he have to accept a history that made him a loser, even when he was president?

Nixon's struggles with his personal demons also distorted his foreign policy, despite his stunning victories of 1972, especially the opening to China and the negotiation of the Strategic Arms Limitation Treaty (SALT) with the Soviet Union. Public revelations about the Watergate break-in and the president's continuing efforts to cover up his role occupied more and more of his attention. The topic begins to dominate the discussions in the Nixon tapes by early 1973.

Nixon's distrust of traditional elites and his conspiratorial inclinations led him to hold tight personal authority over the key elements of his foreign policy. He gave unprecedented power to Special Assistant for National Security Affairs Henry Kissinger, who often carried out the president's policies without informing the secretary of state, the secretary of defense, or members of Congress. This arrangement helped to preserve secrecy and decrease bureaucratic hurdles to policy change, but it also created a strange co-dependency and isolation. Nixon mixed strategic and emotional considerations in his policy orders, and Kissinger struggled to make sense of the president's inclinations. Kissinger also quickly learned to manipulate Nixon's emotions, especially in his depressed moments.[38]

The first example of this dynamic occurred in October 1969, when the president demanded that Kissinger find a way to frighten the Soviet leadership into offering him assistance in procuring a favorable settlement to the Vietnam War. Nixon called this his "madman" strategy; it was based on the proposition that the adversary will give in to a leader who appears unhinged and dangerous. Kissinger ominously told Soviet Ambassador Anatoly Dobrynin: "the train had just left the station and was now headed down the track."[39]

To put evidence behind these warnings, Kissinger designed a bluff that would satisfy the president's "madman" pretensions, signal seriousness to the Soviet Union, and keep the entire matter secret from the American people. During the second half of October 1969, the United States went on alert, sending nuclear-armed B-52 aircraft on eighteen-hour missions over the northern polar ice cap, toward Soviet territory. This was a simulated nuclear strike. The alert extended to Strategic Air Command bombers and Polaris nuclear-armed submarines, all of which adopted communications silence and increased readiness for battle.[40]

The Soviet Union surely noticed these threatening maneuvers, and the American public did not learn of them as planned. There is little evidence that anything else went as Nixon and Kissinger expected. The Soviets never responded to the nuclear alert with assistance in Vietnam, and American military leaders did all they could to counteract the president's orders. Secretary of Defense Melvin Laird and his subordinates believed that the White House was acting in reckless ways that could endanger the entire world—and with little to gain. Laird was, of course, correct.[41]

This pattern repeated itself almost exactly four years later in the days after the October 6, 1973 Egyptian and Syrian attacks on Israel. Nixon and Kissinger worked to broker a cease-fire and then a peace settlement for a war that had almost destroyed the Jewish state. American leaders sought to make the United States the dominant power in the region, excluding the Soviet Union from the influence it had previously exercised through Cairo, Damascus, and other Arab capitals. On October 24, when Moscow threatened to send its own forces to the region, Nixon and Kissinger decided once again that they needed to display overwhelming strength, and some "madman" characteristics, to deter Soviet intervention. Kissinger anticipated this response a few months earlier when he explained to Israeli Ambassador Yitzhak Rabin: "I have learned that when you use force it is better to use 30 percent more than is necessary than five percent less than necessary . . . whenever we use force we have to do it slightly hysterically."[42]

On the night of October 24, 1973, the United States initiated a new nuclear alert, raising the status of its forces to "Defcon III," the state of readiness perlilously close to actual nuclear war. When questioned, Kissinger spoke explicitly of the threat to regional stability:

> The United States does not favor and will not approve the sending of a joint Soviet-United States force into the Middle East. . . . The United States is even more opposed to the unilateral introduction by any great power, especially by any nuclear power, of military forces into the Middle East in whatever guise those forces should be introduced.[43]

This time American actions might have deterred the Soviet Union, but they also created grave international concerns about American overreaction. Unlike the alert in 1969, the "Defcon III" decision immediately became public. The president and his closest advisors never considered the panic their actions would create. Remarkably, Nixon missed the meeting that initiated the alert. Kissinger made the decision with Alexander Haig, then White House chief of staff. "You cannot be sure how much of this is due to our domestic crisis," Kissinger told Haig. "I don't think [the Soviets] would have taken on a functioning president." Nixon's incapacity and distraction on 24 October 1973 were driven by his preoccupation with Watergate.[44]

On October 25 Kissinger and Haig discussed the alert and its aftermath with the clear understanding that they, not the president, had made the key decisions:

> KISSINGER: You and I were the only ones for it. These other guys were wailing all over the place this morning.
>
> HAIG: You're telling me. Last night it seemed like someone had taken their shoes away from them. You really handled that thing magnificently.
>
> KISSINGER: I think I did some good for the President.
>
> HAIG: More than you know.[45]

Kissinger then called Nixon, who was focused on his domestic "enemies" rather than the dangers overseas. The president's personal demons clearly detracted from his ability to manage a major international crisis. He empowered his chief foreign policy advisor, by default, to make decisions that involved the most dangerous weapons in the world. This was a reprehensible departure from the constitutional expectations of the nation's commander-in-chief.

This analysis of a distracted and sometime depressed president brings us back to the Lincoln Memorial in the early morning hours of May 9, 1970. Nixon arrived there neither to condemn nor to persuade his young opponents camping out to protest his invasion of Cambodia. Besieged by his critics at home and stymied in his efforts to find a path to victory in Vietnam, Nixon had a sleepless night of depression. He reached out to the image of Lincoln and the students gathered around the monument as a plea for help. Like other people suffering from depression, he wanted a way out. He wanted to find solace, security, and friendship. He wanted to feel like everything was going to be all right. He looked desperately to the Lincoln Memorial that morning, hoping that setting would give him the emotional sustenance he needed.

It never did. His depression deepened in the coming months and recurred more frequently as circumstances at home and abroad worsened. Even a decisive reelection in November 1972 could not stop the pain. Nixon felt himself sinking. As he punched at those whom he feared were pushing him under the water, he only gave them more ammunition to hasten his drowning. Depression bred hatred and illegality, which made the most powerful man in the world a sobbing wreck, forced from the office he had struggled so hard to attain.

When Nixon reached out to the protesting students on May 9, 1970, he was trying to halt his slide. It was one of the most sincere moments of his presidency. It was also one of the most tragic . . . and depressing.

NOTES

1. For accounts of the ubiquitous public protests and controversial foreign policy decisions in this era, see Maurice Isserman and Michael Kazin, *America Divided: The Civil War of the 1960s*, 4th ed. (New York: Oxford University Press, 2011); Jeremi Suri, *Power and Protest: Global Revolution and the Rise of Détente* (Cambridge, MA: Harvard University Press, 2003); Martin Klimke, *The Other Alliance: Student Protest in West Germany and the United States in the Global Sixties* (Princeton, NJ: Princeton University Press, 2010); Niall Ferguson, Charles S. Maier, Erez Manela, and Daniel J. Sargent, eds., *The Shock of the Global: The 1970s in Perspective* (Cambridge, MA: Belknap Press of Harvard University Press, 2011).
2. For an excellent discussion of President Nixon's visit to the Lincoln Memorial on May 9, 1970, and new evidence about this strange moment and its deeper meanings, see the PBS News Hour interview with Professor Melvin Small on November 25, 2011: http://video.pbs.org/video/2170891424 (accessed 13 May 2014). See also Melvin Small, *The Presidency of Richard Nixon* (Lawrence: University of Kansas Press, 1999), 218; Anthony Summers, *The Arrogance of Power: The Secret World of Richard Nixon* (New York: Penguin, 2000), 364–66; Robert Dallek, *Nixon and Kissinger: Partners in Power* (New York: Harper Collins, 2007), 203–04; Tom McNichol, "I Am Not a Kook: Richard Nixon's Bizarre Visit to the Lincoln Memorial," *Atlantic*, November 14, 2011: http://www.theatlantic.com/politics/archive/2011/11/i-am-not-a-kook-richard-nixons-bizarre-visit-to-the-lincoln-memorial/248443 (accessed 13 May 2014).
3. Among the many books on this topic, see Jeffrey Kimball, *Nixon's Vietnam War* (Lawrence: University of Kansas Press, 1998); Rick Perlstein, *Nixonland: The Rise of a President and the Fracturing of America* (New York: Simon and Schuster, 2008).

4. On the 1968 election and its legacies, see Lewis Gould, *1968: The Election that Changed America*, 2nd ed., (Chicago: Ivan R. Dee, 2010). Walter LaFeber, *The Deadly Bet: LBJ, Vietnam, and the 1968 Election* (New York: Rowman and Littlefield, 2005).
5. The US military officially became an all-volunteer force in July 1973, ending a long history of mandatory conscription of citizens in times of war and national emergency. See Beth Bailey, *America's Army: Making the All-Volunteer Force* (Cambridge, MA: Belknap Press of Harvard University Press, 2009); Christian G. Appy, *Working-Class War: American Combat Soldiers and Vietnam* (Chapel Hill: University of North Carolina Press, 1993).
6. On this point, see William Bundy, *A Tangled Web: The Making of Foreign Policy in the Nixon Presidency* (New York: Hill and Wang, 1998); Kimball, *Nixon's Vietnam War*, esp. 177–248; Pierre Asselin, *A Bitter Peace: Washington, Hanoi, and the Making of the Paris Agreement* (Chapel Hill: University of North Carolina Press, 2002).
7. See Tim Spofford, *Lynch Street: The May 1970 Slayings at Jackson State College* (Kent, OH: Kent State University Press, 1989); Christine M. Lamberson, "In the Crucible of Violence: The Remaking of American Political Culture in the 1960s and 1970s," Ph.D. diss., University of Wisconsin-Madison, 2012.
8. On the events surrounding the US invasion of Cambodia and the public protests in the United States, see John M. Shaw, *The Cambodian Campaign: The 1970 Offensive and America's Vietnam War* (Lawrence: University Press of Kansas, 2005); William Shawcross, *Sideshow: Kissinger, Nixon, and the Destruction of Cambodia* (New York: Simon and Schuster, 1979); Tom Wells, *The War Within: America's Battle Over Vietnam* (Berkeley: University of California Press, 1994); Jeremy Varon, *Bringing the War Home: The Weather Underground, the Red Army Faction, and Revolutionary Violence in the Sixties* (Berkeley, University of California Press, 2004).
9. See Will Swift, *Pat and Dick: The Nixons, an Intimate Portrait of a Marriage* (New York: Simon and Schuster, 2014), 249–50.
10. Ibid., 257–58. On the "silent majority," see Perlstein, *Nixonland*; Matthew D. Lassiter, *The Silent Majority: Suburban Politics in the Sunbelt South* (Princeton, NJ: Princeton University Press, 2006); Michael W. Flamm, *Law and Order: Street Crime, Civil Unrest, and the Crisis of Liberalism in the 1960s* (New York: Columbia University Press, 2005). On the relationship between Eisenhower and Nixon, see John W. Malsberger, *The General and the Politician: Dwight Eisenhower, Richard Nixon, and American Politics* (New York: Rowman and Littlefield, 2014).
11. For a sympathetic, poignant portrait of Nixon's inner demons, see Tom Wicker, *One of Us: Richard Nixon and the American Dream* (New York: Random House, 1995). See also Elizabeth Drew, *Richard M. Nixon* (New York: Henry Holt, 2007).
12. See H. R. Haldeman diary entries, 9–11 May 1970, in H. R. Haldeman, *The Haldeman Diaries* (New York: G. P. Putnam, 1994), 195–97; Henry Kissinger, *White House Years* (Boston: Little, Brown, 1979), 509–17, quotation on 514; Dallek, *Nixon and Kissinger*, 200, 205–44.
13. See Keith W. Olson, *Watergate: The Presidential Scandal that Shook America* (Lawrence: University Press of Kansas, 2003), 14–16.
14. See note 1.

15. This description of Nixon's visit to the Lincoln Memorial and his discussions with students comes from a variety of accounts, especially those in endnote 2. See also Nixon's personal reflections, recorded on a dictabelt on 13 May 1970: http://www.nixonlibrary.gov/virtuallibrary/recordings/dictabelts.php.
16. See the widely read accounts of Nixon's unsteady policy-making, and his early morning visit to the Lincoln Memorial, in Max Frankel, "Nixon: He Faces a Divided, Anguished Nation," *New York Times* (10 May 1970), 157; Tom Wicker, "In the Nation: Getting Through to the President," *New York Times* (10 May 1970), 173.
17. See Nixon's May 13, 1970, reflections on his visit to the Lincoln Memorial a few days earlier: http://www.nixonlibrary.gov/virtuallibrary/recordings/dictabelts.php.
18. See Swift, *Pat and Dick*, esp. 243–65; Stanley I. Kutler, *The Wars of Watergate: The Last Crisis of Richard Nixon* (New York: W.W. Norton, 1990), 77–125.
19. See Henry Kissinger, *Years of Upheaval* (Boston: Little, Brown, 1982), 73–74, 1182; H. R. Haldeman diary entry, 24 April 1970, in *Haldeman Diaries*, 184–85.
20. See Kutler, *The Wars of Watergate*, 77–125, 161–84.
21. The fullest and most accessible collection of the Nixon tapes is available at http://nixontapes.org. This website is largely the result of extraordinary efforts by Dr. Luke Nichter. The Nixon tapes include approximately 3,700 hours of phone calls and meetings that President Nixon secretly recorded between February 1971 and July 1973. The National Archives has released approximately 2,300 hours of the tapes so far. For two sets of published transcripts from Nixon tape selections, especially regarding Watergate, see Stanley I. Kutler, *Abuse of Power: The New Nixon Tapes* (New York: Free Press, 1997); Douglas Brinkley and Luke Nichter, *The Nixon Tapes: 1971-1972* (Boston: Houghton Mifflin, 2014).
22. Audio Recording of President Nixon with Press Secretary Ron Ziegler, May 11, 1973, 8:27 a.m., Oval Office, transcribed in Kutler, *Abuse of Power*, 452–53.
23. Audio Recording of President Nixon with John W. Dean III, Counsel to the President, March 14, 1973, 9:50 a.m., Executive Office Building, transcribed in Kutler, *Abuse of Power*, 229.
24. See Dean's detailed and personal account in his book, *The Nixon Defense: What He Knew and When He Knew It* (New York: Viking, 2014).
25. This point comes through in a number of the memoirs, including those from advisors who remained favorably inclined to Nixon as a leader. See, for example: H.R. Haldeman with Joseph DiMona, *The Ends of Power* (New York: Times Books, 1977); William Safire, *Before the Fall: An Inside View of the Pre-Watergate White House* (New York: Tower Books, 1975); David Gergen, *Eyewitness to Power: The Essence of Leadership, Nixon to Clinton* (New York: Touchstone Books, 2000), 19–104. See also Dallek, *Nixon and Kissinger*. See also Suri, *Henry Kissinger and the American Century* (Cambridge, MA: Belknap Press of Harvard University Press, 2007), 201–11.
26. Audio Recording of President Nixon with H. R. Haldeman and Henry Kissinger, July 1, 1971, 8:45 a.m., Oval Office, transcribed in Kutler, *Abuse of Power*, 9. On the history of the Pentagon Papers and the political controversy surrounding their release by the *New York Times*, see David Rudenstine, *The Day the Presses Stopped: A History of the Pentagon Papers Case* (Berkeley: University of

California Press, 1996); James C. Goodale, *Fighting for the Press: The Inside Story of the Pentagon Papers and Other Battles* (New York: CUNY Journalism Press, 2013); Daniel Ellsberg, *Secrets: A Memoir of Vietnam and the Pentagon Papers* (New York: Penguin, 2002).

27. Audio Recording of President Nixon with H.R. Haldeman and John Ehrlichman, 3 August 1972, 9:44 a.m., Oval Office, transcribed in Kutler, *Abuse of Power*, 112–13.
28. See Dallek, *Nixon and Kissinger*, esp. 89–103; Kutler, *Wars of Watergate*, 94–96.
29. See Olson, *Watergate*, 5–21.
30. Stanley Kutler describes the "Huston Plan," designed to allow the president the ability to spy on domestic critics of the administration. FBI Director J. Edgar Hoover opposed the scheme because it circumvented his agency, and he effectively killed it. Kutler shows that Nixon continued to pursue this secret domestic surveillance capability through various White House intelligence operatives. The "Huston Plan" was a model for the White House "plumbers." See Kutler, *Wars of Watergate*, 96–101.
31. Ibid., 102–25; Olson, *Watergate*, 18–21.
32. Audio Recording of President Nixon with Charles Colson, June 29, 1971, 2:28 p.m., White House Telephone; Audio Recording of President Nixon with John Mitchell and Henry Kissinger, June 30, 1971, 2:55 p.m., Oval Office, transcribed in Kutler, *Abuse of Power*, 6.
33. See Kutler, *Wars of Watergate*, 161–84.
34. These points about a pattern of Nixon administration behavior and the president's knowledge of the break-in are central to the two best books on the topic: Kutler, *Wars of Watergate* and Olson, *Watergate*. See the evidence from the Nixon tapes in Kutler, *Abuse of Power*, especially 43–185.
35. Audio Recording of President Nixon with H.R. Haldeman and Charles Colson, June 21, 1972, 9:30 a.m., Oval Office, transcribed in Kutler, *Abuse of Power*, 54.
36. Ibid., 55.
37. This was the phrase used by John Dean on March 21, 1973. See Audio Recording of President Nixon with H. R. Haldeman and John Dean, March 21, 1973, 10:12 a.m., Oval Office, transcribed in Kutler, *Abuse of Power*, 247. In this remarkable meeting Dean outlines for the president the details of the Watergate break-in, the White House connection, and the subsequent White House cover-up. Nixon listens and then pledges to continue the cover-up, soliciting more money to pay off those who might reveal information incriminating the president. See also Dean's *The Nixon Defense*.
38. See Suri, *Henry Kissinger and the American Century*, 201–11; Dallek, *Nixon and Kissinger*, 89–103.
39. Memorandum of Conversation between Kissinger and Dobrynin 27 September 1969, Folder: Dobrynin/Kissinger 1969 [Part 1], Box 489, Henry Kissinger Office Files, NSC files, Richard M. Nixon Papers, Richard Nixon Presidential Library, Yorba Linda, California [hereafter Nixon papers]. See also Suri, *Henry Kissinger and the American Century*, 216–18; Kimball, *Nixon's Vietnam War*,

63–86; idem., ed., *The Vietnam War Files: Uncovering the Secret History of Nixon-Era Strategy* (Lawrence: University Press of Kansas, 2004), 11–24, 53–120.

40. See Jeremi Suri, "The Nukes of October: Richard Nixon's Secret Plan to Bring Peace to Vietnam," *Wired Magazine* 16 (October 2008); William Burr and Jeffrey Kimball, "Nixon's Secret Nuclear Alert: Vietnam War Diplomacy and the Joint Chiefs of Staff Readiness Test, October 1969," *Cold War History* 3 (January 2003), 113–56.
41. See Scott D. Sagan and Jeremi Suri, "The Madman Nuclear Alert: Secrecy, Signaling, and Safety in October 1969," *International Security* 27 (Spring 2003), 150–83.
42. Memorandum of Conversation between Kissinger, Rabin, and Peter Rodman, January 24, 1973, Folder: Rabin/Dinitz, Sensitive Memcons, 1973 [2 of 2], Box 135, Kissinger Office Files, Nixon papers.
43. Quoted in Kissinger, *Years of Upheaval*, 594–95.
44. See transcript of telephone conversation between Kissinger and Haig, October 24, 1973, 10:20 p.m., available through the U.S. Department of State's Freedom of Information Act website: http://foia.state.gov/SearchColls/CollsSearch.asp [hereafter FOIA]; Kissinger, *Years of Upheaval*, 585–88.
45. See transcript of telephone conversation between Kissinger and Haig, October 25, 1973, 2:35 p.m.; transcript of telephone conversation between Kissinger and Nixon, October 25, 1973, 3:05 p.m., State FOIA.

Shot only weeks into his presidency, Reagan in time recovered. The near-death experience changed him, and through him, the Cold War. [Courtesy Ronald Reagan Library.]

11

Governing During a Time of Crisis

The Reagan Presidency

KIRON K. SKINNER ■

The 1980s presented stunning tectonic shifts in the landscape of international relations. The Soviet Union unraveled. Colonialism in Africa made its final stand. The global war on terror emerged. Within the United States at the start of the decade, the attempted assassination of the nation's fortieth president, Ronald Wilson Reagan, dramatically changed the personal and political undercurrents of his tenure in office.

The assassination attempt laid bare the confusion and lack of consensus among the president's top aides on constitutional and legal issues surrounding presidential disability and succession, as well as their inadequate understanding of nuclear command-and-control procedures. The darker side of any presidency—in this instance, the power grabs by Cabinet members and senior White House staff—was exposed once Reagan was shot. Soon, during the crisis that ensued, Secretary of State Alexander Haig told reporters that he was in charge at the White House. Reagan's advisers would ultimately convince the president to ask for Haig's resignation in the wake of his so improperly overstepping his bounds—at least in a rhetorical sense; but the secretary of state's dismissal did not taper the political disarray that became apparent upon the attempt on Reagan's life. The White House environment in the first hours after the president nearly died set the conditions for the Iran-Contra scandal, which diminished his second term.

Second, through it all, George H. W. Bush quietly emerged in the aftermath of Reagan's near-death as one of the most influential vice presidents in US history. During the nearly two weeks that Reagan spent in the hospital, Bush demonstrated respect for the Oval Office and unwavering loyalty to the president that earned him loyalty in return. Afterward Reagan increasingly sought Bush's counsel on diverse issues and policies, burnishing the vice president's credentials and his White House bid in 1988. In many ways, Bush's vice presidency, which nearly ended only weeks after beginning due to the president's brush with death, was forged in the aftermath of assassination.

Finally, and most significant of all, his being shot was the formative event of the Reagan presidency. The rending experience added to the urgency with which Reagan infused his messianic view that Soviet Communism could be defeated by anticlassical thinking about nuclear deterrence into US foreign policy. Through sheer force of will, even while recovering from his wounds, Reagan halted the White House and State Department machinery that was intent upon sustaining conventional Cold War thinking in his Soviet policies and strategies. The attempt on Reagan's life, in other words, helped transform the man who did so much to transform the world.

The seventieth day of President Reagan's White House tenure began predictably. He had a breakfast with political appointees, meetings with his senior advisers, including Vice President Bush, National Security Adviser Richard V. Allen, Chief of Staff James Baker III, Deputy Chief of Staff Mike Deaver, and Counselor to the President Edwin Meese III. Baker, Deaver, and Meese became known as "the troika." (They were given this moniker because they would have greater access to Reagan than most of his cabinet secretaries.) Shortly after his lunch meeting, the president transitioned to the south grounds, where his motorcade was waiting to drive him to the Washington Hilton Hotel, where he was scheduled to deliver a speech.[1]

Countless times throughout his career, Reagan had stood before large audiences and offered an impassioned defense of democracy. He was thus on familiar ground as he spoke before a gathering of the national conference of the Building and Construction Trades Department, part of the American Federation of Labor and Congress of Industrial Organizations. At 2:03 p.m., he began his remarks, which were familiar fare: "We've gone astray from first principles. We've lost sight of the rule that individual freedom and ingenuity are at the very core of everything that we've accomplished. Government's first duty is to protect the people, not run their lives." Even discussion of his economic recovery plan—it would "ease some of our problems"—reflected the promises he made during the 1980 presidential race. Reagan argued that increasing the defense budget was necessary to redress the military imbalance that favored the Soviet Union. He described members of Solidarity, the Polish workers' union then engaged with a struggle against their communist regime, as "sentinels on behalf of universal human principles." These positions were consistent with the broader critique Reagan had been making for years that détente amounted to US appeasement of its principal adversary.[2] Delivered in characteristically good form, the speech was warmly received though it did not garner overwhelming approbation from the audience. Less than thirty minutes after commencing, Reagan headed back outside for the short walk to his limousine.[3] He appeared happy and relaxed as he strolled past reporters and spectators cordoned off behind a rope barricade, waiting to get a glimpse of him or shake his hand. Not stopping to take questions or press the flesh, Reagan smiled as he walked, waving his left arm.[4]

John Hinckley Jr. was in the crowd. Obsessed with Jodie Foster, a young actress who was then an undergraduate at Yale University, the twenty-five-year-old Hinckley thought he could gain her "respect and love" by assassinating the president. He opened fire with a .22-caliber revolver. The first bullet hit White House Press Secretary James Brady in his head. The second shot struck police officer Thomas Delahanty in the back of his neck. Hinckley's next shot missed. Deaver dropped to the ground. Hinckley's fourth bullet hit Secret Service Agent Tim McCarthy in the chest. Reagan, his left arm still raised mid-wave, was hit by the fifth bullet, which ricocheted from his limousine's bulletproof window before entering his side. Instead of exploding, the Devastator-brand bullet lodged in his left lung, close to his heart.[5] The sixth bullet missed its target and passed by the president's car. In a matter of seconds, Hinckley had fired six shots and struck four men.[6] He was apprehended immediately, his actions quickly determined to be the work of derangement rather than part of a wider criminal or terrorist conspiracy.[7]

Reagan's wounds were not immediately apparent. At first, Jerry Parr, the president's chief Secret Service officer, did not know that he had been shot. Covering the president's body with his own he dove the pair into the car. Reagan's coughing up blood led Parr to order them driven directly to George Washington University Hospital instead of the White House. His quick decisions were the first of many that contributed to saving Reagan's life. First Lady Nancy Reagan recalled that doctors at the hospital believed that "if they had driven to the White House, we would have lost him."[8]

Indeed, it was a very near thing. Reagan said he was "almost paralyzed by pain" during the car ride to the hospital. He later recalled that upon arrival, "my fear was growing because no matter how hard I tried to breathe it seemed I was getting less and less air." Laying on a stretcher he told his medical team, "I feel so bad." Although his pulse was nearly normal, his blood pressure was low and he was nearly in shock. "I can't breathe," he continued to complain as IV lines were set up. Doctors heard abnormal sounds from his left lung, which was rapidly filling with blood. Retaining consciousness, Reagan responded to questions and moved his limbs on command. When the insertion of a chest tube failed to stop the internal bleeding, Dr. Benjamin Aaron, the hospital's chief cardiovascular and thoracic surgeon, knew he had to operate. By this time, Mrs. Reagan had arrived. She gave her consent, and within thirty minutes after entering the hospital the President of the United States was being prepared for emergency surgery.[9]

After several unsuccesful attempts in the course of a nearly three-hour-long operation, Dr. Aaron was finally able to locate and remove the bullet. Reagan awoke in the recovery room at approximately 7:30 p.m. His pain continued as did difficulty breathing. The doctors kept him in the recovery room overnight in case they should be forced to operate again. Morphine was administered. Mrs. Reagan and their son Ron were allowed to see him that evening. By the middle of the night he was able to breathe without a respirator.

On March 31, less than twenty-four hours after having been shot and despite having received additional morphine for pain that morning, Reagan signed the Dairy Price Bill in the presence of Baker, Deaver, and Meese. Designed to stop an increase in dairy price subsidies, the bill was the first piece of legislation from the Ninety-seventh Congress he had been expected to sign. The bill itself was not time-sensitive, but for the president's team its signing projected an image of business as usual despite the tumult. We "were convinced," Deaver later recalled, that "the public needed to see that the Reagan presidency would not be sidetracked because of John Hinckley Jr."[10]

The public-relations strategy paid immediate dividends. Two days after the shooting, a *Chicago Tribune* article reported, "President Reagan, making a rapid recovery from a chest wound he sustained during an assassination attempt, resumed his official duties." The newspaper also published a copy of the dairy law, which bore the signatures of President Reagan, House Speaker Thomas P. O'Neill, and President Pro Tempore of the Senate Strom Thurmond.[11] A *Boston Globe* headline read, "Reagan makes rapid progress; signs bill, sees aides." The *Los Angeles Times* likewise declared, "Reagan 'Doing Well,' Signs Bill in Hospital."[12]

Yet the president's condition worsened in the days after the shooting. His fever lingered, and he continued to cough up blood. Dr. Aaron became concerned that more surgery might be required, but Reagan rallied. Although he suffered several medical setbacks—and concern about serious infection persisted—another procedure proved unnecessary.[13]

The president's characteristic sense of humor helped. Soon after being admitted, he asked his aides, "Who's minding the store?" and quipped to the operating room physicians, "Please tell me you're all Republicans!" Before surgery he told Nancy, "Honey, I forgot to duck." In the recovery room, he wrote messages to the medical team, including a quotation from Winston Churchill: "There is no more exhilarating feeling than being shot at without result." The former movie star also scribbled, "I'd like to shoot that scene again—starting from the hotel." In the vein of W.C. Fields, he penned, "All in all, I'd rather be in Philadelphia." Another of his notepad jokes was, "Send me to L.A., where I can see the air I'm breathing!"[14] Several of the president's remarks appeared in newspapers, and Nancy Reagan felt that they "provided a great deal of reassurance to the nation. People reasoned, understandably, that if the president could be so good-natured in the hospital, his injuries must not be too serious."[15]

The public largely marveled at the president's remarkable recovery, but his intense private suffering was not lost on Mrs. Reagan. Her husband revealed the depth of his concern in notepad queries: "What happened to the guy with the gun?" "What was his beef? Was anyone hurt?" "Can I keep breathing?" "How long in the hospital?" "Will I still be able to work on the ranch?"[16] The hospital staff worried about how the president would be affected by the news that three members of his team had been shot and that Brady was grievously injured by a bullet lodged in his brain. Dr. Daniel Ruge, the White House physician, decided to wait until the day after the surgery to inform him about the condition of his colleagues. Reagan was clearly distraught. His eyes filled with tears when he finally learned the full extent of their wounds. Those who visited him also recognized his suffering. William P. Clark, the deputy secretary of state, met with Mrs. Reagan and the head surgeon at the hospital and recalled that the gravity of the president's condition "was far graver than what was reported at the time." House Speaker Tip O'Neill paid a courtesy call and later said, "He was in terrific pain. Much more serious than anybody thought. . . . He thanked me for coming and we squeezed each other's hands."[17]

Already a deeply religious man, Reagan's strong faith in God provided comfort and solace in the aftermath of the shooting, and he actively prayed for the wounded.[18] His faith also compelled him to pray for John Hinckley Jr. In his diaries he would reveal the following:

> I focused on that tiled ceiling and prayed. But I realized I couldn't ask for God's help while at the same time I felt hatred for the mixed up young man who had shot me. Isn't that the meaning of the lost sheep? We are all God's children & therefore equally beloved by him.

> I began to pray for his soul and that he would find his way back to the fold.[19]

From then on, President Reagan's mission became more clearly focused. "Whatever happens now I owe my life to God and will try to serve him in every way I can," he wrote in his diary.[20]

Everyone wounded in the attack survived. Brady and McCarthy also underwent surgery at George Washington Medical Center. Delahanty was rushed to Washington Hospital Center to have the bullet removed from his neck. On April 7, McCarthy was released from the hospital, as was Delahanty a few days later; nerve damage to his left arm eventually forced his retirement from the DC Police force. McCarthy recovered and soon resumed work. Severely injured and partially paralyzed, Brady remained hospitalized until November 23. He was mainly confined to a wheelchair for the rest of his life, and in the years following the shooting suffered numerous medical complications from his injuries.[21] Although never able to work at full capacity again, White House leadership made sure that Brady retained the title of press secretary, and his commensurate salary, until the end of Reagan's term in office.[22]

Reagan left the hospital April 11. "I walked in here—I'm going to walk out," he reportedly told his doctors. Though visibly thinner and weaker and wearing a bullet-proof vest, he indeed walked out twelve days after being shot, escorted by his wife and their daughter. The White House staff greeted him enthusiastically when he arrived at the South Lawn.[23] While continuing his recovery he asked to meet with a minister on Good Friday. Deaver called Cardinal Terrence J. Cooke, head of the Archdiocese of New York, overhearing Reagan explain, "I have decided that whatever time I may have left is left for Him."[24]

A great irony of the Reagan administration is that, while the president would seize control of policy toward the Soviets, he often delegated authority in many other areas. Some delegation of authority began as soon as he was inaugurated in January 1981, but it occurred frequently in the aftermath of the assassination attempt. Several instances offer revealing insights into both the nature of the Reagan administration and what it meant to govern during a time of such grave crisis.

This president was not a micromanager. He delegated authority on the specific aspects of a policy while focusing his attention on setting the conditions for policy implementation through his speeches, writings, and personal diplomacy. He also rarely criticized members of his Cabinet or aides. Thus, the president's ultimate uneasiness about his secretary of state's behavior was at once uncharacteristic and striking. On March 24, 1981, the day he announced that the vice president would chair his newly formed crisis-management group and six days before he was shot, Reagan expressed concern about Haig: "Al thinks his turf is being invaded. We chose George [Bush] because Al is wary of Dick [Allen]. He talked of resigning. Frankly I think he's seeing things that aren't there. He's Sec. of St. and no one is intruding on his turf—foreign policy is his but he has half the Cabinet teed off."[25]

The president's qualms about Haig intensified shortly after the assassination attempt:

> On the day I was shot, George Bush was out of town and Haig immediately came to the White House and claimed he was in charge of the country. Even after the vice-president was back in Washington, I was told he maintained that he, not George, should be in charge. I didn't know about this when it was going on. But I heard later that the rest of the cabinet was furious. They said he acted as if he thought he had the right to sit in the Oval Office and believed it was his constitutional right to take over—a position without any legal basis.[26]

Reagan would complain repeatedly over the next two years about "the Al H. situation," referring to the secretary of state's various battles with Richard Allen, United Nations Ambassador Jeane Kirkpatrick, and Secretary of Defense Caspar Weinberger, among others.[27] Haig had some legitimate policy differences with his colleagues, such as his defense of North Atlantic Treaty Organization countries in the face of Soviet pipeline sanctions, but the bitterness of his bureaucratic infighting was substantial and persistent.[28] Reagan ultimately accepted his resignation on June 25, 1982.[29]

But Haig became a scapegoat for institutional problems that had been brewing even before March 30, 1981. Two features of the administrative arrangement were troublesome. First, in their respective capacities as chief of staff, deputy chief of staff, and counselor to the president, the troika of Baker, Deaver, and Meese assumed unusual power, even though none held Cabinet posts. The secretary of state and the national security adviser typically had to petition the troika to gain access to the president and to have their memos and reports seen by him; this created tension that prevented the Reagan White House from operating smoothly.

Then there was the related problem of cabinet government. Despite having delegated significant power to his troika, Reagan also instituted an administrative structure in which cabinet officials wielded greater authority than in prior administrations. They would have delegated responsibilities for policy but were to stay consistent with the president's vision. Beyond that they largely had free reign. The move significantly downgraded the significance of the national security adviser. Instead of having National Security Council (NSC) working groups and committees chaired by NSC staff, they would be chaired by senior staff members from the Departments of Defense and State as well as the Central Intelligence Agency.[30]

National Security Adviser Richard V. Allen could hardly function in this environment. His access to the president went through Meese, and Haig distrusted him. Allen resigned on January 4, 1982, and Deputy Secretary of State William P. Clark replaced him. Clark was a close and trusted friend of President Reagan, but he, too, faced bureaucratic challenges that made his job difficult, if not impossible. His clashes with administration officials were never resolved, and he soon left to become secretary of the interior.[31] His deputy, Robert McFarlane, replaced him on October 17, 1983; and when McFarlane resigned, his deputy, John Poindexter, assumed the role. The position of national security adviser was a revolving door during Reagan's first term.

This situation did not stabilize until Frank Carlucci assumed the role on December 2, 1986; but in less than a year he was appointed Secretary of

Defense. On November 23, 1987, General Colin Powell became President Reagan's sixth national security adviser. Powell won praise for his performance as well. Even so, the average length of service for each national security adviser under Reagan was barely sixteen months.

It was in this context of fluid leadership and an ensuing lack of institutional oversight that the Iran-Contra initiative took root in the White House. Covert activities and diversion of funds from Iranian arms sales for the Nicaraguan resistance movement, the Contras, were made possible by the lack of managerial leadership at the National Security Council. Indeed they began there. The scandal nearly scuttled Reagan's presidency. In response, he formed the Tower Commission in the fall of 1986 to investigate the wrongdoing, after public revelations that US weapons were being sold to Iran in violation of the US stance of neutrality in the Iran-Iraq war. Reagan and some of his advisers had hoped that the strategic opening to Iran would create a context for Tehran to encourage Shiite Hezbollah captors to release Americans being held hostage in Lebanon. White House aides also planned to use the proceeds of these sales to aid the Contras in direct violation of congressional legislation. The Tower Commission ultimately concluded that the institutional weakening of the NSC in the president's cabinet government allowed the unsupervised White House body to have staffers running afoul of the law and national policy.[32]

Haig seemed to be President Reagan's main bureaucratic and political problem in the months after the assassination attempt, during which time he became the scapegoat for the administration's initial missteps. In the broader context, Reagan's management style produced more systemic problems. This was evident not only in the implication of McFarlane and Poindexter in the Iran-Contra scandal, but also in the stumbles by two members of the troika. While attorney general, Meese was accused of having a conflict of interest in the Iran-Contra investigation. Deaver left the Reagan administration in May 1985 and two years later was convicted of perjury for his congressional and grand jury testimony about his lobbying activities.[33]

President Reagan had placed perhaps too much trust in the troika. They served him well in their commitment to his policy goals, but the overall chaotic environment in which they operated opened the door for a well-organized and disciplined vice president. President Reagan took notice.

By the time Ronald Reagan sought the 1980 Republican presidential nomination, George Herbert Walker Bush had been head of the US liaison office in the People's Republic of China, director of the Central Intelligence Agency, a congressman, ambassador to the United Nations, Chairman of the Republican National Committee, and an oil industry executive. The Reagan team could not ignore such impressive credentials as they considered vice presidential candidates. They also realized that, as a moderate Republican, Bush added political balance to the ticket. Nevertheless, there were concerns about how loyal he would be to the president, especially after a bitter nomination fight and Bush's famous depiction of Reagan's proposed tax reduction as "voodoo economics." In fact, Bush had not been the first to be considered for the number-two spot. Gerald Ford, the former president, discussed the matter with Reagan, but the two decided against teaming up. In his firsthand account of the negotiations for Reagan's running mate, Richard Allen writes, "George Bush was picked at the very last moment and largely by a combination of chance and some behind-the-scenes maneuvering."[34]

Bush quickly proved his detractors wrong. A vigorous campaigner, he worked diligently with Reagan during the 1980 fall campaign and personified calm and reason during the administration's acrimonious early days. Reagan appointed him head of his Task Force on Regulatory Relief, in early 1981, and soon thereafter formally designated Bush as head of crisis management for his administration.[35] The White House announcement on "Foreign and Domestic Crisis Management" made it clear that the vice president had been given potentially sweeping authority:

> During any emergency, the President would of course be available to make all critical decisions and to chair the crisis management team as his presence may be needed. Vice President Bush's role is to chair the team in the absence of the President. Of great importance, he will also engage in forward planning for emergency responses,

develop options for Presidential consideration, and take the lead in the implementation of those decisions.[36]

This announcement was made six days before John Hinckley's shooting spree. Thus, Bush was well on his way to becoming an influential vice president before the assassination attempt. His performance on March 30 only helped elevate his standing. Bush was on official duty in Texas when he learned that Reagan had been shot. The vice president withdrew from his engagements and flew immediately aboard Air Force Two to Andrews Air Force Base. Administration officials suggested that he be flown by helicopter from the base directly to the South Lawn of the White House. Bush decided instead to be driven to the White House. "Only the President lands on the South Lawn," he reasoned, desiring to do nothing that might contribute to the national unease over the president's fate.[37]

Finally ensconced in the White House Situation Room, Bush listened to reports about the president's condition and the security status of the nation. The pending Dairy Price Support Bill was among the policy issues discussed, and Attorney General William French Smith suggested the vice president sign the bill. Bush declined, preferring to wait until the following day for an update on Reagan's recovery. He also refused to sit in the president's chair, an act of respect that he continued throughout Reagan's hospitalization. Assessing the vice president's behavior that day, a supporter commented: "He had a perfect touch. In the moments after the shooting ... the situation was not exactly harmonious among some of the rest of the people in the Administration. But Bush came through like a star."[38]

By the end of the year, Reagan reinforced Bush's role as head of crisis management by naming him chair of the Special Situation Group (SSG) in emergency situations. The president signed the directive on December 14, 1981.[39] This group became an important strategic analysis and decision-making body, especially as the United States invaded Grenada two years later.[40] The president also designated Bush to head the Anti-Crime Task Force for Southern Florida in January 1982 and the Task Force on Regulation of Financial Services in September 1984. In July 1985 he took charge of the Task Force on Combatting Terrorism. Reagan praised the vice president for his leadership in these initiatives and gave him increasing responsibility for national and international efforts. Clearly, Bush's role had begun to take shape in the wake of the assassination attempt and expanded dramatically as other senior advisers came under fire.[41]

President Reagan, his cabinet officials, and his other advisers were mainly seasoned policymakers. Yet on March 30, 1981, they were new to the Oval Office and, in many cases, to each other. It would be an exaggeration to say that a coup d'état was under way soon after Reagan was shot, but the events that unfolded at George Washington Hospital and the White House leave a chilling impression that some senior statesmen were unclear about the provisions for presidential disability and succession in the Twenty-fifth Amendment to the Constitution, as well as about associated emergency powers.

In the White House Situation Room, the cabinet and staff awaited updates on the medical conditions of the wounded and as the status of US alert forces. Shortly after 3:00 p.m. on a secure phone in the White House, Caspar Weinberger called Meese about disability and succession. "Under these circumstances," the counselor to the president explained, "it is my understanding the National Command Authority devolves on you." The secretary of defense replied that the vice president carried that authority, but Meese said he believed the vice president's plane was not equipped with secure communications. In his memoirs, Weinberger wrote "I confirmed that I was the next in line after the Vice President."[42] He also spoke with General David Jones, Chairman of the Joint Chiefs of Staff, to discuss the military's alert levels, for Hinkley's assault might have been the vanguard of a broader enemy attack. Following the assassination of President John F. Kennedy, for example, the Strategic Air Command (SAC), which then controlled the bulk of the nation's nuclear arsenal, had been placed on alert until the situation settled.[43] Weinberger did not authorize a full change in alert status, however. He did upgrade the readiness level for bombers so they might take emergency positions more quickly, especially after General Jones reported that two Soviet submarines were "outside the box": meaning they were closer to the East Coast than was typical. Jones did not consider this development particularly troubling, as this situation had occurred in the past; but it was worrisome on the day the president was shot.[44]

Little evidence supported the conclusion that Hinckley was part of a wider plot. The US military received normal signals about the geopolitical environment, and Chairman Jones reported that the sensors at the North American Air Defense Command indicated normal activity. Weinberger learned that crews manning the National Emergency Airborne Command Post at Andrews Air Force Base operated at a normal state of readiness and saw no reason to change their status. At the same time, he ordered Jones to "be particularly vigilant and on the alert, until further notice."[45]

Meanwhile, Larry Speakes, White House deputy press secretary, was instructed by Baker to go to the Press Room to answer questions in an effort to calm the nation. Answering a question about whether the United States government was on a higher military alert, Speakes said, "Not that I'm aware of." Then a reporter asked, "Who's running the government right now? If the President goes into surgery and goes under anesthesia, would Vice President Bush become acting President at that moment or under what circumstances would he?" Speakes replied, "I cannot answer that question at this time."[46] The press conference was not conveying a sense of calm and certainty within the White House.

Watching this performance on a nearby television, Haig reacted quickly; in response to Speakes, he decided to hold an impromptu press conference of his own and left the Situation Room, headed to the Press Room, with National Security Adviser Allen right behind. By the time Haig made it up the stairs he was out of breath and agitated. The secretary approached the lectern and Speakes moved out of the way. Allen later recalled "standing right next to [Haig], prepared to catch him. I thought that he was going to collapse. His legs were shaking.... It was extraordinary, absolutely extraordinary."[47]

Back in the secure conference room, everyone watched Haig's television performance.[48] "There are absolutely no alert measures that are necessary at this time that we're contemplating," Haig said. But it was his response to a question about the government's decision-making structure that added to the sense of disarray in the White House. His statement would follow him the remainder of his life:

> Constitutionally, gentlemen, you have the President, the Vice President and the Secretary of State in that order, and should the President decide that he wants to transfer the helm to the Vice President, he will do so. He has not done that. As of now, I am in control here in the White House, pending return of the Vice President, and in close touch with him. If something came up, I would check with him of course.[49]

This was not his only misstatement of the day. Around 3:40 p.m., before his television appearance, Haig seemed to demonstrate a lack of understanding of basic constitutional authority. Allen taped the discussion in the Situation Room, including an exchange between David Gergen, White House staff director, and Haig which produced the secretary of state's comment on authority:

> GERGEN: Al, a quick question. We need some sense, more better sense of where the President is. Is he under sedation now?
> HAIG: He's not on the operating table.
> GERGEN: He is on the operating table!
> HAIG: So the . . . the helm is right here. And that means right in this chair for now, constitutionally, until the vice president gets here.

Haig's statement did not create a stir in the Situation Room, but Reagan administration officials were becoming concerned. According to Allen, "The other Cabinet members and senior staff knew better—there were three others ahead of Haig in the constitutional succession. But Haig's demeanor signaled that he might be ready for a quarrel, and there was no point in provoking one."[50] A decorated combat veteran and general, Haig was used to giving orders; in the midst of the crisis, he merely reverted to form.

Haig returned from the podium to find his colleagues increasingly concerned about the sense of crisis emerging from White House statements. Even though they had discussed the alert status of US military forces before he appeared on television, Haig did not seem to understand what Weinberger had done. The secretary of defense said: "Al, one problem with that is that you should know I have already ordered an increase, although a very small one, in the alert conditions of the Strategic Air crews." Haig then asked: "Did you do this simply because of the Soviet subs, or because of the incident?" Weinberger replied that both influenced his decision. He "seemed unable or unwilling to accept that there could be an increase in the vigilance of our Commands," Weinberger later wrote, "without going through all the technical and procedural changes involved in 'raising the DEFCON.' "[51] Haig did not relent. He opposed the heightened alert status. This was a remarkable exchange between two of the most senior members of President Reagan's cabinet. It has been described as "a dramatic moment of angry but controlled confrontation."[52]

On the issue of who was in charge, Haig looked at Weinberger and quipped, "You'd better read your Constitution, buddy." Then he asked Fred Fielding, White House counsel, to endorse his statement. Fielding told the secretary of state that he was wrong.[53] Indeed, the secretary of state was incorrect in his Press Room statement. He conveyed none of the basic information provided by US law, which designates that the line of succession begins with the vice president and then moves to the Speaker of the House of Representatives, followed by the President Pro Tempore of the Senate. The secretary of state is in line behind these elected officials.[54] Bush was traveling back to Washington from Texas, and there was agreement among the administration officials that decision-making conversations should await his arrival.[55] In the vice president's absence as well as in the absence of the relevant House and Senate leaders, Haig could be considered the highest-ranking officer in the *Situation Room*: but only there, and only until Bush's arrival at approximately 7:00 p.m.

Whereas US law establishes the line of succession, the Constitution's Twenty-fifth Amendment outlines the consequences of presidential incapacity and the various transitions of power from the president to the vice president.[56] This distinction also seemed to be blurred in the conversations among Reagan administration officials in the wake of the assassination attempt. The Twenty-fifth Amendment, ratified on February 10, 1967, begins straightforwardly: "In case of the removal of the President from office or of his death or resignation, the Vice President shall become President." According to section two, "Whenever there is a vacancy in the office of the Vice President, the President shall nominate a Vice President who shall take office upon confirmation by a majority vote of both Houses of Congress."[57]

At the time Reagan was shot, the Twenty-fifth Amendment had been invoked only three times, all during the Nixon administration. It was used first to approve Gerald Ford as vice president; then later it provided for his ascension to the presidency upon Richard Nixon's resignation and finally for Nelson Rockefeller's appointment as vice president. Sections three and four had not been invoked in the past but were applicable given Reagan's debilitated condition. However, the president's aides were loath to set a new precedent. Section three establishes the procedures for the president to declare his own disability by sending a written declaration to the Speaker of the House and the President Pro Tempore of the Senate. The vice president then serves as acting president until the president submits written notification to the congressional leaders declaring his fitness to resume office. According to section four, the vice president and a majority of the cabinet (or a body selected by Congress) may declare in written form that a president is unable to perform the duties of the Oval Office. The president may resume his duties with his own written declaration to the congressional leaders, stating that he is fit for office. President Reagan's aides were not prepared to set in motion the last two sections of the amendment.

If the Twenty-fifth Amendment had been invoked during President Reagan's hospital stay, Vice President Bush would have been the highest-ranking official in the US government. But because the amendment was not invoked, it might have been unconstitutional to hand over executive authority to him. Therefore, the entire time Reagan was incapacitated was a gray area. He did not temporarily transfer presidential power to Bush;

yet between the vice president's arrival at the White House on the evening of March 30 and President Reagan's release from the hospital on April 11, Bush acted as the de facto head of government.

Since the Twenty-fifth Amendment was never used, the law on succession was the legal guide for the Reagan White House. Thus Haig was wrong. Article Two, Section One of the Constitution addresses presidential succession. That constitutional provision was clarified in 3 U.S. Code § 19. Adopted in 1947, this law establishes that if there "is neither a President nor Vice President to discharge the powers and duties of the office of the President" the line of succession is as follows: Speaker of the House, President Pro-Tempore of the Senate, and then cabinet members based on when the office was established.[58]

There was a more general lack of understanding of presidential authorities during the crisis. Meese was not wrong when he told Weinberger in their March 30 phone conversation that the National Command Authority (NCA) would fall to the secretary of defense, but that matter was unrelated to presidential succession. Weinberger replied that it was his understanding that the vice president was the next in line.[59] The confusion in this conversation arose because NCA pertains to nuclear and other specific military authorities. Typically, presidents have organized NCA so that the chain of command goes from the president to the secretary of defense for maximum efficiency during a moment of military crisis. NCA was not particularly at issue on March 30, or during President Reagan's hospital stay, because the secretary of defense and his military chiefs had determined that there was no domestic or international threat to the nation. Nor was there any other kind of crisis, such as a severe weather disruption, that would have made it necessary to invoke NCA.[60]

Furthermore, it was unclear how the Reagan administration intended to organize its NCA. Some presidents have given their vice presidents a more direct role in this area. (Herbert Abrams has noted that "the vice-president's role in the National Command Authority was and still is a somewhat ambiguous matter."[61]) Several days after the president was shot, the Defense Department issued a statement that appeared to address the issue: "The chain of command runs from the President, who at all times is the Commander in Chief of the Armed Forces under the Constitution, directly to the Secretary of Defense."[62] On the day of the assassination, however, the White House issued a statement that "national command authorities" had devolved to the vice president.[63]

Although there was close communication between those in the Situation Room and the president's aides at George Washington University Hospital, each group displayed its own dynamics. Dr. Daniel Ruge, the White House physician, said that he kept a copy of the Twenty-fifth Amendment with him but failed to raise the issue of the president's medical incapacity. On the issue of invoking the Twenty-fifth Amendment, Dr. Ruge later admitted, "It never occurred to me." From a medical perspective, he contends that Reagan most likely should have relinquished presidential authority for "a day or two."[64]

Michael Deaver, who was with the president during the assassination attempt, remained particularly shaken even the day after the event when Richard Darman, a deputy assistant to the president, debriefed him. Deaver admitted that transferring presidential authority barely occurred to him: "It struck me at one point to find out where George Bush was. But you never—it was honestly about an hour or more before you really understood what this situation was . . . clearly . . . you had—it kept progressing and it went from a chipped rib to a bullet in the lung, and possibly injuring the heart."[65]

Events were moving fast but some of Reagan's aides were concerned about who was actually in charge. Soon after the president was shot, Baker, Meese, and Lyn Nofziger, head of the White House's political liaison office, huddled in a hospital supply closet to discuss whether the president should temporarily transfer power. They decided against the action as it seemed likely that he would recover and they did not feel it was wise to undertake even a temporary transfer.[66] In the Situation Room, conversely, Fielding, Haig, and Dan Murphy, chief of staff to the vice president, examined two letters prepared by Fielding that would invoke the Twenty-fifth Amendment. In the letter requiring his signature, the president informed congressional leadership that he would temporarily transfer power to Vice President Bush.

The other letter, to be signed by Bush and a majority of the president's cabinet if the president could not sign, also transferred authority to Bush, but did so on the basis of the president's inability to fulfill his White House duties. In his authoritative account of the assassination attempt and its aftermath, Del Quentin Wilber writes, "The sight of Fielding, Haig, and Murphy reviewing the succession documents made him uneasy. In Darman's view, many of the president's aides had responded to the crisis far too emotionally. Darman did not think this was the best time or place to discuss a historic transfer of presidential authority."[67] The deputy assistant to the president has noted, "There had never before been a transfer of power under the Twenty-fifth Amendment. But one quick pass around the room, and the group might have begun the effective removal of the President of the United States."[68]

Laurence Barrett, in one of the earliest accounts of Reagan's presidency, reviewed the deliberations on invoking presidential incapacity through the Twenty-fifth Amendment, emphasizing Darman's decisive role:

> When he spotted the implementing documents related to the Twenty-fifth Amendment, Darman . . . recognized trouble. If the subject came up for general discussion in the Situation Room and word of that got out, it would create questions about Reagan's capacities. Worse, Darman sniffed the possibility, however remote, that the cabinet might actually seize the initiative. He made a quick decision to head off both dangers. Darman quietly told Fielding, Haig and Murphy that neither the subject nor the documents belonged on the table. He suggested that he take possession of the papers.[69]

Darman called Baker and told him of the development in the Situation Room. Baker let the White House staffer know that he and Meese agreed that President Reagan's power would not be transferred and approved Darman's locking the transfer documents in the safe in his office.[70]

Haig had a different recollection: "At no time did those present in the situation room consider invoking the Twenty-fifth Amendment. . . . Discussion of the transfer of authority was premature and inappropriate and I believed it should be avoided." Yet he does not deny that documents to transfer presidential power were circulated in the Situation Room: "Certainly the preparation of papers on the subject [invoking the Twenty-fifth Amendment] was ill-advised."[71]

Such constitutional matters were not solely confined to the immediate aftermath of Reagan's ordeal. He experienced some of the normal after-effects of major surgery by April 3, for example, including a high fever. Dr. Aaron, the surgeon who removed the bullet from the president's lung, wanted to perform a bronchoscopy to see if an infection could be the cause. The White House medical team asked that the president not be sedated for the procedure, however. No major explanation was given to the hospital doctors at the time, but Laurence Barrett later reported that Baker, Darman, Deaver, and Meese discussed using the Twenty-fifth Amendment if the president was given medication that sedated him or caused him to become fully unconscious.[72]

The world did not stop turning merely because the president was shot. On the same day Solidarity was bargaining with its government for political liberalization. In the days that followed, Soviet saber rattling toward Solidarity made a military takeover appear likely. Outright invasion seemed in the offing, repeating Soviet suppression of reform movements in other Warsaw Pact states in 1956 and 1968. Such an action while the American president was incapacitated could lead to a major geopolitical crisis, aides reasoned, but still they decided against invoking the Twenty-fifth Amendment. According to Barrett, "Reagan tolerated use of the bronchoscope without systemic sedation. George Bush never learned that he had come close to being acting President four days after Reagan's chest had been sutured."[73]

But, in fact, Bush had earlier given thought to a temporary transfer of presidential authority to himself. The Polish crisis was on his mind as he sat aboard Air Force Two on the day of the shooting. As the president's surgery was ending, Bush contemplated what he would do as temporary president if the crisis escalated:

> It doesn't overawe me of what might happen because of the good relations between my staff and Reagan's, good relations with the

> Cabinet. Playing it the lowest-key way possible. . . . There's a certain wondering about the unknown but not (being) concerned about it. We've got Poland out there; could be something there tomorrow – tonight. I'm doing my reading. The Soviets could go into Poland, and I'd have to make those decisions. I've got to sort those things out, absorb it, but I don't feel any lack of confidence.[74]

Years later, Richard Allen would write: "The crisis-management team in the Situation Room worked together well. The congressional leadership was kept informed, and governments around the world were notified and reassured. Meese and Baker, at the hospital, where the helm really was, performed calmly and skillfully. The next morning, as the Vice President and the Cabinet assembled for the post-crisis briefing, Haig leaned over to me and said in a low voice, 'Have you got your maniacs under control? They don't look too sharp this morning.' "[75] Recalling these deliberations, Fred Fielding has remarked, "To be very frank . . . when I mentioned the 25th Amendment I could see eyes glazing over in some parts of the Cabinet. They didn't even know about the 25th Amendment."[76] Among the most senior members of the Reagan administration there was no agreement on the essentials of succession. They were lucky.

Reagan worked a reduced schedule in the weeks following his release from the hospital. Yet he became deeply involved in major policy issues on the economy and foreign policy almost immediately. The issue of missile defense captured his attention, as he recalled in his memoirs:

> As I sat in the sun-filled White House solarium in robe and pajamas that spring, waiting for doctors to give me a go-ahead to resume a full work schedule, I wondered how to get the process started. Perhaps having come so close to death made me feel I should do whatever I could in the years God had given me to reduce the threat of nuclear war; perhaps there was a reason I had been spared.[77]

Reagan had already begun to conceive of a radically different approach to US-Soviet nuclear competition before he was shot. On Sunday, March

29, 1981, the day before his speech at the Washington Hilton Hotel, he recalled in his memoir being deep in thought about how to articulate a strategic doctrine that would end the nuclear arms race:

> During the spring of 1981, the arms race was moving ahead at a pell-mell pace based on the MAD [mutual assured destruction] policy. . . . There didn't seem any end to it, no way out of it. . . . Advocates of the MAD policy believed it had served a purpose: The balance of terror it created, they said, had prevented nuclear war for decades. But as far as I was concerned, the MAD policy was madness. For the first time in history, man had the power to destroy mankind itself. A war between the superpowers would incinerate much of the world and leave what was left of it uninhabitable forever. . . . We couldn't continue this nervous standoff forever, I thought; we couldn't lower our guard, but we had to begin the process of peace.[78]

The idea of nuclear disarmament stayed on the president's mind throughout his recuperation. He considered mutual assured destruction (MAD) immoral. Détente was immoral as well because it codified the international status quo, which included Soviet domination of Eastern Europe. Eliminating MAD, abandoning détente, and furthering the significant military buildup begun by his predecessor, Jimmy Carter, were central elements of his strategy to achieve the goals of reducing the likelihood of nuclear war and eventually ridding the world of nuclear weapons altogether. In essence, Reagan wanted to overturn the logic of conventional Cold War thinking, which had premised global survival on MAD, détente, and containment.[79]

He knew there would be trouble. Resistance would come from many of his own political advisers and foreign policy experts who were convinced that there was no alternative to the concepts that had been forged in the 1960s and 1970s. Then there was the matter of explaining his revolutionary thinking to his domestic audience, Washington's allies, and the Soviets. Thus his first order of business after leaving the hospital was to seize control of his Soviet policy.[80]

Reagan did so by writing directly to Soviet General Secretary Leonid Brezhnev. The interagency machinery of foreign policy experts from the State Department and National Security Council had begun to draft a letter for the president to review and sign in response to a March 6 note from Brezhnev, a process that was still underway when President Reagan was shot. On April 18, while working from the White House's solarium, the president took matters into his own hands, drafting a letter of his own on a yellow legal pad. National Security Adviser Richard Allen then oversaw the merger of both letters. Reagan preferred his own draft, however, and soon thereafter both the State Department letter and his more personal note (this time written on presidential letterhead) were sent to Brezhnev.

Reagan's letter was less strident and bureaucratic than what was produced by the interagency process. In it, he sought to open the possibility for US-Soviet dialogue. At the same time, he did not shrink from criticizing the Soviets, expressing his belief that all people desire individual freedom, liberty, and dignity. He asked whether both sides "have permitted ideology, political and economic philosophies, and government policies to keep us from considering the very real, everyday problems of peoples?" He then offered an olive branch in his conclusion, promising to lift the grain embargo that Carter had imposed after the Soviet Red Army rolled into Afghanistan in 1979, hoping the gesture might "contribute to creating the circumstances which will lead to the meaningful and constructive dialogue which will assist us in fulfilling our joint obligation to find lasting peace."[81] The offer was also a blow to his bureaucracy.

Reagan's desire to induce political liberalization within the Soviet Union also took on new urgency after he was shot. Put differently, he wanted to topple the Soviet government. In delivering the commencement address at the University of Notre Dame on May 17, 1981, he said, "The West won't contain communism, it will transcend communism. It won't bother to dismiss or denounce it, it will dismiss it as some bizarre chapter in human history whose last pages are even now being written."[82] Reagan began establishing an intellectual roadmap with that address, delivered merely five weeks after being released from the hospital.

The strategy announced at Notre Dame was enshrined in strategic doctrine the next year, when he signed National Security Decision Directive (NSDD) 32, which declared that one of the "global objectives" of the United States would be "to contain and reverse the expansion of Soviet control and military presence throughout the world, and to increase the costs of Soviet support and use of proxy, terrorist, and subversive forces."[83] This objective was repeated in NSDD 75. Issued on January 17, 1983, and titled "US Relations With the USSR," NSDD 75 asked US foreign policy leaders "to promote, within the narrow limits available to us, the process of change in the Soviet Union toward a more pluralistic political and economic system in which the power of the privileged ruling elite is gradually reduced."[84]

In the 1980s, then, there was a massive doctrinal shift on offense versus defense and containment versus reversal. Reagan was the undisputed source of that shift. His Soviet strategy grew in part out of his pre-presidential thinking.[85] And as president, he played a distinctly personal role in crafting his Soviet policy. His closest advisers took credit for many policies and decisions but not the Soviet strategy. Most were unaware of how he redoubled efforts on the geopolitical front in light of the assassination attempt. They did know, however, that in that arena the president was in charge. As the Reagan military buildup took place, federal budget deficits soared, but the president did not see massive deficit spending as a zero-sum game. Convinced that his decisions were an essential component to bringing the Cold War at last to an end, he said, "I'll take full responsibility for this gamble."[86]

On December 22, 1982, the president called a private meeting with the joint chiefs of staff (JCS). He had invited the military brass to his office to probe their thoughts on starting a program of research and development on missile defense that would not violate the restrictions of the 1972 Anti-Ballistic Missile Treaty. They told him that they would like to see a missile-defense program undertaken. "Let's do it," Reagan replied.[87] He also consulted with the JCS on February 11, 1983, writing in his diary that the two-hour lunch meeting produced "a super idea." He continued:

> So far the only policy worldwide on nuclear weapons is to have a deterrent. What if we tell the world we want to protect our people, not

> avenge them; that we're going to embark on a program of research to come up with a defensive weapon that could make nuclear weapons obsolete? I would call upon the scientific community to volunteer in bringing such a thing about.[88]

These meetings contributed to creation of the Strategic Defense Initiative (SDI).

On March 23, 1983, in a televised address introducing SDI, President Reagan announced that he was "directing a comprehensive and intensive effort to define a long-term research and development program . . . [to] pave the way for arms control measures to eliminate the [nuclear] weapons themselves."[89] SDI was formalized as a presidential order in National Security Decision Directive 119. Issued on January 6, 1984, the directive had the deep imprint of Reagan's thinking and statements since becoming president. "Given the uncertain long-term future of nuclear deterrence," President Reagan wrote in NSDD 119, "I believe that an effort must also be made to identify alternative means of deterring nuclear war and protecting our national security interests. In particular, the U.S. should investigate the feasibility of eventually shifting toward reliance upon a defensive concept."[90]

Reagan was under no illusions about the difficulties of his proposal. Concerning the near-term feasibility of a major breakthrough in defensive technology that could be deployed and used with accuracy, he said in his SDI speech that what he was proposing was a "technical task . . . that may not be accomplished before the end of this century." In recognizing the potential dangerous signal he was sending his Soviet adversary, he said: "This could pave the way for arms control measures to eliminate the weapons themselves."[91] It was something he had been stating since the beginning of his presidency, but many still did not believe him—that he wanted to eliminate nuclear weapons. Many within the military and scientific communities, including members of the president's team, believed both the idea and program infeasible. But Reagan was undeterred, hoping not only for a world freed from the nuclear scourge but, in the shorter term, to help draw the Soviets to the negotiating table.[92]

He found a partner, or at least someone willing to engage in serious negotiations leading to a new global order, in Soviet General Secretary

Mikhail Gorbachev. Brezhnev had died in November 1982, followed in quick succession by the next two ailing Soviet leaders, Yuri Andropov and Konstantin Chernenko. (Quipped Reagan, "How am I supposed to get any place with the Russians . . . if they keep dying on me?") But Gorbachev was different. Young, energetic, and a dedicated reformer, he would go on to change the very nature of Soviet society and political economy with his policies of *glasnost* (openness, somewhat shy of democracy) and *perestroika* (systemic restructuring). Gorbachev was eager to meet with Reagan to discuss potential initiatives that could profoundly alter the international system. They met at four summits. Their first two summits—in Geneva in November 1985 and Reykjavik in October 1986—deadlocked over the president's unwillingness to abandon SDI. Earlier in 1986, anticipating Gorbachev's opposition to SDI, Reagan had sent the Soviet leader a handwritten note. "If there were no nuclear missiles," he reasoned, "then there might also be no need for defenses against them."[93] Gorbachev remained unpersuaded. After the Reykjavik summit, the president wrote that SDI "won't be traded away."[94] Ultimately, SDI was not traded away, but Gorbachev decided not to let it stand in way of a major opportunity.

And so, all the elements came together. On December 8, 1987, Reagan and Gorbachev met in Washington to sign an agreement that would eliminate all intermediate-level nuclear weapons in their arsenals (with further reductions to come). It was, in Reagan's words, "a grand historical moment."[95] Along with the sturdy rapport that these two extraordinary leaders had established, their nuclear disarmament treaty was the palpable result of the fortuitous circumstances that had brought Gorbachev to power in the Soviet Union and, most especially, of the life-threatening presidential crisis that had made Ronald Reagan ever more determined in his path to a safer world. It was the beginning of the end of the Cold War.

NOTES

1. For President Reagan's schedule on March 30, 1981, see Ronald Reagan Presidential Library (hereafter RRPL), "White House Diary," March 30, 1981, http://www.reaganfoundation.org/white-house-diary.aspx, accessed on March 24, 2015; and "The

Presidential Troika," *The New York Times*, April 19, 1981, http://www.nytimes.com/1981/04/19/magazine/the-president-troika.html?pagewanted=7, accessed May 22, 2015.

2. "Remarks at the National Conference of the Building and Construction Trades Department, AFL-CIO," RRPL, March 30, 1981, http://www.reagan.utexas.edu/archives/speeches/1981/33081b.htm, accessed on March 17, 2015.
3. Douglas Brinkley, ed., *The Reagan Diaries* (New York: HarperCollins, 2007), 12 (hereafter *Reagan Diaries*). For similar reports and more general assessments of President Reagan's speech and surrounding events, see Terry Golway, *Ronald Reagan's America: His Voice, His Dreams, and His Vision of Tomorrow* (Naperville, Florida: Sourcebooks MediaFusion, 2008), 69–72; Philip Shabecoff, "In Talk Just Before the Attack, Reagan Assayed Crime Rise," *New York Times*, March 31, 1981; and Del Quentin Wilber, *Rawhide Down: The Near Assassination of Ronald Reagan* (New York: Henry Holt and Company, 2011), 78.
4. Michael K. Deaver, *A Different Drummer: My Thirty Years with Ronald Reagan* (New York: HarperCollins, 2001), 133.
5. Herbert L. Abrams, *"The President Has Been Shot" Confusion, Disability, & the 25th Amendment* (New York: W.W. Norton & Company, 1992), 54; Lou Cannon, *President Reagan: The Role of a Lifetime* (New York: Simon and Schuster, 1991), 164; Patti Davis, *Angels Don't Lie: My Father's Gift of Faith* (New York: HarperCollins, 1995), 26–27; Douglas Feaver, "Three Men Shot at the Side of their President," *Washington Post*, March 31, 1981, http://www.washingtonpost.com/wp-dyn/articles/A38802-2004Jul9.html; and "John W. Hinckley Jr.: A Biography," University of Missouri, Kansas City School of Law, Faculty Projects, http://law2.umkc.edu/faculty/projects/ftrials/hinckley/hbio.htm, accessed on June 17, 2014.
6. The account herein of the Hinckley shooting and its after effects is informed by numerous sources, but in particular the following provide authoritative accounts: Abrams, *"The President Has Been Shot;"* Laurence I. Barrett, *Gambling with History: Ronald Reagan in the White House* (Garden City, New York: Doubleday, 1983), 108; Deaver, *A Different Drummer*, 133; John Pekkanen, "The Saving of the President," *Washingtonian*, March 10, 2011, http://www.washingtonian.com/articles/people/the-saving-of-the-president/, accessed December 30, 2014; and Del Quentin Wilber, *Rawhide Down*, 82.
7. Edwin Meese III, *With Reagan: The Inside Story* (Washington, DC: Regnery Gateway, 1992), 82–84; and Caspar W. Weinberger, *Fighting for Peace: Seven Critical Years in the Pentagon* (New York: Warner Books, 1990), 95.
8. John Pekkanen, "The Saving of the President," *Washingtonian*, March 10, 2011, http://www.washingtonian.com/articles/people/the-saving-of-the-president/, accessed December 30, 2014; and Nancy Reagan, *My Turn: The Memoirs of Nancy Reagan* (New York: Random House, 1989), 18.
9. Marjorie Hunter, "Men in the News: Surgeons to the President," *New York Times*, April 1, 1981, http://www.nytimes.com/1981/04/01/us/men-in-the-news-surgeons-to-the-president.html, accessed June 2, 2015; Pekkanen, "The Saving of the President"; *The Reagan Diaries*, 12.

10. Deaver, 141. See also Laurence I. Barrett, *Gambling with History*, 121; Loretta McLaughlin, G. S., "Reagan Makes Rapid Progress; Signs Bill, Sees Aides," *Boston Globe*, April 1, 1981; John Pekkanen, "The Saving of the President"; and Weinberger, *Fighting for Peace*, 94–95.
11. Steve Neal, "Reagan Told about Brady; 'Oh, Damn, oh, Damn,'" *Chicago Tribune*, April 1, 1981.
12. McLaughlin, "Reagan Makes Rapid Progress"; and Rudy Abramson, "Reagan 'Doing Well,' Signs Bill in Hospital," *Los Angeles Times*, April 1, 1981, http://search.proquest.com/docview/152723992?accountid=9902, accessed March 17, 2015.
13. This review of President Reagan's hospital stay is informed by John Pekkanen, "The Saving of the President"; and Nancy Reagan, 1–19.
14. These jokes are recounted in Deaver, 138–141; John Aloysius Farrell, *Tip O'Neill and the Democratic Century* (New York: Little, Brown and Company, 2001), 552; Steven F. Hayward, *The Age of Reagan: The Conservative Counterrevolution, 1980-1989* (New York: Crown Forum, 2009), 140; Meese, 82; Pekkanen, "The Saving of the President"; Ronald Reagan, *An American Life* (New York: Simon and Schuster, 1990), 260–261; and Nancy Reagan, 11.
15. Nancy Reagan, 12; and "Honey, I Forgot To Duck," *Los Angeles Examiner*, March 31, 1981.
16. Nancy Reagan, 12.
17. The statements by Clark and O'Neill are found in Paul Kengor and Patricia Clark Doerner, *The Judge: William P. Clark, Ronald Reagan's Top Hand* (San Francisco, California: Ignatius Press, 2007), 127; and Farrell, *Tip O'Neill*, 553. The hospital visits by Clark and Speaker O'Neill are not reflected in the daily agenda overseen at the White House that is now publicly available. See http://www.reaganfoundation.org/white-house-diary.aspx, accessed January 4, 2015. It appears that some of the daily agendas are incomplete.
18. *The Reagan Diaries*, 12; and Steve Neal, "Reagan Told about Brady."
19. *The Reagan Diaries*, 12.
20. Ibid.
21. When Brady died on August 4, 2014, the Virginia medical examiner classified his death a homicide from gunshot injuries. See "Brady Campaign to End Gun Violence," http://www.bradycampaign.org/our-history, accessed January 2, 2015; Peter Hermann and Michael E. Ruane, "Medical examiner rules James Brady's death a homicide," *Washington Post,* August 8, 2014, http://www.washingtonpost.com/local/crime/james-bradys-death-ruled-homicide-by-dc-medical-examiner/2014/08/08/686de224-1f41-11e4-82f9-2cd6fa8da5c4_story.html?wpisrc=al_national, accessed January 2, 2015; "Reagan Press Secretary Jim Brady's Death Ruled Homicide," *NBC News,* August 8, 2014, http://www.nbcnews.com/nightly-news/reagan-press-secretary-jim-bradys-death-ruled-homicide-n176521, accessed January 2, 2015; and Wilber, 222–223. On June 21, 1982, a Washington, DC, court found Hinckley not guilty by reason of insanity. He resides in Saint Elizabeth's Hospital, a facility in the capital for the mentally ill. On January 2, 2015, the US Attorney's Office in Washington, DC, issued an announcement stating that federal prosecutors will not move forward with a new case against Hinckley. See

"John Hinckley Won't Face Murder Charges in James Brady's Death," *NBC News*, January 2, 2015, http://www.nbcnews.com/news/us-news/john-hinckley-wont-face-murder-charges-james-bradys-death-n278561 accessed January 2, 2015; Peter Hermann, "John Hinckley Won't Face Murder Charge in Death of James Brady, Prosecutors Say," *Washington Post*, January 2, 2015, http://www.washingtonpost.com/local/crime/prosecutors-will-not-charge-hinckley-with-murder-in-death-of-james-brady/2015/01/02/67de0024-929a-11e4-a900-9960214d4cd7_story.html accessed January 2, 2015; and "Hinckley won't Face New Charges in Reagan Aide's Death," *USA Today*, January 2, 2015, http://www.usatoday.com/story/news/nation/2015/01/02/john-hinckley-no-new-charges-james-brady-death/21197487/, accessed January 2, 2015.

22. Deaver, 142; and Nancy Reagan, 20.
23. Steven R. Weisman, "President Returns to the White House; Says He Feels 'Great,'" *New York Times*, April 12, 1981, http://www.nytimes.com/1981/04/12/us/president-returns-to-the-white-house-says-he-feels-great.html accessed March 19, 2015; Howell Raines, "White House Staff Sees Reagan Return as Best RX for Program," *New York Times*, April 12, 1981, http://www.nytimes.com/1981/04/12/weekinreview/white-house-staff-sees-reagan-return-as-best-rx-for-program.html accessed March 19, 2015; Howell Raines, "Political Drama Surrounds First Speech Since Attack," *New York Times*, April 29, 1981, http://www.nytimes.com/1981/04/29/us/political-drama-surrounds-first-speech-since-attack.html, accessed March 19, 2015.
24. Deaver, 145–146.
25. *The Reagan Diaries*,11. On President Reagan's management style see, David J. Rothkopf, *Running the World: The Inside Story of the National Security Council and the Architects of American Power* (New York: PublicAffairs, 2005), 211; and Peter J. Wallison, *Ronald Reagan: The Power of Conviction and the Success of His Presidency* (Boulder, CO: Westview Press, 2003). On the president's decision to appoint his vice president of head of his crisis-management group see Bernard Gwertzman, "Haig Opposes Plan for New Bush Role but Reagan Moves," *New York Times*, March 25, 1981, http://www.nytimes.com/1981/03/25/world/haig-opposes-plan-for-new-bush-role-but-reagan-moves-text-of-statement-page-a6.html, accessed December 23, 2014.
26. Reagan, *An American Life*, 271.
27. *The Reagan Diaries*, 88. See also pages 87 and 90–91.
28. George J. Church, "The Shakeup at State," *Time*, July 5, 1982, http://content.time.com/time/subscriber/article/0,33009,925497-2,00.html, accessed March 23, 2015.
29. For the exchange of letters between Reagan and Haig confirming the secretary of state's resignation, see The American Presidency Project, "Letter Accepting the Resignation of Alexander M. Haig Jr., as Secretary of State," June 25, 1982, http://www.presidency.ucsb.edu/ws/?pid=42681, accessed March 23, 2015.
30. Richard A. Best Jr., *The National Security Council: An Organizational Assessment* (Washington, DC: Congressional Research Service, 2011), https://fas.org/sgp/crs/natsec/RL30840.pdf; and Rothkopf, *Running the World*, 216–218 and 220.
31. Kengor and Clark Doerner, 251–253.

32. U.S. President's Special Review Board, Report of the President's Special Review Board (Washington, DC: Government Printing Office, 1987), pp. V-1-V-2. Former Senator John Tower and former Secretary of State Edmund Muskie, and former National Security Adviser Brent Scowcroft were members of the commission, sometimes referred to as the Tower Board. See also Wallison, *Ronald Reagan*, 21, 177–178, and 261.
33. Lawrence E. Walsh, *Iran-Contra: The Final Report* (Washington, DC: United States Court of Appeals for the District of Columbia Circuit, Division for the Purpose of Appointing Independent Counsel, Division No. 86–6, 1993), 80, 123, 445–446, and 525; and "Deaver Charged With Perjury," *New York Times*, March 22, 1987, http://www.nytimes.com/1987/03/22/weekinreview/deaver-charged-with-perjury.html, accessed May 28, 2015.
34. See http://news.bbc.co.uk/2/hi/americas/270292.stm, accessed March 24, 2015; and Richard V. Allen, "George Herbert Walker Bush; The Accidental Vice President," *New York Times,* July 30, 2000, http://www.nytimes.com/2000/07/30/magazine/george-herbert-walker-bush-the-accidental-vice-president.html, accessed June 1, 2015.
35. "Executive Order 12291: Federal regulation," National Archives, February 17, 1981, http://www.archives.gov/federal-register/codification/executive-order/12291.html, accessed March 18, 2015. For a review of Haig's displeasure with the crisis system President Reagan was putting in place, see Richard V. Allen, "When Reagan was shot, who was 'in control' at the White House?" *Washington Post*, March 25, 2011; Bernard Gwertzman, "Haig Opposes Plan for New Bush Role but Reagan Moves," *New York Times*, March 25, 1981; http://www.nytimes.com/1981/03/25/world/haig-opposes-plan-for-new-bush-role-but-reagan-moves-text-of-statement-page-a6.html, accessed December 23, 2014; Don Oberdorfer and Lee Lescaze, "Reagan Reassures Haig that He's Still Main Foreign Policy Adviser; Resignation Avoided," *Washington Post,* March 26, 1981, http://www.lexisnexis.com.proxy.library.cmu.edu/hottopics/lnacademic/?verb=sr&csi=8075, accessed December 23, 2014; and Martin Schram, "White House Revamps Top Policy Roles; Bush to Head Crisis Management; White House Moves to End Disarray on Policy," *Washington Post*, March 22, 1981, http://www.lexisnexis.com.proxy.library.cmu.edu/hottopics/lnacademic/?verb=sr&csi=8075, accessed December 23, 2014.
36. "Statement by the Press Secretary on Foreign and Domestic Crisis Management March 24, 1981," RRPL, http://www.reagan.utexas.edu/archives/speeches/1981/32481b.htm, accessed December 23, 2014.
37. Mark O. Hatfield, with the Senate Historical Office, *Vice Presidents of the United States, 1789-1993* (Washington, DC: US Government Printing Office, 1997), http://www.senate.gov/artandhistory/history/resources/pdf/george_bush.pdf; and Andrew Johns, ed., *A Companion to Ronald Reagan* (Malden, MA: John Wiley, 2014), 498.
38. Steven R. Weisman, "Bush Prizes His Behind-The-Scenes Influence," *New York Times*, February 28, 1982, http://www.nytimes.com/1982/02/28/us/bush-prizes-his-behind-the-scenes-influence.html, accessed March 16, 2015; Lynn Rosellini, "Behind the Scenes is Fine, He Says," *New York Times*, October 28, 1981, http://www.

nytimes.com/1981/10/28/us/behind-the-scenes-is-fine-he-says.html, accessed March 16, 2015; and Johns, 498–499.

39. NSDD 3 was declassified in 1996. See "National Security Decision Directive Number 3," RRPL, December 14, 1981, http://www.reagan.utexas.edu/archives/reference/Scanned%20NSDDS/NSDD3.pdf, accessed January 1, 2015.
40. Johns, *A Companion to Ronald Reagan*, 498–499.
41. Ronald Reagan, "Statement Announcing Establishment of a Federal Anti-Crime Task Force for Southern Florida," RRPL, January 28, 1982, http://www.reagan.utexas.edu/archives/speeches/1982/12882b.htm, accessed June 2, 2015; "Blueprint for Reform: the Report of the Task Group on Regulation of Financial Services," *United States Government Publishing Office*, July 2, 1984, https://archive.org/details/blueprintforrefo01unit, accessed June 2, 2015; "National Security Decision Directive 179," RRPL, July 20, 1985, http://www.reagan.utexas.edu/archives/reference/Scanned%20NSDDS/NSDD179.pdf, accessed March 18, 2015; Concerning the South Florida Drug Task Force, President Reagan reported: "The South Florida Task Force, which we established under the leadership of Vice President George Bush, has, in the opinion of virtually all knowledgeable observers, been highly successful in slowing the illegal flow of drugs into the United States." See Ronald Reagan, "Remarks Announcing Federal Initiatives Against Drug Trafficking and Organized Crime," *The American Presidency Project*, October 14, 1982, http://www.presidency.ucsb.edu/ws/?pid=43127, accessed March 17, 2015.
42. Weinberger, *Fighting for Peace*, 85; and Richard Darman, *Who's in Control? Polar Politics and the Sensible Center* (New York: Simon and Schuster, 1996), 55.
43. Barrett, *Gambling with History*, 119; Weinberger, *Fighting for Peace*, 86–87; and "Chaos Reigned Day Reagan was Shot," *Washington Times*, March 21, 2001, http://www.washingtontimes.com/news/2001/mar/21/20010321-021706-7656r/.
44. Weinberger, *Fighting for Peace*, 87.
45. Ibid., 88.
46. Barrett, *Gambling with History*, 117.
47. Ibid., 117–118.
48. Weinberger 89. Weinberger's recollection of events is slightly different in a later memoir; see Caspar W. Weinberger with Gretchen Roberts, *In the Arena: A Memoir of the 20th Century* (Washington, DC: Regnery, 2001), 298–299. For Haig's telling of these events see Alexander M. Haig Jr., *Caveat: Realism, Reagan, and Foreign Policy* (New York: Macmillan, 1984). Excerpts of the specific section of his memoir that address the White House dynamics on the day President Reagan was shot may be found in *TIME* magazine: "Alexander Haig," *Time*, April 2, 1984, http://content.time.com/time/subscriber/article/0,33009,954230,00.html, accessed on December 23, 2014.
49. Steven R. Weisman, "Bush Flies Back From Texas Set to Take Charge in Crisis," *New York Times*, March 31, 1981, http://www.nytimes.com/1981/03/31/us/bush-flies-back-from-texas-set-to-take-charge-in-crisis.html?pagewanted=all, accessed June 3, 2015; and Wilber, *Rawhide Down*, 175.
50. Richard V. Allen, "The Day Reagan Was Shot," *The Atlantic*, February 4, 2011, http://www.theatlantic.com/magazine/archive/2001/04/the-day-reagan-was-shot/308396/, accessed June 2, 2015. See also Wilber, 167–168.

51. Weinberger, *Fighting for Peace*, 89–90. Allen, President Reagan's first national security adviser, placed a tape recorder on the table in the Situation Room. Years later he published some of the transcript in the *The Atlantic*. The memoirs, books, and articles herein cited that recount the events in the Situation Room are remarkably consistent with the transcript of the actual conversations among the cabinet and staff members. See Allen, "The Day Reagan Was Shot."
52. Lou Cannon, "The Day of the Jackal in Washington; A Chronicle of How an Ordinary Spring Afternoon in Washington Turned Into a Day of the Jackal for the President and His Country," *Washington Post*, April 5, 1981, A1.
53. Barrett, 118–19; and Weinberger, *Fighting for Peace*, 90.
54. "3 U.S. § 19: Vacancy in Offices of Both President and Vice President; Officers Eligible to Act," *US Government Printing Office*, January 3, 2007, http://www.gpo.gov/fdsys/pkg/USCODE-2006-title3/pdf/USCODE-2006-title3-chap1-sec19.pdf, accessed December 23, 2014.
55. Weinberger, *Fighting for Peace*, 85; and Wilber, 164.
56. "25th Amendment," Cornell University Law School Legal Information Institute, http://www.law.cornell.edu/constitution/amendmentxxv, accessed January 3, 2015.
57. "Report of the Commission on Presidential Disability and the Twenty-fifth Amendment," Miller Center Commission No. 4, 1988, http://web1.millercenter.org/commissions/comm_1988.pdf, accessed on December 23, 2014.
58. "3 U.S. Code § 19 - Vacancy in offices of both President and Vice President; officers eligible to act."
59. Weinberger, *Fighting for Peace*, 85.
60. "Department of Defense Directive," December 2, 1971, Number 5100.30; and Richard Darman, *Who's in Control?* 53–55.
61. Abrams, *The President Has Been Shot*, 112.
62. Stewart W. Taylor Jr., "Disabling of Reagan Provokes a Debate over Nuclear Authority in Such Cases," *New York Times*, April 4, 1981, http://www.nytimes.com/1981/04/04/us/disabling-of-reagan-provokes-a-debate-over-nuclear-authority-in-such-cases.html, accessed December 23, 2014.
63. Ibid.
64. "Reagan Doctor Says 25th Amendment Should Have Been Used in '81," *Los Angeles Times*, February 21, 1989, http://articles.latimes.com/1989-02-21/news/mn-112_1_25th-amendment; and Lawrence K. Altman, "Presidential Power: Reagan Doctor Says He Erred," *New York Times*, February 20, 1989, http://www.nytimes.com/1989/02/20/us/presidential-power-reagan-doctor-says-he-erred.html, accessed January 3, 2015.
65. For Deaver's interview on March 31, 1981, see "Michael Deaver Testimony," *Rawhide Down*, http://rawhidedown.com/wordpress/wpcontent/themes/RawhideDown/PDFs/DeaverStatement.pdf, accessed June 2, 2015.
66. Barrett, 114–115.
67. Wilber, 181.
68. Darman, *Who's in Control?*, 53.
69. Barrett, 115–116.
70. Wilber, 181. See also Abrams, 180.

71. Haig, *Caveat*, 157.
72. Barrett, 121–122.
73. Abrams, 101; Barrett, 122; John Darnton, "Polish Ruling Body Reaches An Impasse on Adverting Strike," *New York Times*, March 30, 1981, http://www.nytimes.com/1981/03/30/world/polish-ruling-body-reaches-an-impasse-on-averting-strike.html, accessed May 29, 2015; John Darnton, "Polish Strike in Abeyance as Pact is Signed," *New York Times*, March 31, 1981, http://www.nytimes.com/1981/03/30/world/polish-strike-in-abeyance-as-pact-is-signed.html, accessed May 29, 2015; and Haig, *Caveat*, 243–244.
74. Vice President Bush's memorandum for the record is found at "Office of the Vice President," RawhideDown, March 30, 1981, http://rawhidedown.com/wordpress/wp-content/themes/RawhideDown/PDFs/TranscriptOfBushInterviewOnAirForce2.pdf.
75. Allen, "The Day Reagan Was Shot."
76. Altman, "Presidential Power: Reagan Doctor Says He Erred."
77. Reagan, *An American Life*, 269; and Wilber, 216.
78. Reagan, *An American Life*, 258.
79. Lou Cannon and Carl M. Cannon, *Reagan's Disciple: George Bush's Troubled Quest for a Presidential Legacy* (New York: Public Affairs, 2008), 48–49; Kiron K. Skinner, Annelise Anderson, and Martin Anderson, eds., *Reagan, A Life in Letters* (New York: Free Press, 2003), 26–128; and Bernard Weinraub, "Reagan Acknowledges Carter's Military Buildup," *New York Times*, April 6, 1986, http://www.nytimes.com/1986/04/06/us/reagan-acknowledges-carter-s-military-buildup.html, accessed June 2, 2015.
80. Peter Turbowitz, "'The Balancer': Ronald Reagan, Party Politics, and U.S. Grand Strategy," in Jeffrey L. Chidester and Paul Kengor, eds., *Reagan's Legacy in a World Transformed* (Cambridge, MA: Harvard University Press, 2015), 41–43.
81. Reagan, *An American Life* , 269–274; *The Reagan Diaries*, 13; and Skinner et al, *Reagan, A Life in Letters*, 737–739 and 878. According to Lou Cannon, "Reagan's letter [to Brezhnev] is of special interest because it is one of the few foreign policy documents composed by Reagan in the early years of his presidency without the assistance of speechwriters or formal position papers from his various departments." Cannon, *President Reagan*, 256–267.
82. The speech is found at "Address at Commencement Exercises at the University of Notre Dame," RRPL, May 17, 1981, http://www.reagan.utexas.edu/archives/speeches/1981/51781a.htm, accessed January 3, 2015.
83. "NSDD 32: U.S. National Security Strategy", *The Reagan Files*, May 20, 1982, http://www.thereaganfiles.com/nsdd-32-us-national-securit.html, accessed March 23, 2015.
84. "U.S. Relations with the USSR," RRPL, January 17, 1983, http://www.reagan.utexas.edu/archives/reference/Scanned%20NSDDS/NSDD75.pdf, accessed March 23, 2015.
85. For a review of Ronald Reagan's pre-presidential thinking on foreign and domestic policy, see Kiron K. Skinner, Annelise Anderson, and Martin Anderson, eds., *Reagan, In His Own Hand: The Writings of Ronald Reagan that Reveal His Revolutionary Vision for America* (New York: Simon and Schuster, 2001); and Paul

Lettow, “President Reagan’s Legacy and U.S. Nuclear Weapons Policy,” *Heritage Foundation*, July 20, 2006, http://www.heritage.org/research/lecture/president-reagans-legacy-and-us-nuclear-weapons-policy, accessed June 2, 2015.

86. Deaver, *A Different Drummer*, 154.
87. Martin Anderson, *Revolution* (New York: Harcourt Brace Jovanovich, 1988), 80–99; Reagan, *An American Life*, 547; Skinner et al, 429; “The Schedule of President Ronald Reagan,” RRPL, December 22, 1982, http://www.reaganfoundation.org/whdpdf/122282.pdf accessed March 23, 2015; and “The Daily Diary of President Ronald Reagan,” RRPL, February 11, 1983, http://www.reaganfoundation.org/whdpdf/021183.pdf, accessed March 23, 2015.
88. *The Reagan Diaries*, 130.
89. “Address to the Nation on Defense and National Security,” RRPL, March 23, 1983, http://www.reagan.utexas.edu/archives/speeches/1983/32383d.htm, accessed March 23, 2015.
90. “Strategic Defense Initiative,” January 6, 1984, http://fas.org/spp/starwars/offdocs/nsdd119.htm, accessed June 3, 2015.
91. “Address to the Nation on Defense and National Security.” RRPL.
92. Cannon, *President Reagan*, 288; and Skinner et al, 422–431.
93. Reagan, *An American Life*, 611 and 657.
94. Skinner et al, *Reagan, A*, 430.
95. George C. Herring, *From Colony to Superpower: U.S. Foreign Relations Since 1776* (New York: Oxford University Press, 2008), 897.

Bill and Hillary Clinton campaigned together in 1992, offering Americans two capable leaders for the price of one. Their careers forever intertwined with their personal lives, she more than once made his presidency possible. [Courtesy William J. Clinton Presidential Library.]

12

The Clintons

The Politics of the Personal

WILLIAM CHAFE

In all of American history, no presidential couple has exemplified the interplay of personality and politics more vividly than Bill and Hillary Clinton. There were other presidential marriages that came close. Edith Wilson exercised decisive power, particularly after Woodrow Wilson's stroke in 1918, for example. Nancy Reagan and Rosalind Carter were also movers and shakers behind the scene. Eleanor and Franklin Roosevelt perhaps came closest to being precursors for the Clintons. Eleanor persistently advocated liberal ideas with her husband, oftentimes prodding him to do more on issues of racial equality, housing, and the poor. But Eleanor and Franklin had long lived lives that were primarily separate from each other. No longer a "marital" couple, they functioned as distinctive political figures, independent from each other in the plans they initiated and the allies they recruited.

Bill and Hillary were different. In everything they did, they affected each other. Without Hillary, Bill could never have been elected president. Repeatedly, she "saved" his political life: in Arkansas after his defeat in the gubernatorial election of 1980; in 1992 when his presidential candidacy threatened to implode after Gennifer Flowers revealed her sexual affair with Clinton, and above all in 1998; when Hillary's decision to stand by her husband in the face of the Monica Lewinsky scandal proved indispensable to his remaining as president in the face of impeachment proceedings. In return, Hillary achieved more power, explicitly and implicitly, than any First Lady had ever exercised. The personal chemistry between the two partners both defined their successes and served as a primary source for their failures. No personal relationship was ever more decisive in the White House—or more powerful in shaping the politics of the country.

Simultaneously, that same relationship defined and animated the multiple crises of the Clinton Presidency.

* * *

Not surprisingly, the complicated personal dynamics that made the Clintons who they were could be traced back to the problematic childhoods that each experienced. On the surface, it seemed that Bill's journey toward adulthood was so chaotic that nothing in Hillary's life could possibly match it. Bill's mother, Virginia, came from a family wracked by conflict. Her father started off delivering ice to households in Hope, Arkansas. A handsome, convivial charmer, he often stayed behind to visit with female clients while his assistants went on to the next customer. Subsequently, he became the owner of a general store. His clientele was half black and half white. He treated everyone as equals, extending credit wherever it was needed. He also served bootleg liquor under the counter. Virginia's mother was a nurse who took pride in her profession; yet in her bearing she was as "starchy" as the uniform she wore so proudly. Harsh, didactic, and ambitious, she was often frustrated by her husband's casual, "laid back" behavior. Virginia, their only child, loved her father dearly, while feeling intimidated by her mother. But in one important way, she emulated her mother. Always trying to hide her true personality, she early on adopted her mother's habit of spending lengthy periods each morning applying makeup and eye shadow to her face. By the time that Virginia, too, became a nurse, she devoted ninety minutes each day to the ritual of making herself more attractive. Studiously covering up her real features, she dressed in flattering and "sexy" clothes, and also applied a white dye to her brunette hair, creating a riverlike passage down the middle of her head that dramatically called attention to her distinctiveness.[1]

When Virginia left home to go to nursing school she already had a boyfriend, but soon she met a handsome young man named Bill Blythe and fell in love. Bill said he was a salesman, charmed Virginia, and soon they were married. As World War II got underway, Bill joined the army and went to Italy. When he returned, the couple hoped to live in Chicago, but for the time being, Virginia moved back to her parents' home. She was pregnant. On a weekend trip to see her, Bill Blythe ran off the road into a ditch filled with water. Although he survived the crash, he fell into the water and drowned. A few weeks later, Billy was born. Virginia said she had lost her one true love. Only decades later did she learn that Bill Blythe had been married four times before, had sired numerous children, and in fact had not been a salesman when they met; instead, he was already in the army. It would not be the only bizarre marriage in her life.[2]

Initially, Virginia raised Billy in her parents' home. But her mother insisted on making all the decisions and exercising total control over both her grandchild and her daughter. In order to survive, Virginia left Bill with her parents and went off for more nurses' training in New Orleans. Before she left, she had met Roger Clinton, who was in the automobile business. Roger liked to dance and party as much as she did. They flirted a lot and drank to excess. Eventually, they got married. As with Bill Blythe, Virginia did not know that Roger had been married three times before, had numerous children and, in his last divorce, had been charged with spousal abuse. Soon they had their own child, Roger Jr. But they also engaged in daily spats. He accused her of having affairs, and she responded with similar allegations. They drank and fought all the time. Soon, Roger began to beat Virginia on a regular basis.[3]

Such was the household in which Bill Clinton grew up. Early on, he took responsibility for intervening when Roger started to pummel Virginia, warning Roger never ever to hit his mother again. Although Roger and Virginia divorced for a brief time, they soon came back together, and Bill assumed Roger's last name as his own. Bill soon took on a role that psychologists say occurs frequently in homes crippled by alcoholism and spouse abuse. He became the "rescuer," someone who sought to make things whole by bringing pride and success to the family through his own outstanding achievements. Bill was one of the most popular kids in the neighborhood. He excelled in school, in the band, and in groups like Boys Nation, a kind of American Legion for young people. Charming, outgoing, and brilliant, Bill soon demonstrated how much he could accomplish by being chosen as the Boys Nation candidate for US Senator from Arkansas. The one habit he had picked up from his beloved grandfather was a belief in racial equality. At Boys Nation he distinguished himself by winning a major debate on civil rights. His cohort journeyed to Washington for a national conference, where soon they found themselves in the White House Rose Garden listening to a speech by John F. Kennedy. Once it was over, Kennedy moved toward the crowd, and the tall, six-foot Clinton loped to the front of the line, being the first to have his picture taken with the president.[4]

Billy Clinton was on his way to a career of political and social stardom. Indeed, his success put him in a good position to be the "rescuer" of his broken family. To pursue this objective further, he intentionally chose not to go to the University of Arkansas—even though eventually he envisioned being governor there. Instead, Clinton enrolled at Georgetown University in Washington. Immediately he started to cultivate his classmates. Before long, he was elected president of his first-year class, a feat he repeated the next year. Going to work for Senator William Fulbright in his Washington office, Clinton started to develop a network of political connections that soon led him back to Arkansas as a right-hand aide to the state's Democratic gubernatorial candidate. Already in 1968 he had started to develop a network of political "friends" throughout the state. Soon, he joined the elite of the elite when he won the competition to be a Rhodes Scholar at Oxford. Surrounded by a cadre of stars destined to hold major posts in government and business, Clinton accrued plaudits and connections that amounted to exactly the right preparation for a successful political career. Although plagued by anxiety and doubt about whether to accept a draft notice to join the army during the Vietnam War, Clinton eventually found a way out. The path was now clear for the next step. Once more, Clinton acted boldly, applying to Yale Law School rather than to the University of Arkansas Law School.[5]

As he approached this next stage of his life, Clinton's only problem was his inability to commit to a sustained relationship. Following the values personified by his mother, he sought out "beauty queens" with whom he had short-lived affairs. He had told friends that he wanted to marry someone who would be his intellectual equal and a lifelong partner. But he had not been able to make that kind of commitment. When he arrived at Yale in the fall of 1970, Clinton did what many of his classmates were famous for. He skipped classes and became involved in politics, working for a young Democratic candidate for the US Senate. Only in November did he start attending school, borrowing notes from female classmates to "catch up." It was in that context—frustrated, yearning for a more meaningful relationship—that Clinton met Hillary Rodham, a second-year student, who was already embarked on a mission to change the world.[6]

Although Hillary would write in her autobiography that she had an idyllic childhood, the truth was far from that. Hillary's mother Dorothy was perhaps the most important person in her life. She had been born to a fifteen-year-old mother and a seventeen-year-old father. After living eight years on the West Coast, Dorothy's parents put her and her three-year-old brother on a crosscontinental train, alone, to her grandparents' home in Chicago. Once there, life did not improve. Dorothy was abused and exploited as a household worker until finally she moved to a distant relative's home, where she was treated in a more nurturing and kindly way. It was from that home base that she took a job as a secretary in a drapery factory where one person, Hugh Rodham, solicited orders for theater curtains, produced the drapes, and then installed them. Before long, the two developed a personal relationship. They got married and moved together to Park Ridge, a Chicago suburb, where Dorothy eventually gave birth to two boys and a girl.[7]

Hugh was different from most suburban dads. The son of immigrants from Europe, he was a star football player in high school and won an athletic scholarship to the University of Pennsylvania. Brusque and cold, he was neither gregarious nor affectionate. He took pride in being sole proprietor in his business. Each year he purchased a new Cadillac to demonstrate his status as an upper-middle-class suburbanite. But he neither socialized with neighbors, nor did he have the kind of "organization man" peer group of friends characteristic of most suburbanites.

He could also be cruel. When he and Dorothy got into dinnertime rows, he would berate her, asking "Who put that silly-ass idea in your stupid head?" When she left the table to end the argument, he told her: "Don't let the doorknob hit your ass on the way out." Although he encouraged Hillary to do her best in school, and had enormous confidence in her ability, he also treated her and her brothers abusively. If a child left the cap off a toothpaste tube in the bathroom, he would throw the cap out the window—even into the snow in wintertime—and demand that the child go out and find it. Each night, no matter how cold it was, he insisted on turning off the heat in the house.[8]

It was in that context that Dorothy Rodham taught her daughter the most important lesson her life had to teach. Despite the degree to which she was mistreated, Dorothy would not to leave her husband or break up the family. Nothing was more important, she insisted, than keeping the family together, no matter how egregious the behavior of her spouse. Another pivotal lesson Dorothy taught was the importance of religious faith. Dorothy was a devout Methodist, and she urged Hillary to attend church services and become active in the Methodist Youth Fellowship (MYF). Throughout America in the 1960s, MYF groups were instilling in young people a social conscience, calling their attention to social inequalities based on race, class, and gender. Don Jones, the assistant minister at the local Methodist church, took his youth group to Chicago to hear Martin Luther King Jr. preach about the importance of embracing the Social Gospel and working for racial equality. Jones also brought his students to a Chicago art museum with a group of poor Latinos, where the white suburbanites could see how ghetto dwellers viewed paintings like Picasso's *Guernica* with vastly different eyes than they did. While Hillary also attended after-school sessions with a deeply conservative social studies teacher, and followed her father's example in supporting Barry Goldwater's candidacy for the presidency in 1964, Don Jones and her mother provided the lasting influence on her life.[9]

While Hillary was neither glamorous nor a beauty queen, she was attractive, friendly, and a good companion. Still, her high school years did not feature passionate crushes. She thought more about the future and making a difference in society. With her mother's encouragement, she applied to Wellesley College, one of the "Seven Sisters" women's colleges that since the late nineteenth century had turned out generations of intellectually committed women. (Hugh Rodman was adamantly opposed to Hillary's going to Wellesley.) While Hillary experienced ups and downs in college, she quickly became a campus leader. She was elected president of the Young Republicans, and did volunteer work in the black neighborhoods of Roxbury. She also began a romance with a Harvard student who had a black roommate and spent many a weekend night debating issues of civil rights. While remaining a Republican—and even attending the 1968 Republican convention—Hillary also campaigned for anti–Vietnam War candidate Eugene McCarthy in the 1968 New Hampshire primary. By the time she was a senior she had become class president. Her style was to work with, not against, the school administration, seeking to keep doors open to those in authority as she campaigned for more black faculty and students at Wellesley.[10]

In short, Hillary was both a reformer and a coalition builder, seeking consensus for change rather than polarization. As the class president, she became the first student in campus history to be asked to speak at graduation. Although her prepared speech consisted of countercultural clichés about the need to find a new and better way of communicating about humanist issues in political discourse, she became an overnight sensation after Edward Brooke, the US Senator from Massachusetts, adopted a condescending tone toward student protestors. Hillary took him on directly, criticizing his denigration of her generation of activists. Shortly thereafter, her speech was featured in a *Life* magazine article. Now a prominent spokeswoman for women activists, she headed off to Yale Law School to pursue her determination to "make a difference."

* * *

When Bill Clinton finally started to attend classes at Yale in November of 1970, he found himself staring at a young woman named Hillary. She was already a leader in the student body, having played a major role in campus demonstrations around the trial of Black Panther leaders in New Haven. Consistent with her role at Wellesley, she tried hard to find common ground with students of all persuasions, as well as the deans at the law school. Hillary was the exact opposite of Bill's mother, Virginia, both in appearance and style. While Virginia boasted of spending ninety minutes every morning applying her makeup, Hillary almost never used lipstick or rouge. While Bill's mother was flirtatious, wore sexy clothes, and partied on a regular basis, Hillary dressed plainly, almost never wore nylon stockings, and was deeply serious.

But Clinton was attracted to her precisely because she personified the intellectually focused career person he had told his friends he wanted as his lifelong partner. Once acquainted, the two connected immediately. Although Hillary was already involved with a boyfriend in Vermont who shared her political sympathies, it did not take long before she decided that Bill was the person she wanted to be with. The two became a couple and moved in with each other. He accompanied her to California that summer where she was working for a left-leaning law firm.

The summer after that they went to Texas to work on George McGovern's presidential campaign. Hillary did voter registration work in San Antonio, while Bill coordinated the overall state campaign with Taylor Branch, who subsequently wrote a three-volume biography of Martin Luther King Jr.[11]

The Texas summer proved pivotal. Hillary and Bill saw each other often. They frequently argued. All along, she had been focused and hard reasoning, while he was more committed to building relationships, being emotional, and appealing to people's feelings. On a traditional scale of masculine-feminine, Hillary was the masculine, Bill the feminine. They almost split up in Texas. Meanwhile Hillary became close friends with Betsey Wright, her San Antonio roommate, who was also politically committed and tough minded. Wright told Hillary that she should be the first woman president of the United States. She believed that Hillary, already a star, had exactly the combination of feminist values and political smarts to go all the way to the White House. Hillary listened carefully and took Wright's injunction seriously. At the same time, she remained in love with Bill; after they sorted out their differences, she decided to stay in the relationship. She made this decision even after she had met Virginia, who reacted to Hillary as if she were toxic—not only no makeup, but barefoot, with little sense of fashion, no hairdo—*plain, plain, plain*. Yet as Bill made clear, if he had to make a choice, it would be for Hillary.[12]

While Bill completed his final year at law school, Hillary started to work for Marian Wright Edelman in what eventually became the Children's Defense Fund. She cared passionately about children's rights as well as women's rights. Then, at the end of the academic year, Bill moved to Arkansas to take a position at the University of Arkansas Law School.

Yet more than anything else, he remained committed to pursuing the political connections he had already started to develop across the state. After one year of teaching, he decided to make his first political move as a candidate for Congress. The Watergate scandal had eroded support for Arkansas Republicans, including John Paul Hammerschmidt, a long-serving congressman. Clinton decided to challenge him and quickly made substantial inroads. Hillary, meanwhile, went to work for John Doar in Washington as part of the Watergate investigative commission.

After Bill returned to Arkansas, he maintained his relationship with Hillary but resumed his old pattern of having serial affairs with the beauty queens his mother had encouraged him to cultivate. Hillary quickly realized what was happening and asked her father and brother to go to Arkansas, theoretically to work on Bill's campaign, but in reality, to keep tabs on Bill's sexual affairs and discourage him. Eventually, when the Watergate investigation concluded and Richard Nixon resigned, Hillary herself journeyed to Little Rock, where she soon took on a prime role in managing his campaign (to the dismay of Bill's political team). For a brief period, chaos reigned, with Bill's staff rushing his current girlfriend out the backdoor of the office as soon as Hillary was spotted coming in. But eventually, the "girlfriend" was hired as a "nanny" by the campaign manager and ceased appearing at headquarters. Still, Hillary now understood well Bill's predilection for such affairs, even as he continued to express his desire to make her his permanent partner. Although he had proposed marriage, she was sufficiently wary about both Bill and his mother's influence on him—that she held back, pondering whether a commitment to marriage made sense.[13]

Bill narrowly lost the congressional election. Some blamed Hillary for vetoing a last-minute proposal to funnel thousands of dollars into a vote-buying campaign in the largest city of the district. In the meantime, Hillary took a post teaching at the University of Arkansas Law School. A very different professor than Bill, she offered tightly organized, rigorously administered classes—as opposed to Bill's off the cuff, freewheeling discussions. Then one day in 1975, while driving to the airport, Hillary noticed a house for sale and commented on how attractive it was. While Hillary was away, Bill purchased the home. When Hillary returned, Bill told her he had bought the home so that they could get married. This time she said yes, though her ambivalence could be inferred from her decision not to buy her wedding dress until the day before the ceremony. Indeed, she spent almost no time planning the wedding, nor was there an immediate honeymoon.[14]

For a long time Hillary had debated whether it was better for her to try, on her own, to fulfill the dreams that Betsey Wright had encouraged her to pursue; or whether she had a better chance to achieve her goals while working in a political and personal partnership with Bill. It was a hard call. But in 1972—notwithstanding the many gains women had made in recent years—it was hard to imagine an independent woman running for the presidency. Both because she loved Bill, and because it seemed far more likely that they could achieve their joint goals by working together as partners, she opted for marriage.

In the meantime, Bill proceeded with his plans for a political career. He already had developed a substantial political reputation. He knew that the easiest race to win was for attorney general, and put together a progressive campaign for that office based on correcting abuses and promoting fairness for all Arkansas citizens. With little opposition, he soared to victory. As he prepared to move to Little Rock from Fayetteville, Hillary took a position with the most prominent law firm in Little Rock, where she was guaranteed an affluent and prestigious clientele, as well as congenial and stimulating partners.[15] Two of these, Webb Hubbell and Vince Foster, became her closest friends. Hillary was particularly close to Foster. On his birthday she threw a party for "Vincent Fosterini," and hired a belly dancer to perform. It was an exciting team, and a rewarding professional experience—soon made even more so when Bill moved up the ladder and in 1978 was elected, at age thirty-two, as the youngest Governor in Arkansas history.

* * *

Almost immediately, the new gubernatorial administration started to fall apart. Hillary had played a major role in the campaign, both from a managerial and advisory perspective. Two of her closest friends immediately became part of Bill's inner staff, joined by two of his closest associates. But the two groups disagreed about who was in charge and what Bill's legislative agenda should be, almost exactly the situation that occurred fourteen years later in the White House. With no head honcho, chaos reigned. Meanwhile, Bill loved to be out of the office, touring the state, inviting people to come see him at the governor's office. Except that when they appeared, he had no time in his schedule to see them. In the meantime, Clinton initiated a road construction project to modernize Arkansas' antiquated transport system. To fund it, he proposed a significant new vehicle tax on automobile owners. The problem was that he ended up apportioning the tax based on the weight of the owner's vehicle. This meant that the oldest and heaviest cars were taxed the most, while the lightest and newest cars were taxed the least. Working-class and middle-class drivers, who owned the heaviest cars, revolted. Their anger was further inflamed after President Jimmy Carter consigned thousands of Cuban refugees to camps in Arkansas. When the refugees rioted and widespread disorder ensued, Clinton got the blame. Two years after scaling the heights as the youngest governor in history, he crashed to a resounding defeat in the 1980 election.[16]

Never before had Clinton felt so dejected and disconsolate. "What did I do wrong?" he asked each person he saw on the street. Befuddled, depressed, and confused, he seemed to fit exactly one person's sarcastic description of a Rhodes Scholar: someone whose best years were behind him. Moving into a small law office where there were no exciting clients, Clinton pondered being at the end of his career.

But then Hillary came to his rescue. First, she invited Betsey Wright to Little Rock to become Bill's chief advisor and the person who would run his office and help reinvigorate his political career. Second, she brought back to Arkansas the best political organizer around, Dick Morris. Once the head of a group of New York college activists dubbed the "Junior Mafia" by local politicians, Morris had become a consummate political tactician. He and his associates held endless focus sessions, crafted nuanced questions designed to tease out voter preferences, and he ended up designing strategies for appeals to voters that would hit on key words and values that were most likely to elicit a positive response. Morris had helped Clinton with strategy in 1978. Now, Hillary made sure he returned to work his magic on Clinton's now-energized bid for reelection. Finally, Hillary herself became the overall person in charge, making the final decisions. Now, Clinton, preaching a message that embodied both reform and centrist proposals, once more resonated with the broad middle of the electorate. In 1982, two years after suffering an ignominious defeat, Clinton rose again to the top ofthe heap—largely because of Hillary.[17]

In what became a lifelong pattern, the help that Hillary gave to her husband quickly led to an ever greater political role for her. Soon she became the chief of a task force devoted to proposing education reform, the new number-one priority of the Clinton administration. Education was what he cared about most, Clinton declared, and in order to make sure the needed reforms occurred, he was placing the person closest to him in charge of the reform effort. In a procedure that she would later duplicate, Hillary hired experts for her task force and toured the state holding hearings with education officials. In the end, she generated a series of proposals that won plaudits from state legislators, some of whom wondered why she rather than her husband was not the governor. It was a tour de force. A center of power in the new administration, she won widespread support for her initiative, her executive ability, and her capacity to organize and innovate. So popular were the results that Bill was reelected in 1984 and 1986 with growing majorities.[18]

As governor, Clinton also became known for the "new" Democratic politics he represented. Clearly a centrist, he helped start, then popularize, the New Democratic Coalition (NDC), a group of prominent officials who insisted that the party should cleave to the middle of the road, become a model of efficiency and reform, and win back the Reagan Democrats who had abandoned the party to follow the patriotic rhetoric of the former movie star. Personifying the middle-of-the-road politics that seemed most likely to win back voters, Clinton became the "star" of the NDC. By the mid-1980s, Clinton was nationally known, a governor who spoke across the country at party meetings, seen by many as an ideal candidate to take the national stage.[19]

By the end of 1987 Clinton had become seriously committed to the prospect. After the Mondale defeat in 1984, a fresh face was needed. Mario Cuomo, New York's governor, clearly had the inside track. But it was by no means clear that he would run. Others had raised the flag and then dropped out. As he toured the country and consulted his old Rhodes Scholar friends, Clinton announced that he would hold a press conference on his plans for national office. His best friends flocked to town in anticipation.

But two days before the press conference, Betsey Wright asked to see the governor. What was he going to do, she asked, when confronted by allegations of womanizing? Wright already had the names of thirty women with whom Clinton had engaged in one-night stands while he was governor. She knew who they were from state police; repeatedly, she had tried to call him where he was staying overnight without ever getting through. Clinton listened carefully, acknowledged the problem, and then added the names of additional women he had affairs with.

Colorado Senator Gary Hart had already been forced out of the current presidential race because of his dalliance with a model. Clinton was now forced to consider seriously Wright's concern. In his autobiography, Clinton focuses on the question his daughter Chelsea asked him the next night. "Where are we going for vacation next summer," the eight-year-old queried. "Well, honey," Clinton responded, "I may be running for president and not able to go on vacation."

"Oh, okay," Chelsea replied, "then just mommy and I will go." Clinton said that the question, and Chelsea's response, made him realize that he might lose his only chance for a genuine father-daughter relationship. But in the end, it seems more likely that Betsey Wright's intervention provided the critical catalyst. In any event, the next day Clinton declared he would not be a candidate for the presidency. Instead, he would devote more time to his family.[20]

Rather than clarify his life situation, however, the decision not to run for president triggered in Clinton a new era of depression and confusion. For the first time in his marriage, he initiated a deep, long-lasting love affair. Clinton seemed lost, not knowing where to go or what to do. The woman he fell in love with was a person his own age, accomplished, intellectually independent, with a career—in short, another potential partner. She had been married, had a family, and then went to graduate school and became a business professional. Unlike all of Clinton's other relationships, this was not a one-night stand with a beauty queen. So smitten was Clinton that he asked Hillary for a divorce.

But she said no. Following the deeply imbedded voice of her mother Dorothy, Hillary insisted that she and Bill stay together as a family, seek therapy and find a way to put their marital lives back together. He agreed. The process took two years. Some insist that Clinton continued the affair, even as he was elected president. But for the moment, dissolution of the family was put aside. Both Clintons spent more time in church, they entered intensive counseling and by 1991 had reached enough of an agreement on their future that they could start talking about a renewed presidential candidacy in 1992.[21]

Significantly, Hillary was now well prepared to deal with the allegations of womanizing that she knew would come up in the 1992 campaign. It had become a custom for Godfrey Cheshire, national correspondent for the *Christian Science Monitor*, to host regular breakfasts in Washington with major political figures and other correspondents. Bill and Hillary volunteered to attend such a breakfast in the summer of 1991. When the reporters did not raise the issue of womanizing, Hillary herself initiated a conversation about the subject.

Yes, she and Bill said, they had experienced conflicts in their marriage, as most Americans did. "But we love each other." The two proclaimed their intention to be together the rest of their lives and declared their marital relationship sound and healthy. From there the campaign took off. Clinton did splendidly in his early campaigning. He thrived in the Iowa caucuses and then moved on to New Hampshire where he surged forward, holding a strong second-place position, and gaining on frontrunner Paul Tsongas, Senator from the neighboring state of Massachusetts.[22]

Then came the bombshell. Gennifer Flowers went public in the tabloid press with claims of having had a lengthy affair with Clinton, documented by tape recordings of Clinton's phone calls and arrangements for their meetings together. Soon the mainstream press joined in. Clinton plummeted in the New Hampshire polls. His candidacy was imploding. At this point Hillary intervened once again. "We need to confront the issue head" on, she told Bill, just as they had at the Godfrey Cheshire breakfast. They arranged an appearance on *60 Minutes.* The timing could not have been better. The show aired immediately after the Super Bowl game, with the largest TV audience in America. Once on the air, Hillary did an almost exact repeat of the conversation with Cheshire. "Yes," she said, "we have had marital problems, like most of our audience tonight." "But we love each other," she went on, and intend to be together for a very long time. The Clintons' appearance was a stunning success. It not only halted the rapid deterioration in Clinton's political position but also galvanized heartfelt grassroots sympathy for the pain and anguish the Clintons were experiencing. Hillary had stood by her man, testified to the couple's love, and evinced an empathetic response from millions of viewers who, indeed, had suffered similar pain in their marital relationships. Within days, Clinton's poll numbers in New Hampshire started to rise. By primary day he had once again become a close second to Tsongas. From there, he went on to victory after victory. Hillary had saved his political life and made it possible for him to become president, just as in 1980, she had saved his political life and made it possible for him to be reelected governor.

As a result, in 1992, just as in 1980, Hillary moved to a new position of power and influence. In the spring of 1992 Bill started talking about a "co-presidency." The country, he said, would be "getting two executives for the price of one." Hillary had saved her husband from almost guaranteed defeat. In return, she ensured that her own power in the White House would reach heights never before approached by a First Lady.[23]

* * *

Significantly, Hillary wished to take no chances. She moved aggressively to ensure that no one would question the position of power she had earned. First, she argued adamantly against her husband appointing a strong chief of staff, lest that person begin to give orders that she too would have to obey—a situation starkly reminiscent of Little Rock. Rejecting suggestions of a powerful personality at the helm, like James Baker (Ronald Reagan) or Sherman Adams (Dwight Eisenhower), she instead supported the appointment of Mack McLarty, Clinton's kindergarten classmate from Hope, Arkansas, (dubbed "Mack the Nice" by his peers), as chief of staff.[24]

Second, Hillary insisted that she have her own staff as fully involved in White House affairs as that of the president and vice president. For the first time in history, the First Lady would occupy office space in the West Wing of the White House, side by side with the president and vice president. All three would have to sign off on any actions taken by the executive branch, another first.

Finally, she repeated the role she played after helping Bill win back the governorship. At that time she took charge of the number-one item on Clinton's statewide agenda: education. Now, Hillary would be in charge of the president's most important domestic objective: health-care reform. Although Vice President Al Gore considered requesting responsibility for Clinton's health-care initiative, Hillary dismissed that idea. She would take charge, appoint a staff, hire outside experts, and hold hearings around the country about the new health-care bill—the same scenario she had used with education reform in Arkansas. Bill announced that on an issue of reform this central to his administration's vision for change, he wished to ensure that the person closest to him would be in charge.[25]

Hillary soon demonstrated just how much her power would affect the West Wing of the White House. On day one, she ordered that the inner offices of the White House be sealed off from the press corps. This was unheard of. For decades, reporters had been able to go to the White House Press Secretary's office and ask questions of staff members as they passed through the halls. No more, Hillary said. The door would be closed, and the press secretary would meet with reporters only in the official White House press room. The shock was palpable. Enraged, reporters declared they had never seen anything like this. Indeed, so furious was their response that within a week the order was withdrawn. But the damage had been done.[26]

Next, Hillary gave orders to fire the travel staff who helped reporters make arrangements when the president left Washington—securing visas to enter foreign countries and helping to arrange flights, hotel accommodations, and meals. The travel office was indispensable. But some people accused it of fudging funds and being inefficient and uneconomical. So Hillary fired the staff, proposing to replace them with a firm headed by a distant cousin of Bill's. Again, the fury was instant. It reached such a pitch that Hillary ordered her old friend and law partner, Vince Foster, now deputy counsel at the White House (and Bill's friend since childhood in Hope), to expunge from the record any hint of Hillary's involvement in the travel office scandal. He did so, at great personal cost and anguish.[27]

Why had Hillary placed the administration in peril this way? Fundamentally, it was because she detested the Washington press corps and hated the Washington "establishment" with its air of being in control of all social life and defining, a priori, what was "acceptable" and "not acceptable." From the beginning, Hillary believed that the *Washington Post* judged her and her husband unfairly, dismissing them as "hicks." At a dinner party in December, Kathleen Graham, the *Post*'s publisher, had signaled her suspicion of Hillary's ambitions, suggesting she adapt herself to the traditional role of a First Lady rather than try and carve out a more assertive presence. Through all the tumult and turmoil with her husband and all the stories of his affairs, Hillary had become increasingly angry, not at the "message" the press was printing, but at the "messengers." Others urged her to reach out to the "establishment," to invite them to White

House social occasions, to build bridges, and to seek reconciliation. But with disdain, she refused. Why should she show anything but contempt for "the enemy"?[28]

In all of this, Hillary had come to display an adversarial tough-mindedness significantly different from the commitment to consensus building and reconciliation that she had practiced at Wellesley and at Yale. At some point in the 1980s, defending Bill and their joint dream of making America a better place had translated into "getting" their enemies. While Bill still thought he could reach out and win over the opposition, Hillary developed a fortress mentality that caused her to dig up dirt on her foes, resist compromise, and remain in battle mode. Her way was the right way. It was the only means of holding on to what she had won and being able to move toward to the goals she and Bill shared for the country. The "new" Hillary was neither soft nor accommodating. She had earned the turf she had won by saving Bill's political career. No one was going to take that turf away. She was in charge, and strong self-assertion rather than responsive listening had now become her modus operandi.

The same approach carried over to her work with health care. As she began her leadership on the health-care task force, Hillary did not consult the heads of the congressional committees who would eventually have to pass health-care legislation. Nor did she talk to Cabinet and sub-Cabinet members who had the most experience dealing with health care on a federal level. Many of these individuals had important suggestions to make, but when they offered their advice, she dismissed them—often condescendingly. She hired Ira Magaziner, one of Bill's old Rhodes Scholar classmates, and a brilliant intellectual, to run the health-care operation. But Magaziner was also tone deaf when it came to hearing political perspectives different from his own. Thus, instead of widespread interaction with people in Washington who were "in the know" about health care, Hillary and her task force set off on a round of sessions with "experts" who filled their files with suggestions but demonstrated little awareness of, or attention to, the realities of Capitol Hill.[29]

During all this time, another potential disaster loomed in the background. "Whitewater" was the name of a real estate development in Arkansas.

During Bill's governorship, a political associate, Jim McDougall, had approached Bill and Hillary about investing in the project, offering attractive vacation real estate to prospective clients. Bill was uninterested, but Hillary liked the idea, seeing it as an effective way of increasing the family's wealth. The Clintons signed on. Eventually, the project went bust, and scandals arose about how it was managed, leading to state criminal investigations.

From all the evidence, there was no link between the Clintons and any criminal activity in Whitewater. But the so-called Whitewater papers involved not just the real estate project; they contained other documents from Hillary Clinton's papers dealing with her business activities during those years when her husband was governor. These included exchanges she had with state agencies where she was acting on behalf of clients, a possible violation of the code of ethics barring such conversations, given her husband's position as governor. In addition, some thought that the papers might include evidence that Hillary had overbilled clients. Hence, the "Whitewater" papers not only dealt with a real estate scandal but perhaps also contained evidence that would reflect negatively on Hillary's "ethics" as a lawyer and her character as a public figure.[30]

This conundrum set the stage for perhaps the most important dilemma that confronted the Clintons during the first nine months of their presidency. Whitewater had continued to blare in the headlines. Bill was also concerned that his administration was too much at polar opposites with the Washington establishment. To rescue the situation, in June of 1993 Bill recruited David Gergen to join his team. A former aide who played a pivotal role in the administration of three Republican presidents—Nixon, Ford, and Reagan—Gergen, it was hoped, could use his connections with Washington power brokers to defuse the acrimony that had emerged between the administration and the press corps. Well regarded as a public commentator and columnist with *US News and World Report*, Gergen was ideally suited to build bridges to the press. After being on the job for a while, he approached the editorial board of the *Washington Post* with a proposal: if the Clintons turned over all the Whitewater papers in their possession, the *Post* would promise to review them carefully and fairly.

If they found no evidence of criminality in the papers, they would say so, loud and clear, and the putative Whitewater scandal would be over. The *Post* accepted the proposal. Clinton's key aides also thought it made sense. The president himself agreed. There was only one problem. Gergen would have to secure Hillary's agreement. Setting out to do so, he made one appointment, which at the last minute was cancelled, then another, also cancelled. A few days later, he received a copy of a letter in which Hillary refused categorically to share the Whitewater documents.[31]

The uproar was immediate. Scores of stories on Whitewater appeared. More and more politicians, some Democrats as well as Republicans, demanded that Clinton appoint a special prosecutor to look into Whitewater. In the end, he caved in to unbearable political pressure. Soon Kenneth Starr was appointed to the post, and he was intent on skewering the Clintons. In the beginning, he focused primarily on Hillary Clinton and her role, then later—after the Monica Lewinsky scandal became public—he turned on Bill for the crime of committing perjury about his affair with Lewinsky, an act that had nothing to do with Whitewater. Clinton, of course, had created the crisis over his affair with Lewinsky, and it would have exploded no matter what the circumstances. But with a special prosecutor in place (because of Hillary' failure to turn over the Whitewater papers) there was now a federal prosecutor ready to use Clinton's action as a basis for impeachment. Hillary's decision not to cooperate with the *Washington Post*, White House aide George Stephanopoulos later said, was the one moment in the Clinton administration that he would want to have back, because the appointment of Kenneth Starr led inexorably to the debacle of impeachment.[32]

* * *

Clearly, the intersection of personality and politics that arose from the Bill and Hillary relationship helped to define the Clinton presidency. Nothing highlighted this fact more than the total failure of the Clinton health-care initiative. During nine months of hearings and deliberations, the task force consulted five hundred experts and had thirty-four different working groups, with every hearing conducted in secret. Yet there was still no bill to bring to Congress. Clinton had experienced a series of ups and downs as 1993 unfolded. In what eventually became his most dramatic achievement, he succeeded in getting congressional support, by one vote, on a deficit reduction package that eventually led to two years of surplus budgets at the end of the administration and the beginning of bringing down the national debt. He also scored significant successes in getting ratification of the North American Free Trade Agreement (an end to tariffs with Mexico and Canada), the creation of Americorps (a kind of domestic Peace Corps), and passage of the Brady Bill, a gun control measure prompted by the assassination attempt against President Reagan.[33]

But health care was still the "big" dream, the transforming vision. On that, Bill made a promising start with a speech to Congress in September 1993. Demonstrating total mastery of his subject matter (after a near disaster when speechwriters loaded the wrong speech into the teleprompter), the president was persuasive. Support for health care climbed overnight. But with still no legislation before Congress, that support faded. Criticism mounted, especially about the lack of consultation with Congress and Hillary's insistence on secret hearings. When, finally, the 1,342-page bill was sent to Congress in December, it bewildered most of those who read it. The measure called for increased federal regulation of insurance companies, then a "market" system by which those companies would compete in selling their policies to businesses, with the government subsidizing those who lacked the wherewithal to pay. Such a plan, thus rooted in private companies, could never be denounced as "socialized medicine." Still, in its complexity and detail—and above all, due to the secret process by which it had been developed—the plan drew heavy fire, especially when Hillary seemed insistent on getting the whole package passed exactly as she had written it.[34]

The prospects for health care went downhill as Hillary came under increasing fire for her involvement in Whitewater, and the demands for a special prosecutor increased. When the First Lady went on a nationwide tour to mobilize support for health care, angry crowds greeted her. Things were imploding. In December, a national story about Clinton's multiple love affairs while governor hit the media, including allegations that the state police helped procure women for Clinton and that one of the women he propositioned was a state clerical worker named Paula Jones. The year ended with the Clintons in disastrous shape.[35]

At that point, it might still have been possible to resurrect some health-care advances. Key Republicans, including people like Senator John Chaffee of Rhode Island, were willing to compromise. But at just the time when a "deal" might have been struck on a plan that would have covered 95 percent of the American people, Hillary dug in her heels further. No compromise, she pronounced. Indeed, she insisted that her husband put into his State of the Union message in January 1994 the explicit statement that he would veto any health-care bill that fell one iota short of what Hillary demanded. That decision destroyed any chance that any health-care legislation would be enacted. Hillary's bill never even came up for a vote.[36]

In the meantime, Republican congressional leader Newt Gingrich was campaigning for a Republican revolution that would cut Medicare, reduce federal welfare programs, and create a "Contract with America" that would accelerate the dramatic shift toward conservatism that Ronald Reagan had begun. When pollster Stan Greenberg showed Clinton public opinion surveys indicating how much the American people had turned against him, he could not believe his eyes. But the polls were right. And, on Election Day 1994, the Democrats suffered a worse political beating than at any time since Harry Truman was buried under GOP votes in the Congressional elections of 1946. Both houses of Congress were now controlled by Republicans, and the candidate from Hope, who had campaigned on the theme of Fleetwood Mac's "Don't Stop," ("Don't stop/ thinkin' about tomorrow," went the chorus) could now look back only wistfully at what seemed quite possible two short years earlier.[37]

Bill went into a funk resoundingly similar to the one he had experienced in 1980 after losing his first bid for reelection as Governor of Arkansas. The press saw him as almost irrelevant, so beaten and downtrodden that rebounding in 1996 seemed impossible. Hillary was almost as despondent. With health care over, she retreated to an unfamiliar role—the more domestic image of housewife and mother. No longer the fiery leader possessed by a desire for equal standing with the president and vice president, she took a back seat and focused on issues of children's rights. She began to write a book, *It Takes A Village*, to reflect on how an entire community had to come together to support the raising of healthy, intellectually vibrant families.[38]

Yet on another level, she was the first to reflect on the defeat and fight back. While Bill sulked, she was determined to set things right. Her first, and arguably most important, step was to reach out to Dick Morris, her old ally after the Arkansas defeat. Although now working almost exclusively for Republicans, including Republican Senate leader, Mississippi's Trent Lott, Morris agreed to come on board. He would work in secret, never appear during daytime in the White House, and would be known as "Charlie." But at night he would meet with Hillary and Bill. There he began to craft a comeback message. Suddenly there started to appear in Clinton speeches whole new pages and paragraphs. Where did they come from, his staff wondered? "Charlie wrote them," the staff was told. These were passages that focused on narrow issues, some cosmetic in nature—issues like special tax breaks for parents with children in college, more police on the streets. None was particularly controversial, but all had a "niche" audience of voters who might be persuaded to take a second look at Bill Clinton because he was speaking out on behalf of their interests. All were like the centrist reforms he proposed, at Morris's bidding, back in Arkansas. They aimed at redefining Bill Clinton's image, even as Hillary was redefining her own image as a more "traditional" woman.[39]

Then came Oklahoma City. On April 19, 1995, a terrorist bomb blew up the federal office building there, destroying a daycare center where scores of children of federal employees were killed and injured, as well as large numbers of government workers. Bill Clinton was brilliant. Flying to Oklahoma City immediately, he insisted on not blaming foreign terrorists, like Islamic militants, until police found evidence leading to the killers. He also reached out with a healing hand to the injured and their families. Always a person with a bent for religious expression and healing, the president now reached new heights of effectiveness in injecting love, leadership, and spiritual inspiration to the victims' families. Of course, it turned out that the terrorists were not foreigners but American right-wingers incensed at the role of the federal government in killing a group of extremist Branch Davidians in Waco, Texas, two years earlier. But the important point was that, overnight, Bill Clinton had become a new, lovable leader, a person who cared, who inspired, and who healed. This was, once again, a person who could be believed in.[40]

Meanwhile the Republicans overplayed their hand. Not ready to let Clinton simply be a comforting leader, they set out to drive him and his party out of the White House. Led by Speaker Newt Gingrich, the Republican House of Representatives raised the ante. They not only introduced legislation that sought to dismantle more and more of the Great Society advances of the 1960s; they also insisted on passing a budget that allowed no compromise on legislation that would help children, reach out to the elderly, and improve the environment. Gingrich was even reckless enough to propose tax cuts of $773 million for the wealthy: exactly the same sum by which he proposed cutting Medicare. These extreme actions made Clinton's response credible—that his Republican foes wanted to take money away from senior citizens who were sick and give it to rich people who did not need it.

All of this came to a head when Gingrich twice insisted on shutting down the federal government for days at a time rather than reach a compromise on the budget. Although he was taking a gamble, Clinton made the best political bet of his life when he called Gingrich's bluff. Americans did not like the idea of a political faction shutting down their government, especially at a time when the president was recovering his poise, healing the nation after it was wounded by terrorists, and passing "niche" reforms that appealed to middle-class families.[41]

By the time the 1996 presidential campaign came around, Clinton was back in the driver's seat. He was the centrist, Gingrich the extremist. Hillary had regained popularity by traveling the world, sometimes with Chelsea, as an exemplary defender of children's rights. She also went to China where she returned to taking up the cudgels for women's rights, linking the issue of justice for women and children. "Charlie's" true identity had now been revealed and now, in an open role, he worked alongside Clinton's other staff to shape a presidential election bid that increasingly looked like a no-brainer. Bob Dole, the prospective Republican nominee, was a respected moderate conservative. But he was uncharismatic and somewhat passive, and he could not hold a candle to the ebullient, ever more confident candidate of the Democratic center. Glowing with confidence, Bill Clinton and Hillary, together, laid plans to commence their second term in the White House, this time perhaps better prepared to make a real difference.

* * *

But whenever Bill Clinton was at the height of his powers, it was time to watch out. There was something in him, something self-destructive, that almost guaranteed that, as he reached a peak, he was preparing to plummet downward to disaster. Whether Clinton had initiated sexual contacts in the White House remains a question. Some women claimed that he grasped their breasts and tried to embrace them. But the White House was a hard place to get away with anything. Not only were Secret Service officers everywhere but so were staff. Almost no private space existed, even a small study. But during the government shutdown, people were scurrying everywhere, and some who had never gotten access to the Oval Office now had the chance to see what it was like.

One of these was Monica Lewinsky. A college graduate from a well-off California family, she had secured a job as a White House intern in 1995. On two or three occasions, she had caught the president's eye as he walked past and exchanged sexually charged, soulful looks with him. There was definitely something in the air. One night during the shutdown, she came into Clinton's office. She quickly gestured sexually to him, bending over to expose her black-thonged underwear to him. Later she returned to deliver a pizza. Soon they were embracing and she was performing oral sex on the president of the United States. He became captive to the relationship. Soon he was seeing Lewinsky regularly. Some on his staff were aware of the intensity of the relationship; they knew of the phone calls that ensued, even if they were not privy to the phone sex that accompanied those calls. Although at different times Clinton tried to cut off the affair, it lasted for more than sixteen months. He never had intercourse with Lewinsky, but in one encounter he did stain her blue dress.[42]

Lewinsky was passionately in love with Clinton. She also believed that he might leave Hillary after his term as president ended. When staff members became suspicious of the frequency of Lewinsky's visits to the Oval Office, they arranged for her transfer to the Pentagon. There, she met another woman who had once been a secretary in the White House Counsel's office, and who befriended Lewinsky immediately. The woman was Linda Tripp, an ardent conservative, though she did not disclose her politics. Before long Lewinsky was talking to Tripp about her affair with the president, how much she loved him, what they did together, and how much she hoped they might be together in the future. Lewinsky told her about the blue dress and her plans to have it cleaned. "No, don't do that," Tripp said. Lewinsky might want to hold on to that as evidence of her love relationship with Clinton.[43]

Tripp secretly recorded each of those conversations on a tape machine hidden in her purse. She soon possessed a collection of incriminating evidence sufficient to create a national scandal. She was also in close touch with a right-wing literary agent in New York, with whom she shared her information on Lewinsky. That agent, in turn, contacted Kenneth Starr. Not with standing his most ardent efforts, Starr had not been able to get enough evidence on Hillary Clinton to indict her on Whitewater. But now he had something even better: dramatic, firsthand evidence that Clinton was having an affair with an intern barely older than his daughter Chelsea. If only he could find a way to trap Clinton into committing an impeachable offense. It need not have anything to do with Whitewater.

Suddenly, that became possible. Paula Jones, the state clerical worker in Arkansas who had been quoted in the December 1993 story on Clinton's sexual escapades while governor, was now suing for damages. Clinton was called as a witness in January 1998. He had to testify. But as it turned out, few of the questions were about Clinton's relationship with Paula Jones. Instead, her lawyers asked him whether he ever had sex with a woman named Monica Lewinsky. "No," Clinton said, he had not. Later, he would claim that he was not lying. In his view, sex meant intercourse, and he had not had intercourse with Lewinsky. But that reasoning seemed both antiquated and a devious rationale for avoiding the truth. Then there was a blue dress. Clinton's semen was on it. And once a DNA test were administered, the truth would come out.[44]

Clinton had denied the truth, in effect committing perjury. Initially he was confused, terrified, and muddled. On the evening the charges were first made public that he and Lewinsky had a sexual relationship, he went on the *News Hour* with Jim Lehrer on PBS. He seemed flustered, unsure of himself, blurting out "there is no sexual relationship with Ms. Lewinsky," not that "there has never been a sexual relationship." His friends gathered at his side, panicked at the trouble he seemed to be in. Clinton himself asked Dick Morris to do an overnight poll to find out whether the American people could tolerate the truth and not punish him. "No," they would not accept a Clinton confession, Morris reported. Clinton pondered the possibility—perhaps the probability—that within a week, Democratic leaders might come and tell him he must resign, just as Republican leaders had done with Nixon in 1974. What could he do? Where should he go?

It was at that point that Hillary once more intervened. Bill had told her that nothing had happened with Lewinsky, that Lewinsky was a person in trouble who had come to ask his help and he had tried to counsel her. For whatever reason, Hillary believed him. The next day, she went to New York City to appear on the *Today Show* on NBC. As soon as she appeared, the host Matt Lauer asked her about the Lewinsky allegations. Immediately, she claimed they were lies, and did so vociferously. This was all a "vast right-wing conspiracy" to destroy her husband, Hillary declared. He was guilty of nothing. As she had done on *60 Minutes* six years earlier, Hillary stood strongly by her husband. According to Hillary, he was innocent.[45]

If nothing else, her performance gave Bill Clinton no choice but to match her in the fervor and strength of his denial of an affair. Hillary had provided the stiffening spine that Clinton himself showed no evidence of in his previous commentary. Now he, too, went on the offensive, matching the absoluteness of Hillary's declaration of his innocence. He was now taking Dick Morris's advice. Whatever else might happen, Hillary had helped him to buy time, hoping against hope that the American people would believe him, at least until such a time as they could absorb and forgive his sins. Hillary had once again made it possible for him to survive.

There was one additional occasion. Eventually, Lewinsky turned over the blue dress to the special prosecutor. Linda Tripp trapped her for an intimate conversation, this time at a restaurant outside the Pentagon with her tape recorder in hand. But this time, Kenneth Starr's deputies were there as well. They seized Lewinsky and rushed her to the special prosecutor's office. Soon thereafter, Starr subpoenaed the president to appear before a federal grand jury. Before that appearance, Clinton finally told Hillary that, in fact, he had engaged in an affair with Lewinsky. Shattered, Hillary could not believe her ears. She would not speak to her husband for days. She insisted that he be the one to tell Chelsea, in person, the truth. The next day, after testifying before the grand jury and acknowledging an "inappropriate relationship" with Lewinsky, the presidential family left for a week for Martha's Vineyard. The photo of Chelsea walking between her mother Hillary and her father Bill—holding each of their hands—toward the waiting White House helicopter has now become iconic. Nothing could more powerfully demonstrate the strain that had come over the First Couple.[46]

The grand jury revelation led immediately to charges of perjury. These charges, in turn, caused Republicans in the House of Representatives to hold hearings on impeachment. Again, the Republicans overreached, exhibiting extremism in their determination to humiliate the president. Democrats, meanwhile, were back on their heels, pondering how long to hang in there before making that trip to the White House to tell Clinton he must go.

Then, one final time, Hillary saved Clinton's presidency. Acknowledging just how much she had been wounded and betrayed, she told her husband that she still loved him, that she would stand by him, and that she hoped the American people would give him one last chance. It was a critical moment and, because Hillary acted as she did, Democrats chose not to bring Clinton down. Instead, they rallied to vote against impeachment. Then, when the House proceeded to indict anyway, Senate Democrats united to prevent the two-thirds vote necessary to remove the president from office. The Republicans had only themselves to blame. They had gone too far.

In the time Hillary had bought for Bill in her January defense of him, public opinion had moved to his side. Yet again people had learned to live with the idea that their president was a flawed human being. One last time Bill Clinton had only his wife to thank for rescuing him from a fate he had done all too much to deserve.[47]

* * *

There is no way to explain the multiple crises of the Clinton presidency, or the successes and failures of the administration, except by probing the interpersonal chemistry that shaped both the marriage and the political careers of the Clintons. Bill Clinton could never have been reelected governor or chosen as president had not Hillary Clinton saved his career, repeatedly. And she could never have exercised the power she did without rescuing her husband, which gained her a degree of control and influence never before exercised by a First Lady. Each had helped make the other's political career possible. In the end, Hillary had been right in 1975 when she decided to marry Bill. Together, they might do things that neither alone could ever have envisioned achieving. At the same time, the nature of their relationship helped explain their worst moments.

Postcript: Even as she decided to save her husband one last time, Hillary Clinton was simultaneously talking with Democratic Party leaders from New York State about becoming a candidate for the US Senate to replace the retiring Daniel Patrick Moynihan. On the day the Senate voted to acquit her husband of the charge levied during his impeachment, she was making plans to announce her candidacy. Through her final act of rescue, she had now liberated herself to pursue the independent career as a politician that Betsey Wright had envisioned for her back in San Antonio, Texas, during the McGovern campaign in 1972.

NOTES

1. All of what follows is based on William H. Chafe, *Bill and Hillary: The Politics of the Personal* (New York: Farrar, Strauss and Giroux, 2013). On Virginia Clinton's childhood, See Virginia Kelley, with James Morgan, *Leading with My Heart: My Life* (New York: Simon and Schuster, 1994), 14, 19–30, 40, 42, 51; David Maraniss, *First In His Class: A Biography of Bill Clinton* (New York: Simon and Schuster, 1995),

20–22; Margaret Polk interview with Michael Takiff, *A Complicated Man: The Life of Bill Clinton by Those Who Knew Him* (New Haven: Yale University Press, 2010), 12.

2. Kelley, 42–43,54, 64; Maraniss, 21, 24–28; Gail Sheehy, *Hillary's Choice* (New York: Random House, 1999), 94–95.
3. Kelley, 69–71, 80–86, 90–94, 107–09, 146–49; Maraniss, 31–35; Sheehy, 98, Bill Clinton, *My Life* (New York: Alfred Knopf, 2004), 19, 52.
4. Maraniss, 11, 14–16, 20, 33–38, 42; B. Clinton, 45–46, 51, 58, 60–62; Kelley, 45.
5. Maraniss, 75, 83–85, 140, 148, 166, 174, 190–93, 198–200; B. Clinton, 84–85, 90–93, 104, 118, 135, 144–45, 149, 151–56, 173.
6. Maraniss, 225–35; B. Clinton, 175–77, 181; Sheehy, 76–78.
7. For Hillary Clinton's idyllic view of her childhood, see Hillary Rodham Clinton, *It Takes A Village* (New York: Simon and Schuster, 1995), and Hillary Rodham Clinton, *Living History* (New York: Simon and Schuster, 2003). See also Maraniss, 249–51; Carl Bernstein, *A Woman in Charge: The Life of Hillary Rodham Clinton* (New York: Vintage Books, 2008), 11–12, 13–16, 21–22, 26–27, 29–30; and Sheehy, 16, 20.
8. Bernstein, 15–26; Sheehy, 16, 23.
9. Sheehy, 33–37; Bernstein, 34–37, 250–59.
10. Bernstein, 43–60; Maraniss, 255, 355–58; Sheehy, 40–50, 56–50, 63–70.
11. Maraniss, 246–50,263–64,269–71, 275–77; B. Clinton, 181–82; Bernstein, 85–87.
12. Maraniss, 275–77.
13. B. Clinton, 210–15; Maraniss, 294–97,307–11,316, 319–21; Bernstein, 103–03, 107–07, 113.
14. Bernstein, 109–13; Sheehy, 121–26.
15. Maraniss, 346–49, 351; Bernstein, 124–26, 129–32.
16. Bernstein, 183–88; H.R. Clinton, *It Takes A Village*, 34.
17. Maraniss, 391–92, 396–97, 403–10; Richard Morris, *Behind the Oval Office: Getting Reelected Against the Odds* (Los Angeles: Renaissance, 1999), 45–52; B. Clinton, 301–303.
18. Maraniss, 412–14; Bernstein, 172–75; B. Clinton, 309–12.
19. B. Clinton, 319–22, 365–67; Maraniss, 458–59.
20. Bernstein, 176–80; Maraniss, 440–44; B. Clinton, 332–35.
21. Bernstein, 183–87; Maraniss, 450; H. R. Clinton, *It Takes A Village*, 34.
22. Jeff Gerth and Don VanNatta Jr., *Her Way: the Hopes and Ambitions of Hillary Rodham Clinton* (Boston: Little Brown, 2007), 92–95.
23. Michael Isikoff, *Uncovering Clinton: A Reporter's Story* (New York: Crown Books, 1999), 31; Bernstein, 197, 200–02; Sheehy, 199–201; B. Clinton, 385–91; George Stephanopoulos, *All Too Human* (Boston: Little Brown, 1999), 62–68.
24. Bernstein, 209–13; J. Klein, *The Natural: The Misunderstood Presidency of Bill Clinton* (New York: Doubleday, 2002), 117; Nigel Hamilton, *Mastering the Presidency* (New York: Public Affairs, 2007), 39.
25. Hamilton, 46–47; Stephanopoulos, 109–11; Bernstein, 214–16, 262–70; B. Clinton, 482.
26. Bernstein, 248–49; Klein, 106; John Harris, *The Survivor: Bill Clinton in the White House* (New York: Random House, 2005), 146–47.

27. Bernstein, 324–37; Gil Troy, *Hillary Rodham Clinton: Polarizing First Lady* (Lawrence: University of Kansas Press, 2008), 122–24; Stephanopoulos, 145. Suffering from clinical depression, Foster went into a deep funk and fatally shot himself on July 20, 1993, while sitting on a bench in Fort Marcy Park, in Virginia.
28. Sally Quinn, "Beware of Washington," *Newsweek*, December 21, 1992; Hamilton, 9–10; Harris, 3–4, 35–37; Bernstein, 316–20.
29. Hamilton, 100, 225; Bernstein, 223–25, 284–94; Klein, 106, 118.
30. Maraniss, 373–75; Bernstein, 149–51, 195–97; B. Clinton, 273, 372; Gerth and Van Natta, 92, 94, 107–10; Sheehy, 205–07; Harris, 4–9.
31. Isikoff, 35; David Gergen, *Eyewitness to Power: The Essence of Leadership, Nixon to Clinton* (New York: Simon and Schuster, 2000), 286–90; Stephanopoulos, 226; Bernstein, 335, 35; Klein, 111.
32. Stephanopoulos, 251; Gergen, 290; Bernstein, 9.
33. Klein, 57; Hamilton, 160–71, 177; Stephanopoulos, 178–81, 270; Harris, 101–02; B. Clinton, 547, 557–58.
34. Stephanopoulos, 202–03; Bernstein, 395–96; Sheehy, 252.
35. Hamilton, 201–12, 237–48; Bernstein, 365–66, 373; Sheehy, 248–49; Stephanopoulos, 228–29; H. R. Clinton, *Living History*, 206; Gergen, 319.
36. Klein, 122–24; Bernstein, 397–99.
37. Gergen, 315; Bernstein, 400.
38. Bernstein, 409, 418, 423, 447; Hamilton, 547–50; Sheehy, 259.
39. Morris, 94, 115–16, 123–35; Stephanopoulos, 328–41, 399; Bernstein, 410–11; Sheehy, 258; Klein, 133–34.
40. Hamilton, 437–48, 450–51; Klein, 143; Harris, 178–79; Taylor Branch, *The Clinton Tapes: Wrestling History with the President* (New York: Simon and Schuster, 2009), 238.
41. Hamilton, 520, 548–49, 563–71; Branch, 297, 300, 303; Morris, 183; Stephanopoulos, 403–08.
42. Hamilton, 540–43; Harris, 223–27; Jeffrey Toobin, *A Vast Conspiracy: The Real Story of the Sex Scandal That Nearly Brought Down a President* (New York: Random House, 1999), 86, 235.
43. Toobin, 167, 216, 246–49; Isikoff, 221.
44. Hamilton, 273, 275; Isikoff, 54, 60, 91; Bernstein, 383–87; Toobin, 208–10, 293.
45. B. Clinton, 776; Bernstein, 497–99; Toobin, 258.
46. Toobin, 264–79.1
47. Bernstein, 505, 526–30; Stephanopoulos, 330–33; Klein, 179–81; Toobin, 290, 323–28; Sheehy, 322.

INDEX

Aaron, Benjamin, 260
Adams, John Quincy, 22
Adams, Sherman, 310
Addison's disease, 190
Kennedy, J. F., contracting, 194, 195
airplanes
Kennedy family and crashes in, 189, 194
Roosevelt and air travel, 162, 171, 179, 199
1932 dangers of, 171
Allen, Richard V., 280
on Haig and succession, 271
on Twenty-fifth Amendment, 278
Alliance for Progress, 223
American Federation of Labor, 140
American peace commission, 113
American Revolution, 52
Annenberg, Walter, 201
annexation, of Texas
Calhoun securing, 53
Democrats and, 54
executive power and, 55
Mexican-American War and, 55
Tyler, J., and, 52–55
Anti-Ballistic Missile Treaty (1972), 281
Anti-Crime Task Force for Southern Florida, 268, 287n41
anti-Germanism, 119
Article II, Section 1, of Constitution (U.S.), 59n12, 110, 123
assassination attempt, on Reagan, R., 9, 281, 283n1, 289n48
Brady Bill and, 315
Bush, G. H. W., on succession and, 268, 277–78
Fielding and, 272
government response to, 269–70
Haig after, 257, 264–65, 270, 274, 276–77
by Hinckley, 259–60, 261, 263, 268
line of succession in, 272–73, 275, 276–77
NCA and, 274–75
Situation Room and, 275–77, 289n51
Soviet policies and, 258
Twenty-fifth Amendment and, 273–74, 276, 277, 278
Weinberger increasing security after, 269, 272
Atlantic Conference (1941), 178

Baker, Ray Stannard, 110, 125
Bachelder, Toi, 168
Baines, Rebekah, 212
Baker, James, III, 310
as "the troika," 258, 265
Balaguer, Joaquin, 226
Baldwin, Henry, 30
Bank of the United States
Jackson challenging, 20, 31
McDuffie defending, 24
recharter of, 31
Second, 41–42
Barrett, Laurence, 276, 277
Bay of Pigs Invasion, 200

Bennett, W. Tapley, 220
Benoit, Pedro Bartolome, 222
Big Three. *See* Grand Alliance
Bingham, Robert, 193
birth rates (1920s), 152
Black Panthers, 302
Blythe, Bill, 297
Bosch, Juan, 221
Boys Nation, 298
Bradlee, Ben, 203–4
Brady, James, 285n21
  injuries of, 263
  shooting of, 259, 262
Brady Bill, 315
Branch, Taylor, 302
Brezhnev, Leonid, 280, 291n81
Briand, Aristide, 133, 152–53
Brooke, Edward, 301
Browning, Orville H., 92, 97
Bruenn, Howard, 180, 181
Budget and Accounting Act, 144
Bullitt, William C., 126n15
Bull Moose Party, 150–51
Bundy, McGeorge, 224–25
Busby, Horace, 214
Bush, George H. W., 258
  Anti-Crime Task Force for Southern Florida and, 268, 287n41
  authority of, 267–69
  as chair of SSG, 268
  credentials of, 267
  Dairy Price Support Bill and, 268
  on succession and assassination attempt, 268, 277–78
Bush, George W., 1

Calhoun, John C., 2, 15, 32. *See also* Jackson, Andrew
  annexation of Texas and, 53
  Eaton affair and, 17, 19, 20
  1818 criticism of Jackson by, 22–23, 24
  innocence proclaimed by, 25
  Jackson confronting, 23–24
  Jackson rebuttal of, 27–28
  Lacock supporting, 30–31
  on nullification, 17, 20, 22–23
  on protective tariff, 20, 22–23
  Seminole War controversy published by, 26–27, 36n21
  Van Buren replacing, 23
  on veto power, 49
Carlucci, Frank, 265
Carter, Jimmy, 279
  Cuban refugees and, 305
  grain embargo of, 280
Carter, Rosalind, 295
Castro, Fidel, 211, 221–22
Caulfield, John, 243–44
Cheshire, Godfrey, 308
child labor, 105
Children's Defense Fund, 303
Christian Science Monitor, 308
The Christian's Defense (Smith, J.), 96
Churchill, Winston S., 261
  at Atlantic Conference, 178
  at Tehran summit, 178, 179, 180
Civil Rights Bill (1964), 215
Civil War, 4
  death toll of, 83
Clapper, Raymond, 175–76
Clark, William P., 262
Clay, Henry
  "American System" of, 16
  bank bill of, 47
  on executive power, 49–50
  Harrison and, 45
  Jackson and, 14–15, 20
  Tyler, J., accepted by, 46–47
Clemenceau, Georges, 119–20
Clinton, Bill, *294*
  as attorney general, 304
  Clinton, H., meeting, 299, 301–2
  Clinton, H., saving political life of, 295, 306, 309, 321–23
  Congressional campaign of, 303–4
  Cuban refugees and, 305
  early life of, 297–98
  Flowers affair with, 295, 309
  government shutdown and, 318, 319
  as Governor, 305, 306–7

health-care reform of, 3, 310, 312, 314–15, 316
impeachment proceedings of, 296, 314, 322
infidelity of, 3, 295–96, 303, 307, 308, 309, 315–16, 321
Kennedy, J. F., and, 298
Lewinsky scandal and, 295–96, 319–21
marriage counseling for, 308
Morris and, 306, 317, 318–19, 321
mother of, 296–97, 302–3
NAFTA and, 315
national debt and, 315
New Democratic Coalition and, 307
1994 Congressional elections and, 316
Oklahoma City bombing and, 317–18
presidential campaigns of, 307, 308–9
relationships of, 299, 308
as "rescuer," 297
as Rhodes Scholar, 298, 305–6, 307
Starr and, 314
wedding of, 304
Whitewater papers and, 312–13
Wright, B., and, 306, 307, 308
Yale Law School years of, 298–99, 301–2

Clinton, Chelsea, 307–8, 318

Clinton, Hillary Rodham, *294*
at Children's Defense Fund, 303
Clinton, B., congressional campaign and, 303
Clinton, B., meeting, 299, 301–2
Clinton, B., political life saved by, 295, 306, 309, 321–23
Clinton, V., and, 302, 303
education reform and, 306
First Ladies compared to, 295
health-care reform and, 3, 310, 312, 314–15, 316
on infidelity of Clinton, B., 308–9, 321
It Takes A Village by, 317
Jones influencing, 300
at law firm in Little Rock, 304–5
Lewinsky scandal and, 295–96, 321
in *Life* magazine, 301
marital values for, 300, 308
marriage counseling for, 308
Morris and comeback message for, 317
new self-assertion of, 312
press corps and, 311–12, 313
as Republican, 301
rights of children and, 303, 317, 318
Senate candidacy for, 323
"traditional" image of, 317
travel office scandal of, 311
on Watergate investigative commission, 303
wedding of, 304
at Wellesley College, 301
in West Wing, 310
Whitewater papers and, 312–14, 315
Wright and, 302, 304, 306, 323
Yale Law School years of, 299, 301–2

Clinton, Roger, 297

Clinton, Virginia
Clinton, H., and, 302–3
early life of, 296
makeup for, 296, 302
marriages of, 297

Coffee, John, 13

Cold War, 6, 7, 9. *See also* Reagan, Ronald Wilson
MAD and, 279
nuclear disarmament and, 278–79, 283

colonialism, 257

Colson, Charles, 245

Compromise (1850), 66–67
Missouri Compromise and, 78

Congress on Racial Equality (CORE), 216

Contras, 266

Coolidge, Calvin, *130*
on budget and tax, 134, 149–50, 151–52
college years of, 135–36
community of mourners and, 154
conservatism of, 139, 150
Coolidge, C., Jr., death of, and, 5, 131–33, 147–48
Coolidge, C., Jr., relationship to, 139
Coolidge, G., marrying, 137
Coolidge, G., relationship to, 144

Coolidge, Calvin (*Cont.*)
death of father for, 151, 154
depression of, 132
early life of, 134–35
early political career of, 137–38
economy under, 150
on excess profits tax, 143
failure and, 134–35
on farm subsidies, 147
Ford endorsing, 149
as governor of Massachusetts, 139–41
Great Depression and, 132, 133, 155
Harding-Coolidge program of, 142–43
Kellogg-Briand Pact and, 133, 152–53
law career of, 136
Lincoln, A., and, 134, 135, 136, 140, 142, 146, 156
lion cubs and, 151
Lord meeting with, 151
Mellon and, 146
as minimalist, 150
national debt and, 142, 143, 152
1919 challenges for, 139–40
1924 election for, 133
"normalcy" promoted by, 142–43
perseverance of, 133
Phonofilm video of, 149–50
police strike and, 140–41
political favors and, 138
pragmatism of, 138
presidential style of, 154–55
presidential succession of, 131, 146
on protectionism, 142
"the reign of law" for, 141, 153
tariffs and, 155
Coolidge, Calvin, Jr.
burial of, 148
Coolidge, C., relationship to, 139
death of, 5, 131–33, 147–48
Lincoln, W., compared to, 131
Coolidge, Grace Goodhue, 138–39
Coolidge, C., marrying, 137
Coolidge, C., relationship to, 144
mourning in white for, 148, 153
religious faith of, 153
vice presidential years and, 145
Coolidge, John (son), 131, 132
birth of, 137
CORE. *See* Congress on Racial Equality
Costigliola, Frank, 185n1
Covenant of the League of Nations, 6
Article 10 of, 116, 121, 122
senatorial reservations to, 106, 121–22
ratification fight of, 111
Crawford, William, 22
Credentials Committee, of Democratic Convention, 217, 218
deadlock of, 219
two-seat compromise of, 219–20
Cuban Missile Crisis, 6
Cuomo, Mario, 307

Dairy Price Bill, 261, 268
Darman, Richard, 275, 276
Davis, David, 85, 101n49
Davis, Jefferson, 4, 80n9
Confederate government and, 70
death of son for, 79–80
Pierce, F., relationship to, 70–71, 75–76, 80
Davis, John W., 150
death of wife and, 154
Davis, Varina Howell
death of son for, 79–80
Pierce, J. and, 70, 73
Dawes, Charles, 147, 154
Dean, John, 242, 261
death
in Civil War, 83
Coolidge, C., and, 5, 131–33, 147–48, 151, 154
Davis, J., and, 79–80
Davis, J. W., and, 154
of FDR, 183
of Harding, 131
of Harrison, 39–40, 58n2
Jackson and, of spouse, 2, 13
Lincoln, A., impacted by, 84, 88–89, 90, 91
of Lincoln, W., 88–89, 90, 91

Marshall and, of son, 154
of Monroe, J., 28–29
Pierce, F., and Pierce, J. and, of sons, 4, 65, 66, 67, 79
of Tyler, 56
Tyler and, of wife, 51
Deaver, Michael, 275
perjury conviction for, 266
as "the troika," 258, 265
Debs, Eugene, 116
prison sentence for, 119
as Socialist Party candidate, 115
Delahanty, Thomas
medical retirement of, 263
shooting of, 259
DeLoach, Deke, 217
Democratic national convention (1936)
"Auld Lang Syne" sung at, 177
FDR falling at, 174–75
FDR speech at, 176–77
Democratic National Convention (1964), 211
Democratic Party, 4. *See also* Watergate incident
annexation, of Texas and, 54
Credentials Committee of convention for, 217, 218, 219–20
1854–55 elections for, 78
1842 election for, 50
Jackson in, 41–42
MFDP and, 8, 211, 212, 216–17, 218–20
1936 Democratic national convention, 174–75, 176–77
1912 election for, 115
1916 election for, 115–16
1918 election for, 117–18
1920 election for, 164
1928 Democratic convention, 169
1924 Democratic convention, 166–67
Pierce, F., congressional meeting of, 76–77, 79
Pierce, F., factional warfare and, 73–74
Tyler, J., in, 41–42
Dempsey, Jack, 170
Dennis, Alfred Pearce, 136–37
Dercum, Francis, 108
Dickens, Charles, 51
disability
crutches as symbol of, 169
medical textbook on, 165
Doar, John, 303
Dobrynin, Anatoly, 248
Dodd, William E., 124–25
Dole, Bob, 319
Dominican crisis. *See* Dominican Republic, intervention in
Dominican Republic
Bosch in, 221
civil war in, 8, 224
Hoover, J., on communism in, 225
PRD in, 221, 222
Reid Cabral in, 221
Trujillo Molina dictatorship in, 221
Dominican Republic, intervention in (1965), 211
background of, 221–22
communism and, 221, 222, 223, 224–25
Fulbright and, 236
inter-American peacekeeping force at, 226
marines deployed to, 220–21, 222
McNamara on, 224
OAS and, 222–23
OAS charter violated by, 226
Dominican Revolutionary Party (PRD), 221
Donelson, Emily, 18
Douglas, Stephen A.
on Compromise of 1850, 78
Kansas-Nebraska bill and, 74–75, 81
Dred Scott case, 4
duels, 33
Durant, Will, 169–70

Eaton, John, 13
duels and, 19
resignation of, 18
as secretary of war, 17

Eaton, Margaret "Peggy," 2
 Jackson defending, 18
 ostracism of, 19
 reputation of, 18
Eaton, Margaret "Peggy," affair, 35n7, 35n9
 Calhoun and, 17, 19, 20
 Jackson and, 19, 32, 33
 nullification and, 19
economy
 Coolidge, C., and, 150
 FDR and, 174
 in 1924, 150
 wartime, 117–18
Edelman, Marian Wright, 303
Edison, Thomas, 149
Edwards, Elizabeth, 94
Ehrlichman, John
 Nixon personal politics and, 243
 victimhood of, 240
Eisenhower, Dwight D., 195
 Nixon and, 237, 252n10
electoral college, 21
Ellsberg, Daniel
 Nixon and, 244–45
 Pentagon Papers released by, 244

Fair Housing Act (1968), 220
FDR. *See* Roosevelt, Franklin Delano
Federal Reserve System, 105
Federal Trade Commission, 105
Fielding, Fred, 272, 275
Fields, W. C., 261–62
Fitzgerald, John "Honey Fitz," 192
Fleetwood Mac, 316
Florida, conquest of. *See* Seminole War controversy
Flowers, Gennifer, 295
 Clinton, B., affair publicized by, 309
Ford, Henry, 149
Forsyth, John, 24
Fortas, Abe, 222–23
Foster, Jodie, 259
Foster, Vince, 305, 325n27
 travel office scandal and, 311
Fourteen Points, 117
 criticism of, 118
Freedom Summer (1964), 216
French, Benjamin Brown, 69
Freud, Sigmund, 126n15
Fuess, Claude, 154
Fugitive Slave Act (1850), 77
Fulbright, J. William, 106, 212, 298
 as critical of Dominican intervention, 236

Gadsden Purchase, 74
Gardiner, Julia, 52
George, Alexander, 126n18, 127n19
 Woodrow Wilson and Colonel House: A Personality Study by, 112
George, Juliette, 126n18, 127n19
 Woodrow Wilson and Colonel House: A Personality Study by, 112
George III (king), 176
Gergen, David, 313
Germany, 112
Gilbert, Robert, 132
Gingrich, Newt, 316
 government shutdown and, 318, 319
glasnost (openness), 283
Gorbachev, Mikhail, 9, 282
 nuclear disarmament treaty and, 283
Gore, Al, 310
Graham, Kathleen, 311
grain embargo, 280
Grand Alliance, 7, 177–78, 183
Grant, Ulysses S., 56
Grayson, Cary M., 106
 Wilson, W., medical papers of, 107–8
 Wilson, W., stroke hidden by, 107, 111
Great Britain
 emancipation and, 53
 Grand Alliance with, 7, 177–78, 183
Great Depression, 7
 Coolidge, C., and, 132, 133, 155
 FDR and, 155, 177
 government intervention and, 155, 159n74
 tariffs and, 155

Great Society
of LBJ, 8, 105, 211, 227
Republicans dismantling, 318
Great War. *See* World War I
Greenberg, Stan, 316
Gurney, Eliza P., 97

Haig, Alexander, 287n35
Allen on succession and, 271
"Defcon III" decision and, 249–50
Reagan, R., assassination attempt and, 257, 264–65, 270, 274, 276–77
resignation of, 265
Haldeman, H. R., 237, 239
as brooding, 240
Nixon personal politics and, 243
Hall, Edward, 154
Hamer, Fannie Lou, 217, 219, 220
Hamilton, James A., 13, 24–25
Hammerschmidt, John Paul, 303
Harding, Warren G., 111
Budget and Accounting Act of, 144
death of, 131
Harding-Coolidge program of, 142–43
"normalcy" promoted by, 142–43
Veterans Bureau scandal of, 145
Harrison, William Henry, 3
campaigning by, 43, 58n7
Clay and, 45
death of, 39–40, 58n2
inauguration of, 44
in Whig party, 42–43
Hart, Gary, 307
Hawthorne, Nathaniel, 65
Pierce, F. and, 69
Hay, John, 95
health. *See* mental health; physical health
Henry IV (Pirandello), 215
Herndon, William H., 84, 96
Hinckley, John, Jr.
assassination attempt by, 259–60, 261, 263, 268
Foster, J., and, 259
survivors of attempt by, 263
Hitchcock, Gilbert, 110, 113, 117, 122
Hitler, Adolf, 171
Holt, Michael F., 4
Hoover, Herbert, 155
Hoover, J. Edgar
on communism in Dominican Republic, 225
as FBI director, 211, 217
LBJ influenced by, 224
Hopkins, Harry, 172
Hotel Embajador, 226
Howe, Louis M., 164, 172
Hubbell, Webb, 305
Humphrey, Hubert, 216, 234

Ickes, Harold, 177
The Impact of Illness on World Leaders (Park), 114
Indian removal, 18
infant mortality, 152
influenza, 145
Internal Revenue Service (IRS), 243
internationalism, 116, 117, 120, 121, 122
internationalist movement, 117, 118, 119
International Labor Organization, 121
Iran-Contra scandal, 9, 257–58
fluid leadership and, 265–66
Iran-Iraq war, 266
IRS. *See* Internal Revenue Service
Israel attacks (1973), 248–49
It Takes A Village (Clinton, H.), 317

Jackson, Andrew, 13*f*. *See also* Calhoun, John C.; Seminole War controversy
advisors of, 33–34
Bank of the United States challenged by, 20, 31
Calhoun confronted by, 23–24
Clay and, 14–15, 20
controversy and, 32
death of spouse of, 2, 13
in Democratic Party, 41–42
duels of, 33
Eaton, M., defended by, 18
Eaton affair and, 19, 32, 33
1818 Calhoun criticism of, 22–23, 24

Jackson, Andrew (*Cont.*)
on electoral college, 21
ignorance of, 15
Indian removal and, 18, 35n6
Jefferson birthday dinner toast of, 21
Lacock questioned by, 30–31
mental health of, 25–26, 32–33
Monroe, J., and, 22, 23–24
nullification and, 19, 42
paranoia of, 25–26, 32
Parton and, 15
presidential accomplishments of, 16–17
on protective tariff, 20, 36n22
rebuttal to Calhoun by, 27–28
"Rhea letter" and, 27–28
strict constructionism, 27
temperament of, 33
Van Buren and, 16, 23
Jackson State College, 236
Jefferson, Thomas
birthday dinner of, 21
Kentucky Resolutions of, 41
Jenkins, Walter, 218
Johnson, Claudia Alta "Lady Bird," 228
LBJ marrying, 213
Johnson, Lyndon B. (LBJ), *210*, 228n1. *See also* Dominican Republic, intervention in
Civil Rights Bill and, 215
civil rights for African Americans and, 220
communism and, 223, 224, 225
CORE and, 212
early political career of, 213–14
foreign policy team of, 220
Great Society of, 8, 105, 211, 227
illegal political espionage of, 217
intellectual limitations of, 227
Johnson, C., marrying, 213
Kennedy, J. F., campaigning against, 198
mental health and depression of, 214, 215, 219, 220, 227, 228
MFDP and, 216–17
mother relationship with, 8, 212
1964 presidential win of, 220
overreaction of, 226
paranoia of, 220
physical health of, 215, 228
poverty reduced by, 215
Russell called by, 219
schooling of, 213
SNCC and, 212
split personality of, 214
Vietnam War and, 211, 220, 227, 228
wire-tapping MFDP for, 212
Johnson, Paul, 217
Johnson, Sam Ely, 212, 213
Jones, Don, 300
Jones, Paula, 315–16

Kansas, 81n20
slavery in, 79
Kansas-Nebraska Act (1854), 4, 69, 81n20
Missouri Compromise and, 76
Pierce, F. and, 69–70, 73, 75, 76–77, 78–79
Pierce, J. and, 69–70, 73
slavery and, 76, 79
Keckly, Elizabeth, 89, 94
Kellogg, Frank, 133, 152–53
Kellogg-Briand Pact, 133
campaigning for, 152–53
success of, 153
Kendall, Amos, 14
Kennedy, Edward "Ted," 189
Kennedy, Eunice, 189
illness of, 190
on mental retardation of Rosemary, 204–5, 207
Kennedy, Jacqueline Bouvier, 190–91, 199
Kennedy, John Fitzgerald "Jack," 5–6, *188*, 189
Addison's disease and, 194, 195
assassination of, 233, 269
back pain of, 194, 195
Bay of Pigs Invasion and, 200
at Chelsea Naval Hospital, 193–94
Clinton, B., and, 298
college years of, 192–93
compartmentalizing private and public life of, 204, 207

early political career of, 194–95
health-care bill of, 205–7
illness of father in speech by, 206
inauguration of, 199
LBJ, campaigning against, 198
medications of, 196
Monroe, M., singing to, 206
"National Plan to Combat Mental Retardation" of, 204–5
in navy, 193
1960 presidential campaign of, 198
on physical fitness, 199
physical health of, 190, 192–93, 194, 195, 196, 198, 202–3, 208
scarlet fever of, 191–92
surgery for, 195–96
Kennedy, Joseph P. "the ambassador," 5–6, 190
on Bay of Pigs Invasion, 200
children advised by, 197, 200–201
golf played by, 201–2
illness of, 197
Kennedy, J. F., cared for by, 191–93, 194, 195
impact of stroke of, 202, 206, 207
treatment after stroke of, 203–4
Kennedy, Robert "Bobby," 189, 202, 216
Kennedy, Rose Fitzgerald, 190
decision-making and, 203
diets monitored by, 191
Kennedy, Rosemary, 6
health problems of, 190
hiding condition of, 196–97
lobotomy of, 190
publicizing condition of, 204–5
Kennedy family
airplane crashes and, 189, 194
diets of, 191
exercise for, 190
women of, 189
Kent State University
Lincoln Memorial protest and, 237
National Guard shooting students at, 236
Kentucky Resolutions (1798), 41
Khrushchev, Nikita, 223
King, Martin Luther, Jr. (MLK)
assassination of, 233
Hoover, J., and, 211
MFDP and, 218–19
MYF and, 300
wiretap reports on, 217–18
King John (Shakespeare), 89
Kinsley, Philip, 175
Kissinger, Henry
"Defcon III" decision and, 249–50
"madman" strategy and, 248–49
Nixon and, 8–9, 237, 243
power of, 247–48
victimhood of, 240

Lacock, Abner, 29
Calhoun supported by, 30–31
Seminole War controversy, 30–31, 36n26, 37n30
La Follette, Robert, 143
Laird, Melvin, 236, 248
Lansing, Robert, 110, 111
Lauer, Matt, 321
LBJ. *See* Johnson, Lyndon B.
League of Nations, 6, 106, 107. *See also* Covenant of the League of Nations; Treaty of Versailles
Lodge reservations to, 121–22
machinery of, 116–17, 120
Republican internationalists and, 120–21
sovereignty and, 121, 122
U.S. not joining, 124
Wilson, W., and, 111, 117, 121, 123
Lebanon, 266
LeHand, Missy, 172
Lehrer, Jim, 321
Leuchtenburg, William, 155
Lewinsky, Monica, scandal, 295–96, 314
DNA test in, 321
intercourse and, 319, 320
perjury in, 321
Tripp recording and, 320–21
Liberty Bonds, 142
Life magazine, 301

Lincoln, Abraham, 4–5, 57, *82*
assassination of, 84
children of, 84–85, 86–87
Coolidge, C., and, 134, 135, 136, 140, 142, 146, 156
domestic sadness for, 85–86
faith of, 91, 96–97, 98
at funeral of Lincoln, W., 89
on God and slaves, 97–98
as lawyer on Eighth Judicial Circuit, 85
Lincoln, R., relationship to, 85–86
Lincoln, T., relationship to, 95–96
Lincoln, W., death of, for, 84, 88–89, 90, 91
Lincoln, W., relationship to, 87
McCullough advice from, 91
Meditation on the Divine Will by, 96–97
peace convention and, 55–56
Second Inaugural Address of, 96, 97–98
Union Army setbacks and, 83
Lincoln, Mary Todd
children of, 84–85, 86–87
Edwards as sister of, 94
guilt of, 92
mourning of, 92, 93–94
psychological imbalance of, 84, 92, 101n56, 102n60
spiritualists and, 94
as thief, 92–93
Lincoln, Robert, 84
on relationship with father, 85–86
Lincoln, Tad, 84–85, 86, 87
illness of, 88, 90
relationship with father for, 95–96
temperament of, 95
Lincoln, Willie, 4–5, 84–85
Coolidge, C., Jr., compared to, 131
death of, 88–89, 90, 91
funeral for, 89
relationship with father for, 87
temperament of, 87–88, 100n26
Lincoln Memorial protest (1970)
Kent State and, 237
media coverage of, 239
Nixon visiting, 233–34, 237–39, 250–51, 251n1, 251n2, 253n15
students at, 238–39
Link, Arthur S., 113, 114
Lippmann, Walter, 182
Lodge, Henry Cabot, 111–12
League of Nations and reservations of, 121–22
Wilson, W., relationship with, 120
Lodge, Henry Cabot, II, 194–195
Lodge Reservations, 121–22
Lord, Herbert Mayhew, 151
Luce, Henry, 198–99

MAD. *See* mutual assured destruction policy
"madman" strategy, 248–49
Magaziner, Ira, 312
Mann, Robert, 222
Marmor, Michael, 114, 126n19
Marsh, Charles, 215
Marshall, Thomas R.
death of son for, 154
as vice president, 110, 123, 144
Maysville Road Veto (1830), 27
McCarthy, Joseph, 181
McCarthy, Tim, 259, 263
McClure, Alexander K., 93
McCullough, Fanny, 91
McDuffie, George, 21
Bank of the United States defended by, 24
McFarlane, Robert, 265
Iran-Contra scandal and, 266
McGovern, George, 302, 323
McLarty, Mack, 310
McNamara, Robert, 220
on Dominican intervention, 224
Meditation on the Divine Will, 96–97
Meese, Edwin, III
Iran-Contra investigation and, 266
as "the troika," 258, 265
Mellon, Andrew
Coolidge, C., and, 146

results of tax plan of, 152
"Taxation: The People's Business" by, 147
on tax cuts, 147
Wal-Mart Principle and, 144–45
mental health, 2, 208
Coolidge, C., depression and, 132
Jackson, A., and, 25–26, 32–33
LBJ and, 214, 215, 219, 220, 227, 228
Lincoln, M., and, 84, 92, 101n56, 102n60
Nixon and, 234, 235, 239–40, 241, 242–43, 247, 250–51
Methodist Youth Fellowship (MYF), 300
Mexican-American War
annexation of Texas and, 55
Davis, J., in, 70
Pierce, F., in, 70, 72
MFDP. *See* Mississippi Freedom Democratic Party
Mississippi, 215–16
Mississippi Freedom Democratic Party (MFDP), 8, 211
establishment of, 216
Hamer speaking for, 217
LBJ meeting with, 216–17
MLK and, 218–19
two-seat compromise rejected by, 219–20
wire-tapping of, 212
Missouri Compromise (1820)
Compromise of 1850 and, 78
Kansas-Nebraska Act and, 76
slaves and, 41, 74–75, 76, 78
MLK. *See* King, Martin Luther, Jr.
Monroe, James
Calhoun defense and, 25
death of, 28–29
Jackson criticism and, 22, 23–24
Rhea letter and, 28
Seminole War controversy and, 21
Monroe, Marilyn, 206
Monroe Doctrine, 120
Morris, Dick, 306
Clinton, B., confession and, 321
comeback message of, 317
1996 presidential campaign and, 318–19
Morrissey, Frank, 197–98
Morrow, Dwight, 141
Moyers, Bill, 226–27
Moynihan, Daniel Patrick, 323
municipal bonds, 142
mutual assured destruction policy (MAD), 279
MYF. *See* Methodist Youth Fellowship

NAFTA. *See* North American Free Trade Agreement
National Command Authority (NCA)
Reagan, R., assassination attempt and, 274–75
Reagan administration and, 274
national debt
Clinton, B., and, 315
Coolidge, C., and, 142, 143, 152
World War I and, 142, 143
National Security Council (NSC), 265
lack of leadership at, 266
National Security Decision Directive 32 (NSDD 32), 281
National Security Decision Directive 75 (NSDD 75), 281
National Security Decision Directive 119 (NSDD 119), 282
NCA. *See* National Command Authority
NDC. *See* New Democratic Coalition
New Deal, 7, 155
benefits of, 162
wealthy enemies of, 176
New Democratic Coalition (NDC), 307
News Hour, 321
Nicaragua, 266
Nixon, Richard, 194, 228, *232*. *See also* Watergate incident
advisors of, 240–41
cover-up of, 245–46, 254n37
"Defcon III" decision and, 249–50
Eisenhower and, 237, 252n10
Ellsberg and, 244–45
foreign policy and, 247–48

Nixon, Richard (*Cont.*)
illegal activities of, 241, 242, 244, 245, 247, 251
IRS and, 243
Kissinger and, 8–9, 237, 243
Lincoln Memorial protest and, 233–34, 237–39, 250–51, 251n1, 251n2, 253n15
"madman" strategy of, 248–49
mental health and depression of, 234, 235, 239–40, 241, 242–43, 247, 250–51
1973 Israel attacks and, 248–49
1968 campaign of, 235
personal intelligence office of, 243–44, 254n30
personal politics of, 243, 253n25
"The Plumbers" created by, 244–45
popularity of, 237
Soviet Union and, 248–49
succession and, 273
tapes of, 241, 244–45, 253n21, 254n34
urban violence under, 234
validation for, 241
victimhood of, 240, 242, 247
Vietnam War and, 234, 235
Nixon tapes, 241, 244–45, 253n21, 254n34
Nobel Peace Prize, 111
North American Free Trade Agreement (NAFTA), 315
NSC. *See* National Security Council
NSDD 32. *See* National Security Decision Directive 32
NSDD 75. *See* National Security Decision Directive 75
NSDD 119. *See* National Security Decision Directive 119
nuclear command-and-control procedures, 9
nuclear crises (1969), 9
nuclear crises (1973), 9
nuclear weapons
1987 nuclear disarmament treaty, 283
Reagan, R., on disarmament of, 278–79, 283
SDI and, 282
nullification, 16
Calhoun on, 17, 20, 22–23
Eaton affair and, 19
Jackson and, 19, 42

OAS. *See* Organization of American States
O'Brien, Larry, 206
Oklahoma City bombing, 317–18
Oldroyd Collection, 154
O'Neill, Tip, 262
openness (*glasnost*), 283
Organization of American States (OAS), 222
charter of, 226
inter-American peacekeeping force from, 226
"Ostend Manifesto," 74

Panic of 1837, 42
election during, 43
Paris Peace Conference, 6, 106, 108, 112–13, 119–20
Park, Bert E., 114–15, 123
Parker, Dorothy, 132, 155
Parr, Jerry, 260
Parton, James, 15
peace convention, 55–56
Pearl Harbor, 163, 177
Pendergast, Tom, 167–68
Pentagon Papers, 253n26
Ellsberg releasing, 244
perestroika (systemic restructuring), 283
Perkins, Frances, 164, 167
Pershing, John, 154
Phipps, Joe, 214
physical health, 2, 6, 208. *See also* Kennedy, John Fitzgerald "Jack"; Roosevelt, Franklin Delano
Kennedy, E., and, 190
Kennedy, J. P., and, 197, 206
Kennedy, R., and, 190
LBJ and, 215, 228
Lincoln, T., and, 88, 90
Tehran summit and, 180

Tyler, L., and, 51–52
Wilson, W., and, 112–15, 124
Pierce, Benny, 67, 69, 71, 73, 77, 79-80
Pierce, Franklin, *64*
alcoholism of, 71–72
background of, 65–66
Davis, J., relationship to, 70–71, 75–76, 77, 80
death of sons and, 4, 65, 66, 67, 79
Democratic congressional delegation meeting and, 76–77, 79
Democratic Party factional warfare and, 73–74
on foreign policy, 74, 77–78
Fugitive Slave Act and, 77
Hawthorne and, 69
inauguration of, 64–68
as Jacksonian Democrat, 66
Kansas-Nebraska Act and, 69–70, 73, 75, 76–77, 78–79
in Mexican-American War, 70, 72
Pierce, J., relationship to, 66, 71–73, 77
slavery and, 77
temperament of, 68–69, 80n1
Whig party and, 74
Pierce, Jane Appleton
Davis, V., and, 70, 73
death of sons for, 4, 65, 66, 67, 79
Kansas-Nebraska Act and, 69–70, 73
Pierce, F., relationship to, 66, 71–73, 77
surrogate sons for, 73, 79–80
temperament of, 71
Pirandello, Luigi
Henry IV by, 215
Six Characters in Search of an Author by, 214–15
Place, Edward, 192
"The Plumbers," 244–45
Poindexter, John, 265
Iran-Contra scandal and, 266
polio
of FDR, 7, 161, 165
Warm Springs and, 163, 168–69, 183, 185n21
Polk, James K., 72, 74
Post, Jerrold, 114, 123, 126n19
Powell, Colin, 266
PRD. *See* Dominican Revolutionary Party
presidential election (1828), 2, 13
presidential election (1840)
campaigning in, 43–44
voter turnout in, 44
presidential election (1844), 54, 54
presidential election (1912), 115, 116, 150–151
presidential election (1916), 115, 116, 121
presidential election (1920, 111, 143, 164
presidential election (1924), 133, 147, 150
presidential election (1932), 170–71
presidential election (1936), 174–76
presidential election (1944), 164, 182
presidential election (1960), 198
presidential election (1964), 211, 220
presidential election (1968), 235, 301
presidential election (1972), 302
presidential election (1980), 259, 267
presidential election (1992), 308–9
presidential election (1996), 318–19
presidential limits, 9–10
presidential succession, 59n12. *See also* assassination attempt, on Reagan, R.
Article II, Section 1 of Constitution and, 59n12, 110, 123
Coolidge, C., and, 131
line of succession in, 272–73
NCA and, 274–75
during Nixon administration, 273
presidents following, 56
Reagan, R., and, 269–70, 273–74
Twenty-fifth Amendment to the Constitution on, 57, 269, 273
Wilson, W., and, 110, 123
press secretary, 311
Princeton (USS), 53
Princeton University, 112, 193
Progressives, 150
protective tariff
Calhoun on, 20, 22–23
Jackson on, 20, 36n22
Rauh, Joseph, 218

Reagan, Nancy, 260
  Clinton, H., compared to, 295
Reagan, Ronald Wilson, *256*. *See also* assassination attempt, on Reagan, R.; Bush, George H. W.; Gorbachev, Mikhail; Haig, Alexander; Iran-Contra scandal
  Brezhnev written by, 280, 291n81
  conservatism and, 316
  Dairy Price Bill and, 261
  delegating authority, 263–64, 265
  faith of, 262–63
  humor of, 261–62
  on MAD policy, 279
  national security advisers of, 265–66
  NCA under, 274–75
  NSC and, 265, 266
  NSDD 75 and, 281
  on nuclear disarmament, 278–79, 283
  recovery of, 261–62, 263, 278
  SDI of, 281–82, 283
  Soviet policies of, 258, 280–81, 282–83
  speech at Building and Construction Trades Department, 258–59
  surgery for, 260–61
  Tower Commission of, 266
Red Army, 181
Reedy, George, 212, 214, 219
Reid Cabral, Donald, 221
"the reign of law," 141, 153
Reilly, Mike, 176
  as bodyguard of FDR, 173, 174–75
Republican Party, 4
  Clinton, H., and, 301
  Coolidge, C., slogan for, 150
  1856 election and, 79
  1860 election win for, 78
  Great Society and, 318
  1980 presidential election for, 267
  Tyler, J., and, 41–42
  Wilson, W., facing, 118, 120–21
Rhea, John, 27–28, 36n25
Rockne, Knute, 171
Rodham, Dorothy
  childhood of, 299
  faith for, 300
  marital values for, 300
  Rodham, H., mistreating, 300
Rodham, Hugh
  career of, 299
  Clinton, H., education and, 301
  cruelty of, 300
Rogers, William, 236, 237
Roosevelt, Eleanor, 164, 165, 176
  Clintons compared to, 295
Roosevelt, Elliott, 171
  FDR walking with, 169, 178
Roosevelt, Franklin Delano (FDR), *160*
  allies and, 177–78
  and air travel, 162, 171, 179, 199
  at Atlantic Conference, 178
  Clintons compared to, 295
  crawling for, 166
  death of, 183
  destiny and, 163–64, 184
  as "doctor," 163, 170
  driving for, 172–73
  economy under, 174
  falls of, 165–66, 173–75
  Great Depression and, 155, 177
  heart disease of, 180
  hubris of, 164
  Kremlin wire-tapping room of, 179
  mental sharpness of, 181
  New Deal of, 7, 155, 162, 176
  at 1936 Democratic national convention, 174–75, 176–77
  at 1928 Democratic convention, 169
  at 1924 Democratic convention, 166–67
  paralysis, political and personal effect of, 161–62, 163, 173, 184
  personality of, 168, 170, 184
  polio of, 7, 161, 165
  political path of, 170
  presidential style of, 163
  reporters and photographers supporting, 172, 175
  Roosevelt, T., as cousin of, 164
  in Russia, 181–82
  "splendid deception" of, 161, 162, 163, 165, 167, 172, 184
  Stalin, personal ties to, 181–82

Stalin meeting, 179–80
statues of, 184
at Tehran summit, 178, 179, 180
unemployment under, 162, 174
walking technique for, 166, 169, 171–72, 173
Warm Springs and, 163, 168–69, 183, 185n21
Roosevelt, James, 166, 174
Roosevelt, Theodore, 115, 117
Bull Moose Party and, 150–51
FDR as cousin to, 164
Roosevelt's Lost Alliances: How Personal Politics Helped Start the Cold War (Costigliola), 185n1
Ruge, Daniel, 275
Russell, Richard, 217–18, 219
Russia, 7, 177–78, 183. *See also* Stalin, Joseph
Russian Revolution, 117

SAC. *See* Strategic Air Command
scarlet fever
of Kennedy, J., 191–92
mortality rate for, 192
Schlesinger, Arthur M., Jr., 155, 190
SDI. *See* Strategic Defense Initiative
Second Bank of the United States, 41–42
Second Inaugural Address, of Lincoln, A., 96, 97–98
Secret Service, 51
Security and Exchange Commission, 6
Seminole Indians, 21, 22
Seminole War controversy, 17, 21, 35n13
Calhoun publishing, 26–27, 36n21
Jackson on history of, 29–30, 33–34
Jackson rebuttal to, 27–28
Lacock responding to, 30–31, 36n26, 37n30
positive orders claim and, 29
Rhea letter and, 27–28
Senate Foreign Relations Committee (SFRC), 222
Shakespeare, William, 89, 100n39
Sherman Act, 137
Sherwood Forest, 56
Six Characters in Search of an Author (Pirandello), 214–15
60 Minutes, 309
slavery
Kansas and, 79
Kansas-Nebraska Act and, 76, 79
Lincoln, A., on God and, 97–98
Missouri Compromise and, 41, 74–75, 76, 78
Pierce, F., and, 77
Republic of Texas and, 52
Tyler, J., owning, 41, 55–56
Slemp, C. Bascom, 147
Smith, Al, 166, 169, 170
Smith, James, 96
Smith, William French, 268
SNCC. *See* Student Nonviolent Coordinating Committee
Socialist Party, 115
Social Security, 162
Solidarity (Polish workers union), 259, 277
Sorensen, Ted, 206
sovereignty
League of Nations and, 121, 122
Wilson, W., on, 121, 122
Soviet Union. *See also* Cold War; Stalin, Joseph
Brezhnev in, 280
end of, 257
Gorbachev and, 282–83
grain embargo and, 280
Nixon and, 248–49
NSDD 75 and, 281
Speakes, Larry, 270
Special Situation Group (SSG), 268
Stalin, Joseph
FDR meeting, 179–80
FDR personal ties to, 181–82
at Tehran summit, 178, 179, 180
Truman and, 182
Starr, Kenneth, 322
impeachment and, 314
Statistics of Income, 152
Stephanopoulos, George, 314
Strategic Air Command (SAC), 269
Strategic Defense Initiative (SDI), 281–82

in NSDD 119, 282
Student Nonviolent Coordinating Committee (SNCC), 212
Mississippi black voter registration and, 216
Suckley, Margaret "Daisy," 181, 182
systemic restructuring (*perestroika*), 283

Taft, William Howard, 115
as conservative internationalist, 118
tariffs, 155
"Taxation: The People's Business" (Mellon), 147
Teapot Dome, 145
Tehran summit (1943), 178, 179
illness at, 180
Texas, Republic of, 52–55
Thomas Woodrow Wilson, Twenty-eighth President of the United States: A Psychological Study (Freud and Bullitt), 126n15
Threat Matrix, 1
The Tormented President (Gilbert), 132
Tower Commission, 266, 287n32
Treaty of Versailles, 111, 119–20
Wilson, W., health and, 112–13
Tripp, Linda, 320, 322
"the troika," 258
power of, 265
Trujillo Molina, Rafael Leonidas, 221
Truman, Harry S., 164
1946 Congressional elections and, 316
Stalin and, 182
Tsongas, Paul, 309
Twenty-fifth Amendment to the Constitution, 57, 269
Allen on, 278
Reagan, R., and, 273–74, 276, 277, 278
succession line under, 273
Tyler, J., and, 57
Wilson, W. and, 110, 123
Tyler, John, 3, 48*f*
"acting President" term for, 46
annexation of Texas for, 52–55
assassination threats for, 50–51
background of, 41
bank bill vetoed by, 47–48, 50
Cabinet resignations and, 48–49
campaigning by, 43–44
Clay and, 46–47
death of, 56
death of wife for, 51
in Democratic Party, 41–42
executive power and, 40, 46, 47–48, 55
impeachment and, 50, 60n25
as Jeffersonian republican, 41–42
Jeffersonian theories of, 52
protectionist tariff legislation vetoed by, 50
secession supported by, 56
second marriage of, 52
Sherwood Forest as plantation of, 56
slavery and, 41, 55–56
succession of, 40, 45
veto power and, 4, 47, 48, 49, 50, 53, 55, 57
as vice president, 39
in Whig party, 42, 45–47, 48–49
Tyler, Julia Gardiner, 52, 53
Tyler, Letitia, 51–52

unemployment, 162, 174
Union Army, 83
union membership, 158n58
United Nations, 124
Upshur, Abel, 53
US News and World Report, 313

Van Buren, Martin, 14
Jackson and, 16, 23
replacing Calhoun, 23
resignation of, 18–19
as Secretary of State, 18
as Vice President, 19
V-E Day, 183
Veterans Bureau scandal, 145
Vietnam War, 9. *See also* Lincoln Memorial protest
antiwar demonstrations, 236

Cambodia invasion in, 235, 252n8
draft in, 235–36, 252n5, 298
LBJ and, 211, 220, 227, 228
Nixon and, 234, 235
public anger with, 235–36
Voting Rights Act (1965), 220

Wagner Act, 162
Wal-Mart Principle, 144–45
Walsh, Joe, 148
war guilt clause, 112
Warm Springs, 183, 185n21
atmosphere of, 168–69
FDR establishing, 163
Washington Post, 311
Whitewater papers and, 313–14
Watergate incident, 8
cover-up of, 254n37
investigation commission of, 303
motivation of, 245
Nixon acknowledging guilt in, 246
Nixon depression and, 234
victimhood and, 241–42
Webster, Daniel, 39
as Secretary of State, 45
Webster-Ashburton Treaty, 52
Weinberger, Caspar, 264, 289n48
security increased by, 269, 272
Weinstein, Edwin, 112
doubts on work of, 113, 114
on stroke of Wilson, W., 126n19
Woodrow Wilson: A Medical and Psychological Biography by, 112–13
Wellesley College, 301
Wessin y Wessin, Elias, 221
Whig party, 15
1842 election for, 50
Harrison in, 42–43
Pierce, F., and, 74
resignations of Cabinet of, 48
Tyler, J., in, 42, 45–47, 48–49
Whitewater papers
Clinton, H., and, 312–14, 315
Starr and, 314
Washington Post and, 313–14
Wilber, Del Quentin, 276
Wilson, Edith
Clinton, H., compared to, 295
political role of, 106, 109
stroke of Wilson, W., hidden by, 107, 108, 111
Wilson, Ellen Axson, 109
Wilson, Woodrow, *104*, 150–51. *See also* Covenant of the League of Nations; League of Nations
anti-Germanism and, 119
Coolidge, C., on police strike and, 140–41
European reception for, 119
father of, 112
Fourteen Points address of, 117
Grayson and, 107–8, 111
illness impacting, 112–15, 124
international peacekeeping for, 116
international security and, 122
as late reader, 112, 113–14
League of Nations and, 111, 117, 121, 123
legacy of, 124
Lodge relationship to, 120
"New Freedom" legislative program of, 105
1916 reelection campaign of, 115–16
Nobel Peace Prize for, 111
presidential succession and, 110
recovery of, 110–11
Republican Congress and, 118
Republican internationalists and, 120–21
resignation and, 109, 110
social justice legislation of, 116
on sovereignty, 121, 122
speaking tour of, 106–7
stroke of, 6–7, 106, 107–8, 123, 126n19
Treaty of Versailles and, 112–13
Weinstein on, 112–13, 126n19
Woodrow Wilson: A Medical and Psychological Biography (Weinstein), 112–13

Woodrow Wilson and Colonel House: A Personality Study (George, A., and George, J.), 112
Worcester v. Georgia, 30
World War I, 6
  end of, 117
  federal debt after, 142, 143
  political repression and, 119
World War II, 2
  Grand Alliance of, 7, 177–78, 183
Wright, Betsey, 302, 304, 323
  as chief advisor, 306
  on Clinton, B., affairs, 306, 307, 308
Wyzanski, Charles, 197

Yale Law School
  Clinton, B., at, 298–99, 301–2
  Clinton, H., at, 299, 301–2
Yalta summit (1945), 181, 183
Yankee Doodle Dandy, 172

Ziegler, Ron, 241–42, 246